Disability Studies and the Inclusive Classroom

This book's mission is to integrate knowledge and practice from the fields of disability studies and special education. Parts I and II focus on the broad, foundational topics that comprise disability studies (culture, language, and history) and Parts III and IV move into practical topics (curriculum, co-teaching, collaboration, classroom organization, disability-specific teaching strategies, etc.) associated with inclusive education. This organization conforms to the belief that least restrictive environments (the goal of inclusive education) necessarily emerge from least restrictive attitudes (the goal of disability studies). Discussions throughout the book attempt to illustrate the intersection of theory and practice.

Integrative Framework—This is the first comprehensive textbook to use disability studies as a theoretical grounding from which to address inclusive education.

Balanced Coverage—Parts I and II (chapters 1–5) are devoted to the conceptual grounding of disability studies and Parts III and IV (chapters 6–10) are devoted to classroom practices for inclusive education. Other books tilt heavily in one direction or the other.

Broad Research Focus—This book presents cutting-edge research in education, disability, history, sociology, and psychology alongside more traditional knowledge bases in special education in order to be both critical and comprehensive.

Chapter Structure—Chapters begin by introducing large concepts and key knowledge (e.g., laws and policies), then periodically revisit them in order to reinforce and expand that knowledge. Chapters also employ a thematically driven organization that reflects the most current learning and curriculum design theories.

CEC Standards—Concepts and topics reflect the Council of Exceptional Children's professional standards to ensure that the text fits the accreditation needs of university-based teacher education programs.

Susan Baglieri is Assistant Professor at Long Island University's Brooklyn, New York campus. She served as an assistant editor for *Disability Studies Quarterly* during 2005 and 2006 and served on the board of directors of the Society for Disability Studies (SDS) from 2008 to 2011.

Arthur Shapiro was a special educator on the local, county, and state levels for more than 40 years. He was Full Professor Emeritus at Kean University and an adjunct faculty member at Rutgers University.

Disability Studies and the Inclusive Classroom
Critical Practices for Creating Least Restrictive Attitudes

Susan Baglieri and Arthur Shapiro

Routledge
Taylor & Francis Group

NEW YORK AND LONDON

KH

First published 2012
by Routledge
711 Third Avenue, New York, NY 10017

Simultaneously published in the UK
by Routledge
2 Park Square, Milton Park, Abingdon, Oxon OX14 4RN

Routledge is an imprint of the Taylor & Francis Group, an informa business

© 2012 Taylor & Francis

Library of Congress Cataloging in Publication Data
Baglieri, Susan.
Disability studies and the inclusive classroom: critical practices for creating
least restrictive attitudes / Susan Baglieri, Arthur Shapiro.
pages cm
Includes bibliographical references and index.
1. People with disabilities—Education. 2. Inclusive education. I. Shapiro,
Arthur. II. Title.
LC4019.B275 2011
371.9'046–dc23   2011047441

ISBN: 978-0-415-99371-5 (hbk)
ISBN: 978-0-415-99372-2 (pbk)
ISBN: 978-0-203-83739-9 (ebk)

Typeset in Minion pro
by Cenveo Publisher Services

SFI Certified Sourcing
www.sfiprogram.org
SFI-00453

Printed and bound in the United States of America
by Edwards Brothers, Inc.

9/19/12

For Elly
For Mindy and Matthew
For Erik and Rochelle
For Yitzchak, Shoshana, Nathan, Danny, Evan, and Meira
and
For Thomas and Lucien Anderson, Anthony, Edith, and Jill Baglieri

Contents

Part I: Disability and Society   1

1 Why Consider Attitudes Toward Disability?   3
2 Paradigms of Disability   20
3 Language, Labels, and Identity   40

Part II: Disability in History   51

4 Early Attitudes and Their Legacy: A Brief History of Disability 53
5 Era of Civil Rights and Contemporary Issues   81

Part III: Disability and Education   103

6 Conceptualizing Disability in Schools   105
7 Collaborative Practice   125
8 Disabilities and Initial Approaches for Creating Inclusive
   Environments   139

Part IV: Curriculum for the Inclusive Classroom   183

 9 Curriculum Planning for Inclusive Teaching   185
10 Designing Curriculum to Cultivate Least
    Restrictive Attitudes   222

References   256
Index   276

Preface

Disability Studies and the Inclusive Classroom is an extension to the book *Everybody Belongs* (Shapiro, 1999). The updated and expanded text delves further into the process of providing the least restrictive school programs for youngsters with disabilities by integrating knowledge and practice from the *disability studies* and *special education* fields. It not only focuses the broad, foundational topics that comprise disabilities, such as culture, language, and history, but also moves into practical topics such as curriculum, professional and family collaboration, and disability-specific teaching strategies as well. It not only explains the *what* but also the *why* and *how*.

The book is based on the belief that least restrictive environments (the goal of inclusive education) emerge from least restrictive attitudes (the goal of disability studies) and how they interact. It also emphasizes that to fully understand the issues of disability, schooling, and inclusive education, we must critically examine the meanings of disability in culture. By understanding disability as a product of culture, we can better consider our beliefs and attitudes about disability as amalgamations of social messages and personal experiences. Rather than accepting common, often negative stereotypes of disability and difference, we can teach youngsters to respect and appreciate diversity as a positive idea.

Here, the field of Disability Studies is posed, which is extremely instructive in challenging traditional conceptions of disability and special education. Disability Studies offer an alternative to a medical model of disability. Utilizing a social model, disability is perceived in its cultural, sociological, psychological, and historical dimensions. Disability Studies provide the theoretical grounding and activist spirit to move readers toward a broader, deeper, and more insightful understanding of disability than could be presented in the preceding text, *Everybody Belongs*.

We are extremely grateful to Lane Akers for the opportunity to bring this work to fruition and appreciate his unwavering support and patience. We also thank reviewers of the text, including Howard Margolis and Lynne Bejoian, for their feedback and guidance.

A. S. & S. B.

Part I
Disability and Society

1
Why Consider Attitudes Toward Disability?

We begin to form attitudes about disability early in life, from strong cultural influences, including school, media, language, and literature. Stereotypical images, such as the bumbling, blind Mr. Magoo and Dickens's character, Tiny Tim, tell children that they should trivialize and pity people with disabilities. Negative images such as the villainous Captain Hook tell youngsters to fear people with physical variances. The problem is not the accuracy or inaccuracies of these characters, but the limited opportunities children have to learn about people whose abilities, characteristics, ethnicities, cultures, and languages differ from their own. Providing children with experiences of diverse people and cultures is an aim of pluralistic or inclusive education.

Inclusion is the term used to describe school-based arrangements in which students with and without disabilities learn together in general education settings. Historically, inclusion has been an integral step toward equity in education, the expansion of civil rights, and the societal integration of youngsters with disabilities. Students in segregated, special education settings are not afforded the same learning opportunities as their non-disabled peers (Karagiannis, Stainback, and Stainback, 1996). Many educators and parents equate educational inclusion with social equity and democracy (Cummings, Dyson, and Millward, 2003; Gallagher, 2001). Some liken the inclusion of students with disabilities in general education settings with the civil rights of African-Americans to racially integrated schools (Ferri and Connor, 2005).

The term *inclusion* usually refers to integrating students with disabilities into general education settings. A broader, more embracive idea of *inclusive education* exists in education literature. Ballard (1999), for example, argues that inclusive education means the removal of barriers to learning for all children and "must attend to increasing participation not just for disabled students but for all those experiencing disadvantage, whether this results from poverty, sexuality, minority ethnic status, or other characteristics assigned significance by the dominant culture in their society" (p. 2). Similarly, Wotherspoon and Schissel (2001) challenge the implications of "[school] expectations and practices dependent on specified conceptions of normality" (p. 331) for students who are marginalized on the basis of disability, as well as race, gender, and class. Inclusive education strives for pluralistic teaching practices that create contexts for learning in which every student can identify with and connect to the school and to one another.

Although schools are increasingly integrating students with and without disabilities in general education classrooms, many are finding that some benefits of inclusion are slow to be realized. Gains remain subject to critique. Miller (2001), for example, offers an account of an "included" 15-year-old young man who uses a wheelchair and experiences muscular impairment: "No one expects him to do anything but sit out the hour while his fellow students work at the computers" (p. 820). He proposes, "In order for full inclusion to occur, children must become genuine members of the class. They should be fully engaged and accepted by their peers, not just treated politely and professionally by their teacher" (p. 820). He further urges, "We have got to break down these barriers. Instead of pretending everyone is the same, we need first to accept the worries, the fears, the concerns, and the prejudices—our own and those of our students—and then take action" (p. 821). Inclusive education requires integration *and* attention to prejudice-reduction strategies (Armstrong and Barton, 2007).

Attitudes of acceptance toward persons with disabilities are critical for the successful inclusion of children with disabilities. In order to understand issues of disability, schooling, and inclusive education, we must examine the meanings of disability in culture. Rather than taking common, often negative, stereotypes of disability and other differences for granted, we can challenge children and ourselves to respect and appreciate diversity. Understanding disability as a product of culture provides us the opportunity to examine how we arrive at our own beliefs and attitudes.

Learning from Culture

The primary way that communities arrive at shared understandings about the world is through *culture*, which generally refers to patterns of human activity and the systems and symbols that shape the meaning of the activities. Most ideas of culture imply cohesion among groups of people and their shared understandings. Contemporary anthropologists such as McDermott and Varenne (1995), however, offer a way to understand culture as constructed through dynamic social processes:

> The coherence of any culture is not given by members being the same, nor by members knowing the same things. Instead, the coherence of a culture is crafted from the partial and mutually dependent knowledge of each person caught in the process and depends, in the long run, on the work they do together. ... [I]t is made of the voices of many, each one brought to life and made significant by the others, only sometimes

being the same, more often by being different, more dramatically by being contradictory (p. 23).

As we take in the many voices and perspectives of those around us, we determine which views are acceptable and those that are not; we evaluate those features of individuals that are desirable and that are not. We create structures within our social organizations to reward desirable characteristics and suppress undesirable ones. Culture then makes such decisions appear natural. Culture shapes our perspectives about the world and the people around us. Societal knowledge and beliefs about disability are communicated through media, entertainment, art, laws, and language. In schools, beliefs about disability are communicated through their organization and curriculum.

The language and concepts of *exceptionality* and *disability*, for example, communicate ideas about the way people are or "should" be. As we identify particular people or characteristics as exceptional, we simultaneously construct an idea of what is "normal." Although norms reflect the prevalence and the usual appearance of characteristics, we can also discern value systems that favor some traits over others. Why are some characteristics chosen to be meaningful and others not? The assumed neutrality or naturalness of how we define and reward characteristics is a fallacy when we examine the many ways that the meanings and descriptions of disability and ability develop specific to culture and context and change over time.

In contemporary life, exceptional persons—or, those with extraordinary bodies, minds, or ways of thinking, learning, or doing—are often represented as abnormal and undesirable. As disability is persistently characterized undesirably, attitudes toward people with disabilities are likely to be negative. Pity, charity, fear, and aversion characterize common responses to disability (Linton, 1998). It is important to consider how culture shapes our attitudes toward disability. In turn, we can address negative attitudes in schools to change aspects of our culture that harm students with disabilities and which prevent everyone from valuing human diversity.

The Nature of Attitudes

An attitude is the general tendency of an individual to act in a certain way under specific conditions. Attitudes are manifest by what individuals do and say. An attitude may be viewed as a positive or negative emotional reaction to a person or object accompanied by specific beliefs that tend to cause its holder to behave in specific ways toward its object. Though definitions of attitude may vary slightly, most include three interrelated basic elements: (1) a belief or "cognitive" component, (2) an emotional or "affective" component, and (3) an action or "behavioral" component. The components are interrelated, because positive and complimentary beliefs are accompanied by liking and positive feelings; uncomplimentary and negative beliefs are accompanied by dislike and negative feelings. These beliefs and feelings, in turn, represent a tendency to act. Attitude, therefore, is the tendency of an individual to act or react positively or negatively to his or her world based on the values and beliefs gained through his or her social experiences.

Attitudes toward disability are heavily dependent upon the information and experiences one has related to disability. Studies by Carroll, Forlin, and Jobling (2003) and Alghazo, Dodeen, and Algaryouti (2003) suggest that experiences with people with disabilities as peers, friends, and family members in many contexts may inform perceptions differently than in casual encounters, those developed for instructional purposes, or situations of caregiving, teaching, and helping. Furthermore, the benefits of many opportunities for interactions are not limited to relationships and encounters between people with and without disabilities. Because of the variety of characteristics and experiences that the term "disability" encompasses, a person with a disability may not necessarily relate better or more positively to others with similar or different disabilities. Children's development of positive attitudes toward persons with disabilities may be influenced by having many and varied experiences with diverse peers. Children's attitudes are also influenced by the broader culture.

Attitudes and Images Learned Early in Life

We learn attitudes toward disability early in life from such strong cultural influences as school, the media, our language, and literature. Many first encounters with literature, for example, include stereotyped characters in traditional fairytales. These include the childish dwarfs and humpbacked wicked witch in *Snow White*, the *Little Lame Prince*, the evil giant in *Jack and the Beanstalk*, or the sly deformed dwarf, *Rumpelstiltskin*. Franks (1996) found that many various disabilities are used symbolically in fairy tales. For example, in Grimms' Fairy Tales (1945/1995), the story of *Cinderella* ends with her stepsisters having their eyes picked out by doves. The final line reads, "And so, for their wickedness and falseness they were punished with blindness for the rest of their days" (p. 161). Similarly, the prince who climbs up Rapunzel's hair to get into the tower loses his sight by having his eyes "scratched out by the thorns among which he fell" and is forced to "wander about blind in the wood [with] nothing but roots and berries to eat" (p. 132). Few stories that feature characters with disabilities, either as central protagonists or as incidental characters, are widely available for very young children. Those books that are published are often produced in limited numbers and are frequently out of print and difficult to obtain (Matthew and Clow, 2007). Other entertainment media for children demonstrate similar patterns.

The majority of images depicting disability impress on young minds that people with physical or mental differences are to be feared, pitied, trivialized, or ridiculed. From these stories, children learn cultural ideals of physical beauty, that physical beauty symbolizes goodness, and that disability symbolizes evil. Furthermore, the evil disabled characters are always out to ravage the attractive ones. "Our memories of these and other characters often become indelible, impervious to any experiences we may have with disabled individuals in real life" (Bowe, 1978: 109).

Attitudes are acquired through "observational learning" whereby a child observes surrounding behaviors and influences. Unfortunately, many negative influences in our culture teach children early in life to accept the idea that certain human qualities such as physical "wholeness," good looks, high intelligence, and clear speech, are valued and identified with high-status individuals, whereas the qualities of others are demeaned, stigmatized, ridiculed, feared, and degraded. Children learn to assume that people with disabilities are more "different from" than "similar to" persons without them, and those differences minimize their status and set them apart. The consequences of such beliefs result in segregation and isolation, which in turn reinforce negative attitudes.

Attitudes toward human variances appear to be acculturated in children as they grow and develop. Younger children show more acceptance of their peers with disabilities than older children do (Baum and Wells, 1985). Brodkin & Coleman (1993) explains that children notice differences at a young age, but are not born biased. "By age five, children begin to absorb society's messages and fears. Between the ages of seven and nine, children's awareness of differences may be transformed into full-blown prejudice" (p. 75). Unfortunately, many youngsters enter school with stereotypic views and attitudes toward those perceived as different (Salend, 1994).

According to Morris (1991), "prejudice lies at the heart of the segregation which many disabled people experience both as children and adults" (p. 18). Although inclusion is preferred in educational policies and increasing in schools, positive social interaction has yet to prove a natural outcome (Dewer, 1982; Hehir, 2003). Prejudice must be directly addressed in the schools. Simply integrating children with disabilities into general education environments without pedagogically dealing with attitudes is meaningless and, in some cases, increases negative attitudes. Also problematic is the self-concept a child with a disability may develop in relation to his or her experience of negative attitudes.

Negative Attitudes and Self-Concept

Children who are victims of prejudice experience permanent damage to his or her confidence and sense of self-worth (Brodkin & Coleman, 1993). Self-concept refers to the way in which people perceive themselves and plays critical role in the development of personality. One's self-concept is both learned and changeable with each new experience. Thus, children are influenced by their interactions and encounters with others, especially "significant others"—that is, parents, siblings, classmates, and friends. The attitudes of these groups affect the development of the disabled child's self-concept, and the socialization of that youngster into typical community activities.

Also influential are the relationships that the child with a disability may have with professionals with whom he or she comes into contact including teachers, social workers, counselors, psychologists, physicians, nurses, and clergy. In these roles, the educators and rehabilitation practitioners provide information, services, and stability. Their attitudes can have enormous impact on both the medical and psychosocial processes of adjustment to disability that the youngster experiences. The attitudes of these professionals can also strongly influence the attitudes of family and peers (Antonak and Livneh, 1988).

Disability is one of a variety of differences that exist among people. Since attitudes shape, direct, and underlie actions, prejudice (a thought), can become discrimination (an act), making those to whom it is directed the recipients of segregation, exclusion, patronization, negative social policy, and biased treatment. When students with disabilities are placed into special, segregated school programs, for example, a particular difference becomes equated with undesirability and not "fitting in." Separation on the basis of disability, however, can contribute negatively to a child's self-concept. Attitudes of acceptance evinced by the schools, in general, and peers, in particular, can greatly influence the successful integration of children classified as disabled into general educational settings.

Theories of Attitude Change

Various theories exist on changing attitudes toward persons with disabilities. Several are based on Lewin's theory of attitude change. Lewin (1948) identified two forces that affect the modification of attitudes: restraining forces (factors which inhibit any change) and driving forces (factors which promote existing opinion or behavior). In analyzing Lewin's theory, Evans (1976) emphasized:

> Attitude for opinion modification must be thought of as a result of either the reduction in restraining forces or an increase in driving forces surrounding an opinion or behavior. Attitudes are a quasi-stationary equilibrium when driving and restraining forces are equal. Attitude modification thus necessitates an unbalancing or unfreezing of the present attitude by either reducing a restraining force or increasing a driving force (p. 573).

Evans (1976) identified the uneasiness and inhibitions non-disabled persons felt when interacting with disabled persons as a restraining force. Having disabled persons express their feelings about both their disability and the attitudes of others during interviews may reduce this force. By reducing the discomfort (the restraining force), attitudes may change more positively.

Should the experience accentuate the discomfort, a negative attitude could take place.

In developing her theory of information presentation, Donaldson (1980) approached the driving force rather than the restraining force. She indicated that the use of live or media presentations could unfreeze currently held beliefs. Presenters who communicate authentic, rather than stereotypic experiences of disability may result in positive attitude changes, but the possibility of negative change exists if the individual receives information that confirms or presents a negative stereotype of the disabled. In other words, learning activities intended to promote positive attitudes toward disabled persons are chosen purposefully. Donaldson advised those involved in changing attitudes to follow some model that incorporates the ideas that opinion or attitude modification be thought of as a result of either the reduction in restraining forces or an increase in driving forces surrounding an opinion or behavior. For example, when discussing individuals with disabilities, one can seek to reduce the discomfort that occurs when non-disabled persons interact with disabled individuals by presenting a message powerful enough to unfreeze a currently held belief.

Other research on attitude change offers theories of practice that emphasize the cognitive process of the learner. Researchers Steven Brookfield (1990) and Jack Mezirow (1998), for example, emphasize the role of critical reflection in attitude, or ideology change. Mezirow describes critical reflection as the way people form intention to learn and experience learning. In critical reflection people think about the nature of their thoughts, the process through which thoughts are formed, and the meanings that their thoughts purport in order to examine or pose possibilities for change. To change attitudes toward disability requires learners to be aware of their own beliefs and attitudes. Once aware they may actively develop and adopt new beliefs and attitudes. In short, identifying negative attitudes is essential to changing them.

Attitudes toward disability are formed early in life. Prejudices affect how children with disabilities are treated by their peers, which greatly influences development of self-concept. When a child encounters negative attitudes, prejudice and discrimination, the effects may be quite deleterious. Schools, however, can implement activities to change negative attitudes toward disability. Activities designed to build accurate knowledge about disability can be helpful. Helping children to have experiences with persons with disabilities is also useful. Providing contexts to identify negative attitudes toward disability, too, can support children to eliminate them and develop more positive attitudes.

The Importance of Teaching Diversity

Schools have a responsibility to help change negative attitudes that result in discrimination, prejudice, and segregation. A school is sometimes seen as a "melting pot or a kind of glue to hold the American fabric together" (Sadker and Sadker, 1992: 137) and, therefore, has a responsibility to help socialize and unify society. Rubenfeld (1994) stated:

> School, of course, is one of the great defining experiences in our country. Almost more than family life, it is the Great Socializer. It is where we learn to juggle friends, enemies, and acquaintances, to cope with real-world authority and to test the outside of the disciplinary envelope, to work and play together, and from time to time to cut loose in wonderful self-induced mass hysteria. In short, school is where we learn to be functioning members of a culture, not just our parents' kids. And it is this vital piece of learning that special education can never provide (pp. 235–236).

Because a central purpose of our education is the promotion of values and attitudes crucial to our pluralistic society, it becomes especially important to address those beliefs and attitudes that lead to discrimination—the denial of certain members of society the right and opportunity to full social, educational, economic, and political participation. Schools can reduce harmful attitudes by instilling helpful ones, and "and make disability a topic of investigation and discussion in the same way that some schools explore the issues of sexism and racism" (Biklen, Ferguson, and Ford, 1989: 257). Schools can play an important role in bringing about social change by preparing "each generation to examine and, when necessary, to alter existing social values, practices, and beliefs" (Sadker and Sadker, 1992: 140). They can take responsibility to confront bigotry in all its forms.

Supporting Integration: A Matter of Rights and Right

As we work toward societal integration and educational inclusion, our efforts should be informed by the desires and demands put forth by persons with disabilities and their allies (those who support the agendas of disabled persons). A primary reason is that the perception of what constitutes "positive attitudes" may differ between persons with disabilities and those without them. Makas (1990) described:

> [D]isabled people and non-disabled people differ significantly in their perceptions of what constitutes "the most positive attitudes toward persons with disabilities." For the disabled respondents, "positive attitudes" would mean either dispensing with the special category of disability entirely, or promoting attitudes that defend the civil and social rights of disabled persons. For the non-disabled respondents, "positive attitudes" reflect a desire to be nice, helpful, and ultimately place the disabled person in a needy situation. Non-disabled individuals may actually be perceived by disabled people, therefore, as expressing negative attitudes when,

in fact, the non-disabled persons are trying hard to express what they consider to be positive attitudes . . . (p. 30).

People with disabilities have forged a civil rights movement known as *Disability Rights* (Fleischer and Zames, 2001; Shapiro, 1993). They have emerged as a political force—no longer willing to be "done to" and not satisfied with being "done for" (Safford, 1978: 291).

The efforts of Disability Rights activists have resulted in several equity-focused national policies. The Americans with Disabilities Act was first enacted in 1990 and most recently amended by the Americans with Disabilities Act Amendments Act of 2008 (ADAAA) (PL 110-325). The ADAAA guarantees persons with disabilities the right to equal access to all aspects of society including public accommodations, transportation, communications, employment, recreation, and education. With increased access, persons with disabilities are enabled to enter public life (Linton, 1998). Ramps and reserved parking places are now evident. The public is increasingly becoming aware of concepts such as "deinstitutionalization," "integration," "inclusion," "independent living," "supported employment," and "reasonable accommodation."

Internationally, the 1994 adoption of the *Salamanca Statement and Framework for Action on Special Needs Education* by the United Nations Educational, Scientific and Cultural Organization (UNESCO), proclaims the fundamental right of all children to educational opportunity. In 2006, the United Nations (UN) also adopted the *Convention on the Rights of Persons with Disabilities,* which reinforces the UN's *Universal Declaration of Human Rights* (1948), and specifies particular protections for disabled persons—a group most vulnerable to oppression and marginalization.

It is now common for educators and legislators to acknowledge the benefits of integrating students with and without disabilities in schools. In the United States, for example, the 1975 Education for All Handicapped Children Act (EHA) (PL 94-142) first specified the right of students with disabilities to receive a free and appropriate education in the least restrictive environment (LRE). The EHA is most recently amended by Public Law 108-446, The Individuals with Disabilities Education Improvement Act of 2004 (IDEIA). Before discussing educational and social benefits of integration, however, we need some clarification of terms.

Integration and Inclusion

Integration is the direct opposite of segregation, offered as a concept to challenge the provision of separate schools, classes, or services for students with disabilities (Albright, Brown, Vandeventer, and Jorgensen, 1989). The concept of integration, with respect to schooling, is often described with several terms producing confusion among those unaware of their definitional nuances.

The most common of these terms are: (1) least restrictive environment (LRE), (2) mainstreaming, and (3) inclusion.

Least Restrictive Environment

The LRE is a concept featured in IDEIA (2004), which specifies:

> To the maximum extent appropriate, children with disabilities, including children in public or private institutions or other care facilities, are educated with children who are not disabled, and special classes, separate schooling, or other removal of children with disabilities from the regular educational environment occurs only when the nature or severity of the disability of a child is such that education in regular classes with the use of supplementary aids and services cannot be achieved satisfactorily (20 U.S.C. 1412(a)(5)(B)).

The LRE is widely interpreted in its preference for students with disabilities to be educated in the "regular," or general education setting—hence integrated.

Mainstreaming

Mainstreaming commonly refers to the process of integrating some students with disabilities into general education, while maintaining a separate system of special classes, services, and programs for others. Though absent from state and federal law, the term was one of the first used to describe educational integration of students with disabilities, and has been defined in various ways over the years. It is most associated with the process of bringing children with disabilities into daily contact with non-disabled children for social or education benefits.

Inclusion

Inclusion has become the most common term to refer to practices that integrate students with and without disabilities in general education. Special educational supports, including specialized curriculum are provided in the general education setting. The term "mainstreaming" is now sometimes used to refer to integration without the provision of special services.

Changes in the meaning and interpretation of the terms mainstreaming, integration, inclusion, and the LRE continue to emerge. For the purposes of this book, we adopt the language and concepts of *inclusion* and *inclusive education*. These concepts signify the joint endeavors of providing access to general settings and nurturing belonging for all students in schools and classrooms. Inclusive education aims for physical togetherness, social belonging, and curricular cohesion.

A meaningful result of IDEIA and subsequent interpretations of particularly the LRE has been the increasing integration of students with disabilities into "general education" in public schools. Instruction in segregated, special education settings is more restrictive because it deprives children with and without disabilities the experience of learning together. The challenge of bringing children who have been excluded on the basis of a disabling condition back to general education is an exciting, controversial, and dynamic process. The role of the school in the development of positive attitudes is particularly significant if we are to create least restrictive environments with zeal and enthusiasm, and in the spirit of inclusion.

Goals of Inclusive Education

Negative attitudes, prejudice, and discrimination are rooted in lack of information, lack of experience with people with disabilities, and stereotypes. Stereotypes are often unchallenged because of poor knowledge and experience. Inclusive schools aim to diversify children's experiences and peer relationships, which can allow them to develop accurate knowledge about disability and other differences. In turn, this knowledge can enable all to identify and challenge stereotypes. Excerpted from The Institute on Community Integration of the University of Minnesota (n.d.), are the following additional benefits of inclusive school communities:

1. *Preparation for adult living.* The goal of education is to prepare individuals to be contributing members of society. Segregated settings cannot prepare individuals to function in integrated community and work environments, because they do not afford those with or without disabilities, opportunities to develop the attitudes, values, and skills required to get along with one another as interdependent members of society. By attending their local schools, students with disabilities receive instruction in the communities where they live, practicing skills in the communities where they live, practicing skills in the actual community settings where they are needed, gaining familiarity with the locale, and developing a sense of belonging.

2. *Improved learning.* Many types of learning occur best in integrated schools. Students with disabilities who are placed in regular classes have an environment in which to grow socially and academically. Peers are often the best models and teachers of many socially valued behaviors, and in integrated settings, students with disabilities have opportunities to learn many things, including mobility and vocational, social, and communication skills, from students without disabilities. As with all children, those with disabilities need to encounter a variety of experiences and in integrated settings they are exposed to a wide range of activities, people, environments, and ideas.

3. *Growth for peers.* Having students with disabilities in their schools and classes, peers without disabilities learn to develop skills in dealing

with others who are different from themselves. As both adults and peers grow in their abilities to relate to students with disabilities, they serve as models for one another, supporting and reinforcing these new interaction skills. This experience often leads to growth in their self-esteem and interpersonal behaviors, paving the way for the formation of rewarding adult relationships with a variety of people in community, home, and workplace settings.

4. *Friendship development.* Integration affords students with and without disabilities opportunities to become friends with one another. Peer relationships between students with disabilities and classmates without are important now and in the future and are essential to a successful and fulfilling life in the community. Some of the friends students with disabilities make in school today will be their coworkers and fellow community members as they reach adulthood.

5. *Acceptance of individual differences.* People in our society have many misconceptions about persons with disabilities. The best way to overcome these is by bringing people together in integrated settings. As students with and without disabilities interact as classmates and friends, their parents and teachers have the opportunity to witness successful integration in action. This new experience enables many adults to embrace the vision of a society that accepts and values the inclusion of persons with disabilities into all aspects of community life.

6. *Support of civil rights.* As with all students, those with disabilities have the right to attend regular school and regular classes, and to receive an appropriate education within those regular classes. Public Law 94-142 entitles all children with disabilities to a free and appropriate public education in the least restrictive environment possible. Their integration is also a civil rights issue. In a democratic society, every person is to be afforded equal opportunities; segregated settings symbolize society's rejection of one segment of the population. Through participation in integrated schools and communities, students with and without disabilities can experience the richness of a society that values and includes all citizens.

In considering both the personal benefits and legal necessity to seek integrated and inclusive schools and societies for all children and citizens, you might be wondering why schools have been slow to make successful inclusion a reality. Surely, many legislators, educators, students, families, and others have been engaged in decades of struggle to realize the promise of inclusion. To understand factors underlying the resistance of our social and educational systems to lasting reform, we return to a broad idea of culture proposed earlier through McDermott and Varenne's (1995) work.

Disability as Culture: The Medical Model and Special Education

Culture shapes our perspectives about the world and the people around us. Societal knowledge and beliefs about disability are communicated through media, entertainment, art, laws, in the organization and curriculum of schools, and in the language and words we use. Increasingly, persons with disabilities, activists, and academics point out that the ways we make meaning of disability are funneled and focused through cultural ideologies that inherently devalue disability and the lives of persons with disabilities. A *medical model* is the perspective that best describes how we address disability in American schools and society. Shea and Bauer (1997) explain, "this model contends that the disability should be diagnosed, prescriptive programs should be designed, and efforts should be made to remediate the disability" (p. 423). *Special Education* refers generally to the medical model as practiced in schools. The term encompasses the sets of procedures, services, and practices designed to evaluate and instruct students with disabilities in school settings.

Historically, the first special educators were physicians such as Jean-Marc-Gaspard Itard, Edouard Sequin, and Maria Montessori who, according to Shea and Bauer (1997), focused on the causes of a condition and how to diagnose it. The first special education schools were for children who were deaf/hard-of-hearing or blind. Special education schools for children diagnosed with cognitive disabilities (e.g., mental retardation) and developmental disabilities opened gradually, usually associated with hospitals. The 1950s, however, ushered in the "modern" era of special education during which hosts of other school-based disability classifications emerged. Diagnoses of cultural deprivation, emotional disturbance, and learning disability each gave rise to new classrooms and categories under the umbrella of special education.

Although medical diagnostics were not used to identify children with learning and behavioral "disorders," school and psychiatric methods of evaluation sought objective measures and scientific ways to explain these students' struggle in school. Linton, Mello, and O'Neill (1995) point out:

> Even though special education doesn't rely solely on medical diagnosis, the field by definition forefronts the physical, cognitive, and sensory impairments of individuals. The diagnoses and label become the major defining variable of learners, and the pedagogical practice is largely determined by these designations (p. 7).

Thus, students classified as having disabilities are often treated as patients in need of remediation and cure.

Perceiving the problem as primarily medical can lead to all other activities, including future planning, being suspended until the child is cured or remediated.

Students perceived as having problems, like something broken, are sent to resource rooms, special classes, even special schools or institutions, to be repaired and later returned. Unlike a repair shop, however, many students in special education—indeed the preponderance of them never escape the special label and placement (excluding those with speech impairments that are either cured or simply disappear by the time students reach secondary level). They stay in the repair shop (Biklen, Ferguson, and Ford, 1989: 8).

A medical model of disability fundamentally constructs students with disabilities as physically "defective" and most in need of diagnosis and treatment. Diagnosing disability is often seen as a medical process, as is the course of treatment. Defining disability as essentially medical relegates it to the realm of the physiological. In turn, responsibility for treatment is assigned to specialized professionals. Fixing or curing the disability becomes the primary focus in the child's life.

The medical model influences the manner in which children are diagnosed with disability and treated. A significant outcome of the model's prevalence is the focus on the individual as the site of problem and cure. That is, the disability is located *in* the individual and treatment seeks to fix, alter, or influence the individual. The medical model suggests, "difficulties in schooling belong to the student instead of being a product of school and student interaction" (Biklen, Ferguson, and Ford, 1989: 262). Efforts to increase access and change attitudes, however, must be undertaken by schools, communities, and society. The problem of exclusion is everyone's problem, and does not merely belong to the person being excluded. Our efforts to realize inclusive education are stymied by the school's (and larger culture's) construction of disability as an individual predicament.

To engage in lasting reform toward inclusion, Sapon-Shevin (1989) stated the importance of shifting to a new paradigm:

> A new vision of schools must emerge from an understanding of school functions and practices that incorporate historical, political, economic, and professional frames of reference about both education and disability. The underlying notions that have guided special education must now be replaced by a totally new way of viewing children and their differences (p. 93).

The joint fields of *Disability Studies* and *Disability Studies in Education* have much to offer in shaping inclusive education reform.

Introducing Disability Studies

Disability studies are an interdisciplinary field of scholarship that focuses on the contributions, experiences, history, and culture of people with disabilities.

Disability studies seek to expand the ways that society defines, conceptualizes, and understands the meaning of disability. They involve examining the policies and practices of societies to put forth the social and cultural determinants of disability, rather than the physiological (Linton, 1998). Ware (2001) explains, "the new disability studies understand disability as a way of thinking about bodies rather than as something that is wrong with bodies" (p. 110).

The purposes of disability studies are markedly political. When it is thought that people have something wrong with them, we are less likely to consider their claim to equal rights in schools and society. One right, for example, includes equal access and opportunity in schools. By framing disability in its social dimensions, the practice of segregating a child based on his or her extraordinary body or mind becomes unacceptable. Providing instruction that focuses only on the diagnosis and remediation of children with disabilities inequitably constrains their school experience. Disability studies offer tools for analysis that challenge the idea that "the assigned roles of people with disabilities are inevitable outcomes of their condition" (Linton, as cited in Fleischer and Zames, 2001: 206).

One example of change that can result in thinking about disability as something "about bodies" rather than something wrong with them is found in ramps in public spaces. In most areas of recent construction or new sidewalks, ramps and curb cuts (ramps that make a smooth path from the sidewalk to the street) are apparent. These physical features provide access to people who use wheelchairs. They have become part of our built environment largely because of the activism of wheelchair users and their allies to demand changes that increase freedom of movement and make traveling safer. By focusing on the inaccessibility of streets and buildings without ramps, the discussion of disability shifts to locating the problem of movement in the lack of accessible environments, rather than in the wheelchair user. Ultimately, the broader public, such as those pushing baby carriages and strollers, also benefits from ramps and curb cuts.

Disability studies relate to the civil action known as *Disability Rights*. Akin to civil action in America toward civil rights for women, African-Americans, gays and lesbians, and immigrants, the Disability Rights movement seeks political rights and equity for people who experience discrimination based on disability. Longmore and Umansky (2001) explain:

> As with disability rights legislation and activism, the new academic field of disability studies has risen in response to the medical model's deficiencies in explaining or addressing the social marginalization and economic deprivation of many people with disabilities. Disability studies takes as its domain the intricate interaction among cultural values, social arrangements, public policy, and professional practice regarding "disability" (p. 12).

The activism of disability studies is a response or reaction to a medical model of disability. Because disability has been constructed in a medical model, there has been less value assigned to understanding disabled persons' experiences of life in ways other than as "medicalized" experiences. In other words, we have not considered *other* ways to understand meanings of disability or how social and cultural practices affect our understanding and beliefs about disability. The focus of disability studies, then, is to engage in other ways of defining, understanding, and inquiring into disability.

Scholarship in disability studies with particular respect to inclusion in education is burgeoning. Barton and Armstrong (2001) offer a view of inclusion that prioritizes attention on removing barriers to access. In so doing, they shift the focus from the "deficient" student—as in a medical model—to the responsibility of the school and its creation of barrier-free social and organizational structures:

> From the perspectives we have adopted, inclusion is not about placement into an unchanged system of provision and practice, Also, it is not merely about the participation of a specific group of formerly categorized individuals. ... It is about removing *all* forms of barriers to access and learning for *all* children who are experiencing disadvantage. This approach is rooted in conceptions of democracy, citizenship, and a version of the "good" society. ... Thus, inclusive education is not an end in itself but a means to an end—that of the realization of an inclusive society. This necessitates schools adopting a critical stance both internally and externally toward all forms of justice and discrimination (p. 708).

"Inclusion is about restructuring the curriculum and expanding it to include humanistic values that go beyond science and the quantitative world" (Saini, 2001: 155). As with disability studies, disability studies in education (DSE) examine disability and the experiences of students with disabilities differently from a medical model (Gabel, 2005).

Conclusion: The Three R's: Recognition, Respect, and Responsibility

Understanding inclusive education as a moral value is a momentous trend in educational thinking (Biklen, Ferguson, and Ford, 1989). Inclusion benefits children with disabilities and reinforces the values of recognition, respect and responsibility. Realizing inclusive education, however, requires critically examining culture. We can understand the way attitudes toward persons with disabilities, more often negative, have mitigated past efforts. Disability studies in education offer a theory of inquiry and practice that promise to push efforts in inclusive education in new directions. We end this chapter with "The Three R's"—Recognition, Respect, and Responsibility—to describe some assumptions that shape this book.

Recognition refers to the degree of attention that a person or a group receives. Before one can be respected, one's existence must be recognized. Some efforts to reduce the stigma of disability include advice to "see the person, and not his or her disability." While we acknowledge the positive intention that underlies the idea—not dissimilar to approaching equity in racial relations through "color-blindness"—disability fundamentally shapes the way a person experiences the world and the way others in the world experience her or him. Rather than try to ignore the extraordinariness of bodies and other characteristics, recognition of disability and related experiences are essential to forging value for, rather than ignorance of, the lives of disabled persons.

Respect refers to the means by which someone demonstrates regard for the worth of someone else. Respect for others requires one to treat all people as having dignity and rights commensurate with one's own. We presume the worth, dignity, and civil rights of all children and adults.

Responsibility is an extension of respect. In Lickona's (1991) formula, if we learn to respect persons with disabilities, we value them. If we value them, we feel some responsibility for their welfare. Seeking inclusive schools and societies is everybody's concern, and everyone's responsibility. The responsibility for inclusive education reform does not fall only to students with disabilities, their families, and special educators, but to all.

2
Paradigms of Disability

A paradigm is an ideology or frame of reference. It is the way one perceives, understands, or interprets a topic or issue. Individuals interpret (often unknowingly) everything they experience through paradigms, frequently without questioning their accuracy. People simply assume that the way they view things is the way things really are or the way things should be. Paradigms are so ingrained in culture that they seem "natural." They are a primary source of our attitudes and actions. Awareness of the paradigms that structure our experiences and reactions to them can enable us to identify the sources of our beliefs and attitudes. Analyses undertaken in disability studies and in education propose that, in order to change negative attitudes toward persons with disabilities, we need to shift paradigms. That is, we need to find new ways of thinking about disability. In this chapter, we describe the paradigms of the medical model and social model, which shape school and societal responses to persons with disabilities.

The Medical Model

> The medical model has two dimensions: normal and pathological. Normal is defined as the absence of a biological problem. Pathological is defined as alterations in an organism caused by disease, which is a state of ill health that interferes with or destroys the organism. The medical model often referred to as the disease model, focuses primarily on biological problems and on defining the nature of the disease and its pathological effects on the individual. The model is universal and does not have values that are culturally relative. It is based on the premise that being healthy is better than being sick, regardless of the culture in which one lives. (Hardman, Drew, and Egan 1996: 18)

A medical model of disability makes meaning of disabled persons' experiences in terms of objective, innate conditions that limit their ability to participate in communities and learn in the general classroom setting. Described by Hardman, Drew, and Egan (1996), it relies on the distinction between that which is "normal" and that which is "pathological." In this view, school and society employ a discourse of scientific objectivity to position disability as a matter of fact; a law of the real (Stiker, 1997). The medical model recommends a scientific approach to disability. Diagnosing the source of deviance within the individual is the first step, followed by expert guidance and treatment to intervene in, cure, or remedy the source of deviance. Thus, accurate diagnosis and appropriate treatment for disability are the primary concerns put forth in a medical model.

The Medical Model in Education: IDEIA

The dominance of a medical model for addressing disability in schools is evident in The Individuals with Disabilities Education Improvement Act (IDEIA, 2004), which describes the procedure through which students with disabilities may receive special education services. Under IDEIA, a school representative or parent/guardian nominates a child whom they suspect to have a disability to be referred for disability assessment. A multidisciplinary team, which may include the child's teachers, a school psychologist, a social worker, other therapists, an administrator, and family, then develop a prereferral intervention plan to attempt to address the student's difficulties. If the interventions are not successful, the child is then subject to an initial evaluation for disability, for which the school is required to:

A. use a variety of assessment tools and strategies to gather relevant functional and, developmental, and academic information, including information provided by the parent, that may assist in determining—

    i. whether the child is a child with a disability; and

    ii. the content of the child's individualized education program, including information related to enabling the child to be involved in and progress in the general education curriculum, or, for preschool children, to participate in appropriate activities;

B. not use any single measure or assessment as the sole criterion for determining whether a child is a child with a disability or determining an appropriate educational program for the child; and

C. use technically sound instruments that may assess the relative contribution of cognitive and behavioral factors, in addition to physical or developmental factors. [IDEIA 20 U.S.C. §1414 (SEC. 614), 2004]

The primary concerns in a medical model are proper diagnosis of the disability, then determining and implementing appropriate treatment. IDEIA (2004) describes the practice of diagnosis/assessment as one of determining "whether the child is a child with a disability." It specifies the use of a variety of tools and strategies. These include (a) gathering information about the child from those who know him or her—most often teachers and family members, and (b) using "technically sound instruments" to assess cognitive, behavioral, physical, and developmental factors that affect the child's learning and participation in school. Common instruments administered by psychologists or licensed educational evaluators include psychometric batteries such as the Woodcock-Johnson® tests of Achievement (Woodcock, McGrew, and Mather, 2001) or Cognitive Abilities (Woodcock, McGrew, and Mather, 2003), or the *Wechsler Intelligence Scale for Children* (Wechsler et al., 2004).

Another requirement of IDEIA (2004) is that a child found to have a disability and who is eligible to receive special education services have an Individualized Education Program (IEP). The IEP is an annually written educational program for each child with a disability who is eligible for special educational services. Shapiro (1999) likens the IEP to an educational prescription.

IDEIA offers an overview and rules and regulations for the process of diagnosing or assessing disability, then developing a formal course of treatment for the student, which is documented in the IEP. Its requirement of the use of "technically sound" instruments to inform assessment, and its reliance on the participation of educational experts demonstrates the alignment of IDEIA with a medical model. The focus is on the individual and her or his pathology as the primary locus of educational decision-making and practice.

The Influence of a Medical Model in School Placement Practice

In addition to the procedures that surround a child with a disability described in IDEIA, the influence of a medical model is perceptible in past special education placement practices. Placing students with disabilities into classrooms designated by the disability category was once common practice. For example, there would be particular classrooms for students labeled with learning disabilities, another for those identified as mentally retarded, another for "emotionally disturbed" students, and so on. These placement practices reflected a medical model in presuming that the educational setting should align with the disability diagnosis.

> Classification schemes have led to the person being confused with the characteristics being classified when programs are designed and delivered so services are for those with some level of intellectual disability or for "quads" rather than for those who want to learn to cook. And classification schemes are used as the eligibility criteria for inclusion or exclusion rather than interest, aptitude or need (Rioux, 1996: 6).

The assumption that students with the same disability would benefit from the same kinds of services and curriculum exemplifies the assumption of the objectivity of a disability diagnosis. That is, it was assumed that the diagnosis/disability would reflect the same or similar experience, and therefore indicate the same kinds of solutions. The result was that "special education" became synonymous to the placement of a child with a disability into a segregated classroom with groups of students classified with the same disability category.

Taylor (1988/2004) challenged the practice of special education to be a decision of "placement," rather than as the provision of special services. He described that students perceived as having "severe" disabilities—those requiring intensive support—were automatically placed into the most restrictive settings. It was assumed that their needs were primarily medical and therefore could not be met in more inclusive educational environments. He argued that many services could be provided in less restrictive environments, such as the general education setting, rather than in self-contained special education placements. In other words, the degree of need for special services should not be assumed from the disability diagnosis, nor should the setting in which children are educated be determined only according to the kind or perceived intensity of the services required.

The Medical Model: A Broader View

The medical model reflects shifts in social and cultural norms. In the recent past, pregnancy, childbirth, contraception, diet, exercise, alcoholism, other addictions, erratic behavior, hyperactive children, and disability were not considered medical matters (Macionis, cited in Conrad and Schneider, 1992). Abnormal aspects of each are now featured in the *Diagnostic and Statistical Manual of Mental Disorders* (DSM-IV TR) (2000) of the American Psychological Association, which is a catalog of psychological abnormalities and conditions. One effect of medicalization, then, is the increase in number and kind of experiences defined as pathological.

Another effect of medicalization is a change in the way behavior patterns are perceived. Some behaviors, which were previously understood in moral terms, have become medical. The connotation of some labels used to designate normality or deviance changed from moral terms such as "bad" and "good" to medical terms such as "sick" and "well." Medicalization served to transform deviance from "badness" to "sickness," with its social response becoming "therapeutic" rather than "punitive." "Treatment" for deviance in a medical model is construed, perhaps, to be more humane than "punitive" measures, as well as more easily received by the patient. Thus, medicalization serves to remove the moral stigma from seeking treatment for some kinds of illness.

The benefit that comes from the removal of moral stigma releases the patient from blame and shame. However, medicalization has also invited critique, especially related to disability. Medical definitions are, as Oliver (1990) stated, "partial and limited and fail to take into account wider aspects of disability" (p. 5). Similarly, Hirsch and Hirsch (1995) found the medical model to "perpetuate stigmatizing cultural conceptions of disability when applied to such other aspects of a disabled person's life as educational, professional, social, economic, recreational, and civic activities and interests" (p. 23). Tessier (as cited in *People in Motion*, 1995), a disability rights activist and former candidate for Congress, similarly stresses how the medical model, with its emphasis on "cures," results in a narrow view of the lives of persons with disabilities:

> The medical model is a trap. It defines us simply as physical limitations, medical conditions. It is what justifies the cures, the treatments, incarcerations until you're somehow whole again. And it makes it impossible for us to be seen as full, rounded people. That's the core of our oppression (cited in *People in Motion*, p. 2).

Demonstrated by these authors, the medicalization of disability leads to limited understanding of an individual. Medical descriptions fail to fully capture the particular ways that a specific individual may experience a disability. A second problem is the relationship between medicine and cure. As Hirsh and Hirsh (1995) and Tessier (as cited in *People in Motion*, 1995) point out, the emphasis on being cured obscures the possibility for people with disabilities to be capable and fulfilled. An emphasis on cure also influences the ways that the medical and rehabilitation fields have perceived people with disabilities.

Placed in the role of "permanent patient," one loses power and dignity. One feature of medicalization is the exaltation of the role of the doctor or professional in matters of diagnosis and treatment. When a person with a disability refuses to behave like a good patient, the behaviors are often viewed as "symptoms of maladjustment." In fact, refusal to cooperate actively with the source of help to achieve recovery leads to the individual's loss of personal rights and dignity. Society generally sees nothing wrong with placing disabled individuals under the perpetual tutelage of those experts who provide the help.

> It is often difficult to explain what is wrong with this arrangement. The seemingly benevolent impulses that drive these practices belie the paternalism and control these tools serve. The arrangement privileges the medical definitions of people's lives over the social and political definitions. The solution to the "problem" of disability is seen as residing in the resources and facilities of the medical establishment, rather than in legislative bodies and social institutions. The arrangement buys into the assumption that people with disabilities are more concerned with cures than rights, more plagued with their conditions than with discrimination (Linton, Mello, and O'Neill, 1995: 8).

Medicalization ascribes roles to persons with disabilities. The patient role positions persons with disabilities as recipients of care, which limits their power to influence the course of treatment and set a political agenda.

The medical model is a paradigm with varied implications. Medicalization has removed stigma from some conditions, which releases individuals from moral judgments and has enabled the development of therapy rather than punishment. Because disability refers to long-term and permanent conditions, persons with disabilities may be positioned as permanent patients. Their lives may be overly directed toward recovery and they may lose power and dignity relative to the professionals who treat them.

Summary of the Medical Model

The medical model is a paradigm that structures and influences many facets of contemporary life for persons with disabilities in American society. Two distinguishing features of the model are (a) its classification schemes in which characteristics are designated as normal and abnormal, or pathological; and (b) the preference for a course of cure-seeking treatment, as prescribed by a medical or rehabilitation professional. Implications of the model are decision-making that prioritizes medical aspects of disability, which detract attention from other facets of an individual's life; and the less powerful position ascribed to "patients," which prevents their full participation in developing their own social and political agendas for civil rights, as one example. As Rioux (1996) and Taylor (1988/2004) point out, education placement practices that reflect a medical model may overly emphasize the meaning of a child's category of disability or her or his medical needs, which can result in school opportunities that limit other kinds of experiences.

To view disability issues solely as medical is analogous to viewing gender issues as gynecological or racial issues as dermatological. Many people report that the embodied experiences of impaired sight, hearing, learning, or movement actually cause fewer barriers to living full lives than the loss of power, dignity, prejudice, discrimination, and intolerance that they experience in relation to others' perceptions of disability (e.g., see Linton, 1998; Gliedman, 1979; Bell and Burgdorf, 1983; Hahn, 1987; Oliver, 1996; Mackelprang and Salsgiver, 1996; Rioux, 1996). One needs to go beyond physiological or cognitive conditions to gain a fuller understanding of disability (Rioux, 1996).

Social Models of Disability

The medical model is the dominant paradigm of disability and is quite perceptible in American education legislation, such as the IDEIA. Social models of disability provide another paradigm. Social models of disability forefront the influence our economic and social structures and central values have on the ways in which we define disability and respond to persons with them (Oliver, 1990: xii). They focus not only on a disabling feature, but also on the social context in which disability becomes meaningful. Social models aim to understand disability as a total experience of complex interactions between the body and physical, social, and cultural environments. Rather than a primary emphasis on diagnosing an individual's pathology, ostensibly leading to a course of treatment and cure in which one becomes a permanent patient, the focus shifts to considering virtually everything else—including the social, cultural, and political environment and its influence on the meaning made about disability, life opportunities, and quality of life.

A Sociopolitical Orientation to Disability

While there are a variety of theoretical approaches to social models of disability, we begin with a sociopolitical orientation, which is the most common view of a social model applied to education. Inspired by the Civil Rights movement of the 1960s, collective realizations of the impact of a medical model of disability led persons with disabilities to demand control and full access to society in the Disability Rights movement (Mackelprang and Salsgiver, 1996; Fleischer and Zames, 2001). Longmore (2005) describes the efforts of early American activists:

> Instead of attributing disabled people's social and economic marginalization to pathology, their campaign adopted a minority-group perspective. More urgent than remedial measures to fix individuals was the instatement of equal access, reasonable accommodations, and antidiscrimination protections. Rejecting the charity approach that beseeched attention to disabled people's needs, the movement demanded civil rights enforcement to ensure their right of access to society (p. 507).

This demand evolved into grassroots efforts to secure improved quality of life, and which centered primarily on social and political concerns. Emerging together, the new kinds of demands and the rationale for them informed the development and naming of new paradigms through which to conceptualize disability. The "minority group," the "civil rights," the "disablism," and "independence" models are some of the names for early social models. Each purport civil rights, including access to society's spaces, places, and opportunities, and the rights to self-determination and dignity, are the central issues for persons with disabilities. We use the descriptor, *sociopolitical model of disability*, to encompass the variety of models that emphasize a civil rights perspective.

A sociopolitical model of disability generally views variations among bodies and minds and changes in physical or cognitive function as natural parts of the human experience. Variations need not be described as pathologies, but as anticipated and acceptable occurrences. Following this line of reason, it is not acceptable to discriminate on the basis of difference (assuming a society that espouses the equality of all its members, as in the United States). A difference becomes a *disability* when people with particular characteristics are not able to access life opportunities and experiences as a result of inaccessible contexts or other barriers related to the perceived difference. Disability, then, is a condition defined by an interaction, not only in a body.

Some theorists, such as Wendell (1997), differentiate "impairment" from "disability." This emphasizes the distinction between the physical or sensory experience of a particular characteristic and sociopolitical oppression. The term, *impairment*, refers to the pathology; and *disability* refers to political and economic disempowerment that results from societal barriers to people with impairments. Describing characteristics as "impaired" acknowledges a lack or limit in function, but highlights the experience of disability as one based on context.

In Linton's (1998) words, disabled persons "are all bound together, not by [a] list of collective symptoms but by the social and political circumstances that have forged us as a group" (p. 4). "Persons with disabilities" are a collective defined by common experiences of oppression resulting from barriers that make those with physical, cognitive, and/or sensory impairments unable to access places, information, and opportunities. In contrast to a medical model in which diagnosis and treatment of impairments are central, a sociopolitical model "views prejudice and discrimination as the major issues confronting citizens with disabilities" (Hahn, 1987: 184). Waxman (1992) supports Hahn's claim, and offers:

> Disabled people face a pattern of oppressive societal treatment and hatred, much as women face misogyny, gay men and lesbians face homophobia, Jews face anti-Semitism and people of color face racism. [D]ata about rape, child sexual abuse, incest, sexual harassment, battery, neglect, defamation and other forms of violence directed at disabled people indicate that they are much more likely to be targeted for violence than their non-disabled cohorts. Ongoing research estimates that sexual violence directed at disabled people is one and a half times that directed at non-disabled people of the same sex and age (p. 5).

A sociopolitical orientation to disability engages the social and political issues of persons with extraordinary bodies in ways similar to other "minority" groups who experience oppression on the basis of otherwise natural and cultural characteristics or identities.

Other Orientations Within the Social Model

Another approach to the social model of disability, addressed by Thomas and Corker (2002), critiques a sociopolitical model in the way that it differentiates between impairment and disability. They argue that our understandings about the nature of the body and mind as being impaired or not are produced in our social interactions, but originate and are mediated through the ways that language symbolizes our ideas about the human body. This "postmodern" orientation contends that the meaning and connotation of the word "disability" precedes and shapes the initial meaning we make about a body. It is because we are aware of the concept that identifying people as disabled is made initially possible. The very act of assigning the label or identity of disability to someone is an act of power.

Similar to McDermott and Varenne's (1995) view of disability *as* culture, the language we use to describe "normal" and "abnormal" bodies represent a hierarchical relationship between ability and disability. "Disability" is constructed in a hierarchical relationship with "ability." The term "ability" is the norm and is the preferred state. "Disability" is its converse. The result is that those who become labeled or who choose to identify as disabled are positioned on the undesirable side of a dichotomy. They are fundamentally made marginal.

Social Models of Disability in Society: Disability Studies and Disability Rights

Discussions that explicitly refer to "social models" of disability are found mostly in academic research and scholarship. Disability studies and the influence of the Disability Rights Movement and their ideas, products, and outcomes, however, are increasingly perceptible in the public arena. Although disability studies are eclectic, as Gabel (2005) points out, a common tenet is their commitment to social models of disability and bringing to fore the lives, experiences, and political agendas of persons with disabilities. Internationally, academic programs in interdisciplinary studies, cultural studies, the humanities, the health professions, and education with a "Disability Studies" orientation are becoming increasingly available. The passage of the Rehabilitation Act of 1973 and the Americans with Disabilities Act of 1990 demonstrated political acknowledgement that discrimination against persons with disabilities exists, and should be worked against. As societies become more knowledgeable about the lives and experiences of disabled persons and commit to their political goals, perhaps the influence of social models will become even more perceptible.

Social Models of Disability in Education: Inclusion

Education is an enterprise characterized by its dividing and ranking (e.g., grading and testing) of students. We are consistently willing to explain mismatches between school expectations and student performance as resulting from poverty, cultural differences, family life, degree of English language acquisition, intelligence quotient, personal motivation, disability, and so on (Tomlinson, 2004). As Baker (2002) points out, we are not only willing to refer to such categorical explanations, but we actively engage in a "hunt" for them. In other words, we seek pathological explanations to explain differential school performance and justify its resulting unequal distribution of rewards. Described earlier, IDEIA most strongly reflects a medical model, which has been the dominant model in education.

A social model of disability in schools is found in the idea of inclusive education. From a social model perspective, inclusion is seen as an active process of social interaction. Classroom members continuously construct and negotiate the social and academic contexts of schooling to position themselves and others as included and excluded; full or ancillary members in the classroom and learning community (Allan, 1999). Teachers can design instruction to be accessible and engaging to students with and without disabilities (Hehir, 2003). The way that the participation of students is structured, the kinds of talk and expectations that are anticipated, and the way that students interact with others are made routine as social norms that may serve to include or exclude class members (Allan, 1999; Collins, 2003). Teachers can model and set expectations for mutual respect and appreciation of diversity (Shapiro, 1999; Stiker, 1997). They can create learning situations in which all students work together to position all class members as included (Tomlinson, 1999). Teachers may also position disability experiences as valuable and prominent as they choose materials that represent people with disabilities. In addition, they may engage in disrupting stereotypic characterizations of disability through critical thinking activities and interaction (Ben-Moshe, 2006; Gallagher, 2006).

Summary of Social Models

Social models of disability assert that disability is made meaningful in social interactions. A sociopolitical approach utilizes its paradigm to argue that culture and societal structures impact a person's experience of an impairment to position him or her as disabled. A postmodern approach offers a way to examine the meaning we make of or assign to bodies in our words and language practices. The very word "disability" for example, demonstrates the negative comparison made between ability and disability. The thrust of social models is to interrupt the dominance of the medical model, in order to more fully understand *and* challenge the ways that deep-seated assumptions and beliefs about the nature and impairment and disability prevent the equal participation and status of disabled persons.

Paradigms, Position, and Power

Why do paradigms matter? It might seem that the orientation to disability that we have matters less than the significant progress in civil rights and education legislation over the past half-century. Unfortunately, despite provisions for a barrier-free environment and anti-discrimination employment policies, and despite mandates for special education and subsequent amendments and reforms, persons with disabilities continue to struggle. They experience high rates of unemployment and underemployment, are among the more vulnerable populations for abuse and victimization, continue to have limited options for dignified housing and supportive services, and many children are denied the fullest educational opportunity. In short, persons with disabilities continue to experience discrimination and oppression.

Paradigms inform what how we make meaning and what we believe counts as the knowledge used to make meaning. The paradigm through which we conceptualize disability and subsequently act toward persons with disabilities effects social and political interactions that occur in public life. To understand some reasons for the continued oppression of people with disabilities, it is useful to examine the ways that medical and social models of disability influence our everyday perceptions and interactions.

Stereotypes, Prejudice, and Discrimination

One way to examine the paradigm of disability that informs a particular context is to examine actions, reactions, knowledge, and beliefs that seem taken-for-granted, or which persist over time. We develop particular ideas and responses to people and things as we interact with our culture, and adopt its perspectives. Because culture is all encompassing, we are often not aware that some beliefs and actions that we adopt may be inaccurate or harmful. Examining and transforming the paradigms that inform our beliefs and actions are necessary to mitigate ongoing oppression of disempowered groups and individuals.

We can engage in critical reflection and engagement with others to understand distortions in our thinking about unfamiliar experiences and transform them (Mezirow, 1991; Brookfield, 2004). Within disability studies, there are two lines of argument that reflect critical examination of paradigms. (1) Discerning the influence of paradigms on the lives of persons with disabilities in policy and social practices encapsulates. (2) Recognizing and valuing the participation and perspectives of disabled persons is another. These two lines of inquiry are not distinct, but emerge together. As society attends to the voices of disabled persons, others are made aware of their distorted beliefs or perceptions. Likewise, as we examine the influence of a paradigm and are able to understand the basis for its dominance we are able to make conscious choices to adopt or reject related beliefs and actions. Two questions that a social model puts forth are, How does our culture depict disability and disabled persons? and How do these depictions influence our interactions? One way to critically examine culture is to consider its stereotypes.

Disability Stereotypes

To stereotype is to generalize that all people with a characteristic share other characteristics. A stereotype can also be an exaggerated belief associated with a category. An example is the belief that blind people have extraordinary hearing or exceptional musical talent. Stereotypes persist, because (1) they are constantly reinforced by the media, (2) they reflect the human need to simplify and organize people, and (3) they reinforce the prejudice and discrimination that allow those in power to benefit and profit from the subordinate status of the stereotyped groups (Smart, 2001: 185).

In 1972, Wolfensberger, Nirje, Olshansky, Perske and Roos described the varieties of typical attitudes and related stereotypes toward persons with disabilities. They enumerated typical ways in which persons with disabilities are viewed and their implications for institutional (e.g., school) attitudes as well as personal attitudes. Since then, many other scholars have examined attitudes, stereotypes, and tropes that persist in the public purview (e.g., Darke, 1998; Shakespeare, 1994; Mitchell and Snyder, 2001; Thomson, 1997; Nario-Redmond, 2008). Unfortunately, many of the stereotypes or tropes related to disability have not changed since Wolfensberger et al.'s work in 1972. The following describes some disability stereotypes that have persisted over time, and are readily recognizable in media, entertainment, artistic, and other elements of culture.

The object of pity—The diseased or sick patient. Wolfensberger et al. listed five views associated with the view of persons with disabilities as objects of pity: First, the person with a disability is seen as suffering from his or her condition. Second, although the person may be seen as suffering he or she may also be believed to be unaware of his or her deviancy. Third, the person is seen as an eternal child who never grows. Fourth, being held blameless for his or her condition, the person is seen as not accountable for his or her behavior. Fifth, the individual is viewed with a "there but for the grace of God go I" attitude.

Characters such as Tiny Tim in Charles Dickens's (1843) work, *A Christmas Carol*, exemplify this pitiable characterization. Authors often use the stereotype as a device for revealing another character's goodness and sensitivity. For example, disabled characters offer the possibility for spiritual or moral redemption, as Scrooge becomes the savior to Tiny Tim. Disability becomes a device of characterization in order to propel the plot of the story or add dimension to non-disabled characters (Mitchell and Snyder, 2001; Thomson, 1997). Characterizations as objects of pity are also useful to elicit emotional responses, not only in works of art, but also in media events such as telethons. According to Longmore (2005), Tiny Tim was the model for the infantilized image of poster children. The image of the pitiable disabled person serves as "vehicle of others' redemption, existing not for himself or herself, not as a human being in his or her own right, but to provide the occasion for non-disabled people to renew their humanity" (pp. 505–506).

The subhuman organism. Another common stereotype characterizes persons with disabilities as subhuman. Wolfensberger et al. (1972) note that those with intellectual disabilities (i.e., mental retardation) "are particularly apt to be unconsciously perceived or even consciously labeled as subhuman, as animal-like, even as 'vegetables' or 'vegetative.'" He recalled the public statement of a state institution's superintendent who referred to some of the residents as "so called human beings below what we might call an animal level of functioning" (pp. 16–17). This imagery is found in literature by writers such as John Steinbeck (1937) who, in his widely read novel *Of Mice and Men* describes Lennie, an intellectually disabled adult, walking "heavily, dragging his feet a little, the way a bear drags his paws" (p. 10). Steinbeck describes Lennie drinking from a stream "with long gulps, snorting into the water like a horse" (p. 10). The book ends with Lennie being killed by a shot to the back of his head similar to the way an old sick dog had been "disposed of" earlier in the story. The killing by his companion and caretaker, George, is typically interpreted as a humane end to Lennie's life. Viewing disabled persons as less-human than others presents a significant barrier to claims to equal rights and treatment in society.

Sinister or evil: The menace or the monster. Longmore (1987) found that the most common association of disability is with malevolence. "Deformity of the body symbolizes deformity of the soul. Physical handicaps are made the emblems of evil" (p. 66). Fiedler (1996) similarly stated, "[I]n the throes of our paranoia and projection, we convince ourselves that the crippledness of the cripple is an outward and visible sign of an inward state" (p. 41). Bogdan (1988) illustrated how such stereotypes are internalized. He described watching *Treasure Island* on television one evening with his 10-year-old son and his friend:

> Near the beginning of the film my son's friend, Jeremy, who was confused about the plot asked: "Who's the bad guy?" My son replied: "If they look bad, they are bad" (p. vii).

Bogdan, struck by his son's insight, continued:

> In the film, part of being bad is looking bad, and villains were marked by various disfigurements and disabilities, such as missing limbs and eyes. Horror film monsters are scarred, deformed, disproportionately built, hunched over, exceptionally large, exceptionally small, deaf, speech impaired, visually impaired, mentally ill, or mentally subnormal. In fact, the word monster is standard medical terminology for infants born with blatant defects (p. vii).

Kiger (1989) found the messages regarding disability in film are often derogatory, victimize or degrade persons with impairments, and add up over time to "establish distinct patterns of imagery" (p. 155). Garland Thomson (1997) confirms similar patterns in literature, and Darke's 1998 analysis of film supports Kiger's claim that there are distinct patterns of imagery associated with disability. Images that enforce a relationship between monsters and villains and characteristics of disability can be found in innumerable cultural products.

In fairy tales, the evil ones are most often giants, as in *Jack in the Beanstalk*, dwarfs such as *Rumpelstiltskin*, or Quilp, "the monstrous dwarf who stalks 'Little Nell' through the pages of Charles Dickens's *The Old Curiosity Shop*" (Fiedler, 1996: 41). Often, they are also toothless witches with humps on their backs and eye patches. Remember the crooked man who lived in a crooked house? The relationship between outer physique and evilness is exemplified by the characterization of Captain Hook in *Peter Pan* (Barrie, 1911; Kennedy,

Marshall, Molen, and Spielberg, 1991; McCormic, Fisher, Wick, and Hogan, 2003) named for his prosthesis. Similarly, one of the most popular classical literary devices for conveying evil or disparagement is "the twisted mind in the twisted body" (Margolis and Shapiro, 1987). According to Mitchell and Snyder (2001), it is common for authors to use the device of the "deformed" outer body to reflect the "deformed" inner qualities of their characters. Similarly, Davis (1997) found, "If disability appears in a novel, it is rarely centrally represented. ... [S]ufficient research has shown, more often than not villains tend to be physically abnormal, scarred, deformed or mutilated" (p. 19).

The unspeakable object of dread. Closely related to the stereotype of evilness is the "monster" or the "object of dread." Wolfensberger et al. (1972) described the perception of this individual as a "dreadful entity or event" (p. 20). The monster stereotype is often used in terms of retribution for sins, such as the disabled child sent to its parents by God as punishment for their sins. Longmore (1987) described this character as monster or predator or "one reviled by society as repulsive to behold and dangerous to its well-being." The character also has a "violent loss of self-control, living in a moral vacuum where life holds little value" (p. 68). This stereotype appears in classic horror stories such as *The Phantom of the Opera* (Webber and Schumacher, 2004), *Dr. Jekyll and Mr. Hyde* (Saville and Fleming, 1941), and *The Hunchback of Notre Dame* (Berman and Dieterle, 1939; Hahn, Trousdale, and Wise, 1996).

In addition to problem of images of disability that connote fear, horror, and dread, the images of disabled persons as menaces to society and/or as subhuman once provided justification for forced sterilization during the eugenics movement in the United States. The idea that particular members of society threaten the genetic pool reflects the concept of the "social menace" used by the Nazis toward all forms of difference in their quest for "racial purification." While these dangers represent extreme reactions to disability, the negative impact of images that equate disability with fear, horror, and sub-humanness can contribute to feelings of aversion toward people with particular characteristics.

We must realize that images of persons with disabilities as evil, dangerous, monstrous, and menacing has had serious effects on our attitudes and prejudices. By linking unattractiveness (which is, after all, a value judgment) and physical and mental differences with murder, terror, violence, and evil, we create and perpetuate society's prejudices—prejudices that produce fear and avoidance of persons with disabilities, and ultimately their systematic, intentional exclusion from society (Bogdan, Biklen, Shapiro and Spelkoman, 1982).

The holy innocent or the eternal child. In many and various cultures, individuals with disabilities—particularly those with intellectual disabilities—have been viewed as the "special children of God." They are anointed by grace, or portrayed as "'gee-golly,' happy-go-lucky simpletons" (Biklen, 1981:

5). As such, they are usually seen as incapable of committing evil voluntarily, and consequently may be considered living saints. It may also be believed that they have been sent by a higher power for some special purpose. The role of intellectual disability to signify holiness or eternal innocence has been recognized in a number of cultures and eras, and is reflected in films including *Forrest Gump* (Zemeckis, 1994), *I Am Sam* (Nelson, 2001), and *Rainman* (Levinson, 1988). In each, the eternal innocence of the disabled protagonists is a device used to reveal the flaws and foibles of their "normal" adult peers, and often poses situations in which *other* characters can find redemption through their experiences with the protagonist.

Disabled individuals seen as holy innocents were generally considered to be "harmless children" no matter their chronological ages. As a result, families, caregivers, and professionals who work with disabled persons frequently acquire the "Albert Schweitzer" or "Mother Theresa" syndrome, and characteristics such as having outstanding patience and are "doing God's work" are attributed to them. A major effect of the Holy Innocent stereotype is the juvenilization of adults with disabilities. Biklen (1981) believes the important point to be made is that adults with intellectual disabilities "experience the same emotions as non-disabled people, are capable of a broad range of behaviors, and possess individual and complex personalities" (p. 5). Images that depict disabled persons as eternally innocent and child-like can lead to paternalism and a denial of adult rights.

The object of comedy, ridicule and curiosity. Throughout history, people with disabilities have been viewed as funny, incompetent, and odd, from the use of persons with cerebral palsy and dwarfism as court jesters to the exhibition of freaks to contemporary television documentaries about rare medical conditions. Fiedler (1978) traced the historical roots of this stereotype to traditions based on arguments of such philosophers as Aristotle (1992), who viewed persons with physical anomalies as jokes of nature. "The tradition which derives from him, therefore, views such creatures as sources of amusement rather than of terror, thus, justifying showing them off for profit among the lowly, and keeping them for pets in the households of the wealthy" (p. 231). Thomson (1997) explained how "freaks" were put on display to ensure that their physical traits were dominated and highlighted the exhibit:

> On the freak show stage, highlighted characteristics circumscribed and reduced the inherent complexity of such figures as the Dwarf, the Giant, the Bearded Woman, the Armless or Legless Wonder, and the Fat Lady. Showmen barked embellishing adjectives like "wild" or "wondrous" and anachronistic, ironic pseudo-status titles like "King," "Queen," or "General" (as in the case of Charles Stratton, the famous "General Tom Thumb) that emphasized the extraordinary qualities of the body on display (p. 61).

The dramatic use of characters with disabilities "is a theatrical tradition rooted in antiquity" (Klobas, 1988: xi). Such humor has long been a part of Hollywood's history. It can be found in early film, as in Buster Keaton's 1921 silent film, *The Playhouse*; in Disney's creation, Dopey Dwarf, and in the visually impaired cartoon character, Mr. Magoo—the "archetypal incompetent disabled person" in children's media (Barnes, Berrigan, and Biklen, 1978: 59; Jernigan, 1983). Ridicule of impaired speech is also ingrained in our culture. Porky Pig's classic clonic spasm stutter and Elmer Fudd's and Tweety Bird's articulation substitutions have long reinforced a youngster's right to laugh at persons with speech impairments.

The burden. Viewing persons with disabilities as burdens to society and their caregivers promotes the condition of disability as gloomy, pessimistic and unfortunate. Movies such as *Whatever Happened to Baby Jane?* (Aldrich, 1962), *Sorry Wrong Number* (Litvak, Wallis, and Litvak 1948), *Lady Chatterly's Lover* (Globus, Golam, and Jaeckin, 1981), *Passion Fish* (Renzi, Green, and Sayles, 1992), *and What's Eating Gilbert Grape?* (Matalon, Ohsson, Teper, and Hallström, 1993) reinforce this stereotype. When children are regarded as burdens, the result is dependency, inequality, and rights becoming privileges. Education and the provision of rights and reasonable accommodations become acts of generosity. School districts often regard their students who receive special education services as burdens usurping services, taking away resources from "regular" students and, therefore, deserving lesser experiences than their non-disabled peers receive.

The victim of violence. Often, in children's stories characters with disabilities or physical differences are cast as defenseless recipients of violence (Biklen, and Bailey, 1981). Examples include "The Ugly Duckling," "Rudolph the Red-nosed Reindeer," "The Little Humpbacked Horse," "Pinocchio." Other examples where disabled persons portrayed as victims include *The Hunchback of Notre Dame*, the blind heroine in the movie *Wait Until Dark* (Young, 1967), and the deaf character "Mr. Singer" in the *Heart is a Lonely Hunter* (Freeman, Merson, Ryan, and Miller, 1968). A subtle complexity of casting disabled persons as victims lies in the way that this trope becomes linked to those of the object of pity and/or the holy innocent. While disabled persons are victimized in alarming proportions, more often the reasons do not relate to their particular impairments, but to the lack of access to safe and dignified living conditions.

The Supercrip or the Extraordinary Disabled. At the opposite end of the spectrum from the bumbling-incompetent disability stereotype is the romantic, idealized, and overstated super-disabled figure, often called the "supercrip." Media scholar John Clogston (as cited in Haller, 2000) defined the supercrip as:

> The disabled person is portrayed as deviant because of "superhuman" feats (i.e., an ocean-sailing blind man), or as "special" because they have

regular lives "in spite of" disability (i.e., a deaf high school student who plays softball). This portrayal reinforces the idea that disabled people are deviant—and so, for someone who is less than "complete" the accomplishment is "amazing."

Such stories appearing in the media are often received as inspirational stories. Extraordinary fictional characters with disabilities are found largely on television shows, films and in comic books. The character "Joe" in *Family Guy* (MacFarlane, 1999) and the depiction of Christy Brown in *My Left Foot* (Pearson and Sheridan, 1989) are two examples of media deploying the super-crip stereotype. Comic books have also spawned a number of heroes with disabilities, each possessing extraordinary skills that over compensate for the disability, as in *Daredevil* (Arad, Foster, Milchan, and Johnson, 2003).

The Influence of Paradigms

Stereotypes are reflections of paradigms. They are created and circulated over time and reinforce the paradigms on which they were built. Jernigan (1983), an activist with visual impairment comments on misconceptions about blindness "that go to the very root of our culture and permeate every aspect of social behavior and thinking":

> These misconceptions go back to the days when a blind person could not dodge a spear. In today's society, dodging a spear is not an essential ability but the stereotype of helplessness has remained intact, surrounded by a host of other stereotypes: The blind are simple, spiritual, musical; they have a special sixth sense; their other senses are more acute—in short, they are different and apart from the rest of society (pp. 58–59).

Stereotypes and their related prejudices can lead to discrimination in everyday interactions, as well as operate within oppressive social structures and systems. According to Henderson and Bryan (1997), the five most common forms of prejudice and beliefs toward people with disabilities include that they (1) are inferior, (2) are totally impaired, (3) are less intelligent, (4) need charity, and (5) prefer the company of others with disabilities (pp. 70–75). These can each be linked to the stereotypes we described, as well as to the medical model.

Mackelprang and Salsgiver (1996) describe one of the prevailing beliefs rooted in our culture, which reflects a medical model.

> [P]eople with disabilities can not and should not work or otherwise be productive. Contributing to the belief that people with disabilities should not work is the role of sick people in Western culture. People with disabilities, whom society assumes are "sick," are expected to fill this role even when they are perfectly healthy. As with those who are sick,

people with disabilities are to be taken care of and to be provided for. Their only obligation is to be grateful for the help given them, thus subjecting them to a form of benevolent oppression (p. 10).

Nario-Redmond (2008) confirms that the stereotype of disabled persons as unemployed and non-productive persists. Such stereotypes may influence the opportunities one is privy to, as well as one's self-concept. Sutherland (1984) asserted that stereotypes can become "self-fulfilling prophecies," forcing the individual with the disability into a role that can then be used to justify the original treatment. Additionally, he points out, "Someone who is assumed to be stupid is unlikely to receive much intellectual stimulation" (p. 59). Stereotypes lead to behaviors and actions that limit and reduce opportunities for people in that category (Smart, 2001: 185).

Influence of Paradigms on Public Policy

Many have discerned the relationship of paradigms of disability to social policy. Hahn (1987) elaborates on the limitations of the paradigm that defined disability almost exclusively from a medical viewpoint:

Disability was considered a "defect" or "deficiency" that could be located within the individual. From the clinical perspective of medicine, efforts to improve the functional capabilities of individuals were regarded as the exclusive solution to disability, and policy changes were essentially excluded from consideration as a possible remedy for the difficulties confronting the disabled (p. 181).

Similarly, Pope and Tarlov (1991) stress, the problems that disability-related programs seek to address are often viewed as inherent to the individual and as independent of society (p. 244). The emphasis on pathology in the individual detracts attention from issues of equity, which many persons with disabilities find to be the more pressing.

In contrast to the influence of a medical model, Oliver (1990) discusses the benefit of conceptualizing disability policy through a social model. He contends that if disability were defined as social oppression, social policies geared toward alleviating oppression, rather than compensating individuals, would be developed. The most important policy issue would become designing and modifying the environment—including attitudes and social arrangements—to permit access to opportunity for all (Kirchner, 1996).

Conclusion: Shifting Paradigms, Changing Attitudes

Changing paradigms from the medical model to social models is a challenge posed to both individuals and societies. Resisting stereotypes, prejudice, and discrimination are important to changing attitudes and correcting misperceptions about persons with disabilities. It is certainly possible to develop more positive attitudes toward persons with disabilities by identifying and then resisting problematic assumptions. Hockenberry (1995), a reporter and writer with paraplegia, states:

> Each stereotype thrives in direct proportion to the distance from each class of persons it claims to describe. Get close to the real people and these pretend images begin to break up, but they don't go easily. Losing a stereotype is about being wrong retroactively. For a person to confront such assumptions they must admit an open-ended wrong for as long as those assumptions have been inside them. There is a temptation to hold on to why you believed those stereotypes. "I was once frightened and disgusted by a person in a wheelchair." To relinquish such a stereotype is to lose face by giving up a mask (p. 89).

The process of identifying and changing deep-seated attitudes and beliefs is not an easy or comfortable one. In his theory of transformative learning, Mezirow (1991; 1998) describes a way to conceptualize learning processes involved in shifting paradigms. Briefly, transformation begins when a person experiences a dilemma between what she believes and new information. Learners then engage in a process of *critical reflection*, which requires thinking about the nature of their thoughts, the process through which thoughts are formed, and the meanings that their thoughts purport in order to examine or pose possibilities for change (i.e., learning). Through critical reflection, learners question and possibly reshape their paradigms, which constitutes the experience of transformative learning.

Although transforming seems like a straightforward process, our beliefs, emotions and reactions to disability may feel quite uncontrollable. People may feel uncomfortable, because they are unsure of how to act with persons with disabilities. There is fear about saying the wrong thing or using the wrong word, of not doing something that would be appreciated, or of doing something unwelcome (Cohen, 1977). Discomfort can result from the lack of knowledge and experience many people have with disability. Additionally, researchers have linked feelings of discomfort and guilt to an "existential anxiety" experienced by non-disabled persons when encountering disability (Hahn, 1988). Existential anxiety occurs when facing someone with a disability leads one to imagine the potential loss of functional capabilities. Zola (1982) illustrates, "when the able bodied confront the disabled they often think with a shudder, 'I'm glad it's not me'. But the relief is often followed by guilt for thinking such a thought" (p. 202). Other aversions to disability may relate a fear of human vulnerability that images of impairment may invoke.

Emotions that relate to innermost anxieties are difficult to transform. But many aversive reactions reflect a general lack of experience with persons with disabilities. The situation is exacerbated by the prevalence of stereotypes.

Further, knowledge generated in the medical model emphasizes dysfunction and hardship. Linton (1998) calls upon people with disabilities to take charge of developing different knowledge about disabled lives and experiences. She writes:

> The cultural narrative of [the disability] community incorporates a fair share of adversity and struggle, but it is also, and significantly, an account of a world negotiated *from the vantage point of the atypical* [emphasis in original]. Although the dominant culture describes that atypical experience as deficit and loss, the disabled community's narrative recounts it in more complex ways (p. 5).

Increasing the number of rich and authentic accounts of the lives of persons with disabilities available in literature and media can expand the public's knowledge. In turn, increased visibility and interaction with persons with disabilities can help people feel more comfortable with ways of interacting with others in our world. As the number and variety of images of people with disabilities increase, we become more able to resist "group" stereotypes, since the images of disability we might imagine would be diverse.

The paradigm through which we understand disability informs the way we create our environment. If a culture perceives the experiences of persons with impairments only as those of loss and tragedy; and if we understand disability only as an individual's need for cure, we deny people the fullness of their lives. Emphasis on intervention for the individual's body or mind detracts from efforts to remove barriers and increase access to the community, its services, and its opportunities. Social models of disability provide a paradigm that places the physical, social, and political environment as the crucial focus of intervention. Some elements of legislation indicate a sociopolitical approach. The Americans with Disabilities Act mandates accessibility in many public places and services; The Individuals with Disabilities Education Improvement Act favors the Least Restrictive Environment, which indicates a preference for special education services provided in general education settings. Disability issues have been viewed through the civil rights and minority group paradigm only recently. Continued education about these perspectives can raise awareness about physical and attitudinal barriers to persons with disabilities. Greater understanding can broaden the focus on medical intervention to include, if not prioritize, environmental alterations. In turn, the responsibility for creating an inclusive environment may be shared by everyone in society.

3
Language, Labels, and Identity

Language reflects the world around us and also constitutes the ways we understand and experience it. One aspect of the study on disability involves examining the words we use and the ways in which language represents persons and beliefs about them. The language used to talk about disability and disabled persons has changed over time. History, theory, advocacy, politics, and culture influence how disability is expressed and represented (Albrecht, Seelman, and Bury, 2001). The emergence of new paradigms of disability, the disability rights movement and disability studies, and other changes in culture bring attention to the ways that we talk about and depict disability. Examining varied perspectives on disability reveals considerable variation in language related to disability and how it is regarded.

Disability, Impairment, and Handicap

The terms "disability," "impairment," and "handicap" are the most common English language expressions. In general, they are used interchangeably and refer to a permanent loss in physique or functioning, relative to the average person. Professional and advocacy groups in the United States currently prefer the term "disability." More refined distinctions among the meanings of disability, impairment, and handicap can be found in policy. One example of a national definition of disability is in the United States's federal law, The Americans with Disabilities Act Amendments Act (ADAAA) (2008). Under the ADAAA, an individual with a disability is a person who has:

(a) a physical or mental impairment that substantially limits one or more of the major life activities of such individual
(b) a record of such impairment
(c) being regarded as having such an impairment (42 U.S.C. § 12102(2))

According to the ADAAA, an impairment must substantially limit one or more major life activities, or activities that an average person can perform with little or no difficulty. Examples of major life activities include walking, seeing, hearing, speaking, breathing, learning, performing manual tasks, caring for oneself, and working. The relationship between the terms disability and impairment is similar to the distinction made in a sociopolitical model of disability.

40

In other words, *impairment* describes a characteristic of the body; *disability* is the resulting experience of limitation, as compared with others without impairment.

A threefold distinction among the terms "impairment," "disability" and "handicap" is in use internationally (Wright, 1983; Johnson, 1994; Ingstad and Whyte, 1995). In 1983, the United Nations (UN) defined the terms as follows:

> *Impairment:* Any loss or abnormality of psychological, or anatomical structure or function.
> *Disability:* Any restriction or lack (resulting from an impairment) of ability to perform an activity in the manner or within the range considered normal for a human being.
> *Handicap:* A disadvantage for a given individual, resulting from an impairment or disability, that limits or prevents the fulfillment of a role that is normal, depending on age, sex, social and cultural factors, for that individual (UN Decade of Disabled Persons 1983–1992, 1983).

In using all three terms, a *handicap* describes a specific disadvantage that results from the interaction of the person with a disability with a cultural environment. Thus, a person may experience some degree of individual restriction, or disability, as related to impairment, but that restriction becomes a handicap when it results in a social, political, or economic disadvantage. Those with a sociopolitical perspective on disability tend to incorporate the social and cultural environment into the overall experience of being restricted or limited, or "disabled." In other words, handicaps are not distinguishable from disabilities in that the experience of restriction results from the broader structural, social, and cultural environment. To experience disability is defined as persistently encountering handicaps.

In 2008, the *Convention on the Rights of Persons with Disabilities* was ratified by the UN. The Convention recognizes:

> …that disability is an evolving concept and that disability results from the interaction between persons with impairments and attitudinal and environmental barriers that hinders their full and effective participation in society on an equal basis with others,

It defines persons with disabilities as:

> those who have long-term physical, mental, intellectual or sensory impairments which in interaction with various barriers may hinder their full and effective participation in society on an equal basis with others.

By describing disability as an interaction among the individual's health, personal factors, and the environment and context of daily life, the definition emphasizes the social, cultural, and economic factors that influence the degree to which a person may experience disability—as in a sociopolitical orientation.

Understanding disability as interactional places greater emphasis on working toward environmental access and equity in social systems.

Language, Labels, and Stigma

Perhaps, the most objectionable aspect of language related to disability is labeling and the stereotype and stigma attached to labels. To label a person is to use a single descriptor to imply a general sense of a person. Labels tend to overgeneralize or emphasize particular characteristics. They obscure other elements of personhood, which can lead to distorted perceptions of a person. In short, labeling means to classify something by naming it. Labels are often derived from what seem to be neutral descriptions of impairment. However, they frequently work against children and adults with disabilities. They may conjure distorted or diminished expectations and stereotyped images of what particular individuals are like. Labels can take on an encompassing quality.

> A student who was having difficulties in learning becomes a mentally retarded student, a learning disabled student, an emotionally disturbed student, a blind student. The disability, once a suspected characteristic, then an identified quality, now becomes *the* defining factor of the student. With the label and [an educational] placement to go with it, disability achieves what sociologists call "master status." Those who interact with or observe the labeled person have trouble seeing a person; they see instead a disabled person and all of the stereotypes associated with that status (Biklen, 1989: 13).

The label takes the place of the person's individuality, and invites others to define the essence of the person with the disability.

The concept of *social stigma*, popularized by sociologist Erving Goffman (1963), relates to labeling. Stigma is the social phenomena by which particular traits draw severe social disapproval. Stigmatized traits include mental illness, physical disability, and being associated with particular races, religions, or other facets of identity and culture. Those who possess or are thought to possess the devalued trait are treated with aversion and excluded from society. Disability labeling is a process of categorization in which the inabilities, and the unacceptable and inferior aspects of a person are named. In turn, their exclusion from society is legitimated (Barton, 1996).

Labels do not describe a person in ways that capture who they are and how they relate to the world. For example, describing a child as "having a learning disability" does not communicate specific information about her learning needs, nor does it describe the child's achievement, competencies, personality, or interests. The term merely indicates the child's status in relation to his or her "abled" peers. Labels are not specific enough to be useful for developing an individual education plan, but they can have long-lasting negative effects. "The power of naming is such that the labels and letters remain as an influence on social standing and self perception long after their initial judgments were made and have been subsequently modified, overturned, or rendered null and void" (Corbett, 1996: 47).

People-First Language

People-first language is one attempt to resist labels and stigma by emphasizing the person and not the impairment. Phrasing in person-first language includes: "child with a disability," rather than a "disabled child"; "a child with visual impairment," rather than the "visually impaired child"; a "child with a learning disability," rather than a "learning disabled child"; and so on. People-first phrasing is also preferred in the media and is often recommended for professional writing.

People-first language is most related to desires to better express the wholeness of persons with disabilities, rather than emphasize one aspect of him or her. Vash (1981), for example, cautioned against using terms such as "the handicapped" and "the disabled," because they "…carry the hidden cost of summarizing the individual(s) described as nothing more than one of their characteristics, one that conjures up a negative image in the minds of most" (p. 206). Similarly, Wright (1983) stressed the importance of using the verb "have" rather than "be" with disabilities. For example, when called an "epileptic" or "stutterer," rather than "a person who has epilepsy or a stutter," an entire human being is described by just one characteristic (Shapiro and Barton, 1991). In addition, Smart (2001) argues, "everyone has multiple identities, and for people with disabilities, the disability is only one aspect of their identity" (pp. 9–10). Thus, "no one likes to be referred to, or thought of, as only one aspect of his or her nature. No single label can capture the meaning on an entire person's personality and character" (p. 58).

Davis (1995) also explained, "The term 'person with disabilities' is preferred by many to 'disabled person' since the former implies a quality added to someone's personhood rather than the second term's reduction of the person to the disability" (p. xiii). The use of such terms as "disabled person," implies that individuals within a disability are typically alike and that they form a distinct group that is different from the rest of society (Burgdorf, 1980). For example, there is no such thing as a "typical blind person." Within the group of persons with visual impairments, there are variations in severity and types of blindness, as well as other critical factors such as "time of onset." Although two individuals may currently have identical degrees of acuity, one born with blindness (congenitally blind) and one who became blind later in life (adventitiously blind), will have very different concepts of redness, the sunset, the height of the Empire State Building, or traveling 90 miles an hour. In addition, the individual born with blindness, having no memory of being a sighted person or any identity as such, would experience his or her condition as the normal, or expected, state of his or her body. In short, individuals with visual impairments cannot be grouped into the category of "the blind." The variations are too numerous to allow for a typical case. This is true for all categories of disability. In the majority of American school settings as well as in public discourse, "people-first" language is the preferred and recommended way to describe those with disabilities or impairments.

Language and Identity

Awareness of negative language practices has increased among educators, and most agree that medical diagnosis is not equivalent to a description of the whole child and that labeling/stereotyping is detrimental to the child. In addition, terms such as "the disabled," "the blind," or "the learning disabled" are fading from usage as we recognize that individuals grouped in the categories are too diverse for such gross generalizations to be meaningful. Although the use of some current diagnostic terms and people-first language are widely recommended to refer to disability, there are varying perspectives. Consideration of language practices surrounding disability in schools often boils down to finding common, non-biased, and acceptable sets of descriptors to refer to children. While this is a laudable and practical goal, one caveat is the potential to overlook differing ways in which individuals and/or groups of people may choose to talk about themselves.

Vash (1981) explains how changes in language can reflect changes in the status of minority group members:

> Words have the power to shape images of the referenced objects and their choice is important in building or breaking down stereotypes. A group is oppressed, hidden, stripped of power, and made to feel ashamed of the power of its being. Then social conditions shift in a way that permits the lid of oppression to be lifted a bit. A few of the stronger members climb out and hold the lid aside so that more can follow. Before you know it, you have a "movement" and one of the first orders of business is negotiating acceptable language by which to identify the members when it becomes necessary (p. 22).

Just as other identity groups have claimed the right to determine language used to refer to themselves (e.g., People of Color, African-American or Black rather than negro or colored, Asian rather than Oriental, and woman rather than lady or girl), many people with disabilities reject outdated, often derogatory terminology. "In the wake of the American Civil Rights Movement," Hirsch and Hirsch (1995) state, "increasing numbers of oppressed groups are claiming their right to define who they are and what terms should be used to describe them" (p. 23).

Criticisms: People-First Language, Euphemisms, and Political Correctness

Some examples of differences among groups of people and the preferred language to refer to disability surround the use of euphemisms, as well as people-first language. Several euphemisms for disability are quite popular, but rather objectionable to people who may be described with them. Sutherland (1984) observed that "it is for people with disabilities to decide how we chose to define ourselves, and few of us choose to do so according to the prejudices of people who consider themselves able bodied" (p. 14). Persons with disabilities often receive terms such as "physically challenged," "differently abled," "able disabled," and "handi-capable" as patronizing euphemisms. Although the terms claim to refute common stereotypes of incompetence, they are often considered defensive and reactive (Linton, 1998).

There are several reasons that euphemisms are objectionable. One is that euphemisms imply that talking directly about impairment or disability is shameful or impolite. Another is that using "nicer" language obscures the significance that impairment and disability play in a person's experiences. Smart (2001) explains:

> Euphemisms are insulting because their use implies that the reality of the disability is negative and unfortunate. Much of the language used to speak about the disability experience has been condescending, trivializing, or euphemistic. Expressions such as "physically challenged" or "mentally different" are both condescending and euphemistic, suggesting that disabilities cannot be discussed in an open and candid manner. The use of these expressions also trivializes the disability experience, suggesting that disabilities are only minor inconveniences (p. 59).

Most persons with physical impairments do not view barriers as "challenges" that will make them stronger, more courageous, or better citizens by overcoming them and pulling themselves up by their own bootstraps. Thompson (1985) offers, for example, "It is not fun to be disabled. Being disabled is not a 'challenge' we voluntarily undertake. Nor is it that we are merely 'differently abled.' We are 'disabled'; there are just some things that we can't do, at least as quickly or easily as other people" (p. 79).

Other criticisms of terms such as "physically challenged" and "differently abled" relate to the inaccuracy of the terms to describe the experience of disability and/or the ways they actually reinforce negative perceptions about persons with disabilities. Recall that in a sociopolitical perspective of disability, it is the inaccessible environment and context in which impairment becomes meaningful as disability. On the term "physically challenged," Linton (1998) notes:

> Non-disabled people use it in conversation around disabled people with no hint of anxiety, suggesting that they believe it is a positive term. The phrase does not make much sense to me. To say that I am physically challenged is to state that the obstacles to my participation are physical, not social, and that the barrier is my own disability (p. 14).

Finally, Wendell (1997), on "differently abled," states:

> I assume the point of using this term is to suggest that there is nothing wrong with being the way we are, just different. Yet to call someone "differently abled" is much like calling her "differently colored" or "differently gendered." … If anything, it increases the "otherness" of disabled people because it reinforces the paradigm of young, strong, and healthy body perfectly (pp. 271–272).

Two other common and contested euphemisms are "exceptional" and "special," because they invoke a history of segregation. When used in reference to disability, "special" and "exceptional" are instantly recognizable as connoting segregated and inferior (Smart, 2001). They are not innocuous terms because they emphasize difference and thus are polarizing. Individuals in "exceptional" or "special" programs "are then stigmatized as those who cannot 'get by' under programs designed to meet basic needs" (p. 59). Schwarz (2006) similarly observed how *special* creates a double standard:

> In the name of special care, special safety, or special protection, we sometimes take the dignity of independence, choice, and freedom away from people with disabilities. We create a double standard, not letting them do things that non-disabled people take for granted, things that are often the rites of passage into maturity or adulthood (p. 45).

Overall, terms that attempt to veil words associated with impairment and disability and euphemisms are generally poorly received for a variety of reasons. When the occasion arises, using the terms "disabled," "disability," and "impairment" with accurate and candid descriptions of an individual's characteristics is generally preferred. It is not shameful or hurtful to describe bodies, minds, their strengths, and their limits in direct language.

In addition to euphemisms, skepticism toward new terminologies is also present, particularly when changes in language seem like attempts to be "politically correct," but are not related to meaningful shifts in the treatment of people so described. In fact, the concept of being "politically correct" is typically pejorative and became popular in the 1990s as a backlash attempting to discredit groups wishing to alter the language used to describe them (Perry, 1992). For example, deeming use of the term "African-American," merely as a politically correct change in language minimizes the pride movement that initiated it and strips the significance of the change from its relationship to peoples' identities and sense of history. An important distinction is made between changing our language to honor, value, and respect people's preferences or to incorporate new ways of understanding, and simply adopting new terms.

Fiedler (1996), for example, points out that "verbal changes" and "superficial re-labeling" reflect little progress in real improvements in the ways people with disabilities are perceived and treated. She writes:

It seems to me only an easy way of appeasing the guilt we cannot really allay over our instinctive responses to men and women with drastic difficulties in ambulation to stop calling them "gimps" or "cripples" and refer to them instead as the "handicapped" the "disabled"—or, in that ultimately idiotic euphemism adopted after a heart-searching discussions at the last Democratic Convention, as the "challenged." (p. 36).

Hughes (1993), in *The Culture of Complaint*, asks, "Does the 'cripple' rise from his wheelchair, or feel better about being stuck in it, because someone in the Carter administration decided that, for official purposes he was 'physically challenged?' (Garland, 1995: 4). In short, some feel that merely changing the language we use hardly matters if negative beliefs, prejudice, and stereotyping endure.

In a related critique that also notes the shortfalls of language change to signify meaningful changes in beliefs about and attitudes toward disability, Hogan (2003) focuses on "people-first" language. He writes:

In English, word order does not convey the relative importance of concepts. The most important word in a phrase might be the first, last, or somewhere in between. ... "People first" language proponents have never explained why, in regard to disability terminology, but nowhere else in the English language, putting the word "person" first in a sequence necessarily increases its importance (p. 108).

He continues:

If we assume that the overall intent of this practice is to promote the social status of people with disabilities, then its practical aspects must be considered. Unfortunately, in the literature of the "people first" movement there is no evidence such language structures further the cause of disabled people. In fact, the theory that requiring people to communicate in non-normative ways will promote a more normal or positive image of those with disabilities is illogical (pp. 108–109).

Hogan raises questions as to the rationale and strategy behind the movement for "people-first" language. Simply changing words or the order in which we say them is not an effective strategy—alone—for improving lives and demanding civil rights.

Criticism and skepticism regarding changes in disability terminology are often less focused on what the old and new words are and more concerned about the beliefs of people who use them. Euphemisms communicate that the characteristics of a body or mind are too unfortunate or shameful to be talked about candidly and at worst, simply replace objectionable terms with equally problematic patronizing ones. Using people-first language, while generally recommended, does not alone signify more positive attitudes or altered beliefs about disabilities and persons "with" them.

Language and Group Identity

Recognizing the perspectives of persons with disabilities on the language used to talk about disability, while sometimes complex, provides an informed outlook on the language choices we make or the terms we may hear others using. Some terms, even when they are deemed diagnostically appropriate, are considered antiquated and offensive because of the history surrounding them, as in the term "retarded." Others are rejected, because they are received euphemistically and are patronizing. Further nuances and preferences in disability-related language reflect efforts to imbue the words we use with an understanding of disability as a sociopolitical position and/or cultural or group identity.

Albrecht, Seelman, and Bury (2001), for example, describe a sociopolitical perspective in the controversy over people-first language. They write:

> One group historically advocated people-first language, expressed in the term *people with disabilities,* emphasizing the historical roots of American exceptionalism, the importance of the individual in society, and disability as being something *not* inherent in the person. An equally vocal group has more recently denounced people-first language as offensive, claiming that it was promoted by powerful non-disabled people, particularly advocates for persons with developmental disabilities. This second group prefers the term *disabled people,* emphasizing minority group identity politics. ... This heated discourse struggles with expressing values that acknowledge individual difference and inclusion in a society based on civil rights (p. 3).

Two considerations are highlighted. First, whether disabled people or those without a disability identity initiate a new term is a concern that reflects the role of self-chosen language to communicate a group's emerging status (Vash, 1981). Some of those preferring "disabled people" object to the use of people-first language because the origin of the form was not rooted in disabled persons' desires. The phrasing "disabled people" may also be preferred for its grammatical construction, which emphasizes a sociopolitical perspective on disability. To describe someone as a "person with a disability" locates the disability as an attribute belonging to an individual. By contrast, placing "disabled" before "person" is read, grammatically, as a past participle to indicate a position of being dis-abled, or made not-able. This emphasizes a view of disability, as it is made meaningful in social contexts. In this usage, being disabled refers to an imposed social position or set of experiences, rather than a fact of an individual.

In addition to emphasizing a sociopolitical perspective on disability, some disabled people reject people-first language, because it minimizes the role that impairment and/or disability plays in their lives and identities and casts it negatively. "People-first phraseology conceives of disability as a troublesome condition arbitrarily attached to some people, a condition (unlike gender, race, or ethnicity) that is only significant as a remedial or managerial issue" (Titchkosky, 2001: 126). For some, the experience of disability offers membership in disability culture, which values the lives and expressions of diverse bodies and minds and perceives varied individual and group experiences as more complex than conditions to be managed, overcome, or tolerated. Here, identity-first language is preferred; being a "disabled person" is understood as a dynamic and significant facet of identity, a source of group membership, and/ or an occasion for pride.

Another facet of group identity that pertains to language relates to the ways that oppressed groups reappropriate hurtful language or negative characterizations of their features for their own use and meaning. For an analogous example, the term "queer" originated as an epithet for gays and lesbians and the pink triangle that is now associated with gay rights and gay pride was a symbol used in Nazi Germany to identify gay persons for discrimination and extermination. In the 1990s, the declaration "We're queer, we're here. Get used to it!" became an expression of gay pride. Adopting cruel and often jarring terms to self-identify can serve to revalue the label and disempower its effect when others use them (Galinsky, Hugenberg, Groom, and Bodenhausen, 2003). In disability rights and disability cultural movements, disabled persons sometimes refer to themselves and others in the group as "cripple" or "crip" and "gimp." As with the term, *queer*, terms that once referred to "despised distinctiveness," now refer to "celebrated distinctiveness" (p. 231). Kriegel (1991), for example, discusses a preference for his "cripple" identity:

> I am a man who has lived all but eleven of his years here on earth as a cripple, a word I prefer to the euphemistic "handicapped" or "disabled," each of which does little more than further society's illusions about illness and accident and the effects of illness and accident. For to be "disabled" or "handicapped" is to deny oneself the rage, anger, and pride of having managed to survive as a cripple in America. If I know nothing else, I know that I have endured—and I know the price I have paid for that endurance (p. 61).

In disability rights circles, identifying oneself as a "crip" is a testament to the struggle for rights and equity and a reminder of the damaging beliefs and attitudes still held by many.

Somewhat similar to reappropriating negative language, some groups recast the meaning of identifying terms or create new ones that emphasize different relational aspects of naming and identity. "Aspies," for example, is an affectionate, non-medical term that some self-advocates with Asperger's syndrome have adopted to refer to themselves (Aspies for Freedom). Differences in the language and meaning surrounding the term "deaf" provide an example of a widely acknowledged change in words and connotation. Some members of the deaf community believe that people born without hearing should be described as *Deaf* with a capital *d* and those who lose their hearing in later life are *deaf* with a lower case *d*" (Hogan, 2003: 106). The use of *Deaf* with a capital *D* also relates to a cultural view of deafness defined by the shared use of American Sign Language (ASL). Being *Deaf* means to share in a history and community that unite people who use ASL. Being *Deaf* is a cultural identity; being *deaf* is a description of a degree of hearing.

The considerable attention paid to language used to describe a person, an experience or signal group identity indicates its importance to many. This may be because the ways we describe ourselves or are described is key to self-concept and the way others think about us. While most agree that negative language that invites stigma should be avoided, there is much variety in the words and terms, grammar and letter case used and preferred. Critiquing and developing language is one way that people examine and characterize meaning and experience. The variety of beliefs on disability language demonstrates the variety of beliefs about disability.

Conclusion

Language is both descriptive and political. Words are imbued with meaning derived from history, context, and perspectives. The terms, classifications, categories, and labels surrounding language used in schools and society to talk about disability relate to our policies that define disabilities and impairments, as well as to the social practices in which they become meaningful. By teasing out nuances in the terms, disability, impairment, and handicap, we can arrive at better understanding of how medical and social models of disability diverge in perspective. Attention to language changes, particularly those sparked by disability rights movements, reveals the role of language in group politics and identity. Although knowledge about the terms preferred by identity groups related to disability is not as widespread as the preference for people-first language, it is useful for professionals to be familiar with a variety of perspectives. The study of language is one way to gain better understanding of many perspectives on disability.

Part II
Disability in History

4

Early Attitudes and Their Legacy
A Brief History of Disability

Writing history is not merely an enterprise of compiling facts and creating records of "what happened." Histories are interpretations that reflect the perspectives and beliefs of the historian. Historians make decisions of what to include in their works and how to organize events to tell a story. Readers also interpret histories through their particular cultural and social contexts. Although people with disabilities have always existed, they are often absent in histories we write. When disability is noted, it is described as personal tragedy or insult, rather than as an aspect of culture to be explored (Baynton, 2001). Historians in disability studies instead propose that disability "sit[s] squarely at the center of historical inquiry, both as a subject worth studying in its own right and as one that will provide scholars with a new analytic tool" for understanding human relations (Kudlick, 2003: 2–3).

The histories passed down in most school curriculum do not give significant attention to disability. It is important to correct the absence of accounts of disability in the historical record by recognizing the presence and impact of persons so identified. Examining the history of disability also gives insight into the origins of current attitudes toward disability. Attitudes do not arise in a vacuum—they emerge from the customs, laws, and practices of the past. Examining their foundations helps us perceive the long-lasting influence of culture and beliefs about disability on the present. Early attitudes and beliefs toward persons with disabilities and readily discernible differences have influenced greatly how disabilities, and the people who have them, are treated today.

The Importance of Context

Because disability is environmental, any society's treatment of persons with disabilities should be understood within the context of the social environment and cultural conditions of its own time. Bullock and Mahon (1997) caution readers to remember that the treatment of persons with disabilities occurred in a historical and cultural context. They stress that however inhumane past treatment of people with disabilities may seem, most actions followed the standards of the time. Teachers can present the importance of social context when teaching disability history. This is not to justify harmful practices, but to demonstrate that our understanding of disability is always a product of culture.

Primitive Societies

Throughout recorded history, people with disabilities have been present. Archaeologists constantly uncover evidence of persons with disabilities dating back to the Neanderthal Period (Mackelprang and Salsgiver, 1996). Most primitive societies followed the custom that individuals with disabilities had to be sacrificed for the good of the group (Funk, 1987). Early humans were hunters and foragers who lived to their early twenties. People slept on the cold ground and faced daily starvation, stress, trauma, and fear (Scheerenberger, 1983). The harshness of the environment made survival dependent on group cooperation. With the reality of hunger ever-present, each individual was vital to the band for hunting, gathering, and collective defense. Because early humans leading nomadic existences pursued their prey, those unable to work or keep up were left behind to die. The elimination of the incapacitated, old, or feeble was not only accepted but also expected. Accordingly, children who were unable to contribute due to physical, sensory, or cognitive impairments were liabilities to primitive societies, and infanticide was often practiced (Bowe, 1978; Scheerengberger, 1983; Morgan, 1987). For early humans, the severity of life conditions made death or abandonment the usual outcome for people with disabilities.

Early Civilizations

The environment became more accommodating to individuals with disabilities around 12,000 B.C. when humans passed from the age of itinerant hunting to growing crops, reasoning symbolically, communicating verbally, and living in communities (Scheerenberger, 1983). However, people of early civilizations continued to exterminate those deemed to have severe physical or intellectual impairments as a result of superstition and demonology.

Early societies believed in animism—the existence of spirits that incite or perform evil. The treatment of physical and mental disorders were entrusted to the shaman or medicine man, thereby establishing the shamanistic legacy of the medical model (Scheerenberger, 1983). A striking difference or impairment was usually perceived as evil, ominous, or unlucky, with a strong "demonological conception of a power that controlled behavior" (Ross, 1978: 8). Children born with facial differences were treated with hostility and accused of being evil, as were their parents (Charkins, 1996: 38).

The ancient Assyrians assumed that children with disabilities or physical differences were omens. Among their recorded beliefs are these four:

1. If a woman gives birth to a "cripple," her house should be destroyed.
2. If a woman gives birth to a boy with six fingers on the left hand, he will vanquish an enemy.

3. If a woman gives birth to a child with two heads, the nation will be torn asunder.
4. If a woman gives birth to twins joined at the spine, the gods will forsake the people and the king must abdicate his throne (Monestier, 1987: 13).

Ancient Babylonians also practiced teratoscopy, which is divination based on examination of "abnormal" births. Some prognostics for "monstrous births" include:

1. If a woman should give birth to an infant who has the ears of a lion, there will be a powerful king in the land.
2. If a woman should give birth to an infant who has no right hand, the country will be convulsed by an earthquake.
3. If a woman should give birth to an infant who has six toes on each foot, the people of the world will be injured.
4. If a woman should give birth to an infant whose right foot is absent, its father's house will be ruined and there will be abundance in the house of his neighbor (Thompson, 1994).

In early societies, differences were an occasion for meaning. Some characteristics became disabilities, because they impeded survival, and the undesirability of others was marked by superstition.

Infanticide

The birth of a child with a physical or mental anomaly was a dreaded omen—a sign of divine wrath and providence that presaged evil (Fiedler, 1978; Monestier, 1987; Bogdan, 1988; Thompson, 1994; Garland, 1995). The early Mesopotamians viewed diseases and mental disorders as punishment from God or as possession by the devil or evil spirits. Mental and physical diseases were considered "afflictions"—impure, taboo, and the result of sin, a belief still widespread today. Infanticide was sometimes a ritualized response to anomalies apparent at birth. The precise rituals varied. The ancient Melanesians buried their children alive; Indians cast their deformed babies into the sacred river Ganges (Van Riper and Emerick, 1984). Most early Egyptians appear not to have condoned infanticide. In fact, it was later banned by decree (Moores, 1996). Before its prohibition, however, those parents who chose to practice infanticide were made to hug their dead child continually for three days and three nights to express the appropriate remorse (Scheerenberger, 1983). In some cultures, the mother was killed along with her child.

The early Egyptians were among the first to display an interest the causes and cures of atypical characteristics, as well as the personal and social well-being of individuals with disabilities, especially those with visual impairments. According to Moores (1996), "The priests of Karnak trained the blind in music, the arts, and massage. Blind people participated in religious ceremonies and, during some periods, represented a large proportion of the poets and musicians of ancient Egypt" (p. 32). Customs in other parts of Africa varied according to tribe. The South African Kaffir tribe clubbed their sickly or deformed children to death (Van Riper and Emerick, 1984). The East African Wanika tribe destroyed both deformed infants as well as those believed to be unusually precocious, because they were viewed as ominous forecasters of trouble for the tribe. Albinism was considered a severe disability in the Bakongo tribe, because it was believed to cause "humpback and rheumatism" (Ross, 1978).

American Indians (Native Americans) also had rituals that varied by tribe. For example, the beliefs and practices of the Aztec culture were particularly harsh for those with physical impairments. Often believed to possess magic powers, "deformed" individuals were favored for sacrifice by priests who cut out their beating hearts during times of famine to mark the death of a leader (Van Riper and Emerick, 1984). Most Native American cultures valued rather than devalued those with physical and mental differences, and many venerated those with physical disabilities and blindness. The Zuni, for example, believed that those with severe mental retardation had intimacy with good spirits and often regarded their words and sayings as divine (Ross, 1978). Similarly, among the North American plains tribes, youngsters with deafness were often admired because of their skillful use of sign language (Moores, 1996).

Greek and Roman Practices

Both the Greek and Roman cultures sought the perpetuation of physical perfection, beauty, and health. Herodotus (fifth century B.C.), for example, listed freedom from deformity at the top of his criteria for happiness (Edwards, 1996). Thus, the social response to disability and difference was partially determined by religion, with beauty and wholeness favored by the gods and deformity interpreted as divine wrath. Persons with unexpected facial features were believed created by the gods for their own amusement and sent to warn, admonish, or threaten humans (Charkins, 1996: 38). The birth of a deformed child was seen as a punishment inflicted upon its parents by the gods (Garland, 1995). Blindness was considered a Divine punishment for sin, though supernatural powers were believed granted to blind persons and viewed as compensatory gifts of the gods (Hewett and Forness, 1977).

Greece's city-state of Sparta exemplified the philosophy of "rugged individualism" and "a sound mind in a sound body." The laws of Sparta viewed those with disabilities as burdens to be eliminated for the betterment of their militant society. The boundaries of who was considered disabled, however, were flexible. A soldier with an impairment—for example, a limp or the loss of an eye or even a more serious condition—but who could still fight or be of service to the military, was not considered disabled. Artemon, a man who could not walk, served in the role of military advisor and designed siege-engines and was regarded as a man of ability and prestige (Edwards, 1996).

In ancient Greece, infanticide was a legal right invoked by paternal decision. Within the first week of its existence, each infant faced the father's right to terminate its life. However, the same infant was also brought to a place called *Lesche*, before a state council of inspectors (The Committee of Hygiene or The State Health Committee), where it was carefully examined by "triers" or elders of the tribe to which the child belonged. Any child that appeared to be or was suspected of being defective was thrown from a cliff of Mount Taygetus onto the jagged rocks below, or was left to die exposed to the elements (James, 1975; Preen, 1976; Scheerenberger, 1983).

Infanticide of babies with impairments reflected the beliefs and social environment of the times. Greek religious beliefs emphasized that individuals with disabilities had immortal souls, so that their elimination from this life probably meant a more prompt reincarnation—a pleasant prospect than lives of hardship as disabled and stigmatized individuals. This belief encouraged many parents to accept the custom as a blessing, and the best possible course of action for their children (Preen, 1976).

The treatment of disabled persons in Rome varied over the broad span of the Empire's history, roughly from 800 B.C. to approximately 500 A.D. The Romans often placated their gods by sacrificing children with unexpected facial features who were seen as evil (Charkins, 1996). They often sacrificed the mother as well. As with the Spartans, the Romans sought to establish a military state dependent on a physically strong population and believed in killing unsuitable children. For example, Seneca the Elder, an influential teacher and theoretician in the early Roman Empire, compared the drowning of deformed children to the "killing of unwanted dogs or unhealthy cattle" (Ross, 1978).

Under the principle of *patria potestas*, the laws of Rome gave the father extensive authority over the person and property of his family and descendants. Such power included the right to sell, mutilate, or kill his children and extended into the adulthood (Despart, 1965). Children deemed impaired did have some protections. For example, during one Roman period, a child could be exposed only for the first eight days of life (Scheerenberger, 1983). Later, a child was exposed only after being inspected by male members of five neighboring families who unanimously decided the child was unworthy to live. If the decision was less than unanimous, the father could not expose it at any other time during its life (Preen, 1976).

Early Religious Attitudes

Early religions traditionally considered congenital disability and difference as "an example of the capacity of the divine to violate natural law" (Garland, 1995: 59). The birth of a disabled or deformed child was treated as retribution against the tribe or parents for angering the gods, and although seen as an innocent victim of its parents' sinfulness, the child served as a reminder of general human evilness. Many people continue to view disability as a moral judgment and punishment since society, in a sense, finds it difficult to tolerate a world where punishment is dispensed "with an even hand" to both the guilty and innocent alike (Gallagher, 1995). Early religions thus became highly influential in shaping attitudes toward persons with disabilities (Garland, 1995). Unfortunately, "religious teachings have provided some of the most negative attitudes toward disabled people" (UNESCO, 1995: 32). Because of the huge influence the religions Judaism, Christianity, and Islam have had on the forming of attitudes toward persons with disabilities, they warrant some extended examination.

Early Judaism

The Judeo-Christian tradition, prevalent among Europeans during and after the Middle Ages, taught that people with disabilities were expressions of God's displeasure (Mackelprang and Salsgiver, 1996). Disability signified "sinner" to the ancient Hebrews, and people with disabilities were thought to be possessed by evil demons. They viewed madness as retribution afflicted by an angry God and believed it to be supernaturally inflicted on those who sinned. For example, the first book of Samuel describes the details of King Saul's paranoia. As early as the seventh century B.C., Moses told his people in the book of Deuteronomy (28: 15, 28) "[I]f you do not obey the Lord your God and do not carefully follow all his commands and decrees ... the Lord will afflict you with madness, blindness and confusion of the mind" (Bullock and Mahon, 1997: 32).

While beliefs that linked disability and divinity reflected earlier traditions, a new awareness of and compassion for persons with disabilities was also signaled in Judaism. Although the early Egyptians and Indians initiated the idea of charity by giving alms, it was the early Hebrews who made the practice a religious requirement. Judaism prohibited infanticide of newborn children with disabilities and emphasized the importance of charity to "the sick, the old, the handicapped, and the poor" (Barnes, Mercer, and Shakespeare, 1999; Trattner, 1994).

Between 500 and 400 B.C., as the Hebrews began codifying their laws, they explicitly forbade taking advantage of an individual's disability for sadistic, economic, or other reasons. As the Torah, for example, specifically states:

- Thou shalt not curse the deaf, nor put a stumbling block before the blind (Leviticus 14: 14).
- Cursed be he that maketh the blind to wander out of the way (Deuteronomy 27: 18).

Although the laws of the early Hebrews displayed sensitivity toward those with disabilities by forbidding their exploitation or humiliation, certain common presuppositions associating one's purity with one's outer appearance nevertheless arose, producing restricted religious and social roles. The Hebrews required their practicing priests (Koheins) to be without blemish. Such restrictions resemble those imposed by the early Greeks who had a propensity for physical perfection in their religious ceremonies: "Not only did the victims which were offered in sacrifice have to be without blemish, but the priests, too, were required to be physically perfect" (Garland, 1995: 64). The Romans, as well, prohibited men with disabilities from the priesthood of their pagan temples, "a practice embraced by the Roman Catholic Church, which continued, until recently, to bar disabled men from its priesthood" (Gallagher, 1995: 248).

Early Christianity

Early Christianity demonstrated an indecisive response to disability. People with impairments were regarded as needing healing and general support, though impairments were also considered punishments for sin (Barnes, Mercer, and Shakespeare, 1999). As in Judaism, the Gospel stressed the notion of showing charity, sympathy, and pity to those with physical and mental impairments and recognizing them as children of God (Preen, 1976). Jesus Christ, who preached a way of life based on love and mercy, seemed particularly concerned with the well-being of children (Scheerenberger, 1983). He cured their impairments by miraculous healing, drawing upon their faith to achieve the exorcism of demonic influences (Scheerenberger, 1983).

As Mackelprang and Salsgiver (1996) noted, "In the New Testament, people with mental disorders were believed to be possessed. It was thought that people with disabilities had them because of their own or their parents' sins" (p. 8). Another characterization of impairment related to Jesus' miracle healings. "Disabled people existed in order that the works of God might be magnified in him" (Paré, 1840/1982: 4). The healing acts Jesus performed served as object lessons to glorify God or to vilify the unbelievers. Underlying these healing miracles was an assumption that disability symbolized impurity and evidenced a soul to be saved (Bowe, 1978; Ross, 1978). Forgiveness of sin and physical healing are represented as equivalent (Eiseland, 1994: 71). The healing miracles of Jesus, with evil spirits and the Devil as the antagonists had an enormous influence on future attitudes.

Despite the tenet of Christianity to protect and provide for disabled individuals, religious leaders of the Reformation often promulgated strong convictions about the linkage of sin and disability. Both Luther and Calvin, for instance, considered persons with intellectual impairment to be essentially evil, possessed, and filled with Satan. According to Monestier (1987), such beliefs were based on early Christianity's strict notions of good and evil and its interpretation of natural phenomena as attributable to the intervention of either God or Satan. Good and evil were thought to be in constant conflict. Since, according to the Scriptures, God created man in His own image, monsters and "the deformed" had to be creations of the Devil. Similarly, the basic theological attitude toward individuals with mental illness was that such persons were demoniacal possessed, dangerously inferior, and, therefore, not deserving of

Christian charity. The most common treatments for mental disorders were torture on the rack and death at the steak or gallows.

A more lasting influence Jesus had on attitudes toward persons with disabilities was the creation of the provider–receiver relationship typified by charitable causes today. Early Christian philosophy, based on Judaism, preached sympathy and pity; and as the church assumed the role of provider for the less fortunate by furnishing food, protection, and shelter, it awarded itself a position of superiority and control. It based this control on the belief that disability was an indication of impurity and evidence of a soul that needed to be saved. In general, the biblical attitude toward persons with disability is acceptance and protectiveness (Astor, 1985: 40).

Early Islam

Mohammed (569–622 A.D.) composed the Qur'an with 114 chapters (Suras) that proclaim one God (Allah) who is both powerful and merciful. The Qur'an views infanticide as a sin: "Kill not the old man who cannot fight, nor the young children nor the women." It also considers persons with intellectual and psychiatric disabilities to be Allah's innocents:

> Give not unto those who are weak of understanding the substance which God hath appointed you to preserve for them; but maintain them there out, and clothe them, and speak kindly to them.

Islam, as with Judeo-Christian faiths, directed its followers to more humane treatment of people with disabilities in comparison with Greco-Roman traditions (Scheerenberger, 1983).

Similar to other early cultures and religions, the Qur'an includes parables in which non-believers or those who act against Allah are made blind, deaf, or mute. Also, as with other traditions, some impairment is viewed as divine punishment. In the *Sura*, Muhammed states, for example, "Those it is whom Allah has cursed so He has made them deaf and blinded their eyes" (47.23). Haj (1970) notes that visual impairments are by far the most common type of disability mentioned in the Qur'an. In fact, it gives special consideration to individuals with blindness, because education was based on oral ability thereby making it possible for motivated blind students to succeed, even at universities (cited in Moores, 1996: 37).

Shinto, Confuscianism, Buddhism

As in other regions, the people of the varied societies in Eastern Asia also developed cultural practices specific to persons with disabilities. As early as 850 A.D., Japan reserved membership in masseuse guilds for blind individuals, which guaranteed a source of work. The Shinto concept of purity, however, also led to contempt for disabled people. Disabled people came to be included in the category of *hin-nin* or "non-people" (UNESCO, 1995: 33).

In China, persons deemed blind often received special training as fortune-tellers (French, 1932). It was not uncommon to find blind scholars, soothsayers, storytellers, and musicians in ancient China (Hewett and Forness, 1977: 15). Confucius (551–479 B.C.) taught that fundamental to a just and peaceful world was the decent behavior of the individual. His beliefs were rooted in the concept of a moral sense of responsibility toward others, which included kindness, gentleness, and service to those of weak mind (Scheerenberger, 1983). Confucius taught that the "weak minded" had a claim on society which had a responsibility to care for those who could not care for themselves (L'Abate and Curtis, 1975). Family loyalty was an important value and "Everyone calls his son his son, whether he has talents or not." Every individual was regarded as an integral member of the family even if he or she differed mentally or physically (Ross and Freelander, 1977).

Miles (1995), citing the lack of studies available in European languages regarding disabilities in South Asia and China over the past 4,000 years, expressed appreciation for the new translations that are beginning to provide important glimpses of Asian disability history. For example, stories recently translated tell of Confucius's respectful and kind treatment of a music master with blindness; how the princess Gandhari permanently blindfolded herself out of respect for her bridegroom who could not see; and of Buddha's incarnation as a baby prince, who chose deafness, muteness, and immobility because he could not condone unethical behavior (Miles, 1995: 27–28).

Buddhism, originated in approximately 400 B.C., taught that all other forms of righteousness "are not worth the sixteenth part of the emancipation of the heart through charity" (Trattner, 1994: 1). Buddha taught that love was expressed through helpfulness, charity, and generosity (Scheerenberger, 1983). A result of that philosophy was the early establishment of a ministry, in approximately 200 B.C. for the care and treatment of persons with disabilities, which included appointed officials to oversee "charitable works" (Van Riper and Emerick, 1984: 19).

Summary of Early Civilizations

Early responses to disability varied by culture, place, and time. The earliest response to impairment related to the physical demands of survival in nomadic groups. Those who could not contribute to the group's hunting or gathering, or who could not keep pace were left behind. The rise of agriculture and a more sedentary lifestyle meant that people with physical impairments remained part of societies, rather than being abandoned. Impairment and deformity, however, were still cause for attention. Superstitions led people to interpret abnormalities as omens or messages from the divine. Judeo-Christian and Muslim writings similarly characterized impairment as evidence of spiritual offenses. Subsequently, aversion to those with impairment was characteristic of early responses and made abnormality and impairment liabilities—or disabilities.

Aversion to disability led to a range of cultural practices regarding disabled persons. Extermination, as in the practices of infanticide and sacrifice of disabled persons, was one response. Reserving separate and specific trades for people with disabilities, as in China and Japan, was another. Adherents to Judeo-Christian and Buddhist faiths saw the care of disabled people as part of charitable work. Benevolence and compassion toward those with disabilities exemplified spiritual and moral commitment. Although the particular responses of early cultures to disability varied across time and place, themes that recur in societal practices regarding disability throughout time to our modern contexts are evident. First, the presence of impairment and non-typical characteristics are almost always occasions for meaning, whether spiritual or moral. The meanings made of disability turned people with disabilities into spectacles—as objects of fascination or fear, good fortune, shame, or amusement. Second, aversion to disability is the most common response. Whether construed to represent the best interest of the disabled person or the community, extermination or separation from the general public were frequent reactions. In sum, three kinds of reactions to disabled people resonate throughout time and across cultures: Fascination, Segregation, and Extermination. We examine each of these reactions in the following sections.

Objects of Fascination

People with extraordinary, unexpected physical features have long been a source of fascination. Some cultures marveled at and prophesized according to disability, others saw people with disabilities as sources of entertainment. Aristotle, for example, deemed persons with disabilities *lusus naturae* or "jokes of nature," which, in turn, made them appropriate sources of amusement or pets in the households of the wealthy (Fiedler, 1978). As early as 1000 B.C. disabled individuals were used to provide entertainment and amusement in Egyptian, Greek, and Roman cultures. An enduring image of the Middle Ages is the court fool, or jester, who were often little people. The so-called "freak shows" featured individuals with extraordinary characteristics more recently, and one might argue that the proliferation of documentaries about medical mysteries and rare conditions is a contemporary version of human's fascination with disability.

Entertaining the Aristocracy

The earliest use of little persons as court fools was among the Egyptian pharaohs who chose members of the Danga pygmy tribe as mainly a curiosity, but also for amusement (Bullock and Mahon, 1997). It was customary for wealthy men in the Roman Empire to keep half-witted and "deformed" slaves in their houses for purposes of entertainment; further, females were known to keep "physically stunted" and "mentally deficient" slaves as substitutes for "lap dogs and teddy bears" (p. 21). Deformed slaves were used for entertainment in the court of Attila around 500 A.D. (Bullock and Mahon, 1997). The Spaniards under Cortez, invading Mexico in 1519, entered the city of Tenochtitlan (now Mexico City), where they were shown the Aztec Emperor Montezuma's extensive royal zoo. The Spaniards were amazed to see that alongside the many rare wild animals on display, were persons with dwarfism or albinism, bearded women, and other "deformed" humans (Van Riper and Emerick, 1984). During the Hellenistic Period, little people were highly prized as pets and often given as gifts.

By the second century A.D., persons with extraordinary physical traits were commonly found in homes of wealthy Romans to provide household entertainment. The fool or buffoon became a part of entertainment and feasts—making the guests laugh with his so-called "idiocy" or "deformity." "The popularity of statuettes and vase-paintings depicting deformed dwarfs, hunchbacks and obese women strongly suggests that people of this sort were in high demand as singers, dancers, musicians, jugglers and clowns" (Garland, 1995: 32–33). In fact, the Romans established a special market, called the "teraton agora," where legless and armless humans could be purchased along with giants, dwarfs, and hermaphrodites (Durant, 1944).

The ridicule of persons with disabilities continued apace during the Middle Ages. Most individuals with physical or intellectual disabilities were imprisoned or driven from cities into the rural areas to fend for themselves. The nobility, however, boarded some people in return for being on display as curiosities, objects of ridicule, or performers (Snow, 2001). Charles V of France gave exclusive rights to the province of Champagne to supply his court with fools. Ownership of little people was a high-status symbol among the Russian aristocracy.

During the twelfth century, English kings began to make the care and treatment of "idiots" a matter of royal concern and, therefore, their wards. Philip IV of Spain gathered intellectually disabled persons into his court where they were well fed and well clothed and had the freedom to do as they pleased. In 1490, King James IV of Scotland, brought to his court the Scottish Brothers, twins joined in the upper part of the body and having four arms and two legs. The king ordered that the brothers be carefully raised and well educated. Under his patronage and protection, the brothers learned to play musical instruments, sing in harmony, and read Latin, French, Italian, Spanish, Dutch, Danish, and Irish (Thompson, 1968, 1994).

Though little people gained entry to royal homes as objects of curiosity and ridicule, some "court dwarfs" worked themselves into positions of great power (Fiedler, 1978). They gained charge over the master's treasury, under the assumption that a dwarf would be easier to find and catch should he attempt to abscond with the funds. In fact, several court dwarfs became quite influential and found themselves in positions of total trust within the court and noble households. They were given unlimited license of speech, and often became the pets and favorites of their Royal or Court ladies of the time (Thompson, 1994: 188). Once trusted by a king or noble, they often proved capable of moving up from the status of joker to counselor. Emperors Augustus and Tiberius had court dwarves by their sides for consultation on matters of state. In the late Middle Ages, Bertholde, a court dwarf known for his cleverness, became the King of Lombardy's prime minister. Both little people, Jacof Ris became an ex officio counselor to the Imperial court of The Emperor Charles VI of Vienna, and Godeau was appointed Archbishop of Grasse in 1672, by Richelieu (Fiedler, 1978). Though there were exceptions, people with disabilities were generally regarded as the playthings of the aristocracy and more often subject to harsh abuse and ridicule during the Middle Ages.

The spectacle of disability was received in various ways, largely dependent on context, throughout the Middle Ages. Outside of the royal court, some persons with disabilities would beg from the lower classes to make a living. The art of begging, highly lucrative and remunerative, sometimes resulted in self-mutilation and children being purposefully deformed for the purpose— a practice dating back to ancient Rome. From the fourteenth to the seventeenth centuries, people with psychiatric and cognitive disabilities were systematically removed from the streets and into hospitals, almshouses, and institutions. For a small sum, the public could visit some hospitals to view the "patients" who were displayed as exhibits. Most famous were the "antics of the lunatics" at London's Bethlehem Hospital. There, visitors would stare and laugh at the writhing and screaming of the chained inmates. Certain attendants would beat, prod, and agitate inmates with clubs, sticks, or whips to get them to per- form dances and acrobatics to ensure the visitors a good show (Evans, 1983). No longer the privilege of the upper classes, lower classes could also find amusement in the spectacle made of abusing people with disabilities.

Toward Modernity: Medical Curiosities and Freak Shows

The movement of people into hospitals was predicated by a new way of thinking about extraordinary attributes. Non-desirable ways of thinking and behaving became attributable to mental disease or defect, rather than to moral failings or spiritual signs (Foucault, 1965). Physical disabilities were viewed as medical anomalies rather than as evil omens, the results of witchcraft, or paren- tal punishments for past sins (Bogdan, 1988). By the late 1800s, persons with disabilities began to be viewed as medical anomalies, which subjected them to scientific study and classification.

Heightened scientific interest paralleled and furthered the public's fascina- tion with extraordinary and foreign physical features, which fueled the popu- larity of the so-called "freak show," most popular between 1840 and 1940 in the United States. Called a variety of terms, including Sideshows, Ten in One, Odditorium, and Museum of Nature's Mistakes, these shows put people with extraordinary characteristics (some of them false) on display (Bogdan, 1988: 2–3).

The comments of physicians and natural scientists who visited the "human curiosities" served to fan widespread interest and debates as to the nature and origin of the "creatures," who were often presented to the public in ways to parallel then-new scientific theories about human variation (Bogdan, 1986; 1988).

The fascination with "human oddities" was not just a Western phenomenon. China, as well, has a history of producing curiosities. The following describes a method used during the nineteenth century:

> Young children are bought or stolen at a tender age and placed in a *Ch'ing*, or vase with a narrow neck, and having in this case a movable bottom. In this receptacle the unfortunate little wretches are kept for years in a sitting posture their heads outside being all the while carefully tended and fed. When the child reached the age of twenty or over, he or she is taken away to some distant place and *discovered* in the woods as a wild man or woman (*China Mail*, 15 May 1878, cited in Fiedler, 1978: 50).

The freak show continued earlier practices that made disability into spectacle. Bogdan (1988) explained, the idea of the "freak" is a created perspective comprising a set of social practices that create a stage for making features fascinating and exotic. The juggling, dancing, acrobatics, and side-show set and stage created the characterization of disability as curiosity. The famed circus entrepreneur, P. T. Barnum, for example, once reportedly approached an extremely tall man and asked him if he had any interest in becoming a giant. Thus, framing people with unexpected and extraordinary features for entertainment in staged contexts *made* disability into freakery.

Segregation and Institutionalization

Making persons with disabilities into objects of fascination has been one enduring response to difference. Another response with a long legacy is the segregation or separation of people deemed disabled from the general public. As the Renaissance began, the Roman Catholic Church began accepting persons with disabilities into monasteries and asylums for protection and care as wards of the church, thereby removing them from society. Disability became hidden, the prevailing attitude being "out of sight-out of mind." Persons deemed mentally retarded and mentally ill were housed in monasteries, hospitals, charitable facilities, prisons, almshouses, pesthouses, workhouses, warehouses, and other available buildings (Scheerenberger, 1983: 34). Far from offering protection and care, however, many asylums became places of horror.

A typical example of the horrors of asylums emerges from the history of Bethlehem Hospital in London. Later known as "Bedlam," the hospital was founded in 1247, when the sheriff of London gave his estate and land to the Bishop and Church of Bethlehem to build a hospital for the Order of St. Mary of Bethlehem. In 1377, a few patients with mental illness were transferred there from a storehouse thought to be too close to the royal palace (Scheerenberger, 1983). The number of people with mental illnesses at Bedlam grew, and in 1547, King Henry VIII gave the hospital to the City of London as a hospital for "poor lunatics" (Arieno, 1989: 16–17). An investigation in 1815 found that the patients were often chained and manacled to the walls and slept on piles of hay soiled with human waste (Metcalf, 1818).

Early American Practices

The American colonists brought with them from Europe many religious customs, ideas, and attitudes. The prejudices toward persons with physical and mental disabilities that existed in Europe likely followed settlers to colonial America. The major concern within the colonies, however, focused on the problem of dependency and disorder in the developing communities, rather than on impairment or public spectacle (Ferguson, 1994). Throughout the seventeenth and eighteenth centuries, most cases involving those deemed disabled concerned their poverty, unemployment, or vagrancy (Grob, 1994).

> Whether it was because you could not walk or talk, or were old or orphaned, widowed or homeless, the etiology of your indigence was seldom an urgent question. What mattered to the community was, first, whether you were a resident or not; second, who would care for you; and third, how the provisions for care were to be handled (Ferguson, 1994: 24).

During the colonial period, the emphasis was on the social and economic impact of impairment, rather than medical cause.

It was the custom of colonial families with means to care for their own members with disabilities—often out of concern for the preservation of the individual's property rights. The care of persons with impairments remained a family responsibility, so long as family members could provide the basic necessities for life. If, however, the effects of the disability spilled outside the family, care of the individual fell under the jurisdiction of the local community, which, in turn, was required to assist the individual or his or her family.

Gradually, laws codified the process for the public care and treatment of persons with disabilities. The first such law was enacted by the Massachusetts legislature in 1614. Most of the laws described the requirements for receiving public assistance and emphasized the criteria for residency. For example, an individual or family was required to live and work for a period of 3 months to 1 year before legal residence could be established. Determining the residency of a pauper was important, because residency created a responsibility for his or her care. A stranger, by contrast, who could not support himself or herself was banished, unless a resident assumed responsibility (Bowe, 1978; Rothman, 1990; Trattner, 1994). Early American guidelines for handling unemployed persons—a category into which those with disabilities often fell—were generally concerned with where to place the financial burden of care. Thus, they served to both "relieve the needy resident while cutting off and excluding the dependent outsider" (Rothman, 1990: 20).

Disabled colonists without families or those whose families could not or would not support them were "placed out" or "farmed out" to other families who received public assistance for providing them with room, board, shelter, and care. Many times, the agreement included indentured service akin to slavery. In fact, until the latter half of the nineteenth century, many communities "auctioned off" those with physical or mental disabilities to whomever made the lowest bid, and was then free to demand manual labor services from the persons bought during their period of retention to support room and board (Baumeister and Butterfield, 1970; Funk, 1987; Obermann, 1965; Trattnor, 1994).

Different from the infrastructure in European cities, colonial America initially had few systematic approaches to deal with people with disabilities. Those who were not perceived as a threat to public safety were often afforded the opportunity to work. Newcomers to a community believed to have the potential of becoming public charges were often "warned out"; that is, strongly encouraged to leave. It was not uncommon for local officials to force the return of persons deemed insane to the community in which they were legal residents (Grob, 1994: 16). Another practice was "passing on." This consisted of a community kidnapping their own "feeble-minded" and "insane" inhabitants at night and leaving them on the outskirts of strange, far away towns, with the hope that their inability to communicate would effectively preclude their return (Burgdorf and Burgdorf, 1975). Beyond the family, care and treatment was largely up to local officials who minimized the town's burden by keeping insane, destitute, and disabled persons out.

The Growth of Residential Placements

As American infrastructure grew, the colonists were able to enact ideas brought with them from England and Holland regarding the treatment of poor, ill, and disabled persons. Storing society's unwanted in almshouses, poorhouses, and hospitals was a European practice dating back to at least the tenth century (James, 1975). The first almshouse in America was built in Boston in 1660, and others across the colonies shortly followed. The presence of other residential facilities including jails, insane asylums and poorhouses would also grow over the next 100 years (Baumeister and Butterfield, 1970; Crissey and Rosen, 1986; Rothman, 1990; Ferguson, 1994). All of these became places to house colonists with disabilities whose care was charged to the public.

The choice of residential placement usually depended on how the individual with the disability became known to authorities. Those able to work were sent to workhouses or almshouses where rehabilitation into hardworking, useful citizens was the aim. If the offender exhibited behavior deemed disturbed, they were sent to hospitals for the insane; and if caught breaking the law, they were sent to prison (Crissey and Rosen, 1986). The growth of residential placements replaced the need for practices such as banishment and passing on, but placement in them usually resulted in physical and mental abuse and torture. As in Europe, the facilities ultimately became known for their deplorable conditions, mistreatment, and neglect (Funk, 1987: 9).

The Growth of Residential Facilities

In 1773, the Publik (sic) Hospital for Persons of Insane and Disordered Minds opened in Williamsburg, Virginia, marking the first American public facility designated to house those deemed mentally ill. Over the next 100 years, other large asylums, as well as small, private facilities with similar purpose grew. The majority of colonial Americans deemed poor, sick, feeble-minded, and insane, however, were grouped together under the label of "pauper" and were held in jails or almshouses (James, 1975; Scheerenberger, 1983, Trattner, 1994). As early as 1729, officials in Boston sought authorization for a separate facility to keep "Distracted Persons Separate from the Poor." It never happened. In 1764, Thomas Hancock, a wealthy Bostonian, bequeathed £600 for the establishment of a facility exclusively for insane persons. The bequest was never used for the purpose. It was not until the mid-nineteenth century that comprehensive reform would target the care of persons now deemed disabled.

Concern over the appalling conditions found in the almshouse system roused reformers such as Dorothea Dix and Samuel Gridley Howe to crusade for state supervision of institutionalized facilities and for the establishment of state institutions that would provide specialization of care (Bell and Burgdorf, 1983). While teaching a Sunday school program in the East Cambridge House of Corrections, Dix found conditions there abominable—for example, insane women kept in unheated rooms. This discovery inspired her to visit, during 1840–1841, almshouses, jails, and houses of correction throughout Massachusetts, recording lengthy, detailed descriptions of the squalid conditions she observed. Shortly after, Dix argued her case before Massachusetts State and federal legislators. She agitated for State supervision of institutional facilities as well as for specialized care facilities, such as hospitals, to serve those deemed insane, demented, and imbecilic. Her enormous influence resulted in a growth of state psychiatric hospitals and the reform of existing ones over the next 40 years (Burgdorf and Burgdorf, 1975; President's Committee on Employment of the Handicapped, 1977; Bell and Burgdorf, 1983; Scheerenberger, 1983; Shapiro, 1993; Ferguson, 1994).

Responding to the influence of reformers such as Dix, State Legislative Committees began to attack the almshouse relief system as inefficient, wasteful, and ineffective. They began pressing for a shift of public programs for poor and disabled people to those providing more structure and organization with indoor institutional care. In 1846, Massachusetts enacted the first legislation providing for a public facility for persons with feeble-mindedness [sic], part of which required an inquiry into the "condition of the idiots on the commonwealth [and] to ascertain their number and whether anything could be done for their relief" (Baumeister and Butterfield, 1970: 5). Samuel Gridley Howe, director of the Perkins Institute and Massachusetts School for Blind, was appointed head of the commission.

Howe's institute was home to one of many residential educational programs for persons with disabilities that had been established in America. The Massachusetts Asylum for the Blind (later the Perkins Institute) had been established in 1832; The American Asylum for the Deaf was established in Hartford, Connecticut, by Thomas Gallaudet in 1817, followed by the New York Institution for the Deaf and Dumb in 1818; and public programs for deaf individuals followed in many states, with Gallaudet College founded in Washington, D.C. 3 years later. Howe's 1948 findings emphasized the success of these programs and advocated that Massachusetts develop schools, rather than institutions more concerned with restraint and containment of "idiots." Though skeptical, the Massachusetts legislature provided funding to establish an experimental school for the feeble-minded. On October 1, 1848, a wing of Perkins Institute became the first permanent institution in the United States, as it accepted ten children into its new program. After 3 years, having been declared a huge success, the school was incorporated by the state and officially named the Massachusetts' School for Idiotic and Feeble-minded Youth.

The efforts of Dix, Howe, and other reformers of this era, resulted in the distinction of disability from criminality. The subsequent proliferation of residential institutions for individuals with disabilities offered a public alternative to jails and hospitals. The founders of these early institutions saw as the primary goal of their education and treatment programs, the ultimate return of persons with mental retardation to their own homes and communities (Bell and Burgdorf, 1983: 19). It was believed that with proper perseverance, persistence, and skill, such minds might be trained. Howe fought to have each new institution considered a school with education its primary function, rather than as an asylum, with implications of custody being primary. To enhance their success, these first institutions accepted very few students and only those who offered a reasonable prognosis for achievement. Over time, however, developing small-scale educational facilities was replaced with larger projects.

The Rise of Institutions

Between 1870 and 1890, construction on large facilities proliferated. The role of institutions to provide education and vocational training was replaced by the notion that residential facilities best provided protection for a population needing to be sheltered from the demands of the outside world (Burgdorf and Burgdorf, 1975). Increasingly, the institutions, now developed for adults, were characterized as "benevolent shelters." Institutions were now characterized as charitable housing. The result was the development of many large institutions housing great numbers of disabled people far from population centers, which provided no training that might enable their residents to return home. Some residents were taught some basic skills such as farming and gardening to help defray institutional costs (Bell and Burgdorf, 1983: 19). The view of the institution as a school faded and housing for short-term training was replaced with comprehensive care for long periods of time—sometimes even for life (Baumeister and Butterfield, 1970: 9).

Notable shifts in the attitudes toward disability and mental illness occurred in the latter parts of the nineteenth century. Aims to educate people with disabilities were replaced with a focus on long-term custodial care, often in the name of benevolence and protection. Eventually, the belief that containment in institutions was for the protection of those with disabilities also began to change. The sentiment that society needed protection from disabled people grew in the late 1800s and early 1900s (United States Commission on Civil Rights, cited in Bell and Burgdorf, 1983: 19). The eugenics movement had begun, which would signal a dramatic throwback in the treatment of disabled persons.

Eugenics and the Return of Extermination

The earliest responses to disability were abandonment, presumably leading to death. Nomadic groups abandoned impaired members to survive, while later civilizations practiced infanticide of apparently impaired newborns out of pity, tradition, religion, or superstition. Over time, communities turned toward humanism and took up care of the individual as emblematic of the social good. The advent of eugenics turned interest in the social good against the individual, notably those deemed feeble-minded. Women, especially, were targeted in an American campaign for extermination of disability.

In 1883, Francis Galton introduced the term "eugenics," taken from the similar Greek concept meaning "good in stock." Interested in the scientific examination of heredity, Galton proposed that preventing individuals with undesirable social traits from reproducing would better the human race. The concept was based on the assumption that biology, or any physical or psychological variation, predetermined an individual's morality and social status. Also intrinsic to this notion was the belief that the biological progress of mankind required the elimination of those considered hereditarily unfit. The eugenics movement promoted two major efforts:

> First, it sponsored research to investigate the transmission of social traits, especially undesirable ones, and undertook to classify individuals, groups, and nations on a scale of human worth. Second, it proposed biological solutions to social problems and lobbied for their implementation (Friedlander, 1995: 5).

Eugenics quickly gained national and international attention, and its seemingly scientific information became translated into social policy.

The Making of a Social Menace

In 1912, Henry Herbert Goddard, then Director of research at the Training School for Feeble-Mindedness Girls and Boys in Vineland, New Jersey, published the famous study, *The Kallikak Family: A Study in the Heredity of Feeble-Mindedness*. Goddard began his case study with a woman in his institution, whom he named Deborah Kallikak. He proceeded to trace her genealogy through many generations. Goddard described two branches of the Kallikak family born of a single progenitor. Deborah Kallikak and her ancestors—mostly poor and feeble-minded—"demonstrated" the outcome of the progenitor's one-time affair with a barmaid. The progenitor's other children, who were born in marriage to a woman of "good stock," were successful and moral. The different outcomes in the familial branches, Goddard thought, demonstrated the passage of particular traits through a family's lineage. Ultimately, he proposed the heredity of intelligence, mental health, and morality. Thus, feeble-mindedness became closely linked with poverty, crime, and illegitimacy.

In his study, Goddard also coined the term "moron," which became widely accepted for those considered to be "high-grade defectives." They evinced the typical characteristics of intellectual denseness, social dullness and inadequacy, and moral deficiency. The fear, however, was that morons were not afflicted to a degree obvious to the casual observer nor impaired by such adventitious means as brain injury, disease, or other injury. The next-door neighbor could be a family of poor lineage, perhaps hiding a recessive gene predicting feeble-mindedness. Eventually, feeble-mindedness changed from being merely associated with social vices to being their fundamental cause (Trent, 1994; Haller, 1963). The myth of the "menace of the feeble-minded" and the figure of the moron became an icon and force in American social thought. A social response followed. During the early 1900s, cautionary pamphlets and enactments incorporating the principles of eugenics began to appear in states throughout the nation. Titles of the pamphlets include, for example, *The Menace of the Feeble-minded in Pennsylvania* (1913), *The Menace of the Feeble-minded in Connecticut* (1915), *The Burden of the Feeble-minded* in Massachusetts (1912), and *The Feeble-minded, or, the Hub to Our Wheel of Vice* in Ohio (1913; cited in Gilhool, 1997: 269). The materials described plans to segregate the "unfortunates" in remote areas, hence protecting "normal" residents from social ills, as well as grouping people of the same "kind" to prevent undesirable traits from polluting upstanding family lineages. Beyond fear mongering, more dramatic social responses to "the menace" were also on the horizon.

Controlling Feeble-Mindedness and the Unfit

The eugenics movement highlighted Goddard's to raise the fear that the prevalence of congenital physical disability and feeble-mindedness would undermine society (Smith, 1985). The public became afraid that the occurrence of such disabilities was increasing rapidly in modern civilization and that "the spreading of handicapping conditions through heredity was the single most important problem facing American society" (Burgdorf and Burgdorf, 1977: 998). The eugenics movement had all the fervor of a religious crusade, of which American science was at the forefront (Smith, 1985). The early eugenic aim of eliminating unwanted inherited disorders from human populations by selective marriage practices soon evolved into laws enforcing compulsory sterilization, restricted immigration, restricted marriage, and custodial care (institutionalization) to halt the perceived menace of mental disease and delinquency.

The expanding interest in genetics, at the beginning of the century, led to the establishment of the first organization of the eugenics movement, the American Breeders' Association. Organized in 1903 by leading agricultural breeders, renowned university biologists, and others including Dr. Charles Davenport of Harvard and Alexander Graham Bell, the organization established in 1906 several committees to research specific breeding problems. One of their primary committees, the Committee on Eugenics set out "to investigate and report on heredity in the human race" [and] "to emphasize the value of superior blood and the menace to society of inferior blood" (Haller, 1963: 62). In 1911, the American Breeders Association, wanting to "purge from the blood of the race innately defective strains," recommended the following procedures: selective scientific breeding to remove defective traits, restrictive marriage laws, euthanasia, sterilization, and life segregation for all handicapped persons (Burgdorf and Burgdorf, 1975: 887). After 2 years, the Association defined as socially unfit "the feeble-minded," "paupers," "criminaloids," "epileptics," "the insane," "the constitutionally weak," "those predisposed to specific diseases," "the congenitally deformed," and "those having defective sense organs." They further advocated that such humans should, if possible, be eliminated from the human stock if we would maintain or raise the level of quality essential to the progress of the nation and our race (cited in Scheerenberger, 1983: 154). Society would have to be saved from the burdens imposed upon it by these defectives by such methods as marriage restriction, sexual sterilization, and permanent institutionalization.

Already by the mid-1890s, approximately half of the states had passed laws declaring null and void the marriages of insane or feeble-minded persons on the grounds that such persons were not capable of making contracts (Haller, 1963). By the late 1970s, most states carried statutory prohibitions of marriages where one of the partners was mentally ill or mentally retarded (Burgdorf and Burgdorf, 1977). In addition, while some states restricted marriage among persons considered physically handicapped, at least 17 extended such prohibitions to persons with epilepsy. A number of states also restricted or denied the right of persons with mental retardation and those considered "deaf mutes" from entering into any sort of legal contract. Such restrictions also served to control marriages, which are contractual agreements at law.

Sterilization

Compulsory sterilization became practically feasible in the late nineteenth century when safe, effective, and morally acceptable surgical methods were developed. Up to the 1890s, the only surgical procedure available for producing sterility was castration, considered extremely radical, because it was medically dangerous, caused undesirable changes in secondary sexual characteristics, and was widely considered morally unacceptable. Such thoughts, however, did not stop some institution administrators. During the 1890s, Dr. F. Pilcher, Superintendent of the Kansas State Asylum for Idiotic and Imbecile Youth, castrated 44 older boys and men for masturbating (Trent, 1994: 193). Pilcher had 44 boys castrated and 14 girls clitorectomized until public outrage forced him to stop (Burgdorf and Burgdorf, 1977: 999). Martin Barr, a contemporary of Pilcher's, stated in an 1899 journal article, that one of the benefits of castration was the fact that "some nice male soprano voices could be obtained for the institutional choir" (cited in Baumeister and Butterfield, 1970: 12).

By the end of the nineteenth century, the vasectomy (severing the vas deferens) for men and the salpingectomy (the cutting or removing of the fallopian tubes) for women, were developed. Seen as safe and morally acceptable surgical procedures, sterilizations of those deemed feeble-minded increased, especially in institutions, despite the fact that no state had enacted legislation authorizing them (Burgdorf and Burgdorf, 1977). In 1907, however, Indiana passed the nation's first sterilization law, which applied to "inmates of state institutions who were confirmed criminals, idiots, imbeciles, or rapists" (Burgdorf and Burgdorf, 1977: 1,000). By 1930, 28 states had enacted compulsory laws that authorized the sterilization of "inmates of mental institutions, persons convicted more than once of sex crimes, those deemed to be feeble-minded by IQ tests, 'moral degenerate persons' and epileptics" (Friedlander, 1995: 8). By 1938, more than 27,000 forced sterilizations had been performed in the United States (Smith, 1985).

The flood of state statutes authorizing eugenic sterilizations met occasional obstacles in those courts that found such procedures unconstitutional, until 1925 when the Supreme Court of Virginia made its ruling in the landmark case of *Buck v. Bell* (1925) reinforcing the state's right to force unwanted sterilizations. In 1924, Carrie Buck had been committed to the State Colony for Epileptics and Feeble-minded at Lynchberg. Under the authority of the *Virginia Sterilization Act* (1924), which provided for the sterilization of "mental defectives" confined to state institutions when, in the judgment of the superintendents of those institutions, "the best interests of the patients and society would be served by their being rendered incapable of producing offspring" (White, 1993: 404). The superintendent presented to the Colony's Board of Directors, a petition for an order to sterilize Carrie by salpingectomy, alleging that she had the mind of a 9-year-old, was the mother of a mentally defective child, and was the daughter of a woman previously committed to that same institution. The petition was granted.

Carrie's state appointed guardian appealed the decision up to the United States Supreme Court (Burgdorf and Burgdorf, 1977: 1,000–1,005). Justice Oliver Wendell Holmes, writing for the eight-person majority of the Court held that the Virginia Statute was legal and did not violate Carrie's rights under Due Process or the Equal Protection Clause of the Fourteenth Amendment (Friedlander, 1995: 8). Thus, the Court endorsed the eugenic justifications for the state's sterilizing the unfit and the often quoted excerpts of Holmes' opinion entered the language:

> It is better for all the world, if instead of waiting to execute degenerate offspring for crime, or to let them starve for their imbecility, society can prevent those who are manifestly unfit from continuing their kind. The principle that sustains compulsory vaccination is broad enough to cover cutting the fallopian tubes. … Three generations of imbeciles are enough (cited in Burgdorf and Burgdorf, 1977: 1,004).

Holmes' decision opened the floodgates for sterilizations in the United States. In 1927, Carrie Buck was sterilized. Ironically, "Carrie's child, alleged to represent a 'third generation of imbeciles,' actually grew to be an honor student" (Smith, 1994: 234). In fact, Carrie herself left the institution after she was sterilized, married a deputy sheriff and lived a modest, productive, and respectable life. It was later proven that she did not have mental retardation, and careful examination of her family tree would have revealed she was actually descended from a prominent Virginia family (Smith, 1994). Smith (1994) estimated conservatively, that 50,000 people had been sterilized in the United States under that authority. More than 4,000 had been sterilized at the Lynchburg Training School alone.

Nazi Medicalization of Killing

Though touted as American science, the Third Reich, under Adolf Hitler's Nazi regime, would enact eugenic policies with tremendous impact. Having carefully studied American sterilization and institutionalization laws, the National Socialists based much of their philosophy on the "science of eugenics" (Bowe, 1978; Kuhl, 1994; Friedlander, 1995; Pernick, 1996). With much of its rationale grounded in the American eugenics movement, the Nazis attempted to combine ethnic and eugenic racism into a comprehensive program of race improvement. Kuhl (1994) defined eugenic racism as "The demarcation of certain elements within a particular race, followed by attempts to reduce these elements through discriminatory policies" (p. 71).

Race purification and improvement as a cornerstone of Nazi ideology appeared as early as 1925, when Hitler (1925/1971) idealized the "pure" German state in *Mein Kampf*. In 1930, the Nazi Party's National Socialist German Medical Association proclaimed the "primacy of national biology" (Bleul, 1973: 191). Medical policies and practices became a means to enforce social hygiene. In 1933, immediately upon Hitler's assumption of power, the Nazi's established special Health Courts to implement a newly enacted law requiring sterilization of those with hereditary diseases. The Nazi definition of the hereditarily sick included those with congenital mental deficiency, schizophrenia, manic-depressive insanity, inherited epilepsy, Huntington's chorea, inherited deafness or blindness, or "grave physical defect." The law, which forbade the sterilization of "normal persons," was ultimately responsible for the sterilization of between 300,000–375,000 persons perceived as defective by the state (Lifton, 1986; Finger, 1992; Gallagher, 1995). More than half (approximately 203,250) of those sterilized under the act were presumed to have congenital feeble-mindedness (Gallagher, 1995).

The Nazi policy of sterilization quickly led to a much more comprehensive and vigorous eugenics program that soon included "euthanasia" and the medical killing of approximately 200,000 disabled men, women and children (Burleigh, 1994). The belief in euthanizing people with disabilities for the good of the individual and society was prominent in the age of eugenics. The 1920 book, *Die Freigabe de Vernichtung lebersunwertend Lebens; ihr Mass und ihre Form* (*The Release of the Destruction of Life Devoid of Value*) by respected professionals, Binding and Hoche (1975/1920), for example, proved influential in the Nazi regime. The work stressed the economic and social costs to society by "defective" individuals and mounted an academic argument that unworthy life included children with mental retardation, mental illness, and physical "deformities."

The Binding and Hoche book professionalized and medicalized "euthanasia" by stressing its therapeutic aspect and proposing the destruction of life unworthy of life as a healing process (Lifton, 1986: 46). The authors further pictured "euthanasia" as kind, compassionate, reasonable, moral, and economical (Wolfensberger, 1980). Binding argued that "euthanasia" was a compassionate way to dispose of the "'empty human husks' that fill our psychiatric institutions" (cited in Proctor, 1988: 178). Binding and Hoche's book:

> …became the intellectual, social, legal, medical, and moral basis for the widespread advocacy for the destruction of handicapped and enfeebled people during the early years of World War II (Wolfensberger, 1981: 2).

Many other respected eugenicists around the world shared Binding and Hoche's ideas. In 1933, Gould, an American physician, proposed in the *Journal of the American Institute of Homeopathy* that euthanasia helped resolve economic difficulties, citing with approval, the "elimination of the unfit" in ancient Sparta (cited in Proctor, 1988). Similarly, in 1941, American psychiatrist Foster Kennedy, professor of neurology at Cornell Medical College, delineated a proposal to the American Psychiatric Association for killing "defective" and "hopelessly unfit" children, whom he labeled "those helpless ones who should never have been born—Nature's mistakes" (Proctor, 1988; Hollander, 1989; Shapiro, 1993; Gallagher, 1995). In short, the intellectual and scientific context created by eugenics made the killing of disabled persons appear compassionate, perhaps even dutiful.

Following forcible sterilization, the Nazis adopted a policy of direct medical killing of disabled persons, justified by the principle of *lebensunwertes Leben* or "life unworthy of life." The party line stressed that "[A] healthy Reich could not afford sick people because they were too expensive" (Bleul, 1973: 192), particularly in time of war. The Nazi rationale for such killing was to provide beds for wounded soldiers and civilians by emptying mental hospitals, foster homes, and institutions for persons with disabilities (Pross, 1992). Therefore, forcible "euthanasia" was also based on the needs of a wartime economy, or on what Proctor (1992) called "a preemptive triage to free up beds" (p. 35). The medical establishment became obsessed with how much food and resources could be saved with the killing of each defective person.

As with Binding and Hoche, and later Kennedy, Hitler, and the Nazis "medicalized" the issue of "euthanasia" for persons with disabilities, thereby giving it "scientific legitimacy." Doctors became "the guardians of national hereditary health" (Burleigh, 1994: 191). Once medically legitimized, "euthanasia" was then quickly and efficiently implemented by physicians, nurses, aides, technicians, and others seen as healers, who willingly dealt out death by starvation, gas, injections and poison. They believed they were doing it for the "health" of their country (Wolfensberger, 1980) with "doctors [as] the highest echelon of those directly or indirectly involved in mass murder" (Burleigh, 1994: 154). Hitler Nazified the medical profession by redefining its goal as the "promotion and perfection of the health of the German people to ensure that the people realize the full potential of their racial and genetic endowment" (Lifton, 1986: 30). The role of medicine, then, was to protect the state from unwanted citizens thought to be contaminating it. Hitler allowed physicians, and especially psychiatrists, to pronounce value judgments both on individuals on medical grounds and on entire groups on medical–sociological grounds (Wertham, 1980). As Weindling (1989) observed, "The transition from medicine as care for the individual to the welfare of society and future generations attained the most extreme and brutal realization in the killing of the sick and disabled" (pp. 542–543).

While Hitler and the Nazi regime legitimized killing persons with disabilities, the medical experts assumed the crucial administrative role (Weindling, 1989). The German medical community proved itself shockingly amenable to the eradication of whole groups of people. Gallagher (1995) suggested that the reason that the doctors were so willing to comply was their own arrogance "bred of a confidence in science and the prestige of the medical profession" (p. xvii). Part of that arrogance was based fundamentally on the medical model of viewing persons with disabilities as sick people who never get well, and therefore never live a worthy life. Under the assumption that its desire to perfect the human race justified killing, the medical profession used eugenics, genetics, and biology to provide a "rationale" for it actions (Gallagher, 1995). Not all German doctors had a direct hand in the Holocaust, however. Individual physicians did oppose the regime in various ways, even though open opposition meant certain death (Kater, 1989). Weindling (1989) stressed that not all Nazi doctors who favored sterilization favored medical killing, and such doctors became passive onlookers rather than active participators of medical murder (p. 546). The impact of individual doctors who performed the killings, however, was far less damaging than the public and professional perception of the "science" that supported the killings.

The medical community's role helped to sell the public on the idea that Germany's "ills" were not economic or political, but were threats to the "folkish body" from the increasing number of humans who were perceived as "genetically unworthy" and "inferior." According to Müller (1991), those condemned by the government were described as "ballast to society." By making social problems medical, scientific, and genetic, the Nazis gave them an "untreatable hopeless biological cause" that justified a cure of segregation and elimination. Racial hygiene became both science and social policy governing inferiority and disability (Proctor, 1988). As a medical model, it could explain, categorize, and prescribe. The science of racial hygiene allowed the Nazis to determine the value of human beings first by mental and physical characteristics, then later by racial and social ones.

Those first killed in Germany were physically disabled children in a hospital near Wurthberg operated by the Samaritan Brothers. The SS appropriated the program under the state's policy of taking over of church-controlled asylums (Weindling, 1989). The youngsters, already victims of institutionalization and sterilization, were killed by drug overdoses (usually Luminal, a barbiturate) hidden in their food. Those who refused to eat received forced injections or suppositories filled with the poison (Conot, 1983; Smith, 1985). On August 18, 1939, the "Committee began its work by requiring midwives, medical officers, and doctors to register all children born with serious hereditary diseases, particularly "idiocy" and "mongolism" (especially when associated with blindness and deafness); microcephaly; hydrocephaly; malformations of limbs, head, and spinal column; and paralysis, including spastic conditions" (Lifton, 1986: 52).

Finger stated that the parents of the children selected for death were told that their children would receive "special treatments," which were in reality large doses of pneumonia-causing sedatives. Once induced, the pneumonia went untreated (cited in Johnson, 1987: 24). Parents were then informed by a standardized letter used in all institutions that their child had died suddenly and unexpectedly of brain edema, appendicitis, or some other fabricated cause, and that owing to the danger of an epidemic, their child's body required immediate cremation (Proctor, 1988). The condolence letters and death certificates were frequently accompanied with an urn containing ashes (Berenbaum, 1993).

Remak (1969) reported that the full official implementation of the "euthanasia" program began with Hitler's 1939 memorandum authorizing the extension of "the responsibilities of physicians still to be named in such a manner that patients whose illness, according to the most critical application of human judgment, is incurable can be granted release by euthanasia" (pp. 133–134). The signature was backdated to coincide with the invasion of Poland, and basically the beginning of World War II. A war economy sanctioned the Nazis' killing of life unworthy of life. After bombing attacks, for instance, psychiatric institutes and homes for the elderly were regularly emptied (their patients murdered) to make up for lost bed space (Proctor, 1992).

The program labeled "Aktion T-4" (named for Berlin Chancellery Tiergarten 4, which directed it) focused on chronic adult patients and "involved virtually the entire German psychiatric community and related portions of the general medical community" (Lifton, 1986: 65). Aktion T-4 extended the "euthanasia" project to include adults and called for the identification of all patients with more severe disabilities including schizophrenia, epilepsy, encephalitis, chronic illness, cerebral palsy, delinquency, perversion, alcoholism, anti-social behavior, and a number of others (Wolfensberger, 1981; Scheerenberger, 1983; Lifton, 1986; Proctor, 1988; Rogasky, 1988; Gallagher, 1995; Friedlander, 1995).

The first gassing of psychiatric patients occurred 45 days later at Posen, in Poland. In Germany itself, "euthanasia" quickly "became part of normal hospital routine" (Proctor, 1992: 35). Hollander (1989), in fact, noted the ease with which the program was implemented attributable in large part, to the cooperation of the "service providers" (p. 53). Because of the early success of the "euthanasia" program, it soon spread to include those less severely disabled, those with atypical characteristics, but not disabled (e.g., persons with dwarfism), those reported as having behavior problems, those suspected of being racially or genetically tainted, and those who were devalued entirely for other identities including Gypsies, homosexuals, Polish prisoners of war.

"Racial hygiene" as practiced by the medical community implied that persons with mental and physical disabilities were a threat to the "body" of Germany. Hitler medically justified the Holocaust in the same way by espousing the idea that a Jewish "infection" was causing the Aryan race to be "weak and ill." The only cure was to rid the body of the infection, the Jews. The patient was neither the Jews nor the Gypsies nor any other group; it was the Aryan race. "The way of curing the Aryan race was to get rid of whatever had made it ill" (Lifton, 1990: 225). Kater (1989), in fact, emphasized that, the Nazis saw

Auschwitz as a racial "clinic" and the medically logical extension of sterilization and "euthanasia" (p. 182). As Reichsfuhrer Himmler stated, "Anti-Semitism is exactly the same as delousing. Getting rid of lice is not a question of ideology. It is a matter of cleanliness" (cited in Szasz, 1970: 214).

Euthanasia as a Prototype for the "Final Solution"

The "Euthanasia" medical killing program served, then, as a pilot scheme and training model for those who would later implement the Holocaust (Weindling, 1989). As Wolfensberger (1981) observed, "[T]he killing of the Jews evolved out of the desensitization, legitimization, personnel preparation and equipment development associated with the killing of handicapped persons" (1981, p. 3). Conot (1983) termed the euthanasia program a "prototype" for the extermination of millions that was to follow. Berenbaum (1993) and Proctor (1992) point out the gas chambers, method of transport of "patients," and even process for disposing bodies were developed at the killing centers for disabled people.

> The ultimate decision to gas Jews emerged from the fact that the technical apparatus already existed for the destruction of the mentally ill. In the fall of 1941, with the completion of the bulk of the euthanasia operation, the gas chambers at psychiatric hospitals were dismantled and shipped east, where they were reinstalled at Majdanek, Aushwitz, and Treblinka. The same doctors, technicians, and nurses often followed the equipment (Proctor, 1992: 37).

Dr. Andrew Ivy, who helped prosecute the Nazi physicians at Nuremburg concluded, "Had the [medical] profession taken a strong stand against the mass killing of sick Germans before the war, it is conceivable that the entire idea and technique of death factories for genocide would not have materialized" (cited in Gallagher, 1995: 31–32). Gallagher added that "had the doctors acted differently, had they said no, things would have been different. An early link in the chain of events leading to the Holocaust would have been broken" (p. 32). As Fiedler (1996) wrote of the "euthanasia-final solution" link: "It is a development which should make us aware of just how dangerous enforced physiological normality is when the definition of its parameters falls into the hands of politicians and bureaucrats" (p. 150). The horror of the Holocaust exposed, human rights took on new importance, leading to changes in policy and attitudes, which would shape contemporary life for persons with disabilities.

Conclusion

This historical examination of the treatment and segregation of persons with disabilities provides insight and perspective for understanding the origins of our more familiar current common beliefs and attitudes. Throughout time and across contexts, extraordinary characteristics and impairments have been an occasion for meaning. Whether perceived as divine punishment or reward;

considered sin or blessing; or deemed pathological by science, culture's discernment of difference has played a role in the lives of those deemed disabled. In tracing the treatment of disabled persons, we see the origins of paternalism in Greco-Roman times; the benevolent and charitable response in Judeo-Christian traditions; both the aversion to and spectacle made of "monsters" and "freaks" in the Middle Ages and beyond; and the response to rid society of its undesirables in the eugenics movement and under the Third Reich.

The concept of normalcy has been used to justify the differential treatment of society's "undesirables" throughout history. Deeming differences to be pathologies once made allowable the segregation, abuse, and murder of particular people and groups of people. The specific characteristics that have signified a rationale for differential treatment vary according to place and time; religion and culture. To account for this diversity, we must understand how the idea of pathology can be applied to almost any trait, with the resulting position of being "disabled," or made unable to participate and benefit from society's opportunities. Gordon and Rosenbum (2001) make a strong case, in fact, that disability shares many characteristics with American constructions of race, gender, and sexual orientation. They consider how each status is constructed through unceasing social processes in which people are named, aggregated and disaggregated, dichotomized and stigmatized, and deprived of attributes valued in our culture. Linton (1998) writes, "[Disabled persons] are all bound together, not by this list of collective symptoms but by the social and political circumstances that have forged us as a group" (p. 4). It is the power of the group that is highlighted in the next chapter, as we discuss the "Era of Civil Rights."

5
Era of Civil Rights and Contemporary Issues

As Bullock and Mahon (1997) stated, "Two basic views in the ancient world existed regarding the etiology of disability. One attributed illness to supernatural or divine intervention, and the other view was that illness and disability were due to natural causes" (pp. 19–20). Many religious traditions characterized particular physical and sensory differences as inhuman or reflective of sin, and therefore "justifiably" barred particular people from equal participation in worship and other facets of public life (Shapiro, 1999; Stiker, 1997). Changes in ways of thinking about social inequality are noticeable over time. Baynton (2001) describes:

> Since the social and political revolutions of the eighteenth century, the trend in Western political thought has been to refuse to take for granted inequalities between persons or groups. Differential and unequal treatment has continued, of course, but it has been considered incumbent on modern societies to produce a rational explanation for such treatment (p. 33).

In the age of modernity, science arose to produce an explanation for inequality. The justification for discrimination based on individual's impairments became an acceptable response to the "misfortune" of having an atypical body or mind, and served as the rationale for the extreme atrocities committed during the Eugenics Movement and the Third Reich.

The first half of the twentieth century was an internationally tumultuous era, characterized by two World Wars and the Great Depression. While disabled people were still subject to horrific treatment rationalized by the pseudoscience of eugenics, innovation, humanism, and a new face of disability seen in returning war veterans also marked this period of history.

As early as 1914, federal policies including the War Risk Insurance Act (1914) and the Smith-Sears Veterans Rehabilitation Act (1918) were established to address the concerns of disabled veterans. The Disabled American Veterans organization was eventually formed in 1920, and the National Easter Seal Society was established in 1922. Although these organizations and policies did not reflect the contemporary initiatives posed by disabled persons (veterans and others, alike), their emergence signified increasing public interest and organization around disability issues. In 1932, Harry Jennings built the first tubular, folding wheelchair, which became the prototype for those in use today. The League of the Physically Handicapped (1935–1938) formed as one of the first disability organizations to make discrimination in policy and employment its primary issue. President Franklin D. Roosevelt, along with Eleanor Roosevelt, advanced the concerns of people with disabilities through supporting the March of Dimes (1937) and other policy initiatives, respectively. A confluence of scientific, social, and political factors paved the way for a new era of disability rights to emerge.

Deinstitutionalization and Independent Living

After World War II, as the world became aware of the atrocities of the Holocaust with its roots in "race purification," the ideas of eugenicists began to wane in acceptance and influence. Instead, medical researchers, charitable organizations, and disability rights groups—to some extent—focused attention on the dual goals of curing impairments and improving the living conditions of children and adults with disabilities. Among the first areas of business for the new activists were exposing the undignified, at best, and deplorable conditions, at worst, of the institutions, hospitals, and nursing homes in which many adults and children with disabilities were living. To that point, the architecture of most buildings and streets prohibited the free movement of a new generation of wheelchair users. Societal attitudes had accepted the "wheelchair-bound" images of "crippled" people as an unfortunate, but understandably restrictive condition. Children and adults identified with developmental and intellectual disabilities had long been warehoused in institutions.

In institutions and other group-living environments, disabled children and adults were subject to the dehumanizing conditions expected of any large-scale residential facility. Virtually all decisions, from choice of food and activities to the schedule for sleeping and bathing, were imposed by the structure of the facility. The daily routines of institutions were humiliating. As late as the 1960s, Shapiro (1993) described, "it remained common for inmates at state hospitals to be bathed by stripping off their clothes, forming them into a line, and spraying them with water from a garden hose" (p. 160). Blatt (1970, 1981), while observing four state institutions for persons with mental retardation in four Eastern states during the Christmas season of 1965, found remarkably similar conditions to those described over 150 years earlier in the Bedlam and York asylums. He related the following first-hand account:

> As I entered this dormitory, housing severely mentally retarded adolescents and adults … an overwhelming stench enveloped me. It was the sickening, suffocating smell of feces and urine, decay, dirt and filth, of such strength as to hang in the air and, I thought then and still am not dissuaded, solid enough to be cut or shoveled away. But, as things turned out,

the odors were among the gentlest assaults on our sensibilities. I was soon to learn about the decaying humanity that caused them (1981, p. 142).

As with the conditions at the Bedlam and York asylums, Blatt encountered filth, cruel, inhuman treatment, including the common use of restraints and solitary confinement:

> Many dormitories for the severely and moderately retarded ambulatory residents have solitary confinement cells or what is officially referred to, and is jokingly called by many attendants, "therapeutic isolation." Therapeutic isolation means solitary confinement—in its most punitive and inhumane form. These cells are located on an upper floor, off to the side and away from the casual or official visitor's scrutiny. ... Isolation cells are generally tiny rooms, approximately seven feet by seven feet (pp. 143–144).

Neglect and cruelty were characteristic of conditions in many institutions. Residents also suffered far worse indignities during the mid-century.

At the Fernald School, during the 1950s, government-sponsored research was conducted on children with intellectual disabilities without their knowledge or guardian consent. The Advisory Committee on Human Radiation Experiments (ACHRE) (1996) found that groups considered powerless and dependent were targeted for experimentation. These groups included infants, children, minorities, the terminally ill, persons with cognitive disabilities, and those in institutions. Thus, the institutionalization of the nation's most vulnerable members offered a population of people who could be used at scientists' disposal. In the Fernald School experiments, children were told they were participating in a science club activity and fed oatmeal breakfasts with small doses of radioactive isotopes. Through the response of children to ingredients given in milk and cereal, researchers hoped to ascertain if a chemical in oatmeal would interfere with the body's ability to absorb iron and calcium (ACHRE, 1994; "Retarded school alumni," 1994). Such experimentation on "vulnerable populations" occurred between World War II and the mid-1970s on over 16,000 humans with the Atomic Energy Commission's express approval or financial support. For example, during the 1960s at the University of Arkansas Medical Center in Little Rock, children with mental retardation (some as young as 13) who were wards of the Arkansas Children's Colony, a state institution, received "iodine-131" in a thyroid study. In a similar University of Arkansas study, experiments involved infants as young as 9 months. A study completed at the University of Washington between 1954 and 1958 used "mental patients" from the Northern State Hospital in Sedro-Woolley as unknowing subjects (Burns, 1995; Hoversten, 1995a). In time, as with the European hospitals and American Almshouses of earlier times, the deplorable conditions of modern-day institutions would be exposed to the general public.

In 1972, a series of exposés on the Willowbrook State School in New York City was aired on television and brought unprecedented public attention to the conditions in institutions that visitors such as Blatt had described. The result of the exposure was a class-action lawsuit that mandated reforms to the facility. More importantly, however, the publicity generated by the case brought attention to the civil rights of people with disabilities. Rather than merely seek reform of facilities, reform in the systems that placed people in institutions also became a focus. The idea of *independent living* for people with intellectual and developmental disabilities was brought to fore.

Independent Living

The idea of independent living was not a new one in the 1970s. A trend in deinstitutionalization through the 1950s–1960s had burgeoned from the efforts and activism of physically disabled persons. In 1958, for example, Anne Emerman, who was living at the Goldwater Memorial Hospital in New York City, was selected as a test case in independent living. The 21-year-old, quadriplegic, wheelchair user entered the "mainstream" and ultimately completed college and a master's degree, worked as a psychiatric social worker, served as the director of the Mayor's Office for People with Disabilities in New York City, and became a wife and mother (Fleischer and Zames, 2001). This "test case," and others like it, fueled an era of activism in independent living that those with developmental and intellectual disabilities would eventually also benefit from.

Prior even to the test cases in New York, some of the first college programs for persons with disabilities had been established in what are now the Kansas State Teachers College and the University of Illinois (Fleischer and Zames, 2001). Catering to disabled veterans, these schools capitalized on their relatively compact and flat geography to welcome wheelchair users. Subsequently, they developed assistance centers, sports programs, and accessible transportation options as part of the college experience. The National Deaf-Mute College, which changed its name to Gallaudet College in 1954, had been serving students using an array of communication modes since 1880. The successes that came out of these programs offered promising possibilities for people once deemed unable to work or live full lives. These examples aside, although early pioneers such as Emerman and Marilyn Saviola, the first resident of Goldwater to attend college while living there, were quite ready to enter the world, the world was not as ready for them. Getting into and getting funding for college, securing an accessible place to live, getting financial and medical assistance, gaining employment, and negotiating a physical environment that was more often not friendly to wheelchair users were all barriers to independent living. Most of society had not taken a lead from the efforts of those at Gallaudet, Kansas State Teachers College, the University of Illinois, and a handful of others.

The issue of containment posed by institutions and nursing homes quickly shifted to one of restriction posed by the barriers in most of the world outside of them. It was not enough that a few programs had been established as "disability-friendly." Disabled persons deserved access to the society at large. In 1962, Edward Roberts, a quadriplegic polio survivor who spent most of his life in an iron lung, successfully sued the University of California (UC) to gain admission, insisting that he had an equal right to education. Roberts' enrollment at UC-Berkeley, however, also meant that appropriate housing would need to be provided. As other quadriplegics joined Roberts on the campus, organizing for better services, housing, and assistance for living became possible. They formed a political group called The Rolling Quads and worked on getting services such as wheelchair repair, accessible housing, and attendant care (Fleischer and Zames, 2001: 39).

In 1969, the Physically Disabled Students Program was funded as part of a national initiative for minority students. The blueprint for the independent living movement was born, rooted in a new way of conceptualizing the needs and issues central to the lives of disabled people. Shapiro (1993) captures the change:

> The medical model of disability measured independence by how far one could walk after an illness or how far one could bend his legs after an accident. But Roberts redefined independence as the control a disabled person had over his life. Independence was measured not by the tasks one could perform without assistance but by the quality of one's life with help (p. 51).

In 1972, the Center for Independent Living at Berkeley was formed as an agency governed by and for people with disabilities. Its founder, Ed Roberts, became a new kind of "poster-child," symbolizing not charity or pity, but self-determination and the fight for civil rights of disabled people. The recognition of disabled peoples' agendas as centered on rights and access emerged, and the Disability Rights Movement was ushered in, only slightly after the more frequently honored Civil Rights and Women's Rights Movements of the time.

The Disability Rights Movement

By the end of the 1950s, disability policy had begun to adopt a civil rights orientation. There was increasing humanization of disabled people based on qualities of deservedness, normality, and employability. There was also a move from total societal indifference to recognition that the remaining "unfortunates" must receive some minimum level of care (Funk, 1987). The National Association for the Deaf (NAD) had been founded in 1864, and the American Foundation for the Blind (AFB) in 1921. Noted previously, veterans and those with physical disabilities had broken into the "mainstream," and awareness of intellectual disability was growing. For example, Rose Kennedy, the intellectually disabled sister of President John F. Kennedy, gave a new face to "retardation" in 1960, and the exposure of the worst institutions had alerted the public to the ill treatment many with the diagnosis endured. The independent living movement offered a notable shift from the attitudes before then, which Funk describes as tolerant of retaining persons with disabilities in a caste status and assuming that most would always require segregated care and protection.

By the 1960s, the United States entered a time when formal organizations and coalitions of persons with disabilities could, by analogy to other oppressed groups, focus their efforts on civil rights issues pertinent to *all* categorized "disabled." Prior to the Disability Rights Movement, most organized efforts to improve the quality of life for persons with disabilities were specific to a particular impairment—as in the NAD and AFB—or characterized as charity. Leadership and strategic planning for the latter involved, at best, only marginal participation of their intended stakeholders (disabled persons). The upwell of anti-discrimination action surrounding race and gender led disabled people to also challenge their limited employment and housing options and other exclusions. As with leaders of other movements, disability rights activists believed that self-advocacy and grassroots strategies would promise change more aligned with their agendas. In addition, the idea of defining disabled persons as a group brought together by common oppression, rather than defined by specific impairments, emerged (Linton, 1998).

In the wake of early pioneers in independent living, Judith E. Heumann organized the group, Disabled in Action (DIA), in 1970, whose legacy of demonstrations and lawsuits for disability rights began with demands for accessible public transportation in New York City. Eventually growing into the national group, Self Advocates Becoming Empowered (S.A.B.E.), the *People First* movement took cues from organizations in Sweden, Canada, and the United Kingdom, and began advancing the self-advocacy of persons with intellectual disabilities in 1974. The Union of Physically Impaired Against Segregation (UPIAS) organized to issue a proclamation in 1972, which would ignite the Disabled People's Movement in the United Kingdom. Thus, grassroots organizations formed the basis of the Disability Rights Movement in the United States and internationally.

Section 504 of the Rehabilitation Act

Although earlier legislation and policies in the United States had reflected some of the concerns of disabled people, the *Rehabilitation Act of 1973 (PL 93-112)* is regarded as the first civil rights act specific to the group. When, in 1972, President Nixon vetoed early versions of the act, disability rights activists emerged with force. DIA members, including Heumann and 80 others, halted traffic with a sit-in on one of New York City's main thoroughfares. When the act was brought to vote in 1973, a march and rally on the Capitol ensured that the attention of policy-makers and the public would be captured to guarantee its passage.

The *Rehabilitation Act of 1973* was passed into federal law on September 26, 1973. The original act barred employment discrimination, mandated affirmative action in employment, and established the Architectural and Transportation Compliance Board (now named the Access Board). Most significant to solidifying disability rights, however, *Section 504* of the act barred discrimination in all programs receiving federal financial assistance. Thus, the mass of social systems—unemployment, social security, state courts and agencies, schools, hospitals, and more—were now charged with upholding disabled persons' civil rights. *Section 504* stated:

> No otherwise qualified handicapped individual in the United States, as defined by section 7(6), shall, solely by reason of his handicap, be excluded from the participation in, be denied the benefits of, or be subjected to discrimination under any program or activity receiving Federal financial assistance (United States Congress, 1973).

The wording in *Section 504* matched the *Civil Rights Act of 1964*, which abolished discrimination in federally funded programs on the basis of race, color, or national origin.

As thrilling as the passage of the Act was, however, regulations were not in place to specify situations constituting discrimination, nor their remedies. When Howard University law student, James Cherry, was denied the use of a building's elevator and a request for a closer parking space, it became clear that the impact of *Section 504* was limited without specific direction. He initiated a lawsuit demanding that the Department of Health, Education, and Welfare (HEW) develop and enforce regulations for *Section 504*. In July 1976, Cherry won his case. Pushing the government to develop and pass the forthcoming regulations became a cause around which more local organizations of disability rights could join together and rally. "Until this point," Fleischer and Zames (2001) point out, "the disability rights movement had been local and disparate. With this concerted endeavor to obtain implementation of the Section 504 regulations, the movement became national and focused" (p. 52).

The American Coalition of Citizens with Disabilities (ACCD) had been founded through a Rehabilitation Services Agency grant in 1975, and included members such as Judith E. Heumann, Fred Fay, Ralf D. Hotchkiss, Sharon Mistler, Roger Peterson, Al Pimentel, and Eunice Fiorito—all people with disabilities (Fleischer and Zames, 2001). After Cherry's lawsuit, the group exerted pressure on HEW and congress to issue and amend Section 504. When HEW did not meet the ACCD's deadline on April 4, 1977; April 5 dawned with disability rights activists demonstrating at most of HEW's offices in ten federal regions and the nation's capital. Coverage of the longest sit-ins in San Francisco and Washington, D.C. garnered national attention. The regulations were issued and signed on April 28, alongside those issued to amend another disability rights act—*The Education for All Handicapped Children Act.*

The Education for All Handicapped Children Act

At the same time that adults with disabilities were organizing for access to employment and independent living, parents were also agitating for the rights of their children with disabilities to access public education. Advocacy and parent organizations such as the Association for Retarded Citizens (ARC) and the United Cerebral Palsy Association had been fighting for deinstitutionalization at the same time as others. Parent organizations had also successfully lobbied Congress to establish a federal bureau for "handicapped children" and to provide funds for training special education teachers and developing appropriate curricula (Shapiro, 1993). However, access to *public* schools, rather than special, segregated programs was a right yet to be solidified. Children with disabilities could be denied entry to a school, and there were no provisions to guide the implementation of appropriate curriculum and facilities. In the early 1970s, two lawsuits were brought to argue the right to education of *all* children.

In 1971, the Pennsylvania Association for Retarded Children (PARC) won a class-action suit against the Commonwealth of Pennsylvania claiming the right of all children to enter public schools. To that point, children with disabilities could be denied entry to school. Shortly after, the decision in *Mills v. Board of Education of the District of Columbia* (1972) extended the ruling in *PARC v. Pennsylvania* to include "a presumption that among the alternative programs of education, placement in a regular public school class with appropriate ancillary services is preferable to placement in a special school class." With both Courts acknowledging the overdue right of all children's access to schools—granted in 1954 to African-American children in *Brown v. Board of Education*—and, alongside the passage of the Rehabilitation Act, legislation specific to education was on the horizon.

In 1975, Congress passed legislation that guaranteed a free and appropriate education for all of the nation's approximately 8 million children with disabilities—namely, *Public Law 94-142*, the *Education for All Handicapped Children Act* (EHA), which is now IDEIA. The act included six major provisions to ensure disabled youngsters an education appropriate to their individual special education needs:

1. "Zero reject" requires that all children receive free, appropriate education. No child may be denied an education because of the severity of his or her disability.
2. A non-discriminatory evaluation means that the required assessment of a youngster's handicap is conducted by a multidisciplinary team, is not culturally biased and is individually administered (no group testing).

3. An individualized education program (IEP) ensures that the educational program is tailored individually to meet the needs of each child.
4. Parent and student participation in decision-making.
5. Access to the Least Restrictive Environment (LRE).
6. Right to Due Process, or procedures that guide resolutions of conflict between the parent/student and the school.

Children with disabilities are protected under *Section 504,* which guarantees that they receive educational services and opportunities equal to those provided to their peers. The EHA, however, specified that children were also entitled to receive additional special education supports and services to ensure their *benefit* from the learning experiences provided. In other words, Section 504 guarantees equal access and non-discrimination to public schools and their curriculum, but the EHA required schools to ensure that children are benefiting from the educational program. It is not enough, for example, for a child to simply be in a classroom with others; the curriculum must be catered to the unique needs of each child.

Post-Legislation Activism

With the passage of two historical acts, disability activists were able to capitalize on their newfound recognition, and continued pushing for refinement in the provisions and regulations in the courts and the streets. Disability Rights had gained an attentive audience and many disability organizations focused on civil rights and access to public society emerged. *Guide Dog Users* was organized in New York City; the first convention of *People First*, organized nationally as Self Advocates Becoming Empowered, was held; and *Black Deaf Advocates* was established. Disabled in Action mounted several lawsuits and demonstrations focused on securing accessible public transit—most notably in the 1976 Transbus lawsuit (*Disabled in Action of Pennsylvania v. Coleman,* 1976). Following the success of 1982 demonstrations for accessible busses in Denver, Colorado, Wade Blank and residents of the Atlantis Community founded ADAPT, an influential and radical disability rights group. The group organized local events, but sought national influence and took on the federal government in mounting the suit, *ADAPT v. Skinner* (1989). The court ruled that federal regulations requiring that transit authorities to spend only a small percentage of their budgets on access were arbitrary and discriminatory. A smaller profit margin, in other words, is not a rationale for denying people access to public transportation.

The Americans with Disabilities Act (ADA)

Although *Section 504* and the *EHA* provided non-discrimination guidelines for people with disabilities, it would take a more comprehensive law to ensure their full civil rights. As member and chair of the Texas Task Force for Long Range

Policy for People with Disabilities during the 1980s, Justin Dart, polio survivor, activist, and businessman had begun work on the legislation that would become the *Americans with Disabilities Act* (ADA). The ADA would eventually pass the Senate and the House of Representatives by a wide margin. The concerns about the new legislation related not to its passage, but to whom would be included in its coverage, and whether inclusion in the *Civil Rights Act of 1964* would be adequate and even favorable. Having a specific, possibly weaker, civil rights law for people with disabilities could lead to differentiating the rights of those protected in the *Civil Rights Act* from those specified in the ADA. The National Council on Disability, under President Ronald Reagan, determined that disability discrimination is distinctive and substantially different from other kinds of prejudice, therefore requiring its own law. The new law maintained the definition of disability in Section 504, and made more specific the protection of individuals discriminated on the *perception* of disability, even where the individual's "impairment" does not affect one's abilities. In particular, those with AIDS or HIV, learning disabilities, those recovering from cancer or mental illness, and those with facial disfigurement were now explicitly protected by disability law.

President George H.W. Bush signed the *Americans with Disabilities Act (PL 101-336)* on July 26, 1990. More comprehensive than the *Rehabilitation Act*, the ADA extended rights provisions and non-discrimination to the private sector. All public services and facilities, and not just those that received federal funding, would be held to comply with a standard for access and equality. Each part of the law was designed to end discrimination toward persons with disabilities and is thought to be the most significant piece of federal civil rights legislation since the *Civil Rights Act of 1964*.

The ADA prohibits discrimination in both the private and public sectors in employment, public services, transportation, and communication. It also provides a comprehensive mandate to bring persons with disabilities into the economic and social mainstream of American life. The ADA contains strong standards and provides that the federal government play a central role in their enforcement. Basically, the law prohibits discrimination on the basis of disability or impairment and provides civil rights protection similar to that guaranteed to individuals on the basis of race, sex, sexuality, national origin, age, and religion. The legislation answers the following five persistent questions.

1. *Who is considered disabled?* A firm definition of "disability" underlies the authority of the ADA, which defines "individual with a disability" rather broadly. A person may be considered disabled if he or she (a) has a physical or mental condition that substantially limits one or more of the major life functions, (b) has a record of such impairment, or (c) is perceived as having such an impairment. Even if the

impairment is no longer present, the individual may still be considered disabled. Therefore, if an employer fails to hire:

> [an] individual who was once known to have alcoholism, cancer, or mental illness, or may still have a severe disfigurement, that employer may be guilty of discrimination. Not covered under the definition are those with minor, non-chronic conditions that last a short time like sprains, infections or broken limbs.

2. *How are public accommodations affected?* ADA's public accommodations requirements which became effective on January 26, 1992, define public accommodations as "private entities that affect commerce." Thus, the requirements extend to hotels, restaurants, theaters (how many times have you seen wheelchair users at the movies?), doctors' offices, pharmacies, retail stores, museums, libraries, parks, private schools, and day care centers. Not covered under the ADA are private clubs and religious organizations including churches, mosques, and synagogues.

   The ADA also affects ways in which public accommodations determine who may receive their services. For example, a business that requires a driver's license as the only acceptable identification for cashing a check, could be considered discriminatory toward persons with blindness. In addition, the ADA requires appropriate auxiliary aids and services to ensure effective communication with those with hearing and visual impairments. These may include qualified interpreters, assistive listening devices, note takers, large print or Braille materials, or taped texts. The law does not require such aids if they cause an undue burden or basic alteration in the nature of the goods and services provided. The public accommodation must still provide an alternative auxiliary aid. For example, restaurants are not required to have Brailled menus if waiters or other employees are available to read the menu to a customer with blindness. Similarly, stores need not provide Braille price tags if such information is available orally from sales personnel on request. They need not provide sign language interpreters if their sales employees are willing to communicate in writing when necessary. Physical barriers need to be removed only when it is "readily achievable"—that is, carried out without much difficulty or expense. Examples of readily achievable modifications include providing ramps, lowered telephones and urinals, or spaces for wheelchair users in theaters.

3. *How are transportation services affected?* The ADA requires the Department of Transportation to issue regulations mandating accessible public transit vehicles and facilities, and all public transit busses and rail cars ordered after 26 August 1990, must be accessible to individuals with disabilities, including wheelchair users. In addition,

transit authorities must provide comparable paratransit or other special transportation services. As of July 26, 1993, all existing rail systems must have one accessible car per train and all new bus and train stations must be assessable. Finally, all existing Amtrak stations were to be accessible by July 26, 2010.

4. *How are communications affected?* Companies offering telephone services to the general public must offer telephone relay services to people who use telecommunications devices for deaf persons (TDDs) or similar devices.

5. *How is employment affected?* The ADA employment provisions apply to private employers, state and local governments, employment agencies, and labor unions. Specifically, the ADA prohibits discrimination in all employment practices including job application procedures, hiring, firing, advancement, compensation, training, and other terms, conditions and privileges of employment. It applies to recruitment advertising, tenure, layoff and leave procedures, fringe benefits, and all other job activities (United States Congress, 1990).

Since the ADA. The ADA is a landmark specifying the rights of people with disabilities to an accessible and non-discriminatory society. The provision of rights, however, does not erase a history of prejudice, misunderstanding, and long-lasting negative attitudes toward disability. Disabled individuals and activists continue to experience institutional and individual prejudice and discrimination (O'Brien, 2004), and regularly point out that this "largest minority" is the group with the highest rates of unemployment and poverty—almost 20 years after the passage of the ADA. Patterns in high proportions of poverty among African-Americans similarly persist almost 50 after the *Civil Rights Act*. Advances in transportation and building accessibility are too often stymied by businesses and service providers who claim that the cost of renovating existing structures to be accessible outweigh the benefit. Additionally, the courts have heard many employment suits brought under the ADA, with the majority decisions neutralizing the impact of the ADA. Infamously, the rulings in *Sutton v. United Airlines* (1999) and *Toyota Motor Manufacturing v. Williams* (2002) demonstrate situations in which one can be "too disabled" to work, but not "disabled enough" to be protected under the ADA. The ADA has protected businesses, employers, and agencies more readily than disabled people (Russell, 1998). The hearts and minds of many, unfortunately, have not caught up to the ideals forwarded in the spirit of much civil rights legislation. Recently, the ADA was reauthorized as *The Americans With Disabilities Act Amendment Act* (ADAAA) in 2008. The changes aim to clarify what the law covers by broadening its description of disability. The intent is to focus employers on their responsibility to anti-discrimination and accommodation, rather than on analyzing what constitutes disability under the law, as turned out to be key in many lawsuits.

Disability Rights and Education

The relationship of litigation to legislation is provided in the US Constitution. Cases decided in the Court system set national and state precedents for similar situations to follow. Therefore, Court decisions in one case actually clarify and refine understandings of legislative dictates that ultimately apply to the interpretation of the laws at large. *Sutton v. United Airlines*, for example, clarified the definition of disability in the ADA. In education, several landmark cases were brought to the Court seeking refinement in the interpretation of the EHA/IDEIA.

In *Board of Education v. Rowley* (1982), the definition of Free Appropriate Public Education (FAPE) was clarified in favor of the school. At the time, Amy Rowley was a Deaf first-grade student who could access about half of the classroom instruction through lip-reading, but whose parents believed she would progress further with the provision of an ASL interpreter. After a series of appeals, the Supreme Court accepted the case. It found—by a one-vote margin—that FAPE did not specify that a child be entitled to services seeking a *maximum* or potential benefit. Because Rowley was making progress comparable with her peers, the law did not require providing instruction in ASL. The decision in the case upheld the right of a school—over parents—to determine the special education supports and services provided to a child, and also troublingly interpreted the provision of FAPE to specify a minimum, rather than maximum standard for academic progress. In later versions of IDEA, however, ASL is included as a Native Language—protecting Deaf students' rights to be instructed and assessed with it.

As late as 1985, some US Government officials still resisted all assistance to persons with disabilities, and advocated the repeal of *PL 94-142* based on stereotyped ideology. Then Secretary of Education, William J. Bennett appointed as a special assistant for the Office of Educational Philosophy and Practice, Eileen Marie Gardner, who had written for the American Heritage Foundation that "the handicapped constituency displays a strange lack of concern for the effects of their regulations upon the welfare of the general population" and that regulations enacted to aid children with disabilities "probably weakened the quality of teaching and falsely labeled normal children" (cited in Friedberg, Mullins, and Sukiennik, 1992: 10). Gardner is also quoted as stating that:

> [Disabled children] and their parents are selfish. They are draining badly needed resources from the normal school population [to the extent of $1.2 billion]. … Children and all who suffer affliction were made that way to help them grow toward spiritual perfection and that we are violating the "order of the universe" by trying to help these people (p. 10).

In response to opposition, Gardner resigned in 1985, and in 1986, Congress enacted further amendments to *PL 94-142* enlarging the responsibilities of states and school districts regarding the education of children with disabilities.

Given the history of segregation of students with disabilities in schools and the beliefs of figureheads such as Gardner, however, it is not a surprise that many cases have been brought to the courts to clarify the meaning of the Least Restrictive Environment (LRE), with some implications to FAPE. In *Daniel R.R. v State Board of Education* (1989), a suit was brought to contest the removal of Daniel from a "mainstream" pre-kindergarten class into a special education program. Daniel's teacher had modified the general curriculum for the child diagnosed with Down syndrome and cognitive and speech impairments, but objected to the amount of support he required. The school changed his program to one in which he could eat lunch in the mainstream some days and only if his mother accompanied him, and he attended class in a segregated program. The court established a two-prong test to determine whether the LRE was being met: (1) Can education in the regular classroom with the use of supplemental aids and services be achieved satisfactorily? And, (2) If it cannot, has the school mainstreamed the child to the maximum extent appropriate? The court decided in favor of the school by determining that Daniel's need for support detracted from the education of other children in the mainstream class, and that the school was providing other opportunities for him to interact with non-labeled children. Although the decision was not what some disability rights advocates might have hoped, it provided a test for mainstreaming, and specified that the benefits of mainstreaming need not only relate to academic instruction. Social integration was also a goal of the LRE specification.

Undoubtedly, the most contentious element in the law, the provision of the LRE was again clarified in *Oberti vs. Board of Education of the Borough of Clementon School District* (1993). *Oberti* refined the relationship between FAPE and LRE raised in *Daniel R.R.*, and also stated that the burden of proof was on the school to demonstrate compliance with IDEIA and the need for a segregated placement, rather than on the parents to argue that the school was not in compliance and that inclusion was possible. In response to Rafeal Oberti, a boy with Down syndrome, the Court determined, "Inclusion is a right, not a special privilege for a select few." In addition, it specified, "education law requires school systems to supplement and realign their resources to move beyond those systems, structures and practices which tend to result in unnecessary segregation of children with disabilities." In other words, the school is compelled to alter its structures, and curriculum to respond to children and an inclusion initiative, rather than place students according to the existing, problematic school design.

The LRE and inclusion was once again the topic of the courts in the 1994 case, *Sacramento City Unified School District v. Holland*. At the time, Rachel Holland was an 11-year-old diagnosed as moderately cognitively impaired. The school district initially placed Holland in a divided program—half in special and half in general education—and contended Holland was too "severely disabled" to benefit from full-time placement in a regular class. Her parents successfully won their case for full-time placement in general education, and a four-prong test was developed that presumes general education to be the initial, more desirable placement. The four elements to consider in placement decisions are: (1) the educational benefits of placing the child in a full-time regular education program; (2) the non-academic benefits of such a placement, including social and communication skills, and self-confidence; (3) the effect the child would have on the teacher and other students in the regular classroom; (4) and the costs of supplementary aids and services associated with this placement, which, the Court specified, is only a factor if it would adversely affect services available to other children.

The primary focus of this book, inclusion and inclusive education, continues, indeed, to be a most pressing concern in education for students labeled disabled. The medical model clearly informs IDEIA and each of the court decisions that have interpreted the meaning and practice of LRE and FAPE. Developing a school program around a child's impairment emphasizes one aspect of him or her above all others. Additionally, cost-benefit analysis or discussion of the impact a student's presence has on others, while deceptively pragmatic, detracts from attention to the *civil rights* of children labeled disabled (and ignores the benefit to all of gaining familiarity with children who have many unique identities, characteristics, and experiences). Schools are charged with ensuring the academic progress of all children, but they do much more than that. As a massive social system in which all children are compelled to participate, schools' actions must reflect, and even advance, the broader goal of an integrated society. Rationalizing segregation in education based on the perceived "benefit" of separation to address impairment denigrates the intended spirit of the ADA and disability rights. We do not need to fix students, but the educational systems that are ill suited to its constituency.

Disability Rights in the Twenty-First Century

There is no doubt that equity-focused legislation in employment, public spaces, healthcare, and education improved access and opportunity to Americans with disabilities during the latter half of the twentieth century. The ADA is a public statement that discrimination against disabled persons is pervasive and unacceptable, and IDEIA enforces the right of children with disabilities to appropriate public education. Their continual reauthorizations reinforce the rights of people with disabilities to access and gain from public services. International collaboration has similarly brought attention to the injustices around the world. In 2007, the United Nations (UN) adopted the *Convention on the Rights of Persons with Disabilities*, which adds to the UN's *Universal Declaration on Human Rights* (1948) and specifies particular protections for disabled persons. The adoption of the *Salamanca Statement and Framework for Action on Special*

Needs Education by The United Nations Educational, Scientific and Cultural Organization (UNESCO) in 1994 advances children's right to education, as well as to inclusive environments. While much work has been done to secure disabled people's safety and rights, there are still examples of institutionalization, murder, and abuse that make Disability Rights an urgent twenty-first century issue.

Beliefs, Attitudes, and a New Era of Eugenics

Refining, clarifying, and amending legislation and policy regarding disability rights occurs in the court system and government, and is increasingly informed by disabled participants and leaders. Despite the strides made in law, the medical paradigm of disability is still a persistent influence on the general public's perceptions of disability and disability-related political issues. With our media serving as a prime purveyor of beliefs and attitudes toward disability, disability activists acknowledge the relationship between popular culture and the public's view of disability rights. Thus, activism in the twenty-first century targets the media, along with some familiar issues to the movement. In particular, the fight for independent living endures, and a new era of eugenics may be upon us with scientific research on the human genome, prenatal screening, and the availability of new medical treatments targeting people with disabilities.

The Medical Model and Popular Culture

The message of disability rights is really quite simple: People with disabilities should direct the course of their lives. When unable to advocate for themselves, decision-making should be done according to the individual's best interests, which would protect his or her dignity, civil rights, and quality of life with support—noting that such interests are not necessarily the same shared by their caretakers, health professionals, educators, or other systems through which they are served. Enduring stereotypes and prejudice prevent the wide acknowledgement of these values, which, in turn, maintain the hold that a medical model has on disabled people.

Disability in Entertainment

The entertainment industry has a long history of its use of images and representations of disability. In many cases, television, film, and books have expanded their inclusion of disabled characters, which has resulted in more diverse depictions of disability. Offering a variety of depictions of disability lessens the impact that one type of image may have in constructing or perpetuating stereotypes, and is therefore, a favorable phenomenon. Stereotypes, however, have been a topic worthy of public attention. In 1991, for example, members of the National Federation of the Blind protested outside of the ABC network offices around the country in objection to the depiction of a blind character in the sitcom *Good and Evil*, who destroys a chemistry laboratory by clumsily wielding his long white cane, and then attempts to solicit a date with a fur coat on a coat rack, mistaking it for a woman (Shapiro, 1993: 37). Similarly, in 1997, after learning that the Walt Disney Company was reviving Mr. Magoo for a film starring Leslie Nielsen, the National Federation passed a resolution to "take whatever action appropriate to protest" because "The message is that lack of sight means incompetence" ("Mr. Snafoo," 1997: 21).

Two recent foci of disability rights groups have been the films, *Million Dollar Baby* (Eastwood, 2004) and *Tropic Thunder* (Cornfield, McLeod, and Stiller, 2008). *Million Dollar Baby* depicts the story of a boxer, played by Hillary Swank, who has an accident in a match and becomes quadriplegic. Her trainer, played by Clint Eastwood, honors her wishes to end her life at the end of the film, delivering the message that life is not worth living as a disabled person, and that euthanizing/murdering a person with a disability is a merciful response. The disability rights group Not Dead Yet organized national demonstrations at the theaters screening *Million Dollar Baby* and sparked a lively debate in the press and media (Dolmage and DeGenaro, 2005). While the group was not advocating for censorship, they did ensure that the general public realized not all disabled people see euthanasia as a reasonable response to disability.

The protests surrounding *Tropic Thunder* (Cornfield, McLeod, and Stiller, 2008) also garnered public debate and commentary, bringing the "R-word" to center stage. The advice "everybody knows you don't go full retard" is part of the dialog addressed to an actor, played by Ben Stiller, as he is reflecting on his work playing a character named "Simple Jack"—an experience woven through the film. Co-writer Etan Cohen claimed, "Some people have taken this as making fun of handicapped people, but we're really trying to make fun of the actors who use this material as fodder for acclaim" (Adler, Richard, and Horowitz, 2008). In spite of the filmmaker's ironic intent, activists strongly objected to the frequent use of the "R-word" and the depictions of "Simple Jack" and took the opportunity to bring the public into the argument. The production company, DreamWorks, took down a promotional website featuring "Simple Jack," and later, added an announcement discouraging the use of the word "retarded" on the DVD. Not only do these examples attest to the liveliness of the disability activism today, but also demonstrate that the public is interested, and the press responsive.

The New Eugenics?

It may seem odd to discuss issues of disability representation in the media alongside matters of science, medicine, and research. However, the two facets of contemporary life interplay in unexpected ways. What is acceptable in science and medicine is informed by the beliefs and attitudes professed by the cultures in which the disciplines are practiced. In contemporary society, prenatal screening positions disability to be a feature on which life and death may be decided (Parens and Asch, 2000). The Jack Kevorkian-inspired movement emphasizes the "right to die" at cost to efforts supporting the "right to live" (Gill and Voss, 2005), and the increased interest in biogenetic engineering all speak to society's fear and repudiation of impairment/disability. Charity drives, a cultural predilection for medicine and research, and films such as *Million Dollar Baby* perpetuate the beliefs that disability is a misfortune to be eradicated, that medicine poses the greatest hope for improved lives, and that severely disabled individuals desire death.

In a *New York Times Magazine* piece, Johnson, H. M. (2003), Disability Rights activist and attorney, described her reaction to philosopher Peter Singer's argument for a utilitarian perspective that could justify infanticide by withholding of treatment for newborns with significant impairments.

> He insists he doesn't want to kill me. He simply thinks it would have been better, all things considered, to have given my parents the option of killing the baby I once was, and to let other parents kill similar babies as they come along and thereby avoid the suffering that comes with lives like mine and satisfy the reasonable preferences of parents for a different kind of child. It has nothing to do with me. I should not feel threatened (Johnson, 2003).

While the ancient practices of ritual infanticide are not likely to return, prenatal tests, amniocentesis, and chorionic villus sampling (CVS), are regularly performed on women during early pregnancy. Both tests can indicate whether the fetus has or is at risk of having certain disabilities indicated in chromosomes, notably Down syndrome. Because the prenatal tests solely target disability as the basis for a potential decision to terminate a pregnancy, they may be considered discriminatory from a disability rights perspective (Asch, 2000).

In another contemporary news item, the Ashley X story (Kirschner, Brashler, and Savage, 2007) brought "growth attenuation therapy" to the public purview. This course of treatment included the surgical removal of 7-year-old Ashley's uterus and breast buds to prevent puberty, which her parents claimed would make homecare for her impossible, thus reducing her quality of life. Although the procedure was eventually deemed unethical, reports of therapies seeking similar results through hormone regimens have appeared over the last years. The bodies of persons with disabilities continue to be ravaged in the name of "their own good."

Research into the human genome, while not inherently problematic, can be potentially misinterpreted to denote an ideal human form. Because science is generally considered the arbiter of truth in contemporary America, disabled activists and scholars are acting as harbingers, warning of the slippery slope in genetic engineering that can lead us to a new era of eugenics. Avoiding this fate, however, is a matter of cultural, not scientific work. As much as activism reacts, necessarily, to cultural products that purport beliefs antithetical to the goals of disability rights, proactive work to instantiate disability as a valued and valuable perspective and experience is necessary. There is no better place to gain such appreciation than in disability arts and disability culture.

Disability Culture and the Arts

The Disability Rights Movement is marked by local and national organization of groups dedicated to the social, political, and increasingly, cultural issues that affect people with disabilities. Deaf culture has a long and rich history rooted in its members' shared language and concretized in its well-documented community histories (Padden and Humphries, 1988). The concept of *disability culture* is relatively new, by contrast, and debates on its meaning and existence ensue. Mitchell and Snyder's (1995) film *Vital Signs: Crip Culture Talks Back* documents participants at a national conference in disability and the arts. Performances and interviews offer a glimpse into many impressions of disability espoused by conference attendees, as well as the variety of expressions of disability available in art and performance. The filmmakers offer, in a later work, "The point of the film is not merely to present a chorus of voices but to capture the diversity, originality, and vitality of vantage points that characterize contemporary disability communities" (Snyder and Mitchell, 2006: 176). Present among the commentaries, however, are aspects indicating beliefs, ideas, and traditions shared among those who subscribe to an idea of disability culture. These include recognition of a shared history of oppression, a social and political approach to disability rights, and group pride.

Peters (2000) makes an argument for disability culture by examining three approaches to understanding the meaning of culture—historical/linguistic; social/political; and personal/aesthetic. We have, within the scope of this chapter, demonstrated the historical lineage of disability rights, including its "heroes" who are frequent reference points to tell its legacy. Organizations and groups arising out of the rights movement serve as locations for social cohesion, which are also found in communities such as Berkeley, California, known as a "Mecca" for people with disabilities, due to the efforts of Ed Roberts (Fleischer and Zames, 2001). A general orientation to sociopolitical perspectives on disability constitutes a basis for shared understanding around individual experiences of group oppression, which are solidified in community publications such as *Ragged Edge*, on online magazine dedicated to disability activism and rights that originated as the print publication *The Disability Rag* in 1980.

Considered through its personal/aesthetic components, disability culture is noticeable in declarations of pride in the form of one's body. Peters (2000) writes:

> When I say I am 25 years old, I am not referring to my chronological age, but the age at which I became physically disabled and could proudly assert "I am disabled." For those who subscribe to the view of culture as personal/aesthetic, the ability to assert an aesthetic pride in the disabled

body is a necessary prerequisite to political identity and is the source of empowerment (p. 596).

Nowhere is pride in the disabled body more evident than in disability arts. Disability arts encompass the wide variety of authors, poets, playwrights, actors, sculptors, painters, musicians, and performers whose work emanates from experiences of disability. A defining point, *disability art* is specific to works of disabled artists, whose experiences with disability are recognized as an integral force underlying the artistic process. Painter Riva Lehrer, for example, offers dynamic—both in style and content—portraits of disabled figures, taking her cues from the desires of her models/subjects (Snyder and Mitchell, 2006). The works of late playwright John Belluso offer stories told from a disabled, personal point of view (Schou, 2006). Collections including *Staring Back: The Disability Experience from the Inside Out* (Fries, 1997) and *Points of Contact* (Crutchfield and Epstein, 2000) anthologize contributions of disabled writers and essayists to poetry, fiction, and social commentary.

Simi Linton (2008), founder of Disability/Arts, notes the aim of her work, which is "to increase the scope and visibility of the vibrant arts movement emerging from the disability community, and increase the participation of disabled people in all areas of the arts" (http://www.similinton.com/dac.htm). The spread of disability art is a strong indication of the liveliness of disability culture. In addition, pride events, such as the Disability Pride Parade, an annual event in Chicago, demonstrate the celebratory cohesion of disabled people. No longer useful only for political action, the idea of a disability culture emerges in joined celebration of its history, art, and its pride.

The concept of disability culture, as noted previously, is debated among those abled and disabled alike. As with any culture, its centrality for some does not mean that all people who might identify as disabled adopt it. Developing pride specific to disability can be difficult to grasp. As Gliedman and Roth (1980) once stated, "No one argues that mental retardation is good, blindness is beautiful, that doctors should stop research into the causes of cerebral palsy" (p. 23). Even Irving Zola (1982), a founding figure in Disability Studies, made this observation:

> As the melting pot theory of America was finally buried, people could once again say, even though they were three generations removed from the immigrants, that they were proud to be Greek, Italian, Hungarian, or Polish. With the rise of Black power, a derogatory label became a rallying cry, Black is beautiful! And when female liberationists saw their strength in numbers, they shouted, Sisterhood is powerful! But what about the chronically ill and disabled? Can we yell, Long live cancer! Up with multiple sclerosis! I'm glad I had polio! Clearly a basis of a common positive identity is not readily available (p. 208).

The reservations of Zola and Gliedman and Roth, written over 25 years ago, capture complexities in the movement for disability culture and disability pride. We believe, however, that the proliferation of disability arts, recognition of the Disability Rights Movement, and attention to ongoing activism can contribute to reshaping a view of disability that centers on a value for diversity, appreciation of its history, and a source of positive identity and pride.

Conclusion

The modern era of disability is hailed as a period in which disability rights gained recognition and had an impact on policies, law, and social practices, which were influenced by disabled people as never before in history. Simultaneously, the time period is peppered with contradictions. It has been a long difficult trek from the time persons with disabilities were left to die or thrown off cliffs as babies to the *Americans with Disabilities Act,* yet eugenic medical practices and the ideologies of some "right to die" proponents should give us pause in what may be premature celebration. The ideas of deinstitutionalization and independent living have influenced many nations and cultures, but not all; and the depictions of disability in the media, arts, and popular culture have improved through diversification, though the occasion for protest still arises.

This chapter reveals an evolutionary progression suggesting the distance society has come in its acceptance, treatment, and integration of persons with disabilities. However, the influence of a medical model and the prejudices embedded in it continues to overshadow the self-determination many disabled people seek. As Rioux (1996) points out, "Rehabilitation in itself, no matter how effective, will not lead to fulfilling the goals of human rights" (p. 9). The stigma of disability remains a common reality, and persons with disabilities continue to be denied equal opportunity as a result of stereotyped and prejudiced images based on myths and earlier attitudes. Of the continued fight, Russell (1998) writes:

> We must retain enough optimism so vital to ensuring a just society that we can consciousness-raise, educate ourselves and others, and join in public debate through town hall meetings, the internet and local and national referendums that can result in more participation and justice worldwide (p. 235).

With significant rights now won in policy and law, the remaining work is largely cultural, which Russell captures in the idea of consciousness-raising. What better way to raise consciousness than in work with children and schools? Informed with knowledge of history, language, disability rights, and Disability Studies, we believe that educators can play integral roles in advancing the self-determination of disabled people. Educators can both advance integration through implementing inclusive practices for children labeled with disability, and develop curriculum and content that offer views of disability and disabled people in social, political, and cultural contexts. In the next chapters, we provide concepts and practices to guide educational work that honors disability rights and its legacy, and seeks further realization of its goals.

Part III
Disability and Education

6
Conceptualizing Disability in Schools

National and international attention to disability has provided some ways to conceptualize and define disability in a broad sense. The ADAAA, for example, distinguishes impairment from disability to define which persons are covered by its policies. The UN *Convention on the Rights of Persons with Disabilities* defines persons with disabilities in order to appropriately direct a human rights agenda. In education, the Individuals with Disabilities Education Improvement Act (IDEIA) provides the vocabulary used to define disability. Greatly influenced by the medical model of disability, 13 categories of impairment are defined, which describe the students who may receive special education services. The previous chapter provided discussion of many ways that disability language and labels are contested and perceived differently by various stakeholders. Language and labels used in education are similarly subject to the same variety of perspectives. This chapter offers an overview of the definitions of disability described in IDEIA. In addition, it provides discussion on aspects of the labels that have been contested, especially in the Disability Studies in Education field. The aim is to provide candid information about the influential educational policy, IDEIA, while also offering critical examination of the language practices contained in it.

IDEIA Definitions

(1) Visual Impairments (Including Blindness)

A visual impairment is a limitation in vision that, even with correction, adversely affects sight. Blindness occurs rarely in children—in fact, in less than 0.10% of the population between the ages of 6 through 17. The term "blindness" carries various definitions and despite its common use to connote a total absence of sight, the vast majority of people with visual impairments do perceive some degree of visual information. Rather than emphasize dysfunction, the descriptors "partially sighted" or having "low vision" are sometimes preferred.

(2) Hearing Impairments (Including Deafness)

Hearing impairment is a general term indicating a hearing loss that may range in severity from mild to profound. Discussed in earlier chapters, some

Deaf persons who use American Sign Language identify themselves by the language they use, rather than by their degree of hearing, and consider themselves to be part of a linguistic minority.

(3) Deaf-Blindness

Deaf-Blindness is the fourth sensory impairment specified by IDEIA and means concomitant hearing and visual impairments. Educational approaches for children who are blind often capitalize on providing auditory information, and visual information for those who are hard-of-hearing or deaf. Because children with deaf-blindness do not have sufficient access to visual or auditory information, educational approaches require an educational plan or program that attends to the combination of these relatively rare characteristics—less than 0.01% of children with disabilities experience deaf-blindness.

(4) Speech or Language Impairments

According to IDEIA, "Speech or language impairment means a communication disorder, such as stuttering, impaired articulation, a language impairment, or a voice impairment, that adversely affects a child's educational performance" (Assistance to States for the Education of Children with Disabilities, 2006). Van Riper and Emerick (1984) defined speech as "defective" when "it deviates so far from the speech of other people that it calls attention to itself, interferes with communication, or causes the speaker or his listeners to be distressed" (p. 34). In other words, speech is considered defective when, relative to others, it is conspicuous, unintelligible, or unpleasant.

(5) Orthopedic Impairments

Orthopedic impairments are related to the function of the muscles and/or skeleton and may affect mobility, range of motion, and/or reliable control over one's movements. An orthopedic impairment does not necessarily indicate disability. If the individual is able to move on her or his own or to use a mobility device to negotiate the environment, it is possible that she or he would not require additional educational services.

(6) Traumatic Brain Injury

Traumatic brain injury is one of the few disability categories in which a specific etiology is required for diagnosis. According to IDEIA:

> Traumatic brain injury means an acquired injury to the brain caused by an external physical force, resulting in total or partial functional disability or psychosocial impairment, or both, that adversely affects a child's educational performance. Traumatic brain injury applies to open or closed head injuries resulting in impairments in one or more areas, such as cognition; language; memory; attention; reasoning; abstract thinking;

judgment; problem-solving; sensory, perceptual and motor abilities; psychosocial behavior; physical functions; information processing; and speech. Traumatic brain injury does not apply to brain injuries that are congenital or degenerative, or to brain injuries induced by birth trauma (Assistance to States for the Education of Children with Disabilities, 2006).

Noted in the definition, brain injury can manifest in many ways—including physical-motor, cognitive, emotional, social, and/or speech-language impairments.

(7) Other Health Impairment

As with Traumatic Brain Injury, the category "Other Health Impairment" comprises health conditions with specific etiologies that may "adversely affect a child's educational performance" (Assistance to States for the Education of Children with Disabilities, 2006). It means:

> …having limited strength, vitality, or alertness, including a heightened alertness to environmental stimuli, that results in limited alertness with respect to the educational environment, that—
>
> (i) Is due to chronic or acute health problems such as asthma, attention deficit disorder or attention deficit hyperactivity disorder, diabetes, epilepsy, a heart condition, hemophilia, lead poisoning, leukemia, nephritis, rheumatic fever, sickle cell anemia, and Tourette syndrome (Assistance to States for the Education of Children with Disabilities, 2006).

As with the other categories, the diagnosis of any of the mentioned diseases or conditions may not indicate disability. For example, many children have asthma but not all are adversely affected by it in their educational environments.

(8) Multiple Disabilities

The category "Multiple Disabilities" is imprecise and can refer to any combination of impairments. As with "Deaf-Blindness," this designation indicates a child whose educational needs arise from a variety of impairing factors. A student categorized with "multiple disabilities" typically has a sensory or orthopedic impairment, a combination of the two, or one of them in addition to another kind of impairment—usually "mental retardation."

Discussion

Impairments that affect the senses, movement, or physical health are fairly straightforward to perceive or diagnose in a medical model of disability. The "facts" of such differences or non-typical characteristics are made scientific as we use scales to determine visual and hearing impairments and relate an injuring event to disability. The "facts" of orthopedic and speech and language impairment seem self-evident as cultural norms influence our ideas about "normal" and "abnormal" ways to move and communicate. Approaching impairment from a social model, the degree of disability—if any—that these impairments indicate is related to the context and environment. For example, that a brain trauma occurred is a matter of fact; the meaning of that trauma to indicate disability or handicap is subject to the particular culture and environment in which an individual lives, works, and learns. Similarly, that an individual requires a wheelchair to move from place to place due to an orthopedic impairment is a matter of fact; however, whether s/he experiences *disability* may relate more to the degree to which an environment is barrier-free or to the availability and affordability of the mobility device.

Soft Disability

The final four categories of disability described by IDEIA are (10) mental retardation; (11) specific learning disabilities; (12) emotional disturbance; and (13) autism. Distinguishing impairment from disability becomes difficult in what some have called *soft* disabilities. Soft disabilities are those "for which no discernable physical markers are currently known," which makes "the identification process subjective" (Fuchs, Fuchs and Speece, 2002: 33; also see Reschly, 1996). The disabilities most frequently considered soft are learning disabilities, mild mental retardation, and emotional or behavior disorders. Despite decades of medical research to locate physical and neurological linkages between the body/brain and cognition to what appears to be impaired function, science provides little understanding useful to teachers about the majority of disorders deemed neurological, cognitive/intellectual, and psychosocial in nature. The physiological evidence of cognitive-intellectual and psychosocial impairments is found primarily in comparisons of images of brain activity and brain size and development. Current neurological research can show differences among typical and non-typical activity in individuals already characterized by normal and abnormal function, but researchers have not provided precise understanding of types of impairments based on those differences (Bauman and Kemper, 2004; Fiedorowicz, Benezra, MacDonald, and McElgunn, 2001).

It is important to note that some proponents of a social model of disability argue that *all* diagnoses and perceptions of impairment are ultimately subjective, as science itself is informed by cultural beliefs about the "normal" body. In other words, that which a culture perceives as impaired or abnormal is inextricably related to that which is perceived normal and then explained biologically and neurologically. Perceiving learning disabilities, mild mental retardation, and emotional or behavior disorders are particularly subjective processes, because they (a) are diagnosed with tools that rely largely on assessment of the individual's relationship to a particular context—often school; (b) are difficult to distinguish from one another and often seem to overlap in school settings; and (c) seem particularly influenced by the belief systems and demands of a given society, as expressed in changes of diagnostic criteria over time and in variations in diagnostic criteria in different places (Kane and Tangdhanakanond, 2008). Autism is discussed here as a soft disability, because diagnosis relies on assessment of social behavior. Although neurological research is burgeoning, the majority of characteristics associated with autistic individuals are interpreted as soft neurological signs, or abnormalities that are not readily connected to a specific brain region. The final four disability categories in IDEIA are next described, each with extended discussion to elucidate controversies surrounding them.

(9) Mental Retardation, Cognitive Disability, Intellectual Disability

The terms "mental retardation," "cognitive disability," and "intellectual disability" are often used interchangeably in the United States. People diagnosed with mental retardation are also sometimes referred to as having "developmental disabilities" because one criterion is that it is noticeable before the age of 18—thus it emerges during, and has an impact on, development. IDEIA defines mental retardation as:

> significantly subaverage general intellectual functioning, existing concurrently with deficits in adaptive behavior and manifested during the developmental period, that adversely affects a child's educational performance (Assistance to States for the Education of Children with Disabilities, 2006).

The concept of what we presently deem "mental retardation" has evolved over many years. As early as the first century A.D., a Roman aristocrat, Aurelius Cornelius Celsus, used the term *imbecillus* to denote a general weakness or any form of impairment. The term *idios*, the original Greek form, described a private person—that is, one who did not engage in public life. Both terms became descriptors of forms of mental retardation much later in the Renaissance (Scheerenberger, 1983).

During the early fourteenth through sixteenth centuries, the term *ideocy* began to be replaced by *dunce*, a term that had its origins with the activities of John Duns Scotus, a Scot who, in 1303, argued against the King of France's proposal to tax the Roman Catholic Church to finance a war with England. In response, the Pope excommunicated the French King, who in return banished Scotus from France. After 200 years, Renaissance humanists and Reformation leaders hostile to Duns Scotus's defense of the Papacy began to call any follower of his teachings as a "Duns man" or "dunce"—hence, a dull-witted person (Scheerenberger, 1983).

Terminology changed several more times. In 1846, Samuel Gridley Howe defined persons with "feeble-mindedness" as those who ranged in level of incapacity from those with "reason enough for simple individual guidance plus normal powers of locomotion and animal action" to those who were "mere organisms." In 1914, Henry Herbert Goddard subdivided the classification of feeble-mindedness into the subcategories of "morons," "imbeciles," and "idiots" and linked the levels of function to IQ—a then emerging psychological concept (President's Committee on Mental Retardation, 1975: 2). Prior to Goddard's work, the designation of a person as "idios," "dunce," or "feeble-minded" served to describe his or her societal position in relation to the engagement in public life, agreement with the beliefs of those in power, and/or to characterize the perceived intellectual-cognitive abilities of a person. Goddard's linkage of IQ to "feeble-mindedness" provided a scientific perspective on the concept of intellect.

Understanding of how mental retardation became a scientific concept emerges in the ways that IQ became used in and useful to the culture of the United States. Though he ultimately changed his perspective, Goddard began his research to support eugenics. Eugenics is a philosophy made most popular in the early twentieth century, which sought to shape the human population by controlling the genetic characteristics its members passed down through heredity. Goddard advocated measuring IQ in order to determine those most fit to lead the nation to prosperity, and conversely, those who were a detriment to the society. In addition to providing a "scientific" rationale for forced sterilization of women deemed mentally retarded during the eugenic movement, IQ tests were infamously used to make decisions about military assignments, relegating those with the lowest scores to the infantry and those with higher scores for officer training. In schools, IQ and achievement tests were recommended to "track" high-scoring students into gifted and college-preparation programs in efforts to prepare the "most talented" students to contribute to international supremacy during the Cold War era (Rickover, 1957). Thus, the social practices surrounding the meaning of a "low IQ" conformed to the ways that a designation of idios, dunce, or feeble-minded had been used in the past. The subjectivity and cultural construction of the label, however, became obscured in the science touted by the measurability of IQ.

Rick Heber, in 1959, developed the definition of mental retardation that has received the widest contemporary use. Heber offered: "Mental retardation refers to subaverage general intellectual functioning which originates during the developmental period and is associated with impairment in adaptive behavior." He went onto define subaverage intelligence to mean anyone who tested more than one standard deviation below the "normal" limit (100), or having an IQ of approximately 84 or below. Heber's definition also labeled degrees of impairment as "mild," "moderate," "severe," and "profound" (President's Committee on Mental Retardation, 1975: 2).

Apparent in IDEIA's definition, most present medical definitions that are used to diagnose mental retardation still adhere to Heber's two-prong description that considers the individual's IQ and his or her adaptive function, or ability to respond effectively to the social and environmental demands of life, relative to age and cultural group (Grossman, 1983). The criteria for a diagnosis of mental retardation in the DSM-IV are:

1. Significantly subaverage intellectual functioning—i.e., an IQ of approximately 70 or below
2. Deficits or impairments in adaptive functioning
3. Onset before age 18 years

In addition, present definitions in the *DSM-IV* continue to use Heber's distinctions to describe degrees of mental retardation. Although prevalence figures vary, approximately 3% of the United States population may be diagnosed with mental retardation (Beirne-Smith, Patton, and Ittenbach, 1994). By far, the majority (85%) of those estimated to have mental retardation fall into the mild category. Table 6.1 shows the levels, the related IQ score, and the prevalence of each level.

Causes of mental retardation are characterized as biomedical, environmental, or psychological. Biomedical causes include over 200 identified central nervous system pathologies including phenylketonuria (PKU), hydrocephalus, microcephalus, and Down syndrome. About 10–25% of persons labeled with mental retardation fall into this category. Environmental causes include poor nutrition, poor physical health, exposure to lead paint or other toxins, and lack of sensory stimulation. Because diagnosis of mental retardation relies on the measurement of IQ and the subjective evaluation of adaptive function, misclassification as mentally retarded is possible when an individual's characteristics affect the performance on an IQ battery, or affect an individual's *apparent* adaptive function within particular contexts or conditions.

Mental retardation is the term used in the *DSM-IV* and in our federal policies and is, therefore, a professionally appropriate term for educational and rehabilitative contexts. That stated, the term is widely unfavored in everyday contexts and is more often *not* used by school professionals, who increasingly prefer the terms "intellectual" or "cognitive disability/impairment." One reason for this is its common use as an insult—for example, the schoolyard taunts "retard," "mental," or "tart"—which makes the label of "retarded" an epithet.

Table 6.1 Distribution of Levels of Severity of Mental Retardation

Levels	IQ	Percentage of Mentally Retarded Population
Mild	50–55 to 70	85
Moderate	35–40 to 50–55	10
Severe	20–25 to 35–40	3.5
Profound	20–25	1.5

Many professional organizations have changed their names to avoid the stigma and history of *mental retardation*. In 2006, for example, the American Association on Mental Retardation changed its name to the American Association on Intellectual and Developmental Disabilities by member vote. The related organization, the Association for Retarded Citizens, also changed its name to its acronym, "The Arc." Other problems with the term "mental retardation" are raised in critiques of the diagnosis itself.

Many professionals challenge the practice of placing individuals into a delimited category based on IQ scores and subjective ideas of what adaptive function might mean. This is especially important as we consider the rights and quality of life of those deemed intellectually disabled. In the past, a diagnosis of retardation could be used to bar entry to school and as evidence to support the forced sterilization of women. As early as 1979, Sarason and Doris observed that the concept of mental retardation was not scientific, but embedded in culturally situated values for particular kinds of skills deemed intellectual in nature and a particular idea of the meaning of independence. In other words, that which seems important or valuable to a society is embedded in the kinds of activities expected of its citizens, which change over time. The idea of "mental retardation," however, seems monolithic despite changes among contexts and across time. Furthermore, the diagnostic tools of IQ batteries are infamously biased to privilege the particular competencies demonstrated by the most powerful members of a society (Gould, 1981).

Another issue raised by Blatt (1981) suggests the fallacy of linking the presumption of limited neurological or cognitive function to an experience made meaningful and diagnosed in everyday life. He wrote, "...mental retardation is an invented disease [and] mental retardation, itself, can't be appreciated by a study of marbles and holes or neurons and dendrites." (pp. 118–119). In other words, he challenges the utility of a definition that at its heart relies on a *metaphorical* assumption that IQ represents brain function. Theorists in Disability Studies continue to challenge the concept of mental retardation as a measurable and knowable "condition" belonging to an individual. Stubblefield (2007) cites Carlson (as cited in Stubblefield) to explain:

> "mental retardation" defies a medical model or essentialist analysis because the diagnosis itself is subjective and unstable. There is no straightforward etiology for mental retardation, and the label has been, and continues to be, applied to a wide variety of people with a wide range of characteristics. Indeed, the so-called normality from which cognitive disability is seen as a departure is itself an unstable category: there is no absolute quality in contrast to which we can define intellectual abnormality (2003, 158) (as cited in Stubblefield, 2007: 168).

In the absence of an "absolute quality" of intellectual ability, the idea of retardation as a *scientific* concept is revealed to be faulty. Stubblefield (2007) echoes

Bogdan and Taylor (1994), who likewise concluded that the concept of mental retardation is not real but "exists in the minds of those who use it as a term to describe the cognitive states of other people" (p. 7).

It is important to point out that mild mental retardation is the degree that is most often considered "soft" because of the imprecision of diagnostic tools to distinguish "it" from learning disabilities, for example, in the school setting. Perceiving mild mental retardation most often relies on the IQ in conjunction with adaptive function measured in relation to the literacy demands of school activities; and not necessarily in terms of other activities in daily life that may rely less on the specific idea of literacy measured in schools. Skeptics—largely comprising self-advocates (i.e., people with intellectual disabilities) and those involved in Disability Studies—however, argue that the objectivity underlying assertions of intelligence measures is questionable. Further, the notions of independence and adaptive function professed by a culture also rely on far more subjective and mutable factors than a scientific diagnostic process might infer.

Theorists and persons who challenge the concept of mental retardation firmly agree that individuals interact, perceive, and communicate differently from one another. They generally agree that individuals perform differently from one another in school and in everyday life; that many of us utilize supports and services to lead the lives that we desire; and that the degree and nature of an individual's needs is important to perceive and respond to. They disagree with the concept of "mental retardation" as useful to understand and positively affect the diverse experiences of individuals brought together in the scientific category. As Stubblefield (2007) points out, the label is "applied to a wide variety of people with a wide range of characteristics" (p. 168), making the idea of "mental retardation" impractical for understanding individuals and their unique bodies and minds and how to best teach them.

(10) Specific Learning Disabilities

The term "learning disabilities" emerged in the 1960s. Earlier terms used to label youngsters exhibiting a wide variety of the now-familiar symptoms included "minimal brain dysfunctioned," "brain-injured," "minimal cerebral dysfunctioned," "neurologically impaired," "perceptually impaired," "Strauss syndrome," and "attention deficit disordered" (to name only seven). According to IDEIA:

> Specific learning disability means a disorder in one or more of the basic psychological processes involved in understanding or in using language, spoken or written, that may manifest itself in the imperfect ability to listen, think, speak, read, write, spell, or to do mathematical calculations, including conditions such as perceptual disabilities, brain injury, minimal brain dysfunction, dyslexia, and developmental aphasia.

> Specific learning disability does not include learning problems that are primarily the result of visual, hearing, or motor disabilities, of mental

retardation, of emotional disturbance, or of environmental, cultural, or economic disadvantage (Assistance to States for the Education of Children with Disabilities, 2006).

Learning disabilities are defined as permanent disorders that affect the manner in which individuals with average or above-average intelligence receive, retain, and express information. A scientific-cognitive explanation for learning disability proposes that difficultly in learning occurs when messages traveling between sensory organs and the brain seem to "cross wires" or become scrambled and lead to difficulty processing some kinds of information. The resulting problem involves perception rather than acuity. A child with a visual perceptual disability, for example, may have perfect vision but cannot discriminate between the foreground and background on a photograph. He or she may see it but be unable to perceive or interpret it.

As the concept of learning disability has gained popularity, many sub-types have been named. The following paragraph lists six general kinds of learning disabilities and the names that have been given to describe the particular area of difficulty:

1. Reading comprehension and spelling: *dyslexia, alexia*
2. Written expression: *dysgraphia, dysphasia, agitographia*
3. Mathematical computation: *dyscalcula, acalcuia*
4. Coordination: *dyskinesia, apraxia, ataxia*
5. Memory and recall: *dysnomia, aphasia, anomia*
6. Oral language skills: *aphonia, dysarthria*

Learning disability is, by far, the most common disability diagnosis in American schools.

According to the American Psychological Association (2000), approximately 5–6% of the population in the United States is expected to have a learning disability. The DSM-IV-TR (2000) reports the majority—about 4% of those with learning disabilities—to have difficulties in reading followed by mathematical and written expression, each at less than 1%. Currently, there are approximately 3.5 million students identified as having learning disabilities in the United States, which comprises 51% of all students with disabilities receiving special education services in public schools. The 27th Annual Report to Congress (2007) reported a 28.5% increase in children served under IDEA for learning disabilities from 1991 to 2000, which has remained stable to date. The steep rise in students diagnosed with learning disabilities, alongside reports that point out the disproportionate number of African-American students being diagnosed, has raised many questions about the scientific validity of the diagnosis process (Losen and Orfield, 2002). Perhaps the clearest example of "soft" disability, the history of learning disability, the diagnostic processes to identify learning disabilities, and the meaning of the label itself have been perennially called into question.

The most widespread history of learning disability offers an account of its scientific discovery forwarded by European and American researchers who were intrigued by similarities between the characteristics of some children who were struggling in school and adults with brain injury. Between the 1800s and the early twentieth century, European researchers including Franz Joseph Gall, Adolph Kussmaul, John Hinshelwood, and W. Pringle Morgan endeavored to link brain trauma with mental impairment. American contemporaries including Samuel Orton, Grace Fernald, Samuel Kirk, and William M. Cruickshank extended the work of the Europeans throughout the early to middle century, and ultimately arrived at a convincing argument for linkages between brain function and development of reading and other perceptual-cognitive processes. Kirk is credited with coining the term "learning disability" in a 1963 address to parents of "perceptually handicapped" children, thus ushering in the modern era of learning disability, which attributes otherwise inexplicable difficulties in learning to neurological cause (Opp, 1994).

Examination of the circumstances surrounding the rise in popularity of the learning disability label has been prevalent in educational literature. While one explanation for its increasing prevalence is scientific and social progress, which have led to greater awareness of and better ability to identify and diagnose learning disability, other historical accounts propose that social and cultural factors are also responsible for the steep rise in diagnosis. Sleeter (1987), for example, describes the correlation between the rise of the learning disability label in the United States with the Cold War era advent of high-stakes testing intended to group students into educational tracks most suited to their aptitude. As privileged children—those in middle and upper social classes and of White, European descent—did not pass muster on increasingly demanding assessments, new ways of preserving their status emerged. Definitions of learning disability characterize those "afflicted" as intelligent despite their school struggle, which afford this group a higher status than children labeled with mental retardation. Thus, "learning disability" became and continues to be a more socially desirable label for mild disability as compared with others available in special education.

Parents seeking a more favorable diagnosis for their struggling children, then, contributed to the rise in popularity of learning disability. Carrier (1986) asserts that parent-initiated groups, including major organizations such as the Division for Children with Learning Disabilities of the Council for Exceptional Children (CEC) and the Association for Children with Learning Disabilities (now the Learning Disabilities Association of America), pushed schools to adopt the idea of learning disability to gain advantages in school for their children through Special Education. Ferri and Connor (2005, 2006) also describe ways in which the new label was attractive to some parents, as it preserved racially segregated spaces in special education. By creating "learning disability classrooms" which housed mostly White, middle-class students, proportionally higher numbers of Black students in special education were kept separate from them in lower-status classes for children labeled mentally retarded, emotionally disturbed, and culturally deprived. In the mid-century frenzy that surrounded racially integrated public education in the United States, becoming labeled with a learning disability emerged as a way to protect White children struggling in school from being in integrated classrooms with their Black peers.

Each account of the rise of learning disability contributes to understanding its history, which is useful to examining current issues in the field. As Kane and Tangdhanakanond (2008) point out, the number of children estimated by the APA to have learning disability is much lower than the number of children currently identified in schools. In addition, a troubling pattern reveals that African-American and Hispanic/Latino children are identified as having learning disabilities at higher rates than should be expected (Harry and Klingner, 2005; Losen and Orfield, 2002). Social and historical analyses suggest that these are ongoing effects of both the desirability of the learning disability label, relative to others, and de facto racial segregation. As Brantlinger (2003) points out, parent advocacy is still a powerful force to secure access to appropriate special education services, which creates contexts in which parents who are not accustomed to the mores and discourses of schools are less able to access appropriate services for their children. The most prominent point of contention in the identification of learning disabilities, however, is the *discrepancy method* of diagnosis.

The way that learning disabilities have been traditionally diagnosed is according to the degree of discrepancy between the IQ and scores on an achievement assessment. If a child is determined to have an average or above-average IQ but scores much lower than the expected range on an achievement assessment, the child may be determined to have a learning disability. Researchers have found many problems with the method. First, in addition to issues discussed previously in the section on mental retardation, the validity of some IQ assessments for students with language difficulties is contested. It is difficult to determine whether a child who struggles with language is able to demonstrate his or her aptitude on a measure that is language-based. If the score on which the discrepancy is based is inaccurate, the overall formula does not measure what it claims. Second, comparing an IQ and achievement measure presumes that the measures statistically correlate to each other, which they do not (Kane and Tangdhanakanond, 2008). In other words, the scores on an IQ measure and achievement measure are compared to determine a discrepancy, but the scoring methods used on different measures with different purposes may not have equivalent meanings. In the simplest formula for gauging discrepancy, the problem is that a score of 100 on an IQ measure does not mean the same thing as a score of 100 on achievement measures, even when they are properly converted to the respective standard scales.

The most confounding issues in identifying learning disability are noticeable in examining the field of educational practice. The result of vague criteria specified by IDEA, each state was able to develop its own discrepancy formula to determine learning disability. The discrepancy required for a learning disability diagnosis ranged from as low as 2.1% in Georgia to a high of 8.6% in Rhode Island (Clark, 2003). Consequently, a child could be diagnosed with or "cured" of learning disability simply by moving to a different state. Further, while research has led to better understanding of difficulty in phonological processes related to reading and indications that learning disabilities may be hereditary, it has not been able to differentiate between the academic function or improvement in reading, for example, of children whose measurements have a discrepancy between IQ and achievement and those who do not. Ultimately, the precision and usefulness of the learning disability label to better aid individuals' learning are debatable.

It is no doubt that the discrepancy method of diagnosing learning disability is fading from practice. The most current regulations in IDEIA (2004) specify:

> [States] must not require the use of a severe discrepancy between intellectual ability and achievement for determining if a child has a specific learning disability, [and] … must permit the use of a process based on the child's response to scientific, research-based intervention and may permit the use of other alternative research-based procedures for determining whether a child has a specific learning disability..." (CFR 300.307(a)).

The thrust for the change in using the discrepancy method relates not only to its statistical problems, but also to the length of time it may take for a child experiencing difficulty to receive appropriate interventions in school instruction. In the discrepancy method, a child must fail *before* he or she becomes entitled to special services. Instead, considering the child's responsiveness to intervention, known as "RTI," offers a framework in which diagnosis of disability relates to the outcome of efforts to support the child to learn.

In RTI, children who struggle with school-based learning—typically in reading—are offered interventions to improve. If the child responds positively to the intervention, she/he would ideally continue developing and be able to benefit from the "general" curriculum without additional special services. If the child does not respond positively, he or she is incrementally offered more intensive services, and may ultimately be identified as having a learning disability if s/he does not improve from the interventions. RTI circumvents the statistical problems of the discrepancy method, and is likely to lead to lower rates of children identified with learning disabilities—assuming interventions that are provided are effective for many.

RTI, however, does not lead to more precision in refining the *meaning* of learning disability. In the framework, learning disability means, simply, that a child does not learn well from that which is provided in the particular school context. Because school contexts change from year to year, or even class to class, identification as learning disabled is as much a reflection of the school and its practices, as of the individual learner. Varenne and McDermott (1998), for example, observe that the meaning of school struggle is relative, and that whether learning disability is identified as a cause of difficulty depends largely on the teacher and teaching practices in a specific classroom or school (see also, Reid and Valle, 2004). In other words, if children are provided with multiple ways of engaging in learning, there is less likelihood that individuals will demonstrate struggle. Despite sharing similar characteristics with others who may be labeled learning disabled, some children may avoid diagnosis when served in a classroom that is suited to meet a range of educational needs. If we are to believe that learning disability is a matter of an individual's neurological make-up, context should not matter in the way it does.

Other sociocultural analyses of the rise of learning disability focus on the ideology of schools that presumes children do or should develop and respond to instruction in the same ways at the same times. Dudley-Marling and Dippo (1995), for example, propose that the presumption that school *should* be socially efficient and that students *should* be homogeneous and progress in an assembly-line fashion creates a context in which differences become characterized as deficits. Identifying children who struggle within the regimented school curriculum as individually disordered preserves the notion that the structure of teaching in schools is "right," and it is the individual child and his or her body/mind at blame for his or her failure. Ultimately, identifying failing students as learning disabled becomes a way to locate the problem of school failure in the child and justify the "rightness" of the school, which protects it from changing despite the number of students failing to thrive (Tomlinson, 2004).

As with mental retardation, the emergence of learning disability in schools has a complicated history. For those in Disability Studies in Education, criticism of diagnostic processes and skepticism about the meaning made of learning disability relates to the treatment of children who become so labeled in schools, and to the maintenance—even justification—of schools and curriculum that do not adjust to meet the needs of those subject to them. All people vary in the ways they perceive and respond to information, and one term is hardly adequate to describe each of the 3.5 million children who are categorized as learning disabled. Given that significant differences are not found between children who have learning disabilities and those with reading difficulties, it is unclear how useful the meaning of learning disability is for teaching practice.

(11) Emotional Disturbance and Behavioral Disorder

Emotional disturbance is a category of disability described as such only in IDEIA (as compared with diagnostic inventories in the psychology field). Children identified with behavioral disorders are included in this category, and children with psychiatric, personality, and conduct disorders with more specific diagnoses may also be able to receive special educational services under it. IDEIA offers the following definition:

> Emotional disturbance means a condition exhibiting one or more of the following characteristics over a long period of time and to a marked degree that adversely affects a child's educational performance:
>
> A. An inability to learn that cannot be explained by intellectual, sensory, or health factors.
> B. An inability to build or maintain satisfactory interpersonal relationships with peers and teachers.
> C. Inappropriate types of behavior or feelings under normal circumstances.
> D. A general pervasive mood of unhappiness or depression.
> E. A tendency to develop physical symptoms or fears associated with personal or school problems.
>
> Emotional disturbance includes schizophrenia... (Assistance to States for the Education of Children with Disabilities, 2006).

As with learning disability, individual states in the United States are able to define emotional disturbance and specify the criteria to identify children with it. About 0.90% of children receive special educational services related to emotional disturbance, which has been consistent over the course of IDEA. Despite the relatively low numbers of students identified with emotional disturbance, examining the demographic characteristics of those so identified raises questions to the validity of diagnostic processes and the definition in place. Compared with their peers both with and without disabilities, children identified with emotional disturbance are more likely to be male, African-American, and economically disadvantaged. Thus, being a boy, being Black, and/or poor increases one's likelihood of being identified as emotionally disturbed. While some believe that the overrepresentation relates to challenges that affect a child's school performance intrinsic to each of these life circumstances, as Harry, Klingner, and Hart (2005) point out, the majority of education researchers propose the subjectivity involved in diagnosing emotional disturbance is the problem.

Research conducted by the Center for Effective Collaboration and Practice (2001) suggests that the high identification rates for African-Americans and males may be due both to teacher expectations regarding normative behavior (Horowitz, Bility, Plichta, Leaf, and Haynes, 1998; McLaughlin and Talbert, 1992; Metz, 1994) and to a lack of culturally relevant and linguistically appropriate assessment instruments (Harry, 1994). With regard to the overrepresentation of males, it is possible that teachers are more likely to identify students who present disruptive or externalized behaviors, which are more common in boys than girls. Ferguson (2001) further argues that the criteria for emotional disturbance medicalizes what may be otherwise "normal" feelings experienced by poor, Black youth in the sociopolitical context of the United States. For those children and young adults in the most disenfranchised communities, suspicion of and anger toward teachers, peers, school curriculum, and the institutions they represent may be a troubling, but not inappropriate response indicating impairment. The failure of our schools to respond to the needs of the nation's most vulnerable groups is well documented (Blanchett, 2006; Kozol, 1991; 2005; Noguera, 2008). As with learning disability, identifying students who struggle as individually pathological allows schools to continue "business as usual" rather than query other reasons that particular groups of students seem to fail in our schools.

Most in education acknowledge and work to reconcile problematic approaches to the identification of children with emotional disturbance that have led to the overrepresentation of boys who are poor and Black in the category. However, the wide variety of approaches and the subjectivity in diagnosing emotional and learning disabilities continue to plague the field. It is possible that stronger federal guidelines could reduce the number of students ostensibly mis diagnosed with "soft" disability labels. In addition, preparing teachers to work more effectively with culturally, economically, and racially diverse children can mitigate and help teachers better understand and find ways to talk about behavioral challenges that are often the cause to initiate referral to special education (Danforth and Rhodes, 1997). The latter is more promising, as simply revising our practices in diagnosing hardly addresses the underlying questions of validity that our past and fading practices initially raised. If the meaning and diagnosis of these disabilities are so elastic and subjective, it is difficult to have confidence that these labels can ever contribute to meaningful understanding of a child's learning and interactions in school. Their imprecision mitigates their practicality for making educational decisions.

(12) Autism, Autism Spectrum Disorder, Pervasive Developmental Disorder

In *DSM-IV*, "Autistic Disorder" is part of a broader category named, "Pervasive Developmental Disorders." Other classifications in this category are Asperger's syndrome, pervasive developmental disorder-not otherwise specified (PDD-NOS), Rett's disorder, and childhood disintegrative disorder. In school settings, the terms "autism," and "autistic spectrum disorder" or "ASD," are used somewhat interchangeably. Asperger's syndrome is sometimes described as "high-functioning autism," and "PDD" (short for PDD-NOS) is sometimes attributed to older children who demonstrate autistic characteristics, but who developed them later in age than allowed for by the classification of "Autistic Disorder." "PDD" is also often the label ascribed to very young children who have not yet been classified according to one of the more specific developmental disorders.

According to IDEIA:

> Autism means a developmental disability significantly affecting verbal and non-verbal communication and social interaction, generally evident before age three, that adversely affects a child's educational performance. Other characteristics often associated with autism are engagement in repetitive activities and stereotyped movements, resistance to environmental change or change in daily routines, and unusual responses to sensory experiences (Assistance to States for the Education of Children with Disabilities, 2006).

Over the last decade, many have voiced concerns about the increase in children identified as autistic. According to the US Center for Disease Control and Prevention (2008):

> It is clear that more children than ever before are being classified as having autism spectrum disorders (ASDs). But, it is unclear how much of this increase is due to changes in how we identify and classify ASDs in people, and how much is due to a true increase in prevalence.

A recent study performed in the United States estimated that 3.4 of every 1,000 child aged 3–10 years had autism (Yeargin-Allsopp et al., 2003). It occurs in every racial and ethnic group, but is four times more prevalent in boys than in girls.

There have been several theories on the cause of autism over the last 70 years. During the 1940s–1970s, Bruno Bettelheim championed a theory that autism was caused by parents' lack of warmth toward their child, which led to the retrospectively cruel stigma placed on "refrigerator mothers." Contemporary scientists agree that autism is not caused by parental neglect, abuse, or failure to create an emotional bond, and is not a product of psychological factors in the child's environment. In the 1980s–1990s, vaccinations, particularly those that contained the preservative, thimerosal, were suspected of causing autism. In 1999, the pediatric community, public health officials, and vaccine manufacturers agreed to reduce or eliminate its use in vaccinations. Research on the links between autism and vaccines is ongoing, though research conducted by the Center of Disease Control and Prevention in 2007 does not support a connection between thimerosal and neuropsychological function in children (Price, Goodson, and Stewart, 2007). The specific cause of autism remains unknown, although current research suggests that it is neurological in nature and has a genetic basis.

Similar to other soft disabilities, autism is diagnosed through subjective impressions. Individuals with autism are deemed so based on their behavior, affect, and social interaction, which are gauged according to criteria put forth in the *DSM-IV*. Autism is often described as occurring on a continuum or spectrum—hence the emergence of "autism spectrum disorder" as a popular term. In a medical model, autism is not usually described as a soft disability, but one that is conspicuous—as "it" is diagnosed by gauging perceptible typologies of social responses, actions, and interactions. We have chosen to group autism with soft disabilities because of the reliance on cultural and social norms to dictate diagnosis, and in relation to the beliefs of many autistic self-advocates who strongly disagree with a medical characterization of autism as a deficiency or impairment (e.g., Aspies for Freedom; Autistic Self Advocacy Network). Similar to the circumstance presented by severe and profound mental retardation, however, persons diagnosed on the autism spectrum are often perceived as conspicuously "autistic," thus we recognize and acknowledge the unusual, though purposeful, choice to describe autism as a soft disability label.

Another reason that we have chosen to include autism in the description of soft disabilities is because the meaning and experience of autism has increasingly been contested, most notably in relation to breakthroughs in assistive technology and communication methods introduced in the 1970s. Practices such as *facilitated communication* provide an individual with the physical and emotional support to enable her or him to type or point to symbols in order to communicate using augmentative or alternative communication systems. Learning how to type often begins with a facilitator supporting the arm or hand as the communicator develops precision with typing, pressing, and/or pointing. Some individuals may eventually type independently, and others utilize a range of facilitator support throughout their lives. As with all people, those who use assistive technology to communicate demonstrate a wide variety of social and verbal abilities.

In relation to language use, accurately assessing the cognitive ability of individuals with autism can be difficult, especially with children and individuals who experience significant barriers in verbal communication—a skill required by most IQ batteries. This has led to many autistic persons being mislabeled as retarded, which has also served to reveal the limitations of understanding intelligence as measurable by the most common IQ batteries administered in schools. Studies on the use of measures that are non-verbal in nature, such as *Raven's Standard Progressive Matrices* (Raven, 1958), have shown dramatic increases—altering scores by an average of 30 percentile points—in the measured IQ of autistic persons (Dawson, Soulières, Gernsbacher, and Mottron, 2007). This is not to suggest that using better tools increases the validity of the highly contested concept of IQ, but to point out the problems that emerge in our reliance on them.

The increase in attention to assistive technologies such as facilitated communication and our willingness to explore other ways of measuring intellect has led to better understanding of the experiences of a growing number of autistic individuals once deemed "low functioning." Access to communication and increased public interest has enabled many to tell their own stories and contest the descriptors that have been attributed to autism. Sue Rubin, for example, wrote and was featured in the Academy Award nominated documentary *Autism is a World* (Wurzburg and Biklen, 2004); Temple Grandin is a highly accomplished author and professor of animal science (see Grandin and Scariano, 1986; Grandin, 1995; 2007; Grandin and Johnson, 2005). The book *Autism and the Myth of the Person Alone* (Biklen, 2005) features several autistic authors whose stories challenge common assumptions made about autism and autistic lives. The concept of "presuming competence," or initially assuming and treating individuals as though they are intellectually active even when their performance may not suggest typical ways of functioning, is a useful position with which to approach school practices related to those with intellectual disabilities or autism (Biklen and Burke, 2006; Biklen and Cardinal, 1997; Jorgensen, McSheehan, and Sonnenmeier, 2007; Kasa-Hendrickson, 2005).

Discussion

The idea of the "soft" disability label is complicated and to some extent derived from paradigmatic differences between a medical and social model of disability. Diagnostic criteria for the disabilities and related medical-psychiatric conditions we have described as soft *are* established in the DSM-IV and many instruments and rating scales for assessing the variety of disabilities *are* proven scientifically reliable and valid. Despite the scientific acceptability of these measures, however, it is widely acknowledged that the human role in rating characteristics such as behavior, affect, and emotion are simply subjective, by definition. Noted previously, designating any impairment as necessarily indicating a disability is a product of environment and culture, as in a social model of disability.

Conclusion: Conceptualizing Disability in Schools

The perception and diagnosis of disability is inextricably related to the moral, cultural, and geographic context within which a characteristic becomes a barrier, a liability—a marker of abnormality. The influential medical model in education emphasizes a need to determine and diagnose impairment so teachers and professionals can anticipate and address the related educational need and provide special services. An outcome of linking disability categories to educational practice, however, is labeling. Labeling unavoidably promotes stigma and segregation, and therefore reduces the likelihood of achieving equality in educational services. Close examinations of soft disability categories demonstrate, in fact, that such labels can be manipulated and used to invoke de facto racial segregation. Unfortunately, disability is too often used as a rationale to hide racial and economic inequities or preserve excessive standardization. That is, when students do not achieve the explanation is focused on finding the individual to be disordered, rather than on other contextual factors. Understanding that disability is fundamentally conceptualized as a dividing entity in education can help educators seeking inclusive practices to identify and understand deep-seated resistance held in the structures of schools themselves.

7

Collaborative Practice

There are many stakeholders involved in the education of a child. Students, families, teachers, and other school professionals can work together to ensure that learners have positive and productive experiences in school. Among advances in the rights of people with disabilities is the IDEIA, which guarantees a free and appropriate public education to children with disabilities, as well as specifies the need to engage in collaborative planning and practice.

Individualized Education Program

The requirement of a multidisciplinary team to develop an Individualized Educational Program (IEP) for each child eligible for special educational services is often described as the cornerstone of the IDEIA. An IEP must include:

1. A description of the child's current levels of academic performance, which addresses how the disability affects her or his participation in learning and school.
2. Measurable educational and functional goals and objectives that should enable the child to make progress in the general curriculum.
3. A description for how progress toward the goals will be measured.
4. A description of the classroom setting(s), special education services, and supplementary aids that will be provided to the child, which must adhere to the LRE requirement.
5. A description of accommodations required or alternate measures to enable the child to participate in State or school-wide assessments.
6. The dates for beginning the educational program and intermittent assessment of progress.
7. For students aged 16 and older, a description of goals and instruction to support the student to make the *transition* from school to post-school life.

The descriptions of the child and her or his educational program written for the IEP are developed by an IEP Team. The IEP Team includes: (a) the parent(s)/guardian(s); (b) at least one special education teacher or service provider; (c) a general education teacher, if the child is or might participate in general education; (d) a representative of the school district, usually a school administrator; (e) an individual who can interpret the results of educational assessments, usually a psychologist or other licensed educational evaluator; (f) any other parties with supporting knowledge or experience with the child, at the parent(s)' or school's discretion; and—most important, (g) the child, "whenever appropriate" to quote IDEIA.

An IEP should be developed according to the expertise and contributions of all members of the IEP Team. At minimum, the school must hold at least one meeting per year to review the child's progress and plan or review the IEP for the subsequent annual period. The IEP should be agreed upon by all parties, and the parent/guardian consents to its implementation by signing. It is the responsibility of all teachers and personnel who work with a child who receives special educational services to read his or her IEP, and to comply with the goals, objectives, services, assessment methods and schedule, and accommodations described within. To ensure the implementation of an IEP, cultivating collaborative practices among all members of the team is essential.

Students and Families are Experts

A basic consideration for inclusive practice is to invite, welcome, and take seriously the information, ideas, and desires of students and their families in relation to school planning. School professionals contribute a wealth of knowledge to help understand and support students who experience struggle in schools. Teachers and other school professionals have studied curriculum and instruction and spend most of their workday with children, which add to their expertise. While the contributions of professionals are essential, students and their families should also be considered and treated as experts. Consider, for example, Pam Steeves' (2006) reflection on life with her son, Matthew: "It is by living up close with Matthew that I have come to know stories of Matthew as knowledgeable, as using playful and improvisatory ways to participate, communicate, and contribute to the world" (p. 107). She further describes the way her experience of Matthew enabled her to help school professionals arrive at better understanding of her son's attachment to a stuffed toy cat named Tony—a topic of discussion when he changed schools at age 11. She recollects the phone call:

> After a few pleasantries, the "issue" of Tony, the stuffed toy cat, came up. I must admit that, viewed from the outside, it seemed pretty crazy to defend this cat, but I was looking from a different vantage point. I was attending to what Tony meant to Matthew from the inside. Tony helped Matthew be strong; Tony was always there; Tony was funny and could do things that would make other people laugh, and then Matthew could join in, too. Matthew wanted more than anything to belong, to have a place. Tony helped him to do that (p. 109).

Matthew was able to keep Tony with him in school. Steeves notes:

> Matthew shifted the landscape from one where he held a fixed position as a child with disabilities to a child who was trying to figure out how to fit into a situation. For Matthew, Tony was the way in. Matthew was able to participate because Tony created a common ground (p. 109).

Listening to the stories of parents and attending to their understandings of their children is essential to developing a whole portrait of a student, his desires, and needs in school.

Although IDEIA specifies the importance of family participation in IEP development, the majority of recent studies into parents' perceptions of IEP meetings demonstrate their negative experiences (Reiman, Beck, Coppola, and Engiles, 2010). Common sources of parents' negative feelings are: the density of professional talk and confusion about the goals and purpose of the meeting; the failure of school professionals to include them in the planning process; and the undesirability of attending meetings in which negative talk about their child prevails, especially when they feel blamed for their child's difficulty in school (Reiman et al., 2010; Valle, 2009)). These problems are exacerbated for families who speak languages other than English (Kalyanpur and Harry, 1999; Lo, 2008; Salas, 2004). Other barriers to participation include meetings scheduled in conflict with working or caring for other children; securing transportation to the school; and poor translation or interpretation for families who speak languages other than English (Kalyanpur and Harry, 1999; Rogers, 2002).

Collaborative IEP Meetings

There are many practices professionals can implement to make the IEP meeting more positive for everyone. Creating a positive climate concerns the arrangements made before the meeting, as well as interactions during it. In scheduling the meeting, it is useful to offer various options for the meeting time and place, which demonstrate consideration of the family member's work and other responsibilities. Making sure teachers' and other professionals' schedules are clear is also essential so that they are not pressured during the meeting. Providing travel arrangements to family participants is part of IDEIA, so ensuring parents know it is a right and not a "favor" communicates the school's interest in working together. Ensuring translating or interpreter services are arranged and are of high quality is essential for families who speak languages other than English. Parents in one study suggested that IEP forms be provided in advance of the meeting so they could review and be prepared to discuss them (Simon, 2006). An advance phone discussion about any changes or developments may also be warranted, so that parents do not feel ambushed at the meeting. Beginning the collaborative process begins with facilitating parents' ability to attend the meeting and enabling them to be prepared to participate.

When it is time for the meeting, it is useful to have a planned format that aims for collaboration and equal participation among the members of the IEP Team. Kroeger, Leibold, and Ryan (1999), for example, offer a vision of IEP meetings as collaborative processes of educational planning and suggest ways to make them more accessible to students and families. A facilitator, not a "leader," should begin with having members, including the student, set a format for participation and a time frame. Visual cues can help keep everyone on track: a chalkboard, whiteboard, or chart can be used to record participants' knowledge about the learner's strengths, talents, difficulties, and educational needs. A shared vision for the student's goals and desires should be developed through attending to the recorded knowledge, prioritizing areas of need, and arriving at consensus about the best ways school and related services can enable the learner to meet his or her goals. The facilitator's role should aim to cultivate active participation by all, ensure that members understand each other, and keep track of time—to be respectful of participants' schedules and avoid a need to rush to decisions.

Having a protocol that maximizes everyone's understanding of the meeting content and that provides a process for all to participate nurtures collaboration and mutual respect. A format such as this may also be used to resolve disagreements about an IEP (Mueller, 2009). Adding a neutral facilitator and setting ground rules for respectful communication and turn-taking can help turn contentious situations into productive ones. Being able to solve IEP disputes collaboratively is surely preferred to taking them to formal mediation, as IDEIA allows.

Schools are busy places and school professionals are usually working with many students in what never seems like enough time. Additionally, far too many schools are understaffed and poorly resourced. These constraints often lead to IEP meetings feeling rushed and as though they are formalities, rather than collaborations. This is especially the case when the IEP forms are already completed and are merely presented for parents to sign; when parents and students attend a meeting only to listen and nod (Fish, 2008). To practice IEP meetings as spaces of genuine collaboration requires them to be envisioned as such. School professionals must be open to parents' and students' ideas and suggestions about the educational program. School administrators, especially, need to provide time and support so that teachers and other school professionals can devote the necessary time to cultivating relationships and working with students and families.

Student-Led IEP Meetings

Collaboration with families is important, but including the student in the IEP process is essential. It is strongly recommend that students attend their IEP meetings and desirable that they be placed in leadership roles to guide their annual review meetings (IDEIA, 2004; Mason, McGahee-Kovac, and Johnson, 2004; Martin, Marshall, Maxson, & Jerman, 1997). Students can learn about the purpose and structure of the IEP meeting, and should be encouraged to express their thoughts about their educational progress, their immediate goals, and long-term desires. Students of all ages can participate. Mason, MaGahee-Kovac, and Johnson (2004) note:

> Although it is perhaps easiest for teachers to envision students in high school preparing to leave school as IEP team leaders, we have experience implementing student-led IEPs with students as young as 6 years of age. The vocabulary is different, and the degree of responsibility is different; however, the concept of leadership is maintained through the emphasis that is placed on asking the child about what is important to him or her and using that information in planning goals (p. 22).

Some professionals and families may be hesitant to include children and adolescents in IEP planning because of the presumed need to talk about difficulties, which may be upsetting to a child and uncomfortable to professionals; or to protect the child from knowing the disability with which s/he has been labeled. Perhaps the rationale for including students is evident in reasons offered to exclude them: Professionals can learn how to talk about students in candid, but respectful ways; and children and adolescents have a right and need to know the disabilities attributed to them and should not be made to feel ashamed. Providing opportunities for students to learn how to self-advocate and play a role in educational planning places the individual at the center of his experiences, and honors the values of independence and self-determination, most dear to disability rights.

School professionals and families can support students to engage in their IEP meetings by encouraging their early attendance and explaining the process. There are also a growing number of programs and guides to assist available. The Self-Directed IEP, developed by Martin, Marshall, Maxson, and Jerman (1997) is a program that included lessons, video and other materials that can be used to teach students about the IEP meeting and develop skills that can enable them to lead their meetings. Participating in the meetings empowers students to direct their education, as well as provides a forum for others to perceive their competence.

The IEP meeting has long been a source of negative feelings for families of students with disabilities. There are, however, many practices that school professionals can implement in order to use this meeting time as the collaborative space for which it is intended. Recognizing the positive contribution families and students can have in the process is the first step. Planning for attendance and participation is the second, and developing respectful, inviting procedures for collaboration during the meeting is the third. Working proactively and amenably benefits all stakeholders. Students especially benefit, as they participate in their educational planning and self-advocate for their needs and desires, a major aim of disability rights and disability studies.

Building Relationships Between Schools and Families

Practicing collaborative planning at IEP meetings is an excellent way to form strong, productive relationships among students, families, and school professionals. There are also other steps teachers can take to build positive interactions with families.

Try to contact families at the beginning of the school year as an introduction and also to gain insight into their experiences, thoughts, and desires for their child. This can be a great opportunity to listen to ideas about how the child was successful in the past, as well as finding out about her or his interests and/or life outside of school. Initiating early and open communication is a great way to start positively, and will make it easier to reach out to the family if conflicts or challenges arise.

Provide families with contact information and the best times to be reached—for example, during preparation periods or before and after the school day. Although email is not comfortable and accessible to everyone, it is a way to communicate that is helpful for those with conflicting schedules. Offering contact information demonstrates interest in two-way communication.

Although most schools offer special events for families to meet teachers and visit the school, it is also beneficial to extend a personal invitation for family members to visit the class. This may be especially welcome for those who are unable to attend events offered only once.

Sending out periodic newsletters describing what the class is studying can be interesting to families. Students may also enjoy suggesting what to include and participate in creating them. Letters can also be used to invite family members who have related knowledge, experiences, or ideas to be guest presenters or help facilitate a field trip. It is important, however, to ensure that the format is accessible to families—do consider the languages families may be most comfortable with, as well as whether a phone call would be preferred to reading a letter.

Avoid using a "call home" as a threat to students. Communication between families and teachers is better construed as an ongoing relationship, rather than an occasional means of punishment. From another angle, regularly communicating successes and accomplishments is more likely to nurture a satisfying partnership among teachers and families.

There are many ways that teachers and schools can promote positive and productive relationships with students and their families. It is important, however, to take cues from the community and understand that multiple efforts may be required. Not all families (or communities) have had pleasant interactions with schools. Extending oneself is certainly in the best interest of the student, and the benefits of school–family collaboration can be immense.

Collaborative Problem-Solving

Being proactive in building positive relationships with students and families can make dealing with challenges and finding solutions that are beneficial to students and reasonable for families and professionals a smooth process. Problem-solving is a typical part of work in schools. The majority of challenges and conflicts emerge in daily practice and can be worked out quickly and immediately among the affected parties. Occasionally, however, serious conflicts or especially difficult challenges that require the involvement of other professionals or families arise. Ideally, engaging in collaborative problem-solving should be a welcome chance for teachers, school professionals, families, and students to work together toward the benefit of the student. Unfortunately, the experience of talking about difficulties can become an unpleasant situation in which negative talk prevails, families feel as though they are being blamed for the difficulties or that their needs are not considered.

To illustrate one difficult situation, Danforth and Smith (2005) offer the account of Ms. Perez, a school professional who invited Carlos Quiles, father of Victor, to attend a meeting with Victor's teachers, the special education supervisor, and the school resource police officer. In this excerpt, the school's supervisor of special education has recommended that Victor attend a half-day, instead of whole day, of school because of his disruptive behavior. The arrangement proposed is that Carlos pick up Victor from school each day at 11:30.

> The supervisor of special education spoke. "Well, Mr. Quiles, I can understand if you can't pick him up. I think in this case what might be better would be to put Victor on homebound status, and that way you wouldn't have to be concerned with transportation."
>
> There was a flurry of talk from the teachers. They did not want Victor to be put on homebound. … But the supervisor of special education was already preparing the changes on the IEP (Individualized Education Plan) for Carlos to sign. She said, "We will place Victor on homebound instruction, and if you can work out something for transportation, we can meet again and make changes." She moved the papers and a pen in front of Carlos.
>
> "I don't think this arrangement is in the best interest of Victor. I don't think we should send him home," [Ms. Perez] said.
>
> Carlos did not reach for the pen.
>
> "Mr. Quiles," said the supervisor in a soft sing, sing-song voice, "You can take us to court and we can go to court but…" and her words trailed off. She nudged the papers…

> When Carlos picked up the pen and signed the IEP, I was stunned. I didn't know what to say. I have been led to believe by the school administrator that the meeting was to discuss ideas to help Victor be successful in school... (p. 230).

When Carlos left the meeting, Victor was waiting, eager to know what had been said. Carlos replied:

> "They said you are a pain in the neck, and they don't want you here anymore. You curse, you yell, you can't sit and have a conversation. So you have to stay home and have teacher come out to the house to teach you," his father said.

> "Well they can send someone, but I won't be there," Victor said and hopped into the van.

> Carlos turned to me with an outstretched hand. "Thank you, Ms. Perez, for coming to the meeting with me. But now you know why I don't come back. That officer made me look bad in there. I don't like how I feel now" (p. 230).

In this excerpt, a father has been made to feel at fault for his objection and inability to pick up his child at midday and subsequently threatened with engagement in the legal process when he hesitates to agree to home instruction. He is ultimately manipulated into signing an education plan (IEP) that few members of the meeting see as beneficial to Victor, and that Victor clearly intends to subvert.

One more illustration of barriers to problem-solving is drawn from the book *Ability Profiling and School Failure* (2003). Collins illustrates her work and time with Jay, a fourth-grade student. In one scene, Jay's "calling out" during class discussion is the topic of a conference among two teachers, Jay, and his two grandparents:

> "Why are you behaving like that?" Mrs. Armstrong [the teacher] continues.

> [Jay]: "I mean, I like, I have something to say, and I just say it" (p. 17).

Collins further captures a later conversation between she and Jay on the topic of "calling out":

> "Did you think it was wrong to yell out?"

> "No."

> "Why?"

> "*Cause!*" Jay looks as upset as I've ever seen him. "She doesn't *call on me!*" [Emphases as in original]

"Is it wrong to talk when you're not called on?"

"Yeah, but, still." Jay relaxes and looks at me a bit sheepishly. He continues, some measure of confidence returned to his voice, "Sometime things need to be said. You should always say what you're thinking it if it's something good" (p. 188).

Admonitions that Jay must learn "self-control" pervade much of the conversations surrounding his classroom behavior in the rest of the discussion. Jay, however, is not unaware of his "behavior," nor out of control. He takes responsibility for his efforts to be heard; "I have something to say," and "Sometime things need to be said," he asserts. Unfortunately, Jay's understanding of his experience was not considered in the educational decisions made around him. In this example, listening and attending to Jay's own impression of classroom experiences could lead to better understanding and the development of productive classroom practices related to his desire to be heard in class. In both illustrations, a collaborative, problem-solving approach could better enable multiple perspectives to be considered toward more satisfying outcomes.

Collaborative problem-solving requires a dialog, in which all parties are able to contribute their understanding, ideas, and solutions. It is especially important to have a protocol to follow when prior attempts to address the conflict have been unsuccessful. Here is one outline of how to develop a protocol for collaborative conflict resolution:

1. It is useful to have a neutral facilitator. That is, someone who is not immediately involved in the conflict.
2. The facilitator begins by setting a purpose for the conversation—to arrive at a solution.
3. Then, the facilitator describes the situation and challenge.
4. From there, other participants can be invited to ask questions and clarify understanding of what happened. When describing a challenge in need of resolution, be direct, clear, and keep focus on the present issue. Although there may be many things to talk about, focusing on one challenge at a time is more likely to result in clear, specific solutions. It may be useful for the facilitator to point out issues that are off topic and keep a list of them to address at another time.
5. Once everyone has reached an understanding about what happened, participants can take turns posing ideas to reach a resolution to the situation, as well as to generate ideas on how to prevent the problem in the future.
6. Although compromise can be difficult, it may be necessary and represents the strength of the collaboration. After all, if one person believes he or she has all the answers, then why reach out to others to begin

with? In posing solutions, it is a good idea to ensure that parties share in responsibility for the outcome, and that there is a clear plan for following up.

7. Be sure to summarize the outcome and plan at the close of the discussion.

A protocol for a collaborative process can take many different forms. The key is to aim for all parties to have equal opportunity to share their understanding and feedback, and for the resolution to be agreed upon by all parties.

Consider the way that these practices could influence the events in the situations with Carlos and Victor and Jay and his teachers, described earlier. Perhaps Jay's feelings of frustration could be shared and acknowledged by his teachers, which could lead to a productive, rather than adversarial relationship. Perhaps an agreement that enabled Victor to attend school could be reached. At minimum, Carlos's relationship and impression of the school could be improved, which could lead to better interventions for his son in the future. Although a solution to the immediate conflict is a goal, preservation or development of relationships among parties is a longer-term aim. These will subsequently enable more productive interactions, which is in the interest of all parties. Students are usually members of a school for many years, which means that their families are, too. It is wise to encounter every interaction as an opportunity to build a positive relationship for the long-term.

Professional Collaboration is Essential

In addition to collaborating with students and families in educational planning and problem-solving, the inclusive educator should expect to work with a variety of other school professionals. Inviting and welcoming consultation and engaging in collaborative planning and teaching is a necessity in ensuring that the needs of students with disabilities are addressed comprehensively, consistently, and holistically. In addition to sharing specific kinds of expertise to best meet the needs of students, a benefit of collaboration is in building and maintaining relationships that can facilitate a friendly and satisfying work environment. For all collaborations, standards of professional interactions should be followed. In other words, all should be given respect and treated as welcome classroom members or consultants. When working together, members of a professional team should be introduced to all students and adults. Whenever possible, classroom routines and the instructional plans for a given day should be developed together; at minimum, a description of instruction or service provision should be shared with all who may attend a class. Establishing roles and discussing the kinds of instruction or support that are being performed or may be needed can help with negotiating the changing environment of a classroom and ensure that all adults are able to contribute in appropriate and supportive ways. Descriptions of the most common kinds of professional collaboration follow.

Consulting and Supportive Roles

Special educators provide a variety of instructional services that can be performed in many structures and settings, which reflect the continuum of settings and services specified in the IDEIA. Supplemental support, sometimes described as resource rooms, refers to a service in which a special educator works with an individual or a small group of students with disabilities to provide support on curriculum offered in another setting or to provide a specialized curriculum. Supplemental support may be provided within a large-class setting or in a small-group or individual setting. In either arrangement, the special educator should work with students' other teachers to understand their needs and performance in other settings, the design and requirements of grade-level curriculum, and to offer her or his own experience to help other teachers work with shared students.

Collaborative Teaching, or Co-Teaching

Collaborative teaching generally refers to a teaching arrangement in which a general education teacher and special education teacher work together to provide instruction to a class of students with and without disabilities. Collaborative teaching is the arrangement that best relates to inclusive education. Students in co-taught classrooms have the benefit of two teachers with whom to learn and gain support. Just as teachers support students, they can also support each other. To best implement co-teaching, teachers can:

1. Get to know and work with all children in the class, regardless of disability status.
2. Plan curriculum and instruction together, and in a way that allows both teachers to contribute their experience and expertise—ideas for planning inclusive curriculum are addressed in Chapter 9.
3. Share responsibilities and classroom roles.
4. Participate in the assessment and evaluation of all children, regardless of disability status.

In brief, co-teachers work as a team—with equal status and responsibilities. Collaborative teaching is high on the list of initiatives in inclusive education, and resources with ideas for how to structure classes, determine roles and responsibilities, and establish effective planning and teaching practices are widely available.

Paraprofessionals or School Aides

It is possible that a class may have a paraprofessional or teacher's assistant assigned to support class instruction. An individual student may have a paraprofessional or aide assigned specifically to him or her to help with health and personal needs or with instruction.

Specialists and Related Services

Schools employ a variety of specialists who may work with teachers and students to address needs related to learning, health, and/or access to schools and instruction. A related service is broadly defined in IDEIA, and can include anything from school health services to speech therapy to psychological, and even family, counseling. Specialists of all kinds may work with an individual or group of students outside of the usual instructional environment in a "pull-out" arrangement or they may "push-in" to a class and address needs of an individual or group in conjunction with class instruction. Some of the more common specialists and related services are described in terms of typical services performed in schools.

Speech-language pathologists. Speech-language pathologists (SLP) or therapists are specialized professionals who work with children who need help with articulating speech or language development. An SLP is not the same as a teacher who specializes in teaching English to speakers of other languages.

Audiologist. An audiologist is a specialist in hearing, who may diagnose, treat, and monitor auditory disorders. She or he may provide training for teachers or students related to using hearing aids, amplification devices, or cochlear implants.

Interpreters. Students' right to assessment in their native language is described in the IDEIA. Interpreters for languages other than English may be a part of the assessment process, or may assist at meetings with families who require them to participate in school planning. Interpreters for American Sign Language (ASL) may be permanent members of the classroom if there are students who communicate with ASL.

Counselors and psychologists. Schools may provide any variety of mental heath or therapeutic services. Students may receive individual or group counseling or therapy as part of their school program and related services. A mental health counselor, counseling psychologist, or school psychologist is a licensed mental health professional and is different from a guidance counselor, who is a licensed school professional. The school psychologist is part of the IEP team and may perform assessments and/or provide therapy or counseling. Except in crisis situations in which harm to others or self is imminent, counselors and psychologists must respect the confidentiality of students and families. However, collaboration and professional communication among parties can lead to joint efforts to support a student's psychosocial development and goals.

Social workers. Social workers are part of the IEP team, and may also provide services to students and their families. The social worker connects children and families with social resources and networks to improve quality of life, which may include anything from connecting families with support groups to helping them seek better housing; from connecting a student with a potential employer to dealing with issues of abuse or neglect.

Occupational therapist. Occupational therapists (OT) generally provide consultation and instruction to support the fullest participation and independence in life activities for students with physical, motor, or sensory impairments. They may help assess and adapt the physical environment, provide adaptive equipment, or provide exercises or training to enable independence in school tasks and life activities. For example, OTs may provide a pencil grip to enable independence in writing, offer training or exercises to help a student build dexterity in order to better grip a pencil, or work on helping a student use a different method for written expression—such as typing. OTs or orientation specialists may also support students with orthopedic or visual impairments to learn how to negotiate the physical environment using a cane or crutches, for example, as well as how to perform life activities, such as eating, dressing, or cooking. A final role that an OT may fill is in working with students to develop skills and strategies that support social interaction, play, and responding to sensory stimuli in the environment.

Physical therapists. The work of physical therapists may overlap with occupational therapists, though the focus of "PTs" is on improving, developing, or teaching ways of moving the body that aim to strengthen the body and/or manage or reduce pain toward maximizing physical function. In schools, PT may be provided for students who are working on increasing strength and technique to adapt to physical impairment, for example, or as a way to maintain strength or range of motion.

Health professionals. Health professionals typically include nurses or specialized aides who attend to physiological needs, although mental health professionals, or a psychiatrist, may also be a part of this category. Nurses may administer medication or help monitor a student who has had a seizure, for example; aides may assist with health needs such as eating or going to the bathroom.

Related services have traditionally been offered outside of classrooms. That is, the therapist would take a student or small group of students to an office and provide instruction or therapy there. The students would then return to class. The "pull-out" model has long been thought to provide students specialized instruction in a highly focused environment in which to practice a much needed skill. There are also criticisms of the model, however. First, the pulled out students presumably miss the activity that is occurring in the classroom. The students, at worst, miss instruction and have to make up work. At best, they miss social experience and have to catch up with their peers at a later time. Either way, there is a gap in the students' experience with regard to class activities. A second criticism is that skills learned in isolation are more difficult for students to transfer, or generalize, to the classroom contexts in which they will be most useful. For example, using specific reading strategies to decode challenging words is most needed when reading a text in social studies. The ability to grip a pencil is key in mathematics, and using methods to manage frustration or anger are best utilized in the setting where the emotions are likely to occur. Because of these criticisms, it is increasingly recommended that related services be provided within the classroom instruction—in other words, inclusively. When related services are provided in a classroom, collaboration among professionals, similar to co-teaching guidelines, may be appropriate. All professionals should be aware of each other's goals and efforts should be made to integrate aims as much as possible.

Conclusion

The African proverb "it takes a village to raise a child" is a wise comment applicable to the development of collaborative educational practices. Children benefit from families and professionals who work together on their behalf. Whether co-teaching, consulting with professionals, or reaching out to families, working closely with others is a necessity for inclusive education. While there are barriers that can prevent effective communication and partnerships, there are also many ways that teachers can initiate and nurture positive relationships.

8

Disabilities and Initial Approaches for Creating Inclusive Environments

For inclusive education to be realized, it is important for all school profession-als, especially teachers, to be aware of basic and accurate information regarding the most common impairments or disabilities. The approaches in this chapter offer information and practices that reflect general awareness about disability and inclusive teaching. They are starting points and basics for beginning pro-fessional inclusive practice. It is crucial to remember that individuals experi-ence disability uniquely and develop ways to navigate school and society. It is always important to learn about individual students by asking questions about their preferences and needs. Learning from students, families, shared experi-ences, and other professionals can guide teaching practice beyond the basics.

Primary Considerations

Human Variation Is Normal

A basic consideration for working toward inclusive education relates to devel-oping productive dispositions for working with diverse groups of children. Each of us, at all ages, in all life contexts, has different characteristics, prefer-ences, strengths, and needs. The condition of human difference *is* normal (Stiker, 1997; Baglieri and Knopf, 2004). Characterizing children as normal or abnormal, "general" or "special," or dividing the curriculum of a classroom into normal and abnormal practices stigmatizes differences. Even when "normal" and "abnormal" are applied objectively or scientifically, the terms are not neu-tral descriptions. Rather, they form a hierarchy in which the aspect deemed "abnormal" is nearly always perceived negatively and less desirable. By adopt-ing a perspective that acknowledges variation among students as expected and natural teachers can resist characterizing students and teaching practices in ways that segregate and hierarchize.

Another reason to challenge the use of "normal" is variability in culture and experience. What may seem "abnormal" to one person might be quite "normal" to someone else. For example, if a Deaf student uses American Sign Language (ASL) as a primary means of communication, it may not be normal for others, but it is normal for her. Similarly, one research participant featured on the web-site, *Conversations about Learning Disability and Graduate School* (Baglieri and

Leber, 2008), points out that other adults recognize her difficulty with writing, but that her process does not feel "abnormal" to her. She notes: "...I'm comfortable with [my learning disability] because it's a part of me and I accept it. It feels, you know, normal to me..." (http://www.graduateschoolandld.com). Seeking better understanding of how students see themselves and their experiences helps teachers appreciate the many ways that individuals understand themselves and interact with the world around them.

Developing personal attitudes that prepare us to accept and appreciate all of our students as they are is the first and most important step in working toward inclusive education. Making efforts to interrupt our tendencies to perceive and talk about people and classroom instruction as normal and abnormal (or "general" and "special") serve the aims of inclusive education well. Although we cannot possibly anticipate the infinite range of unique characteristics, talents, struggles, and identities that each and every student brings to classrooms, we can adopt beliefs and attitudes that reject the effects of stigma, and make us open to accepting and working with everybody. Inclusive teaching is not a standardized or scripted practice that should be the same across years, or even days. Instead, it is a set of beliefs and practices that enable continual and thoughtful creation of a welcoming and flexible educational environment. Differences among students should be valued in celebration of the diversity of experiences that schools offer through its members.

Everyone Utilizes the Help and Support of Others

Throughout life, all humans benefit from the help and support of those around them. All of us—disabled or not—can surely remember a time when we benefited from help or support to learn something new, to reach a goal, or to manage a particular difficulty. Specifying ways for students to ask for help and ways that class members may offer help can facilitate a classroom and school community in which all are cared for and respected. Understanding that all humans are *interdependent* is useful to develop inclusive attitudes.

Persons with disabilities are more vulnerable to having unwelcome "help" imposed on them, to not receiving the particular help that is most beneficial, and/or to being hesitant or ashamed to ask for help because of others' potential perception of incompetence. Help should always be rendered in a way that maintains the recipient's dignity and fosters independence. If a student has not asked for help, but it seems needed, the offer for support may come in two questions: "Can I help you?" If the answer is "yes," the second question should be "*How* can I help?" The student should be treated as the expert on his or her needs and should have the opportunity to specify the kind of help required. It is acceptable to offer and explain a different suggestion that may be helpful, but attending to the desires of the recipient of support should be a priority.

Because some students are afraid that asking for help will signify weakness or invite stigma, they may accept assistance only when absolutely necessary. With the exception of situations in which safety is threatened, class members should not impose help if their offers are declined, and should not feel offended if help is refused. Care should be taken, however, to build understanding that all of us need help sometimes, and that accepting the help of others is simply a part of being human. Additionally, ensuring that students with disabilities are competent contributors to the classroom community can help balance the need for help and the ability to contribute. A student with a disability should be encouraged to take leadership positions and participate in classroom duties just as other children do.

General Information About Specific Disabilities

The 13 categories of disability described by the Individuals with Disabilities Education Improvement Act (IDEIA) offer explanations of types of disabilities that may necessitate a student's access to special educational services. There are a variety of impairments, syndromes, and medical conditions, however, which may be further specified in consideration of a student's needs. Disability may be experienced in relation to physique and movement, social behavior, communication, or intellect. Some basic information about human variation in these areas can help inform approaches for creating access to physical environments and social interaction.

Variations Apparent in Physique or Movement

"Physical disability" is a general term often attributed to those with impairments or conditions that are conspicuous in physique. Disabilities described as physical generally include those related to movement, motor function, and the appearance of the body. Not all people with physical disabilities require special educational services, and there is tremendous variety in the kinds of services required, depending on the whole of an individual's characteristics. Orthopedic disabilities are relatively rare among school-age populations, as are the majority of conditions that may be perceived in physique. In addition, some conditions and diseases that affect physique may also affect other aspects of function, such as social behavior, communication, or intellectual performance. We describe some physical disabilities, as well as neurological ones that can present with noticeable affects in appearance, found among children in schools.

Arthritis is a rheumatic disease of the skeletal joints, which causes motor impairment and pain, and can occur at any age. Swelling may occur in just one joint or in many, and the amount of swelling can vary from day to day.

Cerebral palsy refers to a group of impairments characterized by paralysis, weakness, incoordination, spasms, and motor dysfunction. It is related to damage to the brain that affects the development of the central nervous system and can occur during the prenatal period, at birth, and up to age three. The underlying damage is attributable to many possible causes. Cerebral palsy is not progressive. It often results in physical impairment of combinations of the limbs—most commonly, hemiplegia (an upper and lower extremity on the same side), paraplegia (legs only), and quadriplegia (all four extremities). Secondary impairments are also common, including difficulty with respiratory control. Limited muscle and respiratory control can contribute to difficulty in articulating speech.

Down syndrome relates to a genetic irregularity on the twenty-first chromosome for which sub-types are identified according to different kinds of irregularities. Trisomy 21, caused by an extra chromosome on the twenty-first gene pair, is the most common form. Although Down syndrome is caused by genetic irregularity, nearly all forms relate to fetal development and not heredity. Conspicuous characteristics of people with Down syndrome can include distinctive facial features such as a flat nasal bridge, epicanthic skin folds on the eyelids, and a protruding tongue. A short neck, low muscle tone, unusual gait, and congenital heart problems are also associated with Down syndrome, as is cognitive disability to varying degrees. The features of people of East Asian descent were once referred to as "mongoloid," as were people with Down syndrome, in relation to their face, nose, and eye shapes. Despite the continued use of "mongoloid" to denote particular characteristics in the medical community, it is a colloquially unacceptable term to refer to people of Asian decent and those with Down syndrome.

Multiple sclerosis has several sub-types, but generally refers to an autoimmune condition that affects sensory and motor systems. Multiple sclerosis usually occurs between the ages of 15 and 50, and is more common among females than males. Symptoms of multiple sclerosis appear as the covering that protects the brain (myelin) and spinal cord become scarred such that messages have difficulty passing from the brain to other parts of the body. Any aspect of neurological function may be affected, including movement, speech, and/or cognition. Multiple sclerosis is rarely fatal, and is neither contagious nor congenital (inherited). Some forms are episodic, and include intervals of spontaneous complete or partial recovery; others are progressive, with symptoms becoming more pronounced with age.

Muscular dystrophy generally refers to a family of congenital, progressive muscle diseases that affect skeletal movement and other body systems. The most well-known childhood form is Duchenne Muscular Dystrophy, which occurs more often in males than females. A progressive condition, it is usually first diagnosed as a child begins to walk. Muscle weakness, loss of muscle mass, and contracture in the pelvic and shoulder areas occur through childhood, often leading to a loss of ambulation by adolescence.

Seizure disorder (formerly called epilepsy) is a neurological condition that can result in recurring seizures, which are irregular discharges of electrical energy in particular brain cells. Seizure disorder refers to recurring seizures, though a single episode can be caused by stress, poor eating habits, or lack of sleep. Seizure disorders are treatable most of the time, and special educational services are usually not required. There are several types of seizures with varied physical affects. People who experience seizures sometimes have hallucinations, distortions of the environment, or strange odors, tastes, and sensations preceding them, which is called "an aura." Although vigorous and sometimes dramatic, seizures are usually brief and simply cause drowsiness or sleepiness after one occurs.

Spina bifida is a congenital condition of the spinal column that affects motor coordination and other body functions. Spina bifida refers to the malformation of a few vertebrae, which causes a lesion in the spinal cord. Most commonly, the leg muscles are paralyzed with the degree of paralysis depending on the location of the lesion in the spinal cord. In addition to orthopedic problems, children may develop difficulties with bones, joints, and muscles, including those that control the bowels and bladder.

Tourette syndrome is a neurological condition of unknown origin that causes repetitive, involuntary movements or vocalizations called tics. Tics may be simple or complex. Simple tics appear as sudden muscle movements such as brief, repetitive blinking, shoulder or head jerking, grunting, throat-clearing, sniffing, making single sounds, or grimacing. Complex tics involve distinct, coordinated movements such as a making a sound combined with a head movement and shoulder jerk. Although the complex tic, coprolalia (the uttering of taboo words), is associated with Tourette, it is uncommon, as are self-injurious tics such as smacking oneself. The majority of tics do not result in impairment.

Extraordinary bodies. Bodies come in all shapes and sizes, with lots of variation in form and features. Some people have extraordinary bodies due to an acquired injury or disease, including amputation; others' have unexpected features that are apparent at birth. Some people may use prosthetics, which are artificial extensions that replace body parts; others may not. The particular special educational needs required by an individual depend on the nature of the impairment or disability. Amputations, for example, usually occur as a result of accidents or diseases such as bone cancer. Because amputations are acquired disabilities, the amount of time and support needed to adjust varies widely among individuals and is based on such factors as age, gender, family support, education, and the extent of the amputation. Those who have had a longer time to learn how to function with their bodies—as with impairments present at birth—may benefit from physical or occupational therapy, or may demonstrate a high level of physical function even at a young age. Specific conditions that are marked by variations in physique include dwarfism and craniofacial disorders.

Dwarfism is an inherited condition that affects the skeleton resulting in short stature. In the past, the term "dwarf" referred to persons of disproportionate short stature, and the term "midget" referred to those of proportionate short stature. While "midget" is now considered pejorative, "dwarf" is still accepted, along with the preferred terms "short," "little," "small," or "persons of short stature." The most important issues regarding the education of youngsters with dwarfism include dealing with the curiosity of others, and addressing access barriers such as the height of water fountains, urinals, chalk, or white boards, and participating in athletics and other school activities.

As with dwarfism, those with craniofacial disorders may not be impaired in the usual sense of the term. Craniofacial disorders refer to non-typical formations of the skull, which affect the appearance of the head or face and can affect brain function. Cleft palate and cleft lip, which are incomplete closures of the top of mouth or throat (the palates), or the lip, are the most common examples. Surgery to close the palate or lip is often performed on children, but speech articulation and eating can be affected. Though not "disorders," other variations in facial features and skin-tone or pattern can be disabling due to the perceptions and responses of others. For example, low self-esteem or constant teasing related to a child's appearance could lead to depression, anger, or negative social behavior.

Experiencing a Physical Disability

The way a person with physical disabilities experiences the world and school depends on infinite factors, including characteristics related to impairment and the context of an individual's life, in general. We offer a few accounts of adults with physical disabilities to demonstrate some pleasures and frustrations in their experiences. In her 2007 memoir, *My Body Politic*, Simi Linton describes the particular pleasure of visiting a New York City art museum from the vantage point of a wheelchair user.

> While [the Guggenheim Museum] has not always been a totally wheel-chair-accessible building (though recent renovations have moved it forward), it is a wheelchair-pleasing building. The wheelchair user, as most visitors do, takes the elevator to the top floor. It is the last stop, but it is not the top of the building. As you leave the elevator, the spiral continues up to the right at a steep angle. ... When I had visited the museum in a manual chair, I would ask someone to give me a push up to the top, but that day, with a head full of steam, we [Linton and Rufus, her motorized wheelchair] went up, up, up to that tip of the spiral, then down to the next landing, and, just because I could, up and then down again. What a sensation!

> While spiraling down, I am reminded of the most dynamic Impressionist paintings. Impressionists employ color and visible brushwork to show the dissolution of form in light and atmosphere. It is said that with the advent of train travel, painters in increasing numbers were leaving Paris to go to the South of France to paint. As the trains moved (more quickly

than horse-drawn carriages) and light caught images and fractured those images, painters began to visualize form in more component parts that the more static view of earlier painters.

A painter on a train going to the South of France, and me spinning down the ramp at the Guggenheim, are different creatures, and we each have used our velocity for different ends. Yet, in our new vehicles, we both have been catapulted into a new way to see art (pp. 187–189).

By contrast, Long (1985/1990) offers a list of frustrating aspects of being physically disabled:

1. The frustration you feel when you are the guest of honor at the "Handicapped Person of the Year" award luncheon but the rest room doors are too narrow for the wheelchair and you have to urinate in a broom closet.
2. The rage you feel when someone says to you, "Oh, you have muscular dystrophy? If that happened to me, I'd kill myself."
3. The annoyance that comes from not being able to turn the radio on or the television off.
4. The indignity of having to see everything from about 4 feet off the ground. (How'd you like to go to a cocktail party where all you can see are rear ends at eye level?)
5. The indignity of having to ask, all the time.
6. The restlessness of having to sit in one place for 9 hours and then to go home and sit in a different chair for 7 hours.
7. The frustration of feeling violence and anger and having absolutely no strong physical way of expressing it (p. 81).

Several frustrations that may affect children with physical disabilities are clear in Long's list, while Linton describes a distinctive pleasure of using a wheelchair. Experiencing pleasures and frustrations are universal aspects of human life, however, we can glean some common-sense approaches that can reduce frustrations. Having equal access to rooms and facilities, providing furniture for others to sit on to facilitate eye-level interaction, plus ensuring control over objects (e.g., televisions, radios) can reduce frustration with the environment. Other frustrations may relate to coping with one's body and function, which necessitates the empathy and non-judgment of others.

Common-Sense Approaches

Creating barrier-free environments that facilitate freedom of movement and access to materials and activities is essential for students with physical disabilities. In addition, a direct approach to addressing questions and curiosity about variations in behavior and appearance is most useful to reducing fear and nurturing belonging and understanding. Classroom adults and peers should attend to talk and interaction about disability, impairment, and difference. Children may demonstrate curiosity about a classmate's variation in physique or behaviors such as tics, and it is not helpful for questions to be avoided, discussed secretively, made "taboo," or overly emphasized. Encouraging adults and children who have questions to ask respectful, direct questions of the person of subject is recommended. Simultaneously, all should learn to respect a person's option to decline to answer. Explicitly teaching responses such as "I don't know you well enough to answer that"; "I'm not comfortable telling you"; or even "That's not your business" can facilitate respectful ways to deal with curiosity. Other precepts useful for addressing needs of students with physical disabilities follow.

1. In the classroom, desks and other furniture should be arranged so that students with physical disabilities can move around the room comfortably, with full access to peers and class materials. Consistency in the layout of furniture and locations of materials is recommended to support the independence of students with visual impairments.

2. When planning off-campus events such as class trips make sure that the transportation and buildings at the destination are barrier free. An in-person "walk-through" of the site by someone who knows the needs of the members of class is best, but a detailed conversation with a site employee may also suffice. Pay careful attention (or be sure to ask about) access to parking lots, walks, ramps, entrances and exits, steps and stairs, floor surfaces, restrooms, water fountains, telephones, elevators, switches, and controls.

3. When planning a recreational or social event, care should be taken to choose an activity with a facility that is generally accessible to all, and which can be enjoyed by all in some facet. In planning a ski trip or trip to an amusement park, for example, a facility that offers accessible, alternative, and/or adaptive activities should be chosen. For students with significant healthcare or mobility needs, advance notice to the family can facilitate careful thought about preparation to travel to an unfamiliar place.

4. Students who use manual wheelchairs may appreciate some help on difficult terrain—for example, steep uphill or downhill grades, dirt or stone paths, high-pile carpeting, pot holes, or curbs. However, peers, teachers, and other school staff should never push a classmate's wheelchair without the occupant's permission, and should always discuss the wheelchair occupant's preference for "cruising speed" and destination.

In general, though, school and classroom members should be provided with an opportunity to learn how to operate the chair safely, which can allow for natural, spontaneous, and safe invitations or offers to give a push.

"Persons accustomed to pushing shopping carts tend not to realize that wheel-chairs are less steady and that hitting even a small bump in the ground can send the occupant face down on the pavement" (Maloff and Wood, 1988: 11). Wheelchairs are heavy and can gain quick momentum on a hill. In addition, people should become familiar with the dimensions of the chair—for example, with how far the footplates protrude out the sides. Maloff and Wood (1988) cited the thoughts of one wheelchair user:

> I hate being pushed in malls. The person pushing me always underesti-mates how far my feed stick out and my foot plates mash people in the ankles. I spend the whole time getting looks and saying "I'm sorry, I'm sorry, excuse me, I'm sorry." It's embarrassing (pp. 11–12).

To avoid embarrassment and injury, people pushing an occupied wheelchair for the first time need to become familiar with the experience slowly and cautiously.

5. In the school cafeteria, in a restaurant, or at a party, it may be difficult for a classmate with motor or craniofacial impairments to eat or manage certain foods because of difficulty moving his or her arms or hands or mouth. Once help is accepted, the meal becomes more manageable if the meat is precut and put back and reshaped, corn is sliced from the cob, or fruit is separated from its rind (Maloff and Wood, 1988).
6. Remember and teach that wheelchairs, crutches, and other orthotics are personal items and should not be touched without their user's consent. Putting an item such as food or a book on the arm of wheelchair is an invasion of the user's privacy.
7. Welcome and become familiar with assistive devices. These include standing tables, wheelchairs, head sticks, protheses (devices designed to replace, partially or completely, parts of the body), and orthoses (devices designed to restore, partially or completely, a lost function of the body, such as crutches or braces).

About Low Vision

The idea of blindness can be both frightening and fascinating for young-sters, who often draw upon images of dark glasses, a white cane, a tin cup, a guide dog, and perhaps a sad life of hopelessness and eternal darkness to form attitudes. The thought of becoming blind may frighten youngsters par-ticularly because of their familiar experiences of stumbling and groping for articles in the dark or perhaps wearing a blindfold—experiences leading to the assumption that blind persons live in a dreary, black world. However, in reality, only about 10% of all persons labeled as blind are totally without sight (Scholl, 1986). Most are able to respond to some visual stimulation such as light and dark, or shadows or moving objects, providing them with some functional vision.

Blindness occurs rarely in children—in fact, in less than 0.10% of the population between the ages of 6 through 17. Thus, the chances are high that a student with blindness will be the only one in his or her school or even community with that disability. The low incidence of blindness in the young can isolate that student, and encourage stereotyped misconceptions on the part of others. As one student with blindness urged, "I want you to know you shouldn't overreact when you see people who are blind, but just treat them like anyone else" (Westridge Young Writers Workshop, 1994: 88).

Depending on the degree of sight, students may benefit from materials with enlarged print, strong contrast, Braille, or audio information. Such students are usually able to distinguish the presence or absence of light, and any partial vision may be used effectively for learning mobility and orientation as well as other tasks. Students considered to be partially sighted or with low vision may be able to see objects near at hand with magnification and proper lighting.

Dispelling common myths about blindness and low vision can facilitate a young person's positive experience in school. Common myths include the notions that persons with blindness cannot see at all, are all alike, have exceptional musical ability and hearing, live a sad and melancholy life, are dependent and helpless, are led around by their guide dogs, need to be taught Braille, and have become blind as punishment for past sins. Although blind persons may rely on hearing to gather information about their surroundings more readily that those with sight, and therefore might be more attuned to aural information, blind persons do not have super hearing, nor does the degree of hearing increase as a result of visual impairment. As for all, some persons with blindness do have natural musical talent, and some develop a musical talent, but a lot do not. In addition, those persons with blindness who use service animals, such as guide dogs, are not taken where they want to go by their dogs. The individual determines the destination, using the dog as a prosthesis and protection against unsafe areas or obstacles.

As with most disabilities, the effect of blindness on an individual's activities and interactions with others relies on several factors such as whether the disability is congenital, adventitious, stable, progressive, hidden, or visible. Because one's motor development depends highly on one's sight, youngsters born with blindness or a visual impairment may have difficulty with both gross and fine motor performance. Their physical skill and coordination deficiencies are generally attributable to environmental factors—for example, seldom being encouraged to participate in physical activities or being unable to see small objects and thereby lacking practice in picking them up. Children should be encouraged to explore their environments and be provided with ways to learn how to orient themselves.

Experiencing Blindness or Visual Impairment

Attending to experiences of blindness invites opportunities to consider varied perceptions of the world around us. Hull (1990), for example, made the following entry in his diary:

> For me, the wind has taken the place of the sun, and a nice day is a day when there is a mild breeze. This brings into life all the sounds of my environment. The leaves are rustling, bits of paper are blowing along the pavement, the walls and corners of the large buildings stand out under the impact of the wind, which I feel in my hair and on my face, in my clothes. ... The sound of the wind creates trees; one is surrounded by trees whereas before there was nothing. ... The misunderstanding between me and the sighted arises when it is a mild day, even warm, with a light breeze but overcast. To the sighted, this would not be a nice day, because the sky is not blue (p. 16).

In a later work, he notes a difficulty related to the mystery of non-verbal communications, in which not being able to see and respond to a smile or a wink affects interactions. Hull (1990) explains:

> Nearly every time I smile. I am conscious of it. I am aware of the muscular effort; not that my smiles have become forced, as if I were pretending, but it has become a more or less conscious effort. Why is this? It must be because there is no reinforcement, there is no returning smile, I am no longer dazzled by a brilliant smile. I no longer find that the face of a stranger break into sudden beauty—and friendliness. I never seem to get anything for my efforts. Most smiling is responsive. You smile spontaneously when you receive a smile. For me, it is like sending off dead letters. Have they been received or acknowledged? Was I even smiling in the right direction? In any case, how could my sighted friend make acknowledgment? (p. 34).

The ability of any individual with blindness to deal with the physical and social environment is affected in various ways. Because blindness affects one's ability to read print, maneuver in unfamiliar places, and perceive one's surroundings and such social cues as a wave, a wink, a smile, or other type of body language, some particular considerations in developing inclusive school environments are recommended.

Common-Sense Responses

In order to interact with persons with blindness in positive and meaningful ways, students should consider the following ten common-sense approaches:

1. When greeting and communicating with students with blindness, remember to communicate verbally. It is important to identify oneself

and anyone else present—for example, "Hi there, this is Susan and on my left is Joe Smith." Obviously, it is rude to leave an individual standing alone without telling him or her.

2. Class members should know that it is considered extremely rude to gesture about a classmate with blindness to someone else who may be present. In addition, it is possible that the gesture would not be as covert as some might think: persons with blindness are often able to perceive movement and can become aware of other cues that signify such gestures.

3. Using common words such as "look" and "see" to refer to experiences will generally not be received offensively. These words are part of everyone's vocabulary, and it is fine to ask a student with blindness if he or she watched a television show or saw so-and-so at the mall. Expressions such as "I'll see you later" are also perfectly acceptable.

4. Class members should practice being relaxed and smooth in supporting a classmate with blindness to move from one place to another if asked. The proper "sighted guide" method involves the student with blindness taking the other's elbow. This enables guidance, rather than propelling or leading, as the person being guided responds to the motion of the guide's body to tell when curbs, steps, or turns are encountered. To avoid surprises, the student being guided may walk a half step behind the guide. It is useful for the guide to verbalize specific directions and numbers such as "on the right two yards" or "seven steps including the landing." Providing precise directions are much more useful than indications such as "over there" or "go straight up and to the left." When facing someone using directions such as right or left, one should specify whose right or left. Pointing is not likely to help.

5. Guiding others' hands to objects can be useful, but a person who may need help to locate an item should be asked if help is needed and whether it is alright to guide his or her hand—do recall that some objects may be more visible than others based on color or the degree of light available, so help may not always be needed. It is not acceptable to grab someone else's hand without asking permission. However, the more familiar class members become with one another, the more they will know about the kind of help that is desired and hence, received favorably as a friendly gesture even without a request. Teaching and using clock directions can help describe more detailed directions or where things are placed in close relation to the person (i.e., in reaching distance). For example, "the pencil is at 3 o'clock." When offering seating to a student with blindness, it can be useful to ask to place his or her hand on the back of the seat and state which way it is facing.

6. Students with visual impairments should be oriented into classrooms and other settings in the school environment, such as restrooms,

the cafeteria, and other common areas. This may be done by either walking around and pointing out places of interest with the student as he or she explores, or guiding the student to varying places. It is best to ask the student how she or he would like to get to know the environment, as it is likely that he or she has a method to remember where things are. These include counting paces from a landmark such as the doorway or a desk or learning the setup of a room by which areas are proximal to others.

In classrooms, students should be made aware of the shape of the classroom setting and where landmarks such as student desks, the teacher's desk, bookshelves, permanent cabinets, lockers, wastebaskets, windows, pencil sharpener, doorways, windows, bathrooms, chalkboards, and bulletin boards are situated. Wastebaskets and other movable items should be made stationary or kept in the same place. The student should be told of any changes in a familiar furniture arrangement. In the restroom, the student with a visual disability should be guided to the location of the toilets, urinals, sinks, towel dispenser, or hand dryer, especially if he or she is in a public facility such as a restaurant.

7. Be familiar with adaptive aids. These include bookstands, Braille writers, large print books, a cane, raised line paper, writing guides, audio books, and talking calculators. There is an ever-increasing array of software that reads digital text aloud.

8. A visually impaired student may sometimes be unaware of events in the classroom, and sighted student seated nearby might inform him or her of helpful, non-verbal cues such as a smile, a facial expression, a nod or a beckoning arm movement. Persons with visual impairments enjoy a wide variety of recreational activities including bowling, movies, and the theater. Just like describing non-verbal gestures, a friend can quietly describe some of the purely visual aspects of movies and theater performances such as opening scenes, costumes, and special effects.

9. Sometimes, youngsters with visual impairments may exhibit certain mannerisms mistakenly called "blindisms," for example, head rolling, eye poking, rocking. However, many children people with blindness do not develop such mannerisms. As for many differences in the ways people appear and act, class members should be encouraged to practice acceptance. The teacher may help the students reduce these mannerisms.

10. Students should be reminded that a service animal is working and responsible for the safety of its master. Such a dog is not just any pet and should not be distracted or petted without the consent of its master, especially while it is working.

Communication and Social Behavior

There are several kinds of human variations and impairments that become disabling primarily in social contexts, meaning those that require communication and interaction with others. Students who are d/Deaf or hard-of-hearing and those with communication disorders may require accommodations to provide or enhance their access to classroom talk and to facilitate their ways of communicating with others. Students identified as on the autism spectrum, or with emotional or behavioral disorders may also have ways of communicating, acting, and interacting that become disabling in the school setting. Descriptions and common-sense approaches for students who require considerations and accommodations to participate in social contexts follow.

About Students with Disabilities in Communication and Speech

Addressing the social disablement of students with variations or impairments in speech, language, and communication is especially important because of the size of this group. Statistics indicate that as many as 20 million Americans have a speech, language, or hearing impairment that affects communication. Because verbal skills are so highly valued, language-judged deviant is quickly targeted for therapy and intervention, and oral methods (practices that focus on speaking and understanding speech) for d/Deaf children and adults often become the priority in school instruction. It is important to remember, however, that there are many ways to communicate, and members in a community should be recognized, valued, and enabled to participate in social contexts.

Speech impairments refer to difficulties or variations in the production of speech or articulation. *Verbal non-fluency*, or stuttering, is the involuntary repetition or prolonged pronunciation of sounds, syllables, words, or phrases, and may also be marked by involuntary hesitations or pauses during speaking, which are sometimes referred to as "blocks." *Lisps* occur when one sound is replaced by another during speech production, and can relate to the formation of or control over the lips, tongue, teeth, or mouth and jaw. A common type of lisp is the replacement of the /s/ sound, with a /th/ or /sh/ sound. Other impediments to speech production can relate to conditions and impairments that affect muscle control and air flow, notably in those with cerebral palsy.

Communication disorders affect the way a person understands or expresses language relative to meaning. *Aphasia* refers to the loss of ability to comprehend or express language, and can affect language received aurally or expressed in speech; and/or in understanding or producing writing. Aphasia can be caused by lesions on language-related areas of the brain, or by other neurological disorders. There are many clinical terms to describe symptoms, causes, and varieties of aphasia, but for the general school practitioner, some common-language descriptions of symptoms are more useful. Symptoms may include difficulty with "finding" or choosing words to express oneself; with making speech cooperate with one's thoughts; and/or with comprehending the meaning of received language. Aphasia can be an underlying cause of learning disabilities, especially dyslexia; or aphasia may be a symptom of a learning disability.

Children with speech and communication impairments often work with an SLP to learn how to form different sounds and/or to develop strategies that can aid in getting through a "block" or finding a word. Care should be taken to follow professional practices in diagnosing speech and communication disorders. Because speech and language are intrinsically related to culture and access to oral language, many variations in speech are not indications of impairment or disorder. Accents and pronunciations related to speaking languages and dialects other than Standard English (in the United States), for example, should not be confused with impairments. Similarly, the need for more time than expected to understand, select, and say words can also relate to a student's prior learning or simultaneous use of another language, and is not an indication of disorder or impairment. In addition, children of Deaf adults, or CODAs, may have learned to say sounds and words without substantive access to speakers on whom to model their talk or who might guide children to "correct" pronunciation.

Experiencing Speech and Communication Disabilities

The problem with having speech impairment is often less that one has difficulty communicating than society's stigmatizing attitudes toward what it considers to be unacceptable speech. When a person with a stutter, for example, says "h-h-h-hello," the listener usually understands. A disabling context arises, because the interaction is uncomfortable for the speaker, the listener, or both. Similarly, a person with a communication disorder can usually participate in communicating, but allowing more time than usual for interacting or the use of supplemental methods to communicate may be required.

Ruch (1967) listed three types of frustration that can arise from disability, and relate strongly to communication: environmental, personal, and conflict. Among the frustrations found in the environment are those related to one's social surroundings. During interaction, the attitudes and reactions of others have an enormous influence on an individual with so-called "deviant" speech. Carlisle (1985) observed:

> ...very few people know what to do when faced by a stutterer. Do you help the guy begin his word? Do you look at him or look away as he struggles to speak? Do you smile encouragingly or sit there like a stuffed dummy? Most people look away, fidget, and think of ways to escape; or if they happen to be holding a cup of coffee, stir it as though their lives depended upon it. Many just flee in alarm as the stutterer battles his way to the next word. Few know what to do, and uncertainty breeds fear with

its attendant tension, rudeness, hostility, and anger. To make matters worse, stutterers' own attitudes vary; some welcome help and others do not. All stutterers welcome a little patience (p. xi).

Although this example relates to stuttering (verbal non-fluency), others who require more time to communicate or are difficult to understand experience similar environmental barriers.

To avoid or counteract frustrations related to communication, teachers and class members can slow down the speed of talk, demonstrate willingness to repeat talk, and take the time to listen. These changes in talking and listening behavior, along with other common-sense approaches listed later, can significantly reduce the frustrations experienced by a child with a speech or communication disability.

About Students Who Are d/Deaf or Hard-of-Hearing

Being d/Deaf or hard-of-hearing (HOH) becomes apparent in social interaction, and may affect a student's understanding of language, mode of communication, and development of identity and culture to varying degrees. The nature of a related disability depends on many factors including the degree of hearing possessed, the age or period of development during which hearing loss occurred, and the response to deafness chosen by the student and family. Teachers and other school professionals need to be aware of the wide range of options in language, hearing, and interventions available to children who are d/Deaf/HOH, and to be respectful of student and family preferences. Two general areas of consideration are whether to enhance a child's access to auditory information with technology and which communication mode or modes to use and teach.

There is a wide range of technologies that can enhance a child's access to auditory information, which include hearing aids, amplification devices, and cochlear implants. The type of technology chosen, if any, depends on the kind of hearing loss and the choice of the family.

Conductive hearing loss relates to an interference in the middle or outer ear and can usually be addressed by medical treatments to remove or relieve whatever is interfering with the conduction of sound—possibly fluid, wax, a tumor, or another foreign body. *Sensorineural hearing loss* relates to problems in the cochlea or auditory nerve and is not medically treatable. However, hearing aids and amplification devices can be useful. Hearing aids are worn by the child on one or both ears and amplify sounds and improve auditory discrimination (the ability to differentiate sounds). Many styles and models of hearing aids are available, and include those placed almost entirely inside the ear, which can be nearly invisible, as well as those that are visible on the outside of the ear, usually as a cuff that forms to the curve behind the outer ear. There are also a variety of amplification devices, such as FM systems, that allow a speaker to wear a microphone in order to broadcast her or his voice to a receiver worn by another person. In the classroom, this can improve a HOH student's access to teacher's directions amidst background noise made by moving chairs and classroom chatter, for example.

Among the more controversial issues for d/Deaf/HOH persons is the cochlear implant, which is a technology developed to provide access to auditory information for those with severe or profound sensorineural hearing loss, but whose auditory nerves function in whole or part. Cochlear implants do not amplify sound, but electrically stimulate working auditory nerves inside the cochlea to produce auditory information. A cochlear implant has both internal and external parts. A stimulator is surgically inserted into the cochlea, which connects to a magnetic receiver that is implanted in the skin of the skull, just above the outer ear. The external microphone, speech processor, and transmitter—contained in a single, connected apparatus—is then magnetically attached to the implanted receiver. Cochlear implants destroy any natural hearing, and as with any surgery, implantation carries risks. These include infection, nerve damage, and paralysis of the face. Those with implants experience a very wide range of outcomes. Some recipients, especially those who developed language before hearing loss and very young children who initially develop language with an implant, regain or gain significant access to auditory information and speech. Others gain minimal access and the surgery can fail entirely, for others. Among the considerations in gauging the success of an individual's cochlear implant are the availability and quality of the speech-language therapy that follows surgery and the preference of the individual to be part of the "hearing world" and adhere to the therapeutic routine (Kelsay and Tyler, 1996; Schramm, Fitzpatrick, and Seguin, 2002).

The central controversy surrounding cochlear implants relates to a second broad consideration for d/Deaf/HOH children regarding the mode of communication chosen and taught. Members of Deaf culture identify themselves primarily by the use of signed languages—ASL in the United States. As with other cultural groups, aspects of shared history, relations to the "hearing world," and the lineage of ASL connect Deaf people to one another, and many see the use and proliferation of ASL as an affirmation of a positive linguistic and cultural identity (Padden and Humphries, 1988; Rosen, 2006). Because cochlear implants are recommended for persons with profound or severe hearing loss— the same group who might otherwise communicate with ASL—some members of Deaf culture see the implant as a threat to their community and culture (Aronson, 2000). It is more likely that a deaf child with Deaf parents will be encouraged to use ASL, but the majority of profoundly deaf children are born to hearing parents, and fewer than 30% of their families use signed languages regularly (Gallaudet Research Institute, 2003).

The National Association of the Deaf (NAD) (2000) opposes the characterization of cochlear implants as a cure to deafness, and due to the variability of success rates, cautions professionals and parents against the automatic implantation of young children and the setting of therapeutic goals that relate only to hearing and speaking. Children who receive implants are encouraged to develop and practice ways of communicating using hearing and speech, and discouraged to use or continue to use other methods, including ASL. In the longer term, an implanted child may not develop hearing useful to understanding speech and language, and being denied the opportunity to learn ASL or other methods of communication during critical periods for language development can have serious impact on a child's development of literacy.

This brief overview of considerations surrounding d/Deaf/HOH children demonstrates the multiple and complicated possibilities and decisions families face with regard to communication mode. It is essential for teachers and school professionals to work with families to understand their ways of communicating, their desires and expectations for their child, and to respect and observe the choices they make. The following list provides descriptions of possible modes of communication.

1. *American Sign Language* is a signed *language*, which means it has an established shared vocabulary and follows standardized rules of grammar and syntax. ASL is performed by using one or both hands and fingers to make distinctive shapes and movements in specific locations relative to the body. Its rules of syntax are reflected in spatial position, orientation, direction, facial expression, and body position. The syntax of ASL is different from spoken and written English, so interpretation of ASL involves much more than "translating" word-by-word. Other nations and cultures also have signed languages, which include the French language, Langue des Signes Française (LSF); Spanish sign languages, with local dialects present in Spain, Mexico, and Columbia, among others; Australasian, in use in Australia and some parts of Asia; British Sign Language (BSL); and Israel, China, Japan, Pakistan, Belgium, Germany, Ireland, and Quebec, among many others, also have signed languages.

2. *Signing Exact English (SEE), Signed English, or Manually Coded English* (MCE) is performed using many ASL signs, but follows the syntax of spoken English.

3. *Finger spelling* is performed by utilizing manual hand signs for the English alphabet. Finger spelling is literally writing in the air; individuals spell out the entire conversation.

4. *Manual communication* refers to a combination of signed language and finger spelling; it may also refer to communication methods that rely on gesturing and pointing to symbols, typing, or writing.

5. *Oral communication or oral method* refers to the use of speech and speech reading as the primary modes of communication. The receptive component of the oral method is often called "lip-reading."

Kisor (1990) explains that the biggest problem with lip-reading is that many sounds look identical:

> *M, p,* and *b* are made by bringing the lips together. *T, d,* and *l* all take shape with the tongue on the roof of the mouth just behind the teeth. As a result, the words *bat, bad, ban, mat, mad, man, pat, pad,* and *pan* all look exactly alike. To the eye there is no difference between *s* and *z*. Sounds formed in the back of the throat are impossible to distinguish from one another. *Cat* and *hat* cannot be told apart, let alone *mamma* and *papa* (p. xii).

In fact, only 6–30% of speech can be read on the lips (National Child Traumatic Stress Network, 2004); therefore, being able to understand and respond to the context of talk is an essential part of making meaning from lip-reading. Developing speech in the oral method requires intensive therapy, as children must learn how to form their mouth structures and control airflow to make sounds, but may have limited ability to hear the sounds they make and self-correct.

6. *Cued speech* is a system of communication in which a selection of eight hand gestures made next to the speaker's mouth cue "listeners" to the initial sound or syllable being spoken. It is a method used to supplement and enhance the information that can be gathered from lip-reading. In ASL, the signs represent words, whereas in cued speech, the signs represent sounds.
7. *Simultaneous communication* means the combined use of speech and signed English.
8. *Total communication* refers to a philosophy that implies the acceptance, understanding, and use of all and any methods that may aid communication. Those utilizing total communication may use any of the above approaches in whole or part.

It is likely that a d/Deaf/HOH individual will use many methods to communicate throughout their lives, and that those methods will vary by context. It may seem like a total or simultaneous communication approach is the obvious philosophy for working with children in schools, because they seem to offer the most flexibility. School professionals should consider, though, that children may be working toward specific language development goals, and that the use of one method (or many) can interfere with development in another. It is very important to work with families and other professionals—usually audiologists or SLPs—to ensure that everyone is aware of how to best support the child to participate in school *and* develop language and literacy.

Teachers who plan to work specifically with d/Deaf/HOH students generally engage in specialized preparation, and specialized schools and classrooms are often recommended for students who are users of ASL. One reason for the recommendation and preference of a separate setting relates to language. Because deafness is relatively rare among children and the majority of teachers do not know ASL, students who use ASL may have better opportunities to fully develop their language when surrounded by children and adults who do. A specialized school or class may comprise children from a broader geographic area, therefore creating a Deaf community. From another angle, the inclusion of Deaf children in integrated school settings offers the opportunity for others to become interested in ASL and Deaf culture (Rosen, 2006), which reflects a value of pluralism generally espoused as a benefit and rationale for inclusive education.

About Autism and Autistic Behavior

Those "on the spectrum" are recognizable mainly through their social behavior. Although there is tremendous variation in degree and effect on the individual, children with autism, Asperger's syndrome, and PDD-NOS experience difficulty with verbal communication and/or understanding and responding "appropriately" to social cues, which can make verbal communication, social interaction, or group participation difficult or awkward. For example, autistic children and adults may not seek out or respond to others, make eye contact, or respond to emotion or other non-verbal cues (i.e., body language) and subtleties of conversational conventions. Needing to raise one's hand to speak in class or knowing when a pause in speech indicates a time to talk may be small mysteries to autistic individuals.

Those with autism often experience sensitivity to sensory stimuli such as touch, sound, or light, which makes some environments or interactions unbearable and a cause for reaction even when others are not affected. Other sensations may be sought through *self-stimulating behaviors*, which include repetitive body movements such as rocking or flapping one's hands. These are usually not harmful, but do attract the attention of others. *Self-injurious behaviors*, such as banging one's head or biting oneself, may be forms of self-stimulation, a response or reaction to a specific event, and/or efforts to communicate, but are harmful and require intervention.

Some autistic persons' preferences for following strict routines can make participation in variable situations difficult. Some autistic students may need the same, detailed regimen to be followed for specific activities; or may demand perfect adherence to the schedule for a day or week. Others tolerate change (or can learn), but may require plenty of warning and preparation when changes in schedule or people in an environment are imminent. Aversions to being touched or hugged and to interacting with others in play or talk are also associated with autistic individuals. Thus, "anti-social" behavior can also raise the concerns of others and can be especially difficult for families.

A final characteristic that is stereotypically associated with autistic persons is the presence of splinter or savant skills. *Splinter skills* are discrete abilities at a level considerably above the person's expected performance. Somewhat similar, those who demonstrate marked exceptionality or talent in an entire area of function may be referred to as having *Savant syndrome* (Young, 2005). An enduring public impression of Savant syndrome is found in the 1988 movie *Rainman* (Levinson, 1988), which featured actor Dustin Hoffman as an autistic character who possessed exceptional memory and ability to manipulate numbers. The terms "autistic savant" and "idiot savant" have been used to refer to the syndrome, but the prior is inaccurate, as savant skills have been noted in persons who are not autistic, and the latter is pejorative. Research into the meaning of savant skills in relation to general intellectual performance is ongoing. A critical view may challenge the underlying premise that intellectual performance is or should be inherently uniform. A variety of interventions for speech, communication, unusual social behaviors, and harmful behaviors are proffered to children on the autism spectrum.

Speech and communication. Individuals with autism develop speech to various levels of proficiency. Common speech peculiarities associated with autism include *echolalia*, the immediate or delayed repeating of sounds, words, or phrases; unconventional word use; and the production of unusual tones, pitches and inflections. Although some children with autism do not develop functional, or reliable, speech, many can learn to communicate through a variety of methods, including sign language. Other options include the use of augmentative or alternative communication systems, sometimes abbreviated by the acronyms AAC, AC, and AACS. *Communication boards* are boards with symbols, pictures, words, or letters to which an individual can point. Software that offers extensive databases of printable pictures and words are commercially available, as are palm-size devices that can display pictures digitally. Other augmentative/alternative systems utilize technologies that enable a person to communicate by typing or using a head pointer to select letters on a keyboard or screen. Communication may then be expressed in writing or "spoken" with a digitized voice. The use of alternative and augmentative communication technology is not exclusive to persons with autism, and is widely used among those with physical disabilities that affect speech articulation.

Learning to communicate with alternative systems takes time and requires skills such as controlling intentional movement, which may be difficult for people with autism (Broderick and Kasa-Hendrickson, 2006). *Facilitated Communication* (FC) is a promising practice in this regard, though has also been a topic of controversy. FC refers to a process by which a communicator is physically supported by a facilitator to enable typing, pressing, or pointing. The facilitator usually supports the arm and creates tension by gently holding it back, which allows the communicator to intentionally point or press. The relationship between a communicator and facilitator is also important, as the partnership can serve as an emotional support, which may help motivate an autistic person to communicate and increase her or his confidence in communicating.

Ideally, a goal of FC is for the facilitator to decrease the support over time as the communicator moves toward independence. Some individuals gain complete independence and others continue to rely on some degree of support beyond the training period.

According to Douglas Biklen, who is credited with popularizing FC in the United States, and coauthor Jamie Burke, a user of an alternative communication system who learned through FC, "controversy about the method of [FC] centers on the question of authorship" (2006: 173). Noted by Biklen and Burke (2006), there are studies that have shown that "a facilitator's physical touch of the typist's hand or arm may influence the person's pointing" (p. 173); an equal number of studies, however, *have* demonstrated authorship. In addition to studies cited by Biklen and Burke (see p. 173), the Academy Award nominated documentary *Autism is a World* (Wurzburg and Biklen, 2004) and the recent book *Autism and the Myth of the Person Alone* (Biklen et al., 2005; see also: Crossley, 1997) offer powerful, FC-user accounts of the benefit of providing the option of FC to autistic children and young adults. Although picture exchange systems (e.g., communication boards) offer an extensive selection of symbols that depict things, actions, and feelings, they do not offer communication as flexible as access to language does, and do not support the development of a sophisticated level of literacy. Therefore, offering a variety of approaches to communication can help to ensure that a child has the opportunity to develop language. Assessing each individual, rather than denying access to an approach, because it has not been proven for others, should determine whether the approach should be introduced or continued. *Any* given educational approach—related to autism or not—may work for some children and not others, and waiting for a resolution to a debate over a non-harmful practice is not a justification for denying a child access to a possibility.

On autistic behavior. It is important to differentiate unusual behaviors from harmful behaviors when considering interventions for autistic children. Some behaviors, such as having an attachment to an object or flapping ones hands occasionally, may be unusual, but not harmful. Trying to change these behaviors may take a lot of time and effort, but actually benefits others who are disturbed by the behaviors rather than substantively improves the life of the autistic person (the effect of stigma aside). Learning or improving behavior related to social interaction can support an autistic person to better participate in school and beyond, but it is important that the behavioral goals consider the desires of the child. A teacher or parent may want a child to initiate conversations or play with others more frequently, for example, but the child may be very satisfied playing alone. Indeed, school should provide opportunities for new experiences and meeting other children, but while introducing and encouraging an autistic child to try new things, she or he should not be wholly denied access to the activities—however unusual or "anti-social"—that are otherwise enjoyed. There are a variety of approaches used to teach desirable behaviors or change harmful ones.

Applied behavior analysis (ABA) refers to a child-specific type of intervention designed to identify undesirable and desirable behaviors, determine the environmental stimuli to which the behaviors relate, and then use rewards or positive natural consequences to increase desirable behaviors and eliminate undesirable behaviors or replace them with more desirable ones. Methods in ABA include *discrete trial training* and *naturalistic intervention*. Discrete trial training is when a child works one-to-one with a "trainer" on a particular skill in a controlled environment in which the training is the main event. The person is presented with a stimulus, prompted to respond, then rewarded for the desirable response—usually with a favorite food, object, or activity. Naturalistic interventions, including Pivotal Response Intervention (Koegel, Koegel, Harrower, and Carter, 1999; Koegel, Koegel, Shoshan, and McNerney, 1999), takes place in the context of a classroom or other daily activities. Trainers or teachers identify desirable behaviors—such as communicating, making choices, or playing with others—and prompt and reward the child as the opportunity to engage in a desired behavior presents itself.

Worthwhile to note, *Lovaas ABA*, named for developer, O. Ivar Lovaas, is a frequently recommended intensive program that utilizes the principles of ABA to improve speech and response to language, and reduce "autistic" behaviors. Francis (2005) describes:

> Skills in receptive/expressive language, attending to social stimuli, imitation, pre-academics (e.g. rote counting, knowledge of spatial relationships, etc.), and self-help that are deficient, are broken into discrete components. They are then taught on a one-to-one basis, in school and/or at home, using rewards for the successful completion of each step. Behavioural techniques of reinforcement (mainly positive), backward chaining (i.e. the process of teaching each component of a behaviour starting with the last step needed to complete the sequence), shaping, and prompt and prompt fading are used. Physical aversives are no longer employed. Initially, food and favourite objects are used as reinforcers, and are later replaced by more social ones, such as praise. Learned responses are repeated until firmly embedded. ... After the initial assessment, the children follow a comprehensive curriculum, tailored to their individual needs for approximately 40 hours per week with their trainers. Parents are also encouraged to contribute to the programme in order to achieve generalization of the skills learned (p. 495).

Generalization—the transfer of discrete skills to real-world situations—is one of the more important and controversial elements to consider in choosing an ABA approach, alongside the cost and intensity of Lovaas ABA, in particular.

The long-term effects of both discrete trial training and naturalistic intervention to increase independence are debatable, though ABA is generally recognized to have positive effects (Francis, 2005; McConnell, 2002).

Despite the dominance of ABA and other child-specific approaches used in a medical model, several inclusive approaches to addressing the social behavior of children with autism are available. Collateral skills interventions emphasizes training in skills that seem unrelated, yet lead to improved social behavior (McConnell, 2002). Practices in this category favor an inclusive setting (one in which autistic and non-autistic children learn and play together), in which all children learn and participate in more structured play activities. The opportunity to play with others in activities designed to facilitate interaction offers a welcoming, predictable environment, which can lead to increased interest in engaging with others in various situations. Somewhat similar, peer-mediated interventions involve the direct teaching of social skills to all children in an inclusive setting. Here, class members learn how to actively invite and involve each other in activities.

Sensory integration therapy. Attentiveness to the sensory experiences of persons with autism is sometimes necessary, and a variety of therapies are being investigated to respond to this need. OTs or other therapists may provide *Sensory integration therapy*, which was first proposed by A. Jean Ayres and aims to improve motor and academic skills by stimulating senses in ways that effect and improve neurological processing of sensory information (Ayres and Tickle, 1980). Sensory integration therapies range from offering deep-pressure brushing or massaging to exercise or movement protocols to special diets to immersion in environments that are flooded with sound and light (Baranek, 2002). Work on theories underlying the linkages made between sensory integration therapy and neurological effect is ongoing; as are investigations into therapeutic outcomes. As with any therapy, careful attention to the needs and characteristics of each individual is necessary to determine which approaches to introduce or continue. For the most inclusive approach to related services, efforts to implement therapies alongside and within general education curriculum and settings are highly desired.

About Emotional Disturbance and Behavior Disorders

Students identified with emotional disturbances or behavior disorders receive special services due to difficulty interacting within the social environment to an extent that interferes with learning. We often find emotional disturbance described through two subgroups consisting of externalized and internalized behaviors. Externalized or "acting out" behaviors are characterized by impulsive, antisocial, hostile, or aggressive actions directed toward others. Boys exhibit this type of behavior much more than girls and, therefore, have a higher identification, referral, and classification rate. Internalized behaviors, more prevalent in girls, are often characterized by social withdrawal, fear, immaturity, shyness, depression, an excessive craving for control and the development of self-directed symptoms such as cutting oneself, bulimia, and anorexia. Internalized behaviors are often hidden or masked (Gearheart, Mullen, and Gearheart, 1993; Hunt and Marshall, 1994; Smith and Luckasson, 1995). Although relatively rare among school-age children, there are a variety of psychiatric and psychological conditions that may underlie behavior and emotional responses that seem "disturbed."

Anxiety is a normal reaction to stress, but persistent or severe anxiety that causes intense fear and distress, which may include shortness or breath and increased heart rate, can disable children from participating in school. Two anxiety disorders of note include *post-traumatic stress disorder* (PTSD) and *obsessive–compulsive disorder* (OCD). PTSD is persistent or severe anxiety caused by trauma. Among children, it can relate to abuse, primary exposure to violence, or personal tragedy, such as a fire in the home, injury, or the death or injury of a family member. OCD manifests as involuntary responses to persistent anxiety, which may cause people to engage in irrational, possibly repetitive behaviors and/or strict routines. Obsessive–compulsive personality disorder, by contrast, relates to voluntary—though irrational—responses to phobias such as fear of germs or crowds.

Depression is characterized by persistent sad, anxious, hopeless, pessimistic, or "empty" feelings, or feelings of guilt, worthlessness and/or helplessness. Irritability, restlessness, fatigue, and loss of interest in activities that were once enjoyed are also symptoms, as are changes in sleeping and eating habits. Thoughts of suicide and suicide attempts may also indicate depression. It is normal for people to experience periods of depression, especially in relation to a traumatic event. More often affecting adolescents and adults, short-term periods of depression or "moodiness" should be differentiated from long-term, recurring, or critical depressive symptoms (e.g., suicidal thoughts or attempts). *Major depressive disorder* refers to persons who experience depressive symptoms to an extent that they interfere with interacting in life activities such as caring for oneself, working, or finding enjoyment in life. *Bipolar disorder*, sometimes called manic-depressive illness, is rare and is characterized by oscillations of extreme highs and lows. *Schizophrenia*, as well as Bipolar disorder, relates to the body's regulation of chemicals (neurotransmitters) in the brain. Among the school-age population, schizophrenia usually first appears in the late-teens for men and in the early twenties for women. The most common symptoms are disorganized talk and thinking, delusions, auditory hallucinations, and paranoia. Schizophrenia is *not* related to dissociative identity disorder, which is sometimes referred to as "split personality" or "multiple personalities" in popular culture.

Behavioral disorders. Who becomes categorized as "emotionally disturbed" due to a behavior disorder generally depends on many ambiguous factors. Society, schools, and teachers set standards for acceptable behavior and expectations for children and adults, and such conditions as the individual's age, the characteristics of the surrounding society, and the conditions under which behaviors occur each influence how people in authority judge the appropriateness of behavior (Smith and Luckasson, 1995). What is disturbing to one person may be viewed as independent, humorous, appropriate, or creative by another. Relevant to the problem of such a subjective category of disability classification, it is important to differentiate between children who demonstrate rational, purposeful, and communicative challenging behavior and those whose behaviors seem aggressive or reactive without an age-appropriate or contextually/culturally germane rationale (Ferguson, 2001).

Oppositional defiant disorder (ODD) is a psychiatric disorder marked by aggressiveness and a tendency to purposefully bother and irritate others. According to the *DSM-IV* (American Psychiatric Association, 1994), ODD refers to:

> A pattern of negativistic, hostile, and defiant behavior lasting at least 6 months, during which four (or more) of the following are present:
>
> 1. often loses temper
> 2. often argues with adults
> 3. often actively defies or refuses to comply with adults' requests or rules
> 4. often deliberately annoys people
> 5. often blames others for his or her mistakes or misbehavior
> 6. is often touchy or easily annoyed by others
> 7. is often angry and resentful
> 8. is often spiteful or vindictive

A further diagnostic note specifies, "Consider a criterion met only if the behavior occurs more frequently than is typically observed in individuals of comparable age and developmental level" (American Psychiatric Association, 1994). The presence and intensity of some oppositional behaviors are expected and typical at varying degrees throughout childhood and adolescence. A *conduct disorder* may include behaviors included in the ODD category, but is additionally noted by aggression toward people and animals, destruction of property, deceitfulness or theft, and/or serious violations of societal, school, or home rules (American Psychiatric Association, 1994).

Students who exhibit behavior disorders need assistance and guidance designed to help them learn how to cope with their environments by establishing positive interpersonal relationships. The goal of inclusive education is to provide an environment that will support the students' development of healthy behavior, enhance the student's feeling of self-worth, and enable the student to reach academic goals. Students seen as exhibiting emotionally disturbed behaviors need to be included in the mainstream of education for three important reasons: (1) to give them a chance to interact with youngsters who are not handicapped, (2) to provide constructive role models for behavior, and (3) to keep up academically (Kirk & Gallagher, 2009).

Common-Sense Approaches

It should be apparent that disabilities affecting communication and social interaction relate to a wide range and variety of access needs, impairments, or psychological conditions. Our grouping of common-sense approaches, however, relates to the similar attitudinal and environmental considerations and accommodations that are useful to facilitate the inclusive school experiences of those whose ways of communicating and interacting necessitate particular attention.

(1) Practice and Teach to Others Acceptance, Tolerance, and Empathy

As stated earlier, variation among humans is normal. In addition to acknowledging differences in appearance, senses, and communication methods, students and teachers need to be aware that people relate to people, objects, and events differently from one another, and some respond unusually or dramatically to sensory stimuli, group environments, or authoritative instruction. When necessary, these ways of responding should be addressed candidly in order to cultivate understanding and acceptance of difference. Class members should be made aware of noises or kinds of activities or interactions that may be uncomfortable for classmates, and helped to avoid them as a show of respect and empathy toward others. Conversely, class members should also be taught and encouraged to practice ways of interacting that are supportive and welcoming to each other. These are essentials for building a sense of *community* among class members, in which working together leads to the betterment of the whole.

Students with disabilities may more frequently seem to be at the center of class interruptions or adult support, and class members should learn to be tolerant during disruptive events. For example, teachers should have a plan in mind for how to deal with dramatic disruptions in the case of a student engaging in self-injurious or aggressive behaviors. Typically, two or more school professionals are available in a classroom that includes students at risk for these kinds of behaviors, and a plan that addresses which adults will manage the safety and security of all students should be agreed upon before an incident might occur. Following an incident, students should be provided an opportunity to respond to and discuss what happened. Keeping communication open and straightforward can reduce fear and stigma, as well as provide opportunities to help all students learn to cope with interruptions and unexpected phenomena, gain understanding about other people, and even develop ways that they can help, when appropriate. Academic learning is integral to school, but so is learning how to coexist respectfully in a diversified world. Adopting an open process for discussing unpleasant occurrences is not limited to disability-related interruptions and can be a useful method for addressing issues of teasing, name-calling, bullying, and other conflicts common in schools, as well. In an inclusive class, the occasion to address aspects of shared experiences toward nurturing acceptance, tolerance, and empathy for others should not be viewed as interruptions in curriculum, but as a central part of it.

(2) Accept, Teach, and Encourage Many Ways of Communicating

Be sure to explain to all class members the many ways individuals communicate, and help students and professionals to learn how to interact with communication boards, assistive or augmentative technologies, or signed languages. In addition, make sure that class members have access to and are comfortable asking a specialist, such as an ASL interpreter or communication facilitator, to help them communicate with users of these methods. To cultivate acceptance, provide plenty of opportunities for communication in a variety of arrangements. For example, ensure that there are times for one-to-one conversations, large-group, and small-group communication built into class instruction, and encourage social conversation during recess, lunchtime, and other non-instructional times. Some students' instructional goals may relate to engaging in social relationships and are, in fact, quite common for students labeled with emotional and behavioral disabilities and autism.

In teaching acceptance and promoting many ways to communicate, it is important to encourage students who use assistive technologies, such as hearing aids, FM receivers, and augmentative systems, to use them. However, it is also fairly common for children to reject technologies as they are getting used to them or in response to teasing, the curiosity of others, and stigma. Adults should be sensitive to the reasons children may reject their technologies in figuring out how to respond. Asking the family about their preferred response is essential, and might even help to reveal a problem with the technology itself. At minimum, teachers should gain basic familiarity with how technologies are powered and operate in case the need to help a student change a battery or troubleshoot arises.

(3) Slow Down the Pace of Talk, Pause Between Topics, and Take Turns

Slowing down the pace of talk can improve understanding for students who need time to process the meaning of language or who lip read, who may need a minute to respond to instructions, and is necessary to support accurate ASL interpretation. In addition, willingness to slow down the pace of conversation and listen more carefully offers a welcoming context for classmates with communication difficulties to join in. A student with a speech impediment, for example, may speak slower than usual, and it will put the speaker more at ease if class members simply accept the fact that the conversation will proceed slower and that there is no need to rush it. Students and teachers should remain calm and relaxed, listen attentively and become the kind of people with whom others like to converse.

Pausing after a classmate with speech impairment speaks or a communicator uses a board or other method can ensure that s/he has finished the thought. Similarly, pausing between ideas offers a natural moment for someone else to interject or offer a new topic. It is important, in other words, to *take turns* during talking, and making an effort to give another person a turn may be needed for those who need more time to "jump in." Pausing and turn-taking are relevant to children who need time to process the meaning of language, who have difficulty pronouncing and articulating speech, those who use augmentative communication or interpreters, those who need help interpreting social cues, those with anxiety, and even those who have trouble keeping quiet for long periods. Making sure that appropriate times to talk are made available can welcome all to communicate and reduce behavioral conflicts.

(4) Model and Teach Respectful Communication Practices

Direct teaching, or explicit instruction, on respectful communicative and interactive practices may help support the positive participation of students with behavioral difficulties or autistic students, and enhance the classroom community overall. Topics may include turn-taking and pausing, described earlier, and may also address other conventions such as initiating conversation, ending one, changing subjects, reading body language, or declining an invitation. Expectations about talking and listening within groups may also be a part of direct instruction on respectful social interactions. Other practices specific to providing access to speech and supporting those with communication disabilities follow.

Talk and questions should be directed to the conversation partner, even if an interpreter or other facilitator meditates the communication method. The interpreter or facilitator will not be offended if the conversers do not look at her or him. Respectful communication also includes attending to the needs of a listener. Even though a speaker's respect is communicated by looking at the person to whom one is talking, it is important to understand and accept that a communication partner may need to look at an interpreter or facilitator, and not at a speaker. Attention should be given to ways that show respect for people who read lips as a primary or supplemental way to understand speech. Body, face, and mouth position can make the difference between being understood or not. Speakers should avoid standing directly in front of a light source, because it darkens and obscures a face in front of bright light. It is best to face persons who are lip-reading squarely, and stand or sit at their level. Be mindful of turning to the side or backwards, and placing books, papers, or hands in front of the mouth. It is also advisable to avoid eating and chewing gum; and a teacher with a moustache or beard needs to know that facial hair often obscures the mouth, making lip-reading difficult. That is not to suggest that a teacher must be clean-shaven, but that he pays closer attention to making himself understood. Finally, it is important to speak clearly and a slightly higher volume than usual may help; but avoid yelling or over-exaggerating speech, as these cause contortions of the lips that make understanding more difficult.

Do not stop, correct, or interrupt a student with verbal non-fluency (i.e., stutter); and encourage him or her to talk as he or she naturally does, as trying to avoid or move too quickly through a stutter or block during talking increases frustration and anxiety and is likely to make communication more difficult. Unless the preference of the speaker/communicator is explicitly known, others should not finish a sentence or assume the meaning of a communication, even if the expresser has difficulty and even if the listener is pretty sure what the end of the thought will be. The "receiver" may be wrong, for one, and denying someone the right to his or her voice is simply disrespectful. Additionally, the way others respond to a person with a stutter will affect his or her speech. It is important to use good manners, hear the person out, avoid finding excuses to leave or end the conversation, and avoid offering unsolicited advice about the speech impairment (Johnson, 1956; Carlisle, 1985; Maloff and Wood, 1988; Lessen, 1994).

It is perfectly permissible to ask a speaker to repeat himself or herself, and requests to repeat or clarify should be respectfully obliged. Clarifying means to rephrase, shorten, or expand; repeating means to restate. Although repeating or listening to a repetition can take time, care should be taken to attend to the entirety of the initial exchange. Although a sentence or idea may be able to be clarified in fewer words, few of us want to participate in a "watered-down" conversation (especially in a mixed group in which others *did* receive the full communication). It is easier, in fact, for students who read lips to grasp a word's content or meaning in context rather than in isolation. Finally, learners deserve to understand the fullness of instructional talk, so differentiating between a need to clarify and repeat is essential for instruction.

(5) Be Aware of and Reduce Environmental Barriers to Positive Social Interaction

Try to reduce unnecessary sounds and noise pollution. It is easier for most to listen when noises and sounds in the atmosphere are reduced, and students who are hard-of-hearing can hear better away from telephones, radios, and other noise sources, including traffic sounds from outdoors and noise from a school corridor. When listening is not essential (i.e., during independent work or reading), some students may prefer wearing headphones that muffle sounds, turning off hearing aids, or moving to a quieter location. Sound-muffling headphones, or ones with music, can also support students with sensitivities to sound to feel comfortable in noisy classrooms and schools. Raising everyone's awareness to sources of disturbing noises and sounds is recommended, and can offer an opportunity to find creative solutions. Students might need to be reminded if they are unknowingly or repetitively making noise, most pertinent to students who are autistic or d/Deaf. A solution to reducing the excruciating classroom noise of chairs scraping the floor when they move, for example, is to apply felt feet to furniture, or even use "gutted" tennis balls to cover them.

The seating arrangement should be suitable for the students and conducive to the attainment of the program goals. Students who sometimes exhibit disturbing behaviors should be positioned for optimum interaction with their teachers and those peers who are appropriate role models, and may be sources of peer help. In addition, students should be provided enough space to feel comfortable. Creating space between children may help to eliminate pushing, shoving, or other contact that may lead to aggression or retaliatory behavior; however, it is also useful to teach how to interact respectfully when proximal to others. After all, it is not possible to avoid being near to others in life. School is a great context to learn how to behave, respect others' personal space, and deal with conflicts. An opportunity may be lost if separation is our only response.

Disabilities related to social interaction relate not only to methods of interacting, but also to access to interactions. Ensuring that school arrangements and environments are friendly to a wide variety of children makes interactions possible. Environmental barriers that can impede a child's access to other children relate to lighting, temperature and even the taken-for-granted presence of many students and teachers talking and moving. Especially, fluorescent lights can cause headaches and discomfort for many people; and the large buildings and rooms of schools, many older, may not have good climate control. It is not possible to eliminate all barriers, but being aware of them, reducing them when possible, and having integrated alternatives can facilitate the inclusion, hence social interaction, of many individuals. Being near a bright window or having an incandescent desk light can reduce the effects of fluorescent lights; dimming lights or turning them off when possible can also be helpful. Moving a whole class to an air-conditioned room or allowing the use of a small fan when it is very warm would be welcome by many, and may be a necessary accommodation for students with low thresholds for discomfort, as may be students with autism or emotional/behavioral disabilities. Finally, making sure to provide breaks, allowing individuals to take breaks, and offering an alternative, less noisy or less hectic setting in which a heterogeneous smaller group can socialize, work, or eat lunch, for example, can be helpful to facilitating inclusive school environments.

(6) Structure Class Activities and Routines for Positive Group Interaction

The pace of activity, talk, and the many explicit and implicit demands that are made of children in classrooms means there is a lot of information and even more rules to negotiate in order to interact as expected in the social environments of schools. Children and adults generally learn the variable expectations and rules of behavior in many different contexts through experience. As we encounter new situations in which we want to participate, we observe and adopt the behaviors of those around us. More experienced members of a group, such as adults and other children, serve as models or may explicitly guide novices to enact appropriate and expected ways of behaving and interacting. The age, family mores related to social behavior and authority, and prior experience of school or other group activities affects the kind of social rules and expectations that children will know and be ready to abide by when they join a new class.

To facilitate positive group interaction, all class members should have ample opportunity to learn the routines and expectations of a class, which may include: *procedures* for taking a turn to talk, asking questions, requesting help, going to the bathroom, taking a break, and accessing learning materials; *rules* that relate to behavioral norms, which often include keeping one's hands to oneself, using "nice" language, and being quiet when others are speaking; and *instructions* for engaging in particular kinds of repeated activities such as a morning meeting, homework review, putting materials away, entering and leaving class, being called to attention, and changing from one activity to another. To deter rule-breaking, teachers may specify types of rule infractions and the consequences, usually punishments, students can expect from a violation. In the same family as ABA, behaviorist approaches that rely on positive reinforcement may be used as a strategy to shape desirable behavior. Examples are: systematically praising by name all students who are sitting down as expected (and not those who are not); or noting the good behavior of students who raise their hand to speak. Ideally, students who are not sitting or raising their hand will begin to in order to earn the praise of an adult, though this approach is highly dependent on whether the indirect instruction is comprehended. Teachers cannot assume that others understand the "hidden" agenda. Systems including *token economies* and behavior charts provide a structure through which individual students or a whole class can earn tokens (such as gold stars, play money, or checkmarks) for predetermined desired behaviors and then exchange them for prizes, privileges, or parties—to name a few common rewards.

Before a systematic reinforcement method is considered, however, it is important to remember that in order for anyone to learn and abide by routines and expectations, individuals need to understand them, be able to perform them, and desire to be a participant in the setting to which they relate. In order to cultivate group understanding, adults and students should cooperatively develop classroom procedures, rules, and instructions. This can ensure that aspects of group participation are reasonable to all and that the language used is understandable to all in the class. It is important for class members, especially adults, to remember that learning and learning from mistakes is part of school and life. It is unreasonable to expect that individuals of any age or ability/ disability status will immediately learn and be able conform to all of the routines and expectations of a class based on a list of rules or single day of procedure-development. Commencing punishment or the denial of a "gold star" in the first days and weeks in a new environment can exacerbate undesirable social behavior if individuals feel as though they have already failed or disappointed, and is a sure way to squash a student's desire to participate. Students should be afforded time and positive guidance to learn and be able to participate in routines and expectations.

The type and topics of class activities have a tremendous effect on students' social behavior. It is important that instructions for each activity be provided, and that teachers or class members ensure everyone's hearing, understanding, and ability to abide by them. Offering instructions in talking and in writing, making sure to clarify understanding, and breaking down complicated tasks can be helpful. Adults should *expect* students to need direction and clarification as they engage in work, as some clarifying questions will not arise until the activities are attempted. Considering students' engagement and motivation with regard to class topics is also essential to reduce problematic social behavior. A teacher should provide challenging and interesting curriculum that is appropriate to the age and skills of students. Students who are engaged in activities that are interesting and that provide success are much less likely to present challenging behaviors. Activities and schedules should provide variety and diversity, be both active and passive, and take place individually, in small groups, and with the whole class. Varied teaching techniques, sports and other extracurricular activities, and interesting materials and resources, such as computers, help arouse and retain student interest. In addition, the instructional program should be appropriate to the student's need, skill level, and learning style. Offering subject matter that is relevant to students' lives and connects to familiar ideas or experiences is always recommended to cultivate engagement.

A final note on structuring a class for positive social interaction relates to schedules and social procedures. Having a consistent flow of class activities and implementing particular procedures for working with others can support students who require predictable activities, need to be alerted to changes from one activity to another, benefit from knowing the time parameter of activities to manage frustration, and help with interacting with others. Autistic individuals often resist changes in their routines, and those who experience anxiety or paranoia may be discomforted by novel situations. Knowing exactly how long they have to attend to a particular subject matter or kind of activity may support students who have low tolerance for frustration. Tolerating something displeasing can be easier when an endpoint is known and having warning about the end of an activity can help students who hate to leave work unfinished. Finally, some class members may need to leave class at scheduled times for health-related needs, supplemental therapies, or academic support. Having a consistent and predictable schedule can make the environment comfortable for many and reduce the amount or kinds of experiences students miss if they must leave the class. For students who need time to adjust to or get ready for an impending change, providing advance knowledge or alerts can be helpful. For example, a student or class may have a class schedule that they set up each day; be alerted to the imminent end or start of an activity and countdown to its close or beginning; or check off or manipulate a pictorial schedule to signify a change. From another angle, individuals may be enabled to work at their own paces if moving on too quickly causes distress.

Incorporating *cooperative learning* or collaborative work and teaching specific social procedures that support cooperation is highly recommended for cultivating desirable and productive group interactions. Cooperative learning is usually performed in small-group activities in which students are to learn from working together. It is often recommended that specific roles and tasks that relate to a whole product or process be specified in order to ensure that all members participate and benefit. The benefit of well-designed cooperative learning experiences is touted frequently as offering a most engaging form of school activity, since students must be active, as well as implementing a demo-cratic vision of classrooms as supportive communities (Johnson and Johnson, 1999; Slavin, 1999). Because the nature of cooperative learning incorporates role defining and purposeful social interaction, its structures are supportive to students who need help to interact, are better enabled to participate in working with smaller numbers of others, and who benefit from clear rules of interaction.

(7) Practice Respectful and Meaningful Individual Interventions for Undesirable Interactions

There are many, many reasons why students may not initially (or ever) adhere to the rules of the social environment of classrooms and schools. The develop-mental period of adolescence is virtually defined by the needs of its members to "test" rules and societal norms in order to define one's own place and identity in the world—often accomplished by dressing and talking in ways different from adults, challenging adults, or defying the rules of adult life in or outside of school. Most adolescents ultimately gain from participating in school, and therefore generally adhere to the rules that allow them to access school and avoid conflict with authority figures. Other children and adolescents, however, either do not or do not feel that they gain from participating in school and may engage in behaviors—purposefully and not—to avoid school, classes, or authority.

The vast majority of undesirable behaviors that arise in the course of a school day are minor and may be annoying to others, but do not indicate a need for planned intervention. Positive guidance or reminding of "the rules" will usually do; as will extending time to talk or time to cool down in the case of a conflict. It is a human virtue to offer acceptance and understanding for children and adolescents who may have acted or reacted unfavorably, but are simply having a bad day or involved in the throes of a peer conflict, which can be dramatic, but are usually not serious. Conflicts and undesirable behaviors are sure to occur in any school setting, and some immediate responses helpful to resolve them are listed in the following text.

A. Reminders of class rules that many students may occasionally neglect to observe may be noted aloud, and the class permitted to continue.

B. In the case of non-compliance with a direction, make sure students have had enough time to respond to it and allow them the chance to get it right before prompting them or repeating it. Additionally, make sure that the direction was clear. For example, saying "Why don't we all put away our notebooks?" or "I think it's time to put away our notebooks" are not the same as saying "Everyone please put away your notebooks." The first is actually a question, the second a comment, and only the third is truly an instruction.

C. Some negative behaviors are best ignored. By purposely avoiding eye contact and overlooking the student's behavior, the teacher may discourage the behavior rather than fuel it. The misbehaving student may be testing the teacher. By ignoring the behavior, the teacher gives the student time and a chance to reduce anxiety or anger. Of course, the application of the strategy of "planful ignoring" always depends on the situation. Never ignore behavior if the student is liable to harm to self or others.

D. Initiate a "signal system." Many teachers use a prearranged signal to alert a student or the entire class to unwanted or unacceptable behavior. Such signals may include turning the classroom lights off and on, raising a hand, sitting down in one's chair, putting a finger to the lips, or using other gestures to indicate a need to control undesirable behavior. However, remember that signals are usually most effective during the early stages of misconduct to keep small incidents from growing.

E. Individual oppositional or refusing behavior should be handled privately and quietly. An adult may go over to a child and address him or her quietly, or ask the child to meet in a private other area. In these cases:

○ The undesirable behavior should be described clearly to ensure that the adult's perception is accurate and that the student understands the problem. Because disruptions happen quickly and in the midst of other activities, it is not uncommon for students to be unsure of the precise problem noted by the teacher, or a teacher to be mistaken (Vavrus and Cole, 2002).

o The student should be asked directly what the class and teacher might do to make the situation better. In just a brief conversation, the teacher can help a student adopt reasonable changes that can be made on the spot.

o Adults should ensure that the student understands and is able to participate in the activity underway. Students may be overwhelmed by an activity and embarrassed or too upset to ask for help.

o The student should be offered the opportunity to start over or take a break to calm down and try again. The object may be to ask for help or clarification, to share an object of conflict, to raise a hand, or exchange a respectful comment or question for a disrespectful one. The meaning of the repeat performance is essential, and offering the opportunity to try again is not the same as demanding a student repeat a routine over and over as punishment.

o Offering a change in the nature of the activity or redirecting the interest of the student can be helpful.

o Individual students should never be made "responsible" for a whole class being punished. Avoid threats or punishments that require a whole class to "pay" for the undesired behavior of one or many. These kinds of practices are more likely to increase antagonism between an individual and adults, and can create conflicts and anger among students.

In the case of recurring undesirable behavior, intense or harmful ones, an assessment and intervention plan may be necessary. Behavior is a form of communication, and students may "act out" to express feelings or exercise control. Common communicative purposes of behavior include expressing frustration, anger, discomfort, or difficulty, seeking attention, avoiding a person or activity, and needing help. The most easily and quickly performed assessment can be done through open communication, which consists of talking with the student to try to figure out the reason for the behavior. Once the reason is established, alternative ways to express needs may be posed or strategies for coping with anger or frustration may be taught. Some coping strategies include:

o Asking for help
o Taking a break from the work
o Counting or breathing exercises to regain composure

- Alternating engaging in the frustrating task with an enjoyable one
- Temporarily leaving the environment to regain composure

In the course of a school day, students are posed with different subjects, kinds of activities, environments, and people. Any number of possibilities may make a situation uncomfortable for a student, leading to behaviors that permit him or her to avoid them. To reduce behaviors performed to avoid a situation:

- The student should be asked how to improve the situation.
- Effort should be made to emphasize the abilities and belonging of the student in relation to the setting or topic.
- Teachers should ensure that tasks are understood and manageable.
- Help should be offered and sustained until the student gains confidence in the activity.
- Consider providing a temporary alternative setting or format of assignment in which the student can gain confidence or tolerance for the activity or setting and return to the group.
- Consider that dealing with disciplinary consequences may feel more desirable than engaging in the activity or setting. Teachers should deal with the conflict in the situation and setting in which it occurred, as students will quickly learn how to repeat or escalate behaviors to escape to the principal's office, for example.

Although the desire for attention is often described as problematic within the context of schools and classrooms, needing affirmation from others and asserting one's presence and belonging in a group are hardly pathological. Children and adolescents who do not feel belonging are more likely to "announce" their presence in undesirable ways. Some helpful ways to instantiate belonging and respectfully reduce negative attention-seeking behaviors are:

- Make sure to emphasize all individuals' strengths in private acknowledgements and public praise. It is essential, however, for praise to be authentic and meaningful. If offered too frequently for the same thing, for every kind of thing, or without enthusiasm, individuals will not feel acknowledged.
- Offer ways for individuals to contribute to the class and recognize those contributions.
- Proactively call on, move near, or attend to students who may need help.
- Offer positive attention when appropriate, and create situations in which a student can be caught "doing good."
- Handle disruptions privately and quickly, which communicates that negative behaviors will not result in the public attention a student may seek.

F. Provide a program that allows students to "let off steam" in acceptable ways. Learning activities should provide relief from tension and exhaustion, which may provoke unwanted behaviors. A student who exhibits disturbing behaviors needs opportunities to drain off anger and frustrations in order to regain self-control. The youngster should have an opportunity to express his or her personal feelings openly to classmates or teachers.

G. Provide direct teaching and support. Sometimes problems arise in the classroom, because a youngster cannot cope with some aspects of the program. If this occurs, specific help—for example, working on the assignment directly with the student—may make what he or she thinks difficult easy. The teacher's focus should be on teaching the child to overcome the learning problem at hand, rather than on the student's misconduct.

H. Provide "teacher proximity." Teachers tend to sense potential problems, and a teacher's physical nearness at such times may help a student control his or her behavior. A teacher may avert an outburst in a stressful situation if the student draws reassurance from the teacher's nearness and support. The teacher can provide the student with a model of self-control, self-concept reinforcement, and on-the-spot encouragement.

I. A teacher can usefully anticipate and allow for changes in the environment. If the youngster is exhibiting a problem in his or her environment, it may be helpful to change that environment until self-control returns. The emphasis should be on ameliorating the unruly behavior and helping the child "get over it."

J. Reinforce and reward positive behavior. Rewards can communicate others' recognition and appreciation for desired behavior, which can encourage a child to "keep up the good work."

K. Avoid threats and blame. Some youngsters who exhibit disturbing behaviors interpret blame as rejection. Always keep the behavior and the individual separate: "I don't like what you are doing but I still like you." However, a teacher who states firmly the consequences of an action may help the child retain self-control. "Positive affirmation" of desirable student behavior builds positive self-concepts. Teachers who call attention to positive peer behaviors promote appropriate role modeling.

Disabilities Affecting Academic Performance

Schools are dynamic, social places and it is often difficult to precisely determine whether barriers to participation and learning in school relate to the social behaviors and interactions of class members or are attributable to differences among the ways learners perceive and respond to class instruction. A learner's ability to perform well on academic tasks expected in school has as much to do with one's particular abilities and prior experiences as the social environments and manner in which instruction is provided. Common-sense approaches for students with identified learning and intellectual/cognitive disabilities presented here relate primarily to accommodations that are often specific to provisions listed on IEPs.

Learning Disabilities

Learning disabilities, according to IDEIA, are permanent disorders that affect the manner in which individuals with average or above-average intelligence receive, retain, and express information. Students deemed learning-disabled constitute the greatest number of children receiving special education services. Biological bases of learning disabilities unknown, many critiques have been raised regarding the diagnostic process and the disproportionate numbers of students of color placed into special education under the category (Blanchett, 2006; Ferri and Connor, 2005; Losen and Orfield, 2002). An argument can be made that variations in learning are natural and the steep number of disability diagnoses indicates the inflexibility of school practices, more than the prevalence of learning disorders in children (Harry and Klingner, 2005; Reid and Valle, 2004). The nature of learning disability notwithstanding, students presumed to have learning disabilities may benefit from support in any or all of the following general areas: reading comprehension and spelling; written expression; mathematical computation; coordination; memory and recall; and oral language skills. No one person would experience all of these difficulties.

Public awareness about learning disabilities has increased over the past decade, and teachers are generally much more informed on the subject. Students with learning disabilities, however, had long been misjudged as lazy, stubborn, or "dumb" by teachers and classmates (Shapiro and Margolis, 1988). Because the category is embrace of many kinds of otherwise inexplicable learning difficulties, it is problematic to compile a list of "classic" characteristics. Further, learning always takes place in context, and how well a person can perform a particular skill strongly relates to their interest and prior experience with the content and the type of performance demanded. For example, a student's performance will depend on whether the task is to read fiction or expository text; to answer a question, write a response, or discuss an opinion. Several aspects of perception and academic performance are commonly assessed in children with learning disabilities.

1. *Visual discrimination* relates to distinguishing visual information. Related skills include matching sizes, shapes, and colors, and distinguishing letters and other kinds of visual information (reversals of letters, however, are typical for children as they are developing literacy).
2. *Memory* relates to being able to retain and recall visual, auditory, or textual information.

3. *Sequencing* relates to perceiving, organizing, or understanding patterns of colors, shapes, objects, pictures, or other kinds of information, including events, time, and quantity.

4. *Figure-ground perception* relates to distinguishing an object from a background. It can pertain to visual or auditory information. This kind of perception influences drawing, coloring, finding hidden figures, finding little words in big words, or discerning material on a crowded page. In relation to auditory perception, distinguishing the origin and volume or sounds is affected.

5. *Visual motor coordination* refers to synchronizing visual information with movement. It relates to tasks including writing, catching a ball, following an outline while cutting, tying shoes, buttoning clothes, reproducing a motor pattern, or skipping, hopping, dancing, or running;

6. *Auditory discrimination* is distinguishing features of sounds. It relates to hearing differences between different musical instruments or letter sounds, identifying where a sound is coming from, or noting subtle changes in tone of voice;

7. *Spatial sense* relates to locating and distinguishing objects in their dimensionality. It also includes perception of one's own location and movement in relation to other objects. We use spatial sense when, for example, we write between the lines on lined paper or move without bumping into things.

8. *Abstract reasoning* refers to recalling and organizing information in imagined scenarios. It relates to problem-solving, and organizing and integrating thoughts.

Common-Sense Responses

The best way to support students with learning disabilities is to be flexible. Learning disability varies from one student to another and, often, affects the same person differently according to the situation and task at hand. Flexibility in teaching practices is helpful, as is flexibility in day-to-day activities. The following suggestions can help teachers begin to create classroom environments that are supportive of students with learning disabilities.

1. *Instruct in varied formats.* Ensure that class instruction and directions are delivered in multiple formats. For example, provide directions aloud and in writing and offer many ways to present and respond to information and assignments.

2. *Provide flexible work environments.* Students may benefit from working on independent activities in an area designed to reduce distractions. For example, cubicles or desks with a carrel may be helpful, if desired by the student. By contrast, students may learn better with a

partner or in a group, where ideas can be presented and thought through by a variety of people.

3. *Get to know the individual.* Create a positive climate in their classrooms by communicating on a personal level with all students and attending to specific needs. Knowing students well enables teachers to develop personalized supports and creates a relationship wherein the student is comfortable asking for help and suggesting new ideas.

4. *Assign meaningful work.* All students should be provided with meaningful work. Even when offering alternate assignments, work should be on topic and appropriately challenging.

5. *Address student questions.* A teacher should address questions such as these from curious peers openly and honestly:

   o How come he's lazy and doesn't pay attention?
   o How come he's so clumsy?
   o How come she is allowed to use a calculator in math and we can't?
   o How come we get more homework than she does?
   o How come he gets good grades with such sloppy writing?

   Refusing to answer these kinds of questions can create suspicion among students and too-brief answers that simply indicate special education or special needs as a reason can lead to stigma. Rather than avoid them, these kinds of questions give the class a chance to discuss disability and diversity, or the broader idea of fairness. One approach is to conceptualize the concepts of equality and equity. "Equality" means everyone gets treated alike; "equity" means everyone gets what he or she needs (Welch, 2000).

6. *Provide supplemental information and organizers.* Students with learning disabilities (and many others) may learn better if provided supplemental instructional guides, outlines, and graphic organizers. For example, a list of the three or four major points to be covered that day with room for developing those points can help to focus attention on the main ideas. A written outline of each unit can also be helpful. Providing frameworks for organizing information, such as outlines with space for fill-in or grids for note-taking, can also be helpful.

7. *Provide clear and organized materials.* Assignment sheets and reading materials should have a clear font with a streamlined, straightforward format. Directions should be positioned prominently.

8. *Set students up for success.* Invite students' participation on aspects of the lesson in which they are likely to succeed. Providing discussion questions or challenging problems ahead of time so that a student can prepare a response may help build confidence and participation.

9. *Use technology.* Learn how to use different kinds of technologies for reading, writing, studying, taking notes, responding to assignments,

or examinations. Welcome and permit students to use them in and out of class.

10. *Be generous with time.* One of the greatest supports a student with a learning disability can have is time—for example, extra time to read, complete an assignment or test, or simply think about the task at hand. Make arrangements for providing extra time in advance so that the student's work is disrupted as little as possible.

11. *Consider self-concept.* School can be very unpleasant and demoralizing for students who have difficulty with academic demands. A critical element in helping the child with a learning disability is building a strong, positive self-image. Providing an understanding environment, honest praise, and tasks that invite success and progress can help build confidence in learning.

About Intellectual Disabilities

Students deemed to have intellectual disabilities are diagnosed based on their IQ and adaptive behavior. Previously discussed at length, both areas are highly subjective and relative to the social context and environment. Some general areas that are assessed in terms of adaptive behavior, however, are:

1. *Social behavior*, which includes interpersonal skills, interaction and play, dealing with conflict and interpreting social cues or body language.

2. *Intellectual and academic performance*, which includes memory, rate of learning, abstract concepts, and applying learned information to new situations.

3. *Speech and language development*, which includes articulation of speech, vocabulary, and understanding the nuances of meaning.

Common-Sense Responses

Mental retardation is diagnosed on a spectrum, from mild to profound. Accordingly, experiences of intellectual disability are tremendously varied. As with working with students with learning disabilities, flexibility in teaching and instruction and getting to know the individual are important guidelines. The following recommendations can also guide educators:

1. *Presume competence.* For example, engage in dialog, offer choices, and age-appropriate materials and activities.

2. *Teach, re-teach, and reinforce.* Offer opportunities and support for repetition, practice, and reinforcement when teaching a new concept or skill.

3. *Provide supplemental materials.* Offer encouragement and provide supplemental materials to aid attention, memory, and avoid frustration.

For example, a multiplication table, vocabulary word list, quick fact sheet, and so on.

4. *Be precise and detailed.* Students with cognitive disabilities may have difficulty reasoning abstractly, which can make it hard to make connections in concepts and instructions. Providing specific details on content and on instructions to complete assignments can be very helpful. Offering practical experiences to support the transfer of learning from one activity to another can also aid understanding and retention of knowledge and skill.

5. *Provide orientation to school and schedule.* Students may benefit from help finding the school office, school nurse, lockers, cafeteria, art room, music room, and lavatories, and so on. Reminders of school schedules and routines can also be helpful. Facilitating relationships and partnerships among peers with the same schedule can be a good way to ensure all students get where they need to go.

6. *Appropriate expectations.* Students with intellectual disabilities are at risk for having poor self-images and low tolerances for frustration. The development of poor self-image can relate to repeated failure on tasks that are inappropriately demanding. On the other end of the spectrum, when students are frequently posed with tasks that are too easy they may resist challenges and develop a low tolerance for frustration. Either situation can lead to learned helplessness, which is when a person acts incapable or waits for others to do for them, based on past patterns, usually of others helping too much. It is important that students are provided reasonably challenging and meaningful work and that they are provided enough support to learn, but not so much that they fail to develop a sense of self-efficacy.

7. *Facilitate relationships.* Another source of poor self-image among students with intellectual disabilities can relate to social isolation. Especially for adolescents, it can be difficult to establish peer relationships when social behavior and language may seem child-like. Teachers can encourage positive social relationships by making interaction a part of class instruction. Cooperative learning and other kinds of group work can help students get to know each other and provide opportunities for relationships and friendships to form.

Conclusion

There is tremendous variation among individuals with disabilities, and the practices that can best support students with disabilities in schools are equally varied. The information this chapter offers is merely a starting point for professional practice. Teachers are encouraged to see the information as useful to demystifying impairment and conditions that may otherwise seem foreign, frightening, or off-putting. The beginning practices should pose initial ways of thinking inclusively about educational practices. It is essential to remember that children are individuals, not labels. The best way to learn how to effectively welcome and educate students is by gaining specific knowledge through building relationships with them.

Part IV
Curriculum for the Inclusive Classroom

9

Curriculum Planning for Inclusive Teaching

The previous chapter offered common-sense responses to reduce a variety of access barriers that can be found in the physical and social environments in schools. In this chapter, we offer an overview of curriculum planning practices useful for inclusive teaching. Curriculum is a course of study in which learners engage over time, and generally refers to the range of classes or areas of study offered by a school or program. For teachers, curriculum planning involves laying out areas of study students will learn, learning teaching methods useful to students' learning in the areas, and developing assessments to understand how students are learning. We begin with a brief history of curriculum in special education, followed by an overview of key concepts in curriculum planning that emphasize Universal Design for Learning. We end with an overview of teaching practices useful to the development of inclusive curriculum.

A Brief History of Curriculum in Special Education

Over the history of public education, there have been many perspectives on the development of curriculum and purposes of schooling (Kliebard, 1995; Winzer, 1993). Special schools for blind and D/deaf children were established earliest, and placements for children deemed "mentally retarded," "backward," "incorrigible," and those grouped in other special education categories emerged over the nineteenth and twentieth centuries (Franklin, 1987; Winzer, 1993). Early special schools typically catered to teaching the orientation and communication skills useful, and often empowering, to students who were blind or visually impaired, deaf or hard-of-hearing, or both (Wright, 1999). Vocational training for boys, "home-keeping" training for girls, and the teaching of basic skills in reading, writing, and mathematics constituted the majority of curricula; the specifics were often determined by the kind and degree of impairment.

The Early Twentieth Century

Early special programs for children with physical and cognitive impairments were often located in hospitals and the curricula of educational programs revolved around the rehabilitation efforts of healthcare professionals. Itinerant teachers—those who traveled from home to home—were frequently the only access that some children had to school forms of learning, and they usually provided academic instruction that reflected the sequence of studies offered in school, but began and ended according to what the child could perform. Special classes within schools—as those for so-called "backward children" in the early twentieth century—had differentiated goals for its students. Separate classes for students who were unable to keep up with the students in the "general" class were created as places in which struggling learners could develop at their own rates, with the goal of "catching up" and rejoining the general class. Others followed a different curriculum that focused on vocational training or life skills. The school curriculum offered to children with disabilities was dependent on many factors: the kind and degree of impairment or disability, the availability and kind of education placement, and the prediction made about a child's future (Franklin, 1994).

Early decisions to segregate students with disabilities from same age peers were intended to be a positive shift for schools and children. The belief was that the specialized setting would benefit them and enable their academic progress. Favorable advances, particularly in reading instruction, for children who were struggling became available to schools. First used during the 1930s, the *Orton-Gillingham* reading program and a family of multisensory approaches to teaching reading emerged to help children for whom other approaches failed. The intensity and individuation of the programs, however, often meant that a child could make progress in some areas, but missed other experiences offered in school. The provision of separate kinds of education fueled the division made between curriculum conceived as "regular" and "special." Schooling became an enterprise in which special and general education operated as parallel systems, in which a child hoping to catch up in special education and return to the general setting never really did. Part of the reason was that a reductive view pervaded beliefs about teaching and learning in the early twentieth century. A reductive view purports that a student should master and be able to express or perform each component of a skill before moving onto a sequential step. Requiring learners to progress in lock-step fashion meant that most students in special education would not "graduate" to the level of their peers in the general classroom. He or she became trapped in special education.

The Advent of "High-Stakes" Schooling

Mid-twentieth-century thinkers advanced the idea of schools as competitive places that should strive to identify those "most talented" in order to provide advanced education for potential leaders who would win the Cold War for Americans (Rickover, 1957). Struggling students who could not keep up with increased academic expectations were increasingly labeled in a new category— learning disability—and placed in segregated environments. Labels such as "culturally deprived" were given to African-American students, and virtually any difficulty with the general curriculum became an occasion for separation into tracked programs. Even students in general education were divided into programs that prepared them for differing post-school opportunities such as college preparation, vocational or technical studies, or basic skills preparation. The parallel system of special education, alongside the development of educational tracks, became a way to maintain racial segregation in spite of the 1950s movement to integrate schools. Black students who had been in sub-par racially segregated schools found themselves again segregated, but this time for what were deemed psychological, social, cultural, and cognitive deficiencies.

In the mid-century, the practice of special education became marked by contradiction. Positive efforts to understand and address the needs of a new category of learning disabled children coincided with negative effects for Black children, who now had a new arbiter of separation to reckon with. Classes for students categorized "mentally retarded," "culturally deprived," and "emotionally disturbed"—majority Black—became places for racial containment (Ferri and Connor, 2005). Needless to say, curriculum in these classes did not seek the high achievement or academic advancement of their students. As with the "backward children" before them, new categories of disability and the resulting segregated placements trapped a new group of students in a parallel system.

The Passage of the EHA/IDEA

Throughout the subsequent decades, American society, especially parents, recognized the poor quality of education offered in segregated schools and programs, and students deemed "severely disabled" were still regularly barred entry into public schools. The passage of the EHA/IDEA in 1975 specified the right to a Free Appropriate Public Education for all and the provision of a continuum of special education services, in accordance with the Least Restrictive Environment. Remediating students' perceived source of difficulty continued to be the primary goal of special education, which reflected the medical model of disability. The cost to children was that the emphasis on remediating one source of difficulty and doing so in a reductive fashion trumped their access to learning higher-order academic skills (Heshusius, 1989). Pugach and Warger (2001) explain special education instruction focused on basic skills, teaching learning strategies in isolation from the curriculum, or offering a watered-down curriculum. Curriculum rarely provided content requiring deep understanding. In addition, all students were denied opportunities to interact with and learn from each other when those with disabilities were segregated for much of the school day.

Mainstreaming and the Regular Education Initiative

Early efforts toward inclusion provided part-time integration that offered children a mixture of social benefits of participating in the "mainstream" and developmentally appropriate academic instruction in a separate setting. In 1986, however, the Regular Education Initiative (REI), developed by Madeline

Will and issued by the US Department of Education Office of Special Education and Rehabilitative Services, challenged the assumption that the self-contained special education classroom was the most effective setting in which to teach students with disabilities (Stainback and Stainback, 1996). A lively debate between those in support of inclusion and major reforms to special education and those wishing to be more cautious emerged in the research field (Andrews et al., 2000; Paul and Ward, 1996). Among the top points of debate were (1) whether to conceptualize inclusion as a moral imperative, aligned with civil rights and a humanistic perspective on the role of schools in society (Gallagher, 2001) and (2) whether to wait for an empirical body of research demonstrating positive outcomes for students with disabilities before moving toward "full inclusion" (Kavale, 2002).

The public had also engaged in debate over the IDEA, with many concerned about a perceived drain on fiscal and human resources presented by special education. On public perceptions gathered in newspaper editorials, Rice (2006) describes the creation of an "us vs. them" dialog:

> Early presentations of special education set students with disabilities up against other children. The early view and regular repetition of this perspective … sets "special education" up for suspicion and resentment. In this narrative, education is a zero-sum game, with "winners" and "losers": the "contest" being between special and general education students (p. 38).

The idea of inclusion and the REI exacerbated the division made between "us vs. them." With schools positioned as places for competition among children, concerns about the amount of time a teacher would dedicate to one student at a cost to others were raised, as were questions about a general educa-tion teacher's responsibility to craft a separate curriculum for an "included" child (Yell and Drasgow, 1999).

The right to due process granted under IDEA led to further interpretation of the LRE and inclusion in the courts. As Yell and Drasgow (1999) and Kavale (2002) point out, the language in IDEA regarding the LRE was (and is) purposefully vague, leading to a "fuzzy" notion of inclusion that placed the impetus on IEP Teams to determine the practices that best fulfilled the needs of an individual and the intention of the law. Initial arguments for inclusion posed social skill development as a rationale for the importance of severely disabled students' inclusion in general education. A principle of the REI, however, also put forth the belief that all students, regardless of the nature of their differences, are more alike than different. Therefore, practices in general education could be developed to meet the needs of a variety of learners. Making accommodations for students with disabilities, offering modified curriculum, and supporting social integration emerged as promising practices for inclusion.

In addition to the proliferation of sourcebooks and practical ideas for providing accommodations to students with disabilities in inclusive classrooms, interest in the application of sociocultural learning theories—including those of Lev Vygotsky (Gindis, 1999; Mahn, 2000)—to special education arose. Theorists advanced ideas that learning is not accomplished by practicing discrete, reductive skills in isolation from their authentic application in social contexts. In fact, preventing a learner from engaging with ideas and activities more sophisticated than what she or he is able to perform, and denying struggling learners access to peers with greater competence and experience limits progress. Similarly, the denial of some kinds of instruction—especially in literacy—to students perceived to be incapable limited educational opportunity (Kliewer, Biklen, and Kasa-Hendrickson, 2006). Some aspects of poor achievement by students in special education settings were intrinsic to both their segregation and the presumption of incompetence that informed curriculum provided to them. In other words, the lesser curriculum provided in special education contributed to low achievement.

Contemporary Issues in Inclusive Education

Many stakeholders in education supported the REI for students with disabilities. However, the assumptions about disability and schooling that led to the creation of parallel systems of education were quite entrenched in both IDEA and the practices of schools that had become accustomed to segregation. The assumptions included:

- Students with disabilities are more unlike than like those not-identified (Will, 1986).
- Segregated systems best serve students with diverse needs (Ferguson, 1995; Skrtic, 1991; Slee, 1993).
- School must resemble assembly-line models of teaching that favor a one-size-fits-most delivery of instruction (Dudley-Marling and Dippo, 1995; Varenne and McDermott, 1998).
- The provision for a continuum of placements—which led to presumptions that students with severe disabilities were best served in the most restrictive designations (Taylor, 1988/2004).

Each assumption prevented the realization of inclusive education, despite the intent of the REI.

Burgeoning work in Disability Studies, as discussed in earlier chapters, began to point out the discrimination proliferating through the medical model, which had influenced the IDEA (Barton, 1986; Beratan, 2006). Early scholars in DSE challenged the presumption that parallel systems of education are an acceptable, democratic response to differences among children that might otherwise be anticipated as quite "normal" in the scope of human variation (Baker, 2002; Skrtic, 1991). The narrow—at best—and discriminatory—at worst—conceptualization of school practices as only being configured to meet the needs of a select segment of children signified a broader problem in school curriculum and teaching.

In addition to a need to reconcile a history of segregation that permeated public attitudes toward persons with disabilities, school structures, and educational policy, movement toward inclusion presents challenges to professionals in the field of education. For example, general educators feel unprepared to address the needs of students labeled with disabilities (Cook, 2002; McLeskey and Waldron, 2002; Mullen, 2001); special educators see challenges to support students' learning outside of specialized settings (Fisher, Frey, and Thousand, 2003; Jubala, Bishop, and Falvey, 1995); and both general and special education teachers negotiate new roles in collaborative environments (Boudah, Schumacher, and Deshler, 1997; Stainback and Stainback, 1996; Stanovich and Jordan, 2002; Walther-Thomas, 1997). The presence of such complex and layered barriers to inclusive education has resulted in slow change in curriculum offered to students with disabilities. Surely, progress is being made in all areas, but many erroneous assumptions about special education and the benefit of segregated environments continue to permeate school practices.

As Heshusius had noted in 1989, Tomlinson, in 2004, points out that special education curricula continues to be informed by a low expectation, favoring remedial over sophisticated curricula. For example, opportunities to engage in conversational discourse, inquiry, critique, and debate are often not provided in special education (Mariage, Paxton-Buursma, and Bouck, 2004: 542). Even in inclusive contexts, students labeled with disabilities are "more likely to encounter curricula focused on drill, seatwork, giving right answers, going over questions, reviewing, and other low-level tasks," as reflective of their placement in "low-group" and "low-track" general education settings (Tomlinson, 2004: 520). Lack of access to high-quality academic experiences exacerbates the division between learners deemed "special" and "general," and greatly affects students' opportunities for achievement and quality of life after they complete school. Further, the legacy of de faco racial segregation through special education is evident. The overrepresentation of Black students in special education and in lower-tracked classes is apparent, which increases the likelihood of a poorer quality of instruction (George, 2005; Losen and Orfield, 2002; Blanchett, 2006; Reid and Knight, 2006; Arnold and Lassmann, 2000; Artiles and Trent, 1994; Harry and Klingner, 2005).

A final issue worthy of note is the intensely competitive, high-stakes climate of contemporary public schools. Characterized by some as an "era of standardization" (Meier and Wood, 2004), policy-makers in the twenty-first century have put academic achievement at the top of schools' agendas. In the United States, the *No Child Left Behind Act of 2001* (NCLB) (PL 107-110) reauthorized the *Elementary and Secondary Education Act of 1965* with a strong focus on the accountability for academic progress made by children in schools. NCLB insists that schools are able to demonstrate students' annual yearly progress, as gauged by their performances on standardized assessments. An ideal of inclusive education coincides with increased standardization of curriculum, with complicated implications. For the first time in national history, schools are held accountable for the progress of students with disabilities on national achievement measures under NCLB. A move toward increased accountability aims to improve the achievement of students with disabilities by better aligning the curricular goals of special education with those of general education (Schumaker et al., 2002).

It is difficult to object to the idea that schools should be accountable for students' learning, and that a general standard for instruction is useful to developing a cohesive education agenda across the nation. However, the heavy emphasis on particular areas of academic achievement has underplayed other aspects of school and learning, leading to substantive reductions in students' opportunities to engage with the arts—areas where students who struggle with reading and writing might flourish—or social studies, for example (Eisner, 2005; Landsman and Gorski, 2007). In addition, pressure to keep up with a standardized curriculum (or what seem to be the demands of the next test students will take) can exacerbate negative attitudes toward the inclusion of students who struggle to "keep up" or present needs that have usually been addressed through individuated remediation. Ultimately, as Bejoian and Reid (2005) point out:

> The NCLB emphasis on standards as measured by regular and frequent standardized testing preserves the need to conform to imposed levels of performance and types of behavior, rather than to promote the acceptance and support of diversity. As a consequence, it promotes further marginalization and separation of those who meet the normative standard and those who do not (Allen [sic], 1999). (p. 224).

Efforts to positively affect the development of the *whole* child are potentially weakened in the relatively narrow aims and ways of measuring student growth in current educational policies and practices.

The educational implications of upholding students' civil rights in inclusive education are tremendous. Whereas IDEIA specifies the requirement to individuate educational programs for children with disabilities, a value for inclusion also supports their participation in classes where attention to other children's programs and goals are also necessary. To develop the idea of a critical practice of inclusive education we call upon the ideals of the civil rights workers who have shaped our national conscience on equality. Separate is not equal, and pitting efforts to progress in one endeavor against progress made in others is unlikely to result in gains for students with disabilities. Failure to include is a failure of civil rights. A renewed interest in ensuring the academic progress of students in particular areas is not a rationale to deny others access to general education. Schools are among the first community places in which children (can) learn that they belong, and indeed, that everybody belongs in society.

Curriculum Concepts for Inclusive Education

Resist Normalizing Practices

The concept of the norm is a statistical assumption, much more than is a reality in the complexity of human lives and experiences. Differences enable our distinctive appearances, talents, and interests, so variety in academic performance should also be anticipated. The central ideals of inclusive education are to query the problem of narrow conceptualizations of normality. It is only when we determine a norm, expect it, and favor those who seem to comply with our expectations that we label and marginalize. A tenet of inclusive teaching practice is to resist beliefs and practices that promote one "normal" way to live and learn. Instead, inclusive education seeks to broaden the range of experiences that can be valued and embraced in schools.

The tradition of parallel systems ingrained in most educators' minds inhibits our ability to think creatively and broadly about all kinds of learning that happens in the "general" environment. Similarly, the idea of a single curriculum in which all children are supposed to do and learn in the same ways is a powerful, long-lasting image of classroom instruction that is simply not viable for inclusive education. Similar to reflecting on what we think about "normal" and "abnormal," thinking inclusively about teaching starts with developing beliefs and images of schooling that emphasize the growth of the *whole* child and all children.

Democratic Schooling

Democratic schooling relates to the creation of curriculum that engages learners in shared dialog and work with others to enable them to be active participants in a democratic society. In the foundational work, *Democracy and Education*, philosopher and education theorist, John Dewey (1916), described:

> A democracy is more than a form of government; it is primarily a mode of associated living, of conjoint communicated experience. The extension in space of the number of individuals who participate in an interest so that each has to refer his own action to that of others, and to consider the action of others to give point and direction to his own, is equivalent to the breaking down of those barriers of class, race, and national territory which kept men from perceiving the full import of their activity (p. 87).

In other words, democracy is a way of life in which communities of people shape their worlds and actions in concert with each other. Engagement in dialog and shared action with many individuals allows many perspectives and experiences to be considered for action toward mutually beneficial goals.

The relationship of democratic schooling to inclusive curriculum is strong. Simply providing access for students with disabilities to schools positions them to be participants in a social organization. Creating curriculum that includes them in work alongside their peers can enable them to participate in shared dialog and action, in which everyone benefits. Oyler (2001) further offers four considerations for teaching that can enable students to learn how to engage in democracy through school curriculum. They are:

1. Searching for strengths in all learners
2. Expanding beyond the whole-class, uniform-lesson format
3. Utilizing flexible grouping strategies
4. Fostering collaborative problem-solving (p. 29)

Engaging in collaborative problem-solving provides further considerations for curriculum development. In addition to offering forums through which to teach and provide opportunities to develop ways of talking and working with others, students may also play a central role in proposing areas of study.

Students of all ages can find problems to investigate in the real world. Incorporating their ideas and making learners' interests central to curriculum increases their engagement and provides experiences in the democratic process itself. In the essay noted above, Oyler (2001), for example, described the shift in a course of study on ancient nomadic life when a student wondered about similarities between nomads and people without permanent homes in contemporary society. The course of study bloomed into an investigation that provided students the opportunity to explore current news media and community resources toward understanding a contemporary problem. A recent book by Schultz (2008) similarly describes fourth-grade students' yearlong investigation into the failure of their city's government to repair or replace their dilapidated school. What began as a group brainstorm of problems that affected students in the class exploded into a vigorous campaign to petition for a new school. Students studied political process and media analysis by studying documents and literature related to their cause and actively engaging in these forums as concerned and informed citizens.

Both Oyler (2001) and Schultz (2008), among many others, have demonstrated the impact that engagement in democratic processes of education has on students. When student-identified interests and problems are taken up as courses of study, we engage them in real and important work—as students in Schultz's class noted; and we allow them to live the benefits of engaging with others in shared study and dialog—as Rachel, in Oyler's (2001) essay, pointed out. Hardly detracting from students' development of academic skills in literacy, for example, Schultz notes the "spectacular" growth of students enabled by this kind of personally meaningful curriculum. To end with Dewey's (1916) words, a democratic society:

> ...must have a type of education which gives individuals a personal interest in social relationships and control, and the habits of mind which secure social changes without introducing disorder (p. 99).

Inclusive education is best developed as practices that engage students in authentic problem-solving, which inherently offers diverse ways of participating, opportunities to learn from others, and the development of content-area knowledge and academic skills.

Constructivism

The basis for democratic schooling primarily relates to ideals in active political engagement, though it is also supported by psychological-cognitive, and social theories of learning and development. Constructivism refers to a family of theories of learning and development, initially posed by Swiss psychologist, Jean Piaget, during the early twentieth century. Piaget was interested in describing and understanding the importance of children's play to their cognitive development. The essential tenet of constructivism is that children generate knowledge (i.e., learn) from their own experiences. Through experiencing the world by engaging with natural phenomena and information gathered through the senses, children build "theories" about how things work and what things mean, then "test" those theories in order to arrive at knowledge. The theories and knowledge that children generate and understand as truth change, however, as varying cognitive abilities develop, as they accrue more experiences, and as they gain access to the knowledge of others, including formal knowledge.

The implications of constructivism for curriculum and teaching center on children's need to learn through experience, or learn by doing. As children actively engage with phenomena to be studied, they are able to build ideas about what is happening from their own perspectives and then test those theories against subsequent experiences, which may include an introduction to a formalized concept. For example, children can learn that *to add* means to increase quantity through manipulating building blocks to create lesser and greater quantities, then matching those quantities to numbers. As the child is able to see and feel the increase of quantity, he or she can understand that adding means to increase quantity. In constructivist approaches to learning, children are provided with authentic (i.e., manipulating blocks), rather than abstract (i.e., only working with numbers and symbols), experiences through which to develop understandings about phenomena.

Constructivist approaches to curriculum and teaching correspond well to inclusive education, because they place the learner at the center of his or her knowledge-making. It is expected that children will develop knowledge and understanding through different means and at different rates, because we all have varied experiences and prior knowledge that will inform the ways we encounter and learn new ideas. Common educational approaches that relate to constructivism include: "hands-on" learning, discovery learning, the Montessori method, named for developer Maria Montessori, and Reggio-Emelia methods, which are named for a region in Italy (Fosnot, 2005).

Social Constructivism

Social constructivist theories of learning, initially described by the Russian psychologist, Lev Vygotsky, are similar to constructivist theories. Both theories posit knowledge to be actively constructed by learners, though social constructivism offers a more extensive focus on the social and cultural contexts in which learners form motivation and intent to learn and acquire the tools to generate knowledge—primarily, language. Although Vygotsky was developing ideas at the same time as Piaget, Vygotsky's work was relatively unknown to the Western world until the English translation of his works during the 1960s. The contribution of social constructivism to educational approaches is most evident in the concept of learning as *apprenticeship*. In this view, children learn through their active engagement with members who are more experienced in the activity. In the classroom, those more experienced may be teachers or other students. Three basic relational stages of growth toward mastering an activity can be characterized as: *novice*, in which the apprentice observes and/or copies actions that seem important to an activity; *dependence*, in which the apprentice can accomplish some facets of an activity with support; and *independence*, in which the learner is able to fully engage in an activity and direct his or her efforts appropriately to a novel task of the same kind.

Three related concepts intrinsic to social constructivism have, perhaps, the greatest influence on contemporary approaches to teaching and efforts to refine instructional methods.

- *Zone of proximal development* (ZPD). ZPD refers to the range of skills or tasks that a child cannot do independently, but can with support. It is this "zone" from which goals and objectives for a child's curriculum should be drawn. Nearly all kinds of classroom-based assessments aim to determine the ZPD in order to meet the needs of children.
- *Scaffolding*. As a child acts as a novice-apprentice, the more experienced "expert" acts to *scaffold* the tasks or activity by providing the necessary support to enable to novice-apprentice to learn the essential skills. Scaffolding learning is analogous to a scaffold in construction—external supports that enable work to be done on a structure before it is internally sound. Modeling, or demonstrating how to engage in a task or activity, is an initial kind of scaffold. Offering guided practice, or leading learners through the steps of an activity, is also a way of scaffolding.

- *Mediation.* Finally, *mediation* describes the context and means by which novices learn from experts. For example, the social context in which a skill is learned, the materials presented to a learner, and the language and style of language in which instruction is offered are each intervening, middle forces, that substantively affect the course of learning. *Cultural mediation* refers to the tremendous impact of culture on the ways in which people learn to use language, think, and behave. Members of varying cultures value and perform ways of interacting and thinking and kinds of knowledge differently from one another. *Sociocultural perspectives* on teaching and learning put forth the implications of cultural mediation to education. Collins (2003) succinctly describes, "a sociocultural perspective suggests examining the intersection of environment and individual to understand how they mutually construct each other" (p. 3). Social models of disability are derived from this family of thought.

The centrality of understanding students' and teachers' prior experiences toward establishing effective ways to construct learning activities cannot be overstated. Construed generally, it is essential to attend to how learners interact with materials and others and how they are enabled to interact with these mediating forces in the classroom. The concept that students performing on varied ranges of competence and with varied backgrounds and experiences learn from each other while engaging in shared activity relates strongly to ideals of democratic schooling. Aside from the innumerable methods for teaching that recommend differentiating instruction according to students' ZPD and practices that act as scaffolds, methods of teaching that strongly relate to sociocultural theories of learning include: Guided Inquiry (Burns, 2005; Palincsar, 1998) and Cooperative Learning (Gutierrez, Baquedano-Lopez, Alvarez, and Chiu, 1999; Johnson and Johnson, 1999).

Universal Design for Learning

Both constructivism and social constructivism offer theories that characterize learning as dynamic processes influenced by the culture and prior knowledge of the individual, in conjunction with the social context in which instruction is provided. Support for these approaches to instruction for students with disabilities is growing (Morocco, 2001). The ideal of the democratic classroom aims to offer school experiences that value and respond to diversity and provide students with knowledge, skills, and dispositions to interact within and be able to influence a democratic society. Universal Design for Learning (UDL) provides a broad framework to conceptualize the kinds of teaching practices that can meet our aims.

UDL is a framework for curriculum development and teaching practice, which is defined by the anticipation of diversity and the presumption of the school's responsibility to take learner variation into account from the start. Architect and wheelchair user Ronald Mace first proposed *universal design* as the creation of physical spaces that are both functional and elegant for the broadest possible constituency (McGuire, Scott, and Shaw, 2006). For example, a building designed universally might feature a gently sloping incline as an entrance, rather than having both a set of stairs and a designated wheelchair ramp. Designing this way provides entry to many, and might also maximize the use of space and be more aesthetically pleasing than building two entryways. UDL seeks the same elegance and functionality in a conceptualization of planning, teaching, and learning that presumes all students possess unique sets of strengths and needs.

Orkwis and MacLane introduced the application of universal design to curriculum development for schools in 1998 (McGuire, Scott, and Shaw, 2006). They described initiatives that could open up access in education by capitalizing on advances in technology, which could make general curriculum more accessible to a variety of learners. Why couldn't schools offer text, digital, and audio versions of a book, for example? Why couldn't a learner type an answer to a question or dictate a response to someone else, instead of performing only in handwriting? Why wouldn't schools presume that many ways of engaging with instruction were possible?

The Center for Applied Special Technology (CAST) is a not-for-profit organization that had been exploring ways of increasing access through technology since 1984. Founding directors David Rose and Anne Meyer discerned three main barriers that prohibited the access of students with disabilities to school curriculum:

1. The mode of *representation* of materials and instruction
2. The mode of *expression*, or how students were enabled to perform their learning
3. The mode of *engagement*, or method by which students were engaged in learning.

Each of these elements of pedagogy, CAST purported, could be construed to meet the needs of broader, more diverse groups of learners. Pertinent to learning theories described previously, readers will note that each element relates to a mediating force in the social context of classrooms.

Finding ways to modify or adapt materials and practices to include students with disabilities in the general curriculum is commonplace work in special education. Offering larger print materials, using digital texts, and adapting or modifying text were ways to open access to classroom materials. The possibility for students to use technology such as computers, word processors, or augmentative communication devices broadened the methods by which students could express learning. Students with disabilities did not need a separate curriculum as much as ways to gain better access to the general curriculum. The shift to imagining inclusion as practices of accessing curriculum signified a shift in the ways inclusion had been thought about, especially for students deemed severely disabled. Wehmeyer (2006), for example, notes that the first aim of inclusion was to provide entry to schools and to "the mainstream"; and the second, to improve teaching practices aimed at supporting students with disabilities in inclusive environments, such as co-teaching. The third wave—current practices— aims to improve access to the general education curriculum, and also seeks to ensure students' benefit and progress through instruction. If not evident already, moving away from the one-size-fits-most model of planning and teaching is essential, as captured in Oyler's (2001) advice to expand "beyond the whole-class, uniform-lesson format" (p. 29).

Offering accommodations and modifications to extend access for students with disabilities to the general education environment is necessary, and highly recommended in the IDEIA and education literature. However, there is one caveat in this way of conceptualizing curriculum planning. The notion that some students require "extra" accommodations or modifications to engage with a course of study can categorize and stigmatize students. In other words, constructing provisions for access as supplemental to an otherwise "normal" course of study partitions children into "general education" students and those with needs deemed "special." Unfortunately, children may become characterized by the modifications and accommodations that are needed, which stigmatizes the individual. In addition, work to support children requiring accommodations and modifications may be seen as "extra" work by teachers. Rather than imagining curriculum as a stock set of practices that can become accessible by making "special" accommodations and modifications, it is useful to envision curriculum as flexible and able to be crafted for diverse needs from the beginning. This way of thinking presumes and anticipates learner diversity, rather than aiming to retrofit curriculum when a student struggles.

Instruction derived through UDL is equivalent to conceptualizing teaching as a way to offer a spectrum of possibility. Planning with the assumption that learners are individuals who will benefit from a variety of materials, interactions, experiences, and opportunities better attends to the tenets of the most noted learning theories. In addition, presuming diversity and planning for an anticipated range of student ability and competencies reduces the problems caused when students must first fail before getting help. Planning for instruction using UDL is also efficient. Spooner et al. (2007) conducted workshops to introduce UDL to undergraduate and graduate students studying to be general or special educators. They propose:

> ...universally designed concepts might save teachers an extensive amount of time by creating modified lesson plans rather than changing them after the fact. By designing lessons before the fact, considering all students

using the components of UDL, teachers have a better opportunity to teach a curriculum that actively involves all students. Participants in this study were given approximately 20 min to complete lesson plans during the posttest, and they were able to create a lesson plan with modified instruction for all students, including those with disabilities, within that 20-min time period (p. 114).

In UDL, curriculum and instruction can already be designed for the many ways that learners can engage learning, thus allowing opportunity to emerge in each new moment, in each new day. UDL promises classroom design that is, in Pisha and Coyne's (2001) words, "smart from the start" (p. 197).

UDL in Practice

Developing teaching practices through a framework of UDL requires attention to three main elements that affect students' access to learning opportunities: (1) planning curriculum; (2) developing instructional methods and materials for daily instruction; and (3) assessing instruction and reflecting on teaching to inform future work.

Planning Curriculum

There are many factors to consider when figuring out which topics and skills to present for students' study and learning. Some schools use a scope and sequence or curriculum map of topics for study and accompanying skills that teachers are expected to follow. Others use programs and material sets, including textbooks, which layout the topics of study. In the United States, individual states also describe standards for learning, and most provide core curriculum for subject areas, which describe the knowledge and skills students are expected to master. In standardized curriculum, benchmarks for progress are provided and assessed at the end of the primary, middle, and secondary grades—for example, fourth, eighth, and twelfth. Despite the interest in ensuring that all students of the same age are able to meet standards, natural human variation and differences in the kinds of school and out-of-school experiences students have make aiming for a singular goal for all impractical. A more useful concept for inclusive teaching is to ensure all students have ample opportunity to make progress toward individualized goals, while having access to and gaining experience toward meeting State-developed guidelines.

Planning curriculum for a whole class, then, has the dual aims of being both cohesive and individualized. *Differentiated Instruction* is a named approach to this kind of curriculum planning, quite popular in contemporary schools. The term had been used, however, as early as 1959 by Donald Durrell and others. John Dewey had also posed the necessity of developing constructivist curriculum to match individual students' needs, lives, and interests in 1938. Although differentiating instruction is a hot topic in current teaching practice, the ideas that instruction is best developed to meet a range of students' needs and competencies is not one new to the field. To describe recommended practices for planning curriculum in a UDL framework, however, we draw from a selection of contemporary literature to best reflect current educational language.

Developing Coherence in Curriculum

Coherence in curriculum is achieved by developing a broad set of related concepts for a class to study over an extended period of time. These are typically organized as *units of study* that can range anywhere from a few weeks to several months, or even a whole year (described in Schultz's 2008 work, noted previously). Organizing curriculum into units supports the natural ways that people learn new information. We organize new knowledge by building on what we already know. If students are presented with many ideas surrounding a central base of concepts over a period of time, they are better able to organize the information for long-term understanding. In addition, sustained study on a set of central concepts offers more time and the possibility of providing many experiences through which students may develop understanding.

Onosko and Jorgensen (1998), among many others, suggest that inclusive curriculum planning begin with identifying a central unit issue or problem to investigate. The issue or problem should relate to students' lives and enable them to refer to their prior knowledge and experiences. Posing instruction as sets of problems to solve or issues to investigate provides a learning context in which children are able to brainstorm what they already know in order to set directions for new learning, then explore and generate ideas to inform their shared goal of problem-solving, and culminate in deeper understanding of an issue. Because there are many ways to solve problems and investigate issues, everyone can participate in the investigation to her or his own levels of comfort. *Big ideas* and *essential questions* are two concepts to help teachers figure out how to pose problems and issues for study.

Big ideas are conceptual organizers that students will revisit multiple times during the course of their education (McTighe and Brown, 2005). In order to determine big ideas, McTighe and Brown (2005) recommend "unpacking" curriculum standards provided by the state to identify conceptual organizers. An example of a "big idea" related to social studies and a unit on immigration, perhaps, is: People move for a variety of reasons, including economic opportunity, greater freedoms, or to escape something (McTighe and Wiggins, 2004). A big idea may also be broadened to apply to a variety of subject and study. For example, instead of focusing only on the immigration of people, a theme of "movement" might also encompass study on animal migrations. Seeking food, shelter, and more favorable climates could be other reasons posed for movements of these kinds. Even broader, a study of movement could include examination of the various ways that individuals move. Opportunities to explore movement technology and access could easily incorporate disability-related study, and certainly encompass movement goals that a child with physical or multiple disabilities may be working toward in replacement of or in addition to content-area learning.

Essential questions capture problems or issues posed for students to investigate, toward conceptual understanding. They may be big ideas written in question form; for example, *How have people come to live all over the world?* Or, *How does moving shape the human experience?* Characteristics of essential questions are:

1. They help students become investigators.
2. They involve thinking, not just answering.
3. They offer a sense of adventure and are fun to explore and to answer.
4. All students can answer them.
5. They require students to connect different disciplines and areas of knowledge (Jorgensen, 1996: 224).

In the two preceding examples, opportunities for students to connect study to their varied, individual lives and experiences are abundant. Students may explore their own ways of moving or places they move, or family histories of movement. They may investigate transportation, any number of mass movements of people over history, or any kind of movement of other organisms. Beginning with a shared big idea and set of organizing concepts offers many possibilities for individuating curriculum.

Key concepts, big ideas, and essential questions may be developed according to students' interests in problems they define; in terms of state standards; and/or in terms of other topics and areas of study provided by the school. It is most likely that teachers will consider each of these sources of curriculum. For example, the teacher may present a broad theme recommended by the state and/or school, and then refine it based on student contributions and questions that emerge along the way.

Individuating Curriculum at the Planning Stage

While developing problems, issues, big ideas, and essential questions to characterize the coherence of a unit and shared work around a theme, it is recommended that teachers also consider ways that individual students will demonstrate their understanding of the big ideas. In the *Understanding by Design* framework, Wiggins and McTighe (1998) describe a process of backward planning. Backward planning begins at the end—that is, thinking about the desired end goals in order to support students' learning toward them. Backward planning with inclusive design requires teachers to consider the many ways students may learn toward a theme and ultimately demonstrate their learning. End products or performances that help teachers assess student learning are called *culminating projects* or products, and should directly relate to the big ideas and essential questions initially posed.

Assessments should require students' demonstrations of understanding, not just recall of information or formulaic modeling. Understanding is best revealed through multiple forms of understanding, including real-world applications, explanations involving the construction of claims and arguments supported with evidence; analysis of perspectives associated with significant debates and controversial issues; expressions of empathy, with students encouraged to walk in the shoes of others; and self-reflection, involving students' growing ability to reflect, revise, rethink, and refine (McTighe and Brown, 2005: 236).

Continuing with the earlier examples related to "movement," varied ideas for culminating projects can suit a range of learners' needs. Some may aim to construct a map, noting the many places people live; others may increase the sophistication of a map by including movement patterns with dates, reasons, and details about cultural or geographic groups that have immigrated over time. Other students may focus on family histories or personal patterns and ways of moving. As we consider the class as a whole unit of problem-solvers and investigators, the great variety of culminating products imagined from the start of curriculum planning can result in a robust and substantive study of movement in which all participate and contribute.

Developing Instructional Methods and Materials for Daily Instruction

Once a unit theme, big ideas, and some possibilities for a range of culminating projects are proposed, attending to instructional methods for daily instruction is in order. A general guideline is that lessons are linked to the central issue or problem and daily instruction should engage students in work that will be useful to the development of culminating products (Onosko and Jorgensen, 1998; Tomlinson and McTighe, 2006; Wiggins and McTighe, 1998). This requires teachers (and students) to consider what is needed to investigate the theme. General areas to consider are:

1. *Increasing knowledge about an area of study*, which may include activities such as: accessing literature and other informational media on the theme; learning vocabulary and symbols pertinent to a new area of study; performing experiments to work with models or observe an area under investigation; working with "expert" guests in or out of school; or finding real-world examples and areas for study in the community.
2. *Developing skills to access information*, which may include instruction in: reading, or particularly useful reading strategies for different kinds of text; searching for and locating resources; interviewing; observing; listening; reading maps, graphs, and charts; or any other forms of data.
3. *Developing modes of inquiry to engage with ideas*, which may include instruction in: collaborative work and discussion; ways of conducting

investigations and experiments; analytical and critical thinking in general, or specific to disciplines (e.g., working with mathematical/ computational systems); or reflection.

4. *Developing ways of performing the knowledge and skills learned*, which often include writing, speaking, word-processing, displaying mathematical algorithms, charting, and graphing (and test-taking). Other forms of expression may also be areas for instruction, including: the visual arts, theatrical and musical performances, and the wide variety of media arts and computer-related forums for expression (e.g., presentation software and web-pages).

Sourcebooks containing ideas for lesson planning, materials, and teaching methods are abundant. For the purposes of considering inclusive, differentiated instruction we offer an overview of methods and material ideas consonant with these aims. The section is organized in terms of (1) assessment; (2) methods; and (3) materials.

Assessment

Assessment involves examining students and their work to support planning and instructional design to best meet their needs. IEP development includes assessment processes, and is one tool that describes goals and areas of study for individuals useful to daily practice. In addition to attending to IEP goals, it is essential for teachers to assess students in the particular instructional environment and in relation to the specific unit of study. For example, a question to guide assessment might be, "How will Juan best benefit from and engage in study about movement?" Or, "How will Shannon's IEP goal of increasing reading comprehension be met in a study of movement?" The overall purpose of assessment is to gauge the competency of students with regard to the four areas described earlier. In other words, (1) What do students know about the area of study, and from what sources?; (2) What skills do students possess that will enable them to access information?; (3) In what modes of inquiry are students able to engage?; and (4) In which kinds of formats are students comfortable performing or demonstrating their learning? Based on general answers to these questions, teachers can develop ideas that will emphasize students' strengths as areas on which to build and help identify areas to pose for growth.

Assessment for planning can take many forms. Inviting student input is, perhaps, the most straightforward way to begin assessment for planning. A number of surveys, tools, and methods for discerning students' interests, learning strengths, and prior knowledge are available. Student interest surveys and simply having group or individual discussions about interests may be used to inform areas of study likely to be engaging. Asking students about the kinds of school activities that they found enjoyable in years past may also help teachers figure out practices that are familiar and likely to be successful. Some questions to guide a conversation include:

- What was your favorite subject last year?
  - o What kinds of work did you do in that class or on that subject?
  - o Do you have any examples of that work from last year?
- What was something you feel you learned very well last year?
  - o What kinds of things did you do to learn that?

If possible, talking to students' past teachers about what was successful and engaging to students can give a new teacher great ideas for where to begin planning.

Having an idea of what students' already know is also very helpful to planning for daily instruction. The KWL Chart was originally developed as a tool for helping students to more deeply engage with and comprehend reading materials (Ogle, 1986). It has subsequently become a frequently used strategy for assessing students' prior knowledge, discerning students' interests, and charting progress throughout a unit of study. KWL stands for What I Know, What I Want to Know, and What I Learned. To create a KWL Chart, simply create a three-column chart with one heading for each column. The class then fills in the chart with what they Know about a given area of study, as well as what they Want to know. Teachers and students then have a shared way of determining areas for study. As the class learns the areas proposed (and others), they can fill in the "Learned" column for a dynamic display of class accomplishment.

In addition to asking students directly, observation and reviewing student work are other straightforward ways to get a sense of students' comfort zones and areas of need. A suggestion for beginning practice is to watch students, as they work on a variety of open-ended tasks on familiar topics. Perhaps the most familiar topic is oneself, and beginning a school year with activities that allow teachers and classmates to get to know each other is highly recommended. For example, asking students to create a product to express what they did over the summer, the previous night, or over the weekend is a way to give a familiar task that can be completed in many ways. Students may choose to write, draw, select pictures from magazines, or any other creative way to present a recent experience. Taking note of which students gravitate to which form can provide insight into the kinds of work students are most comfortable doing. The work samples can provide valuable information about students and their experiences, as well as suggest students' areas of strengths and needs. In addition, many diagnostic tools are available to help teachers determine the ZPD. Being sensitive to what students are able to do and able to do with help in the context of their actual work is most helpful to planning.

While assessment is useful to get a broad idea of the kinds of activities most likely to result in success, sociocultural theories emphasize the importance of context to learners' achievement. It is likely and desirable that students will be able to perform more sophisticated knowledge and skills in the context of authentic problem scenarios and when they have many models on which "apprentice." Rather than imagine assessment as occurring once at the beginning of a year or unit, it is useful to attend to individual students' progress each day and in different kinds of activities that emerge as a unit develops. This kind of attention enables teachers to note and repeat (or further develop) topics or kinds of activities in which students perform best.

Methods

The methods chosen for teaching and learning are greatly determined by the skills, modes of inquiry, and performances of learning that are desired. The educational philosophy of a democratic ideal for inclusive teaching also has significant impact on the kinds of skills and modes of inquiry addressed. For example, engaging in and gaining from shared dialog requires class members to learn how to present their ideas clearly, acknowledge and listen to others, and be able to clarify and incorporate others' ideas and contributions (Palincsar, Magnussen, Collins, and Cutter, 2001). Sociocultural theories of learning offer a framework that supports engagement in shared work, in which students learn by modeling their thought and actions on more experienced class members. Constructivist theories also support the necessity of learners' interaction in authentic experiences that allow them to construct ideas toward the development of conceptual understanding. McTighe and Brown (2005), offer:

> Students learn best when they are engaged in purposeful, active, and inquiry-driven teaching and learning activities, rather than passive variations of didactic instruction. The more learners are situated at the center of their own learning process, the greater the extent of their understanding and mastery of desired outcomes (p. 236).

The family of methods related to guided inquiry and cooperative learning seem well suited for inclusive teaching (Morocco, 2001; Palincsar, Magnussen, Collins, and Cutter, 2001).

Guided inquiry provides students with problems to investigate and an interactive, social forum to share ideas and gain guidance toward developing disciplinary understanding. In other words, students are enabled to develop their own ideas, which are posed to the group (including teachers), and then refined as content-area knowledge through further questioning, clarifying, and investigating. The teacher's roles are to develop or help students develop activities to illustrate and animate the concepts of study; to guide students' thinking and doing toward productive directions by modeling and questioning; and to provide direct teaching of skills, instructions, and information likely to support students' ability to engage in inquiry. Cooperative learning generally refers to work in which students learn by working together (Johnson and Johnson, 1999), and is an integral component of guided inquiry.

Morocco (2001) offers four broad considerations for planning in a guided inquiry method: (1) authentic tasks; (2) cognitive strategies; (3) social mediation; (4) constructive conversation.

1. *Authentic tasks.* Authentic tasks pose students with real-world scenarios and/or actual materials to manipulate in order to investigate concepts or phenomena. A few real-world scenarios are:

   o Preparing for a trip by investigating a place to go, mapping a route, and calculating mileage and costs. The most authentic work might feature actual planning to go on a field trip, though planning for an imagined trip can also be quite engaging.
   o Investigating a current social problem, posing ideas for action, and getting involved in anything from volunteer work to communicating with government official—the closer to students' lived experiences, the more authentic the work.
   o Mathematical problems involving calculating area, volume, perimeter, and other geometric skills are frequently posed through scenarios in which students will plan to paint a room, plant a garden, or build a building. Science experiments and lab work are frequently designed to provide materials to manipulate and phenomena to observe.

2. *Cognitive strategies.* Addressing cognitive strategies relates to the teaching of steps or thinking processes in which people engage to complete tasks. In guided inquiry, teachers may listen for and reinforce desired ways of thinking and talking, as they emerge naturally in student talk and work. For example, a student may be asked to share a particular idea or way of interacting that highlighted an instructional aim. Teachers may also directly teach cognitive strategies to deepen and better enable student understanding. In mathematics, a common example of teaching cognitive strategy is found in supporting students to differentiate important and unimportant information given in word problems. When learners first encounter word problems, teachers or other students may lead them through a step-by-step process to identify the question the problem is asking, the information that seems useful to answering the question, and the information that is not useful to the question. Oftentimes, keywords for operations are highlighted to enable students to figure out how to manipulate the numbers to answer the question (e.g., "altogether" usually refers to addition).

   Another well-documented cognitive strategy is Reciprocal Teaching, which relates to reading comprehension of nearly any kind of text for any kind of content (Lederer, 2000; Palincsar and Brown, 1984; Slater and Horstman, 2002). Reciprocal Teaching provides a series of strategies in which readers actively engage in discussion to arrive at shared meaning during reading. First, a group reads a common selection of text. Next, they generate questions prompted by the selection and try to answer them. After that, readers raise issues that need to be clarified for best understanding of the selection. Summarizing the passage is next, and finally, readers predict what might happen in the subsequent text. The next section of text is read, and the process is repeated. Each of the four steps may be taught in isolation from one another, with the goal to be able to practice them altogether. Ultimately, Reciprocal Teaching breaks down and makes explicit the skills of questioning, clarifying, summarizing, and predicting text in order to gain accurate understandings, while also highlighting the importance of dialog and shared meaning.

3. *Social mediation* and 4. *Constructive conversation.* Learning is an interactive process and can be characterized as exchanges of ideas through which individuals and groups develop shared understandings. In guided inquiry, the sharing of ideas and propositions followed by group discussion to clarify and question supports learners to develop and refine understandings. In the examples in the preceding text, the teacher usually provides directions and demonstrations of each step, and then supports students as they practice the steps with the whole class, and then in smaller groups of students, which increases everyone's opportunity to engage with and practice the strategies. As students practice, they act as models for each other and all refine their understanding of material and gaining competence with the strategies. In this method, it is essential that students have the opportunity to practice and learn how to engage in constructive conversations or communication. Just as cognitive strategy instruction may be provided, strategies for sharing and listening to ideas may also be directly taught and practiced within the context of authentic experiences.

There are many ways that daily lessons can be structured, and the kind of activity in which students will engage is likely to dictate the flow of a lesson. Madeline Hunter (1982), for example, offered a seven-step model of lesson planning for direct teaching that incorporates the teacher's scaffolding, which may be useful when introducing cognitive strategies. Workshop models for teaching reading and writing workshops adds the concept of the "mini-lesson" (Calkins, 1986). The characterization of lesson delivery, or direct instruction, as "mini" emphasizes the need for students' active engagement and time for exploration and dialog. We offer five lesson components that are useful to structure daily planning for a balance of direct and inquiry-based instruction:

1. *Activate prior knowledge or anticipatory set.* Students are invited to consider and share knowledge and experiences related to the objective

for the day; review prior learning from the unit of study; or offered an "attention-grabbing" activity or idea to increase their anticipation of the activity for the day.

2. *Mini-lesson.* Students are provided instruction on a particular cognitive or social strategy of focus that will guide them to be successful in the day's activity, or that will further their development in an ongoing investigation. Introducing new information pertinent to the area of study may also be offered.

3. *Check for understanding and offer opportunities for guided practice.* Students are guided through a model application of the new concept or strategy. Students may role-play, observe, and comment on others' practice; and/or follow along as teachers or peers demonstrate. Care should be taken to provide clear directions and explanations to enable students to understand the purpose and process of the lesson.

4. *Interdependent practice.* Students are provided with authentic tasks or problems through which to practice their new learning, initiate, or continue an investigation. Ideally, this is a time that students work together. Teachers can circulate among groups to ensure understanding of directions and to pose questions or model language to deepen conversations. When groups are enabled to work interdependently, this can also be a time for teachers to have individual conversations with students or provide additional support or enrichment for small groups.

5. *Sharing and reflection.* The class community, in guided inquiry, is thought of as a learning community in which all members learn from each other and contribute to the whole of class accomplishment. Small groups or individuals may present on their learning and activity for the day and/or participate in a larger group discussion or work. This is often a time in which broader conceptual understandings emerge and can be highlighted. Teachers may also take note of understandings, strategies, and concepts that can be emphasized in subsequent lessons.

In planning for a unit and guided inquiry model of teaching, the overall framework is guided by big ideas, concepts, and instruction needed to work toward culminating projects. Topics for the mini-lessons can emerge from students' learning along the way, as areas of need and interests are noted; or relate to more specific skills students are expected to learn.

There are several reasons that guided inquiry and workshop models are recommended for inclusive teaching. First, students work in learning communities on a shared problem or issue. Any given big idea, concept, essential question, and investigation poses the need for many different kinds of information and ways of engaging in joint, culminating efforts. Everyone can contribute to class learning toward a theme while working on individual goals. In UDL terms, guided inquiry and workshop models provide ways of differentiating the mode of engagement in learning. Similarly, as Tomlinson (1999) describes of differentiated instruction, the process by which students practice and perform learning can be varied. For example, a group can work together to search for information on a shared topic, with some doing Internet searches, others watching a documentary; others reading texts, and so on. All members can contribute information from different sources of information. One group or class member may create a visual display of information by making a collage of related words or pictures, while another writes a report of the information, another develops a website, and another presents an oral presentation. Each member can work individually, but in concert toward a shared aim.

Second, because students are working on similar concepts and topics, they are enabled to support and deepen each other's learning. "Students are thought of as having and using distributed expertise" (cited in Mariage, Paxton-Buursma, and Bouck, 2004: 541), which means that it is expected that students will develop understanding and competencies at different rates and through varied means. Engagement in dialogic work provides any individual with several "models" who may act as learning scaffolds. The openness of instruction similarly poses infinite opportunities to arrive at novel ideas and understanding and allows students to interact in ways most familiar to them while gaining experience and instruction. This allows for a valuing of students' ways of knowing alongside the development of culturally dominant styles of interacting (Garderen and Whittaker, 2006; Gutierrez, Baqudano-Lopez, Alvarez, and Chiu, 1999; Mariage, Paxton-Buursma, and Bouck, 2004; Reid and Valle, 2004).

Third, planning in units provides a context for sustained study that deepens over the course of the unit. Spending a greater duration dedicated to related areas of study allows more time for learners to develop understanding or to complete assignments without feeling left behind. Finally, supporting students to work interdependently provides a structure in which teachers are able to plan for small-group or intensive instruction when necessary. Rotating combinations of heterogeneous groups for themed work with homogeneous groups for specific skill instruction can provide flexible teacher and peer support.

Developing ways of teaching that support students toward interdependence can make time for combinations of whole-group, small-group, and individual instruction, as well as position students as teachers and leaders in areas of strength. There is no formula or ideal balance that can apply to all classes of students; and the process of thinking about differentiated instruction can be messy, even chaotic. However, the following ways of thinking about grouping, student strengths, and cognitive and social strategies instruction are a place to start.

- In addition to considering the general guidelines for guided inquiry, there are many guidelines and tools available to support the work of cooperative learning. Johnson and Johnson (1999), for example, provide the following elements of cooperative learning activity design:

o *Positive interdependence:* The task requires all members to contribute in order to complete the assignment. To support positive interdependence, students may choose or be assigned specific roles to fill. These may relate to aspects of a product or process. For example, there may be a timekeeper, material manager, note-taker, and facilitator to support the social process of a shared task; or students may be differently assigned to create a visual display, outline, a writing piece, or a speaking component based on shared understanding of an experiment, piece of text, or problem.

o *Individual accountability:* Individuals' contribution to the group must be acknowledged and assessed. Assigning roles or asking students to describe their contributions support the participation of all members.

o *Face-to-face promotive interaction:* Group work should require students to interact with each other in ways that will advance their pursuit. A jigsaw, for example, is when individual members of a group are responsible for learning different aspects of a task, then come together to share, explain, and ensure that all group members understand all of the varied aspects. Another possibility is that all members need to use their learning toward solving a shared problem. In either case, students must interact to complete the assignment.

o *Social skills:* It is essential that students be provided guidelines and instruction toward respectful and productive interaction. Offering direct instruction in social skills and providing ongoing reinforcement and acknowledgement of good communication is a necessity of cooperative learning, as well as a primary value in democratic schooling. Even if it takes time for students to develop respectful and productive ways of interacting, taking the time to teach students to work with each other is well aligned with the goals of an inclusive classroom. Beyond establishing general norms of mutual respect, instruction in strategies to cultivate conceptually meaningful dialog is a central principle of guided inquiry communities. Students can learn how to acknowledge others' contributions, rephase ideas, form questions, and clarify, and build on each other's ideas.

o *Group processing:* Cooperative learning can be built upon and furthered, as students (and teachers) develop values for shared work and evaluate successful elements of group work. Group work should include a time and forum for the group to identify successes in the group process and areas that can be improved. In fact, these kinds of reflections and learning can be great ideas for follow-up mini-lessons or ways of identifying goals for the next time the group works together.

- Student groupings can be created by interest in a common type of product. For example, all students who wish to create a visual product may work together to share ideas, draft work, share materials, create products, and offer constructive criticism. Assuming a variety in skill level and experience in art-making, peers can support each other to develop better products than they would without each other. A teaching artist or more advanced student of the arts would be an excellent classroom visitor to advance this group's skills.

- Student groupings can be created to gather students with a range of abilities and competencies with the express purpose of their supporting each other. Roles can be assigned by ability, process, or product to appropriately structure students' participation and increase the likelihood of success.

- Student groupings can be created according to affinity or interest groups. These groupings can increase student engagement or support the building of relationships and friendships.

- Students can be grouped according to specific needs of instruction, which allows teachers to provide scaffolded instruction that they are best equipped to facilitate. These groupings and intense instruction benefit students who may need support to engage in an enriching task and those who need support revisiting a concept or skill.

- Teachers can make the most of small-group, intensive instruction by changing groupings regularly and varying the complexity of assignments. For example, when intensive instruction for a small group of students is required, other groups may be assigned to continue work-in-progress or a task that is likely to be comfortable. These help ensure a balance of attending to students' needs with an organized and productive class.

- Most cognitive strategy instruction will be useful to all. To ensure that students are able to make progress, materials and ways of applying strategies in independent work can be differentiated to provide appropriate levels of challenge.

About Cooperative Learning and Attitudes Toward Students with Disabilities

Cooperative learning experiences can promote greater acceptance of differences and interpersonal attraction between students with disabilities and students without disabilities. Direct contact and interaction through cooperative experiences can move students beyond one-dimensional prejudices to multidimensional views of one another. Teachers can help students reduce their prejudices by allowing them to learn cooperatively and encouraging them to value each other (Conrad, 1988). Practiced cooperation leads to spontaneous cooperation, the polar opposite of prejudice. Assigning students with disabilities to work cooperatively with their non-disabled peers creates a pattern of positive interaction. Guidelines to facilitate a productive experience include (Yuker and Block, 1979):

1. The interaction of non-disabled students and their peers with disabilities should rely on collaborating rather than a helping. This orientation must be taught. Many students both with and without disabilities simply lack the necessary skills to interact with each other. Thus, a teacher needs to teach collaboration.

2. The interactions of non-disabled students with their disabled peers should be cooperative rather than competitive. Techniques such as cooperative learning that emphasize group accomplishment and de-emphasize competition nurture self-esteem by building confidence and inviting students to achieve their potential.

3. The interactions of non-disabled students with their disabled classmates should be intimate rather than casual in order to lead to positive attitudes toward one another.

4. The interactions of non-disabled students with their disabled classmates should be frequent rather than occasional.

5. The interactions of non-disabled students and their classmates with disabilities should take place on settings that make them equals. Students with disabilities should not be treated as "guests" who earned their way into the mainstream, but as students who belong in that classroom as much as any other student.

Cooperative learning increases contact between students, gives them a shared basis of similarity (group membership), engages them in pleasant activities together, and encourages them to work toward common goals. The outcome of these kinds of experience can be friendships and long-lasting impressions that counteract stereotypes about disability. An important psychological outcome of cooperative learning is the positive effect it can have on self-esteem and self-confidence. The students' realization enables them to withstand life's disappointments, to be confident decision-makers, and ultimately to be happy and productive individuals.

Variety in Expressing Learning

A final consideration for methods in UDL and differentiated instruction is providing variety in the ways students can perform their learning—that is, varying the mode of expression. Already noted in earlier sections, planning instruction and learning activities around themes provide varied goals that individuals in a class can be working toward, while engaging in shared aims. Earlier described, students may be working on a range of goals. Reisberg (1998), for example, points out:

The infusion of goals, objectives, and activities from the areas of self-help, independent living, and social and learning skills is limited only by a teacher's imagination and subsequent planning. Some skills and knowledge fit better and are more effectively related to particular themes than others; however, through careful planning and development, teachers can address, in the general education classroom, many of the learning goals needed by students with disabilities (pp. 276–277).

Performance-based assessment refers to a way of gauging student growth based on what they are able to perform in an authentic context of application. The most common way of assessing learners on complex projects and application of skills is with evaluation rubrics and task checklists. A rubric is usually formatted as a grid that lists key competencies with a range of criteria that describe performance levels or qualities. Task checklists are lists of components or processes that should be included or performed as part of the assignment.

Ideally, students may use the same rubric to gauge progress over a course of similar study. For example, a rubric for writing an essay may be used for a variety of kinds of essays, but specify general components such as thesis, supporting details, organization, style, and editing. To gauge content-area knowledge and conceptual understanding, a rubric may be developed according to big ideas, key concepts, or essential questions. A range of product types can be assessed according to the range and depth of content and concepts displayed in them. Rubrics can be developed for any goal—academic, social, or other skills— by identifying and describing the range of competence most appropriate for the student. Because the rubric offers descriptive details of different performance levels or qualities, students are provided specific feedback on how to improve. Rather than simply provide a grade or level, assessment can guide instruction and provide a goal for further work, useful to both teacher and student. Using rubrics and descriptive, performance-based assessment practices focus attention to individual progress, rather than emphasize comparisons with others or performance relative to a norm.

Materials

A main tenet of UDL is the provision of varied materials to reduce barriers in the mode of representation. Having multiple formats of a material is one way to diversify. For example, when offering reading material it is useful to have the text version, a larger-print text version, a digital format that can be viewed or read aloud on a computer, an audio version, and perhaps a Braille version. Ideally, these materials would be obtained at the same time to be ready-to-go for anyone who could benefit from them. Preparing for students with diverse needs before a need arises reduces frustration and barriers that can occur when available materials are inadequate to support the class. If varied formats are not available or able to be acquired, teachers may plan to engage the whole class in read-aloud, shared, or partnered reading so that all have access to the text. Similar methods may also be used to include students who cannot read. Of shared reading and reading aloud, Browder et al. (2008) point out that "the two primary outcomes for literacy are enhanced," including "quality of life through shared literature and increased independence as a reader" (p. 3).

In addition to having varied formats of texts, providing modified texts may also be appropriate and helpful. One example of modified texts that are available for purchase is abridged versions of books. They are shortened versions of materials that include main plot elements, characters, and essential story lines. Many "classics" in literature and mythology are available in many versions written or retold in differing levels of sophistication. Educators can certainly create modified text materials, as well. Students may be offered a photocopy of a page with only the main headings or central ideas visible; or a text that is highlighted to alert them to the main ideas, as correlated, perhaps, to individuated instructional goals. Providing modified texts can enable a student to participate in conversation and class activities without becoming frustrated with an overwhelming task. Or, a modified text may be useful for homework or independent work, when sources of classroom support may not be available.

Beyond offering multiple or abridged versions of a shared material, it is recommended that educators collect or locate many kinds of materials that offer similar information in a variety of formats and that relate to and incorporate various cultures and people. Resources of these kinds are necessary for robust thematic and unit planning. Having rich, detailed, and diverse source materials increase the potential to engage and be interesting to the widest range of class members (Onosko and Jorgensen, 1998). Efforts in inclusive education are best designed to create contexts for learning in which every student can identify with and connect to the school's culture and organizational life (see Dei et al., 2000, as cited in Wotherspoon and Schissel, 2001). Inclusive schooling, according to Wotherspoon and Schissel:

> Incorporate[s] social and cultural resources such as the accumulation of significant pools of informal learning, or the presence of individuals with special skills or life histories, that are often ignored in schooling or not considered as legitimate learning resources (Livingstone, 1999). (p. 332).

In other words, when seeking materials, it is useful to consider human resources, community organizations, and all kinds of available experiences that may be related to a theme of study. In general, teachers may consider having books and readings on similar topics on many levels and in many text types (i.e., novels, magazine articles, picture books, textbooks, etc.); a selection of videos; websites; and hands-on materials, all related to a theme, provide many ways for students to obtain information for study. Students can all have a chance to choose materials most interesting to them, gain experience working with varied forms of information, and can expand, enrich, or review learning throughout the duration of study. Garderen and Whittaker (2006) offer an important further note to keep in mind: "regardless of the degree of heterogeneity of a district or classroom, all students should learn about the history and experiences of diverse groups so that they can function in a global society" (p. 13).

Finally, just as material sources of information can be varied and modified, so can assignment handouts, class notes, and any other material provided in class. Supplemental materials and aids, such as reading or vocabulary guides, calculators, or graphic organizers—such as charts, Venn diagrams, concept maps—are also ways of opening access to understanding and participation. The possibilities for providing a variety of materials and supplemental tools for organization or ease of completion of assignments are innumerable and are best derived from considering the needs of individual students as teachers get to know them. Resources containing ideas to modify and develop supplemental materials are abundant. Although IDEIA guarantees the modifications and accommodations listed on a student's IEP, there is no reason that supplemental and varied versions of materials can be offered *only* to students with IEPs. Offering everyone the opportunity to benefit from the range of resources and practices available in a UDL curriculum can maximize learning for many.

Assessing Instruction and Reflecting on Teaching to Inform Future Work

Teaching is dynamic because of the many variable factors that influence joint engagement in shared work. All class members are affected by events, moods, and the ups and downs of life. In addition, many factors influence how an individual or group will respond to class activities on any given day—the topic, prior knowledge, and experience of class members, nature of activity, materials provided, members of a group, and so on. Although planning universally and differentiating instruction can maximize the potential of daily lessons to provide students with success and growth, no degree of planning can account for all of the variations that affect classroom life. Teachers, however, can engage in practices that help increase the effectiveness in planning for teaching.

Students grow through opportunities to revisit and practice ways of thinking and talking over time. Conceptual understanding develops and deepens as students engage in similar processes and encounter similar, related phenomena over time. Deep learning does not "happen" in one day or in a single experience. Therefore, teachers should not be discouraged by students' needs to revisit concepts. In fact, planning a unit emphasizes and builds on learners' needs to engage in sustained study that deepens—through scaffolding—over time and experience. That said, teachers do need to be attentive and responsive to factors in class design that can be improved. Assessment applies not only to gauging students' growth and progress, but also to teachers' growth in the design and implementation of instruction.

It is recommended that teachers take time to consider and reflect on teaching practices in order to inform subsequent planning. Certainly, thinking about the events of a day and making mental notes about what is going well and not, and responding to student work are ways that teachers gain insight into students' learning in order to adjust instruction. However, after a long day of work, details that could inform knowledge about students and effective or ineffective teaching processes are likely to fade in memory. A first step toward being enabled to reflect on teaching practice, then, is to develop a means for noting and recording details of teaching. Taking notes while teaching or right after a lesson, keeping a written or audio journal, or even periodically recording video or audio of a class are possible ways to create detailed accounts of practice.

Korthagen (1999) defines reflection as "the mental process of structuring or restructuring an experience, a problem or existing knowledge or insights" (p. 193), and offers the ALACT process of ongoing reflection and action suggested for teachers. Described as a spiral, the ALACT model is an acronym for stages of reflective practice. Guiding questions follow the stages listed below.

1. *Acting:* The act of teaching. Key questions consider are:

   o What did I want to achieve?
   o What did I want to pay particular attention to?
   o What did I want to try out?

2. *Looking back on the action:* Recording descriptive details of the actions

   o What were the concrete events?
   o What did I want?
   o What did I think?
   o How did I feel?
   o What did I do?

3. *Awareness of essential aspects:* Discerning, from the description, key areas of interest or a problem

   o What is the connection between answers to the previous questions?
   o What is the influence of the context/the school as a whole?
   o What does that mean for me?
   o What is the problem or the positive discovery?

4. *Creating alternative methods of action:* Posing ideas to solve a problem or repeat and further effective practices

   o What alternatives do I see? What are ways to make use of my positive discovery?
   o What are advantages and disadvantages of each?
   o What do I resolve to do next time?

5. *Trial:* Trying out the new ideas. The process then spirals back to the acting stage (p. 197).

In this open design, teachers can aim to describe a particular event or challenge to write a narrative description of a longer period of time. The more that is recorded, the more enriching and comprehensive the process can be. It is important to remember that events and interactions preceding a challenging situation may influence it; so developing descriptions that precede a particular event can give further insight and awareness.

The ALACT model is quite flexible. The process can be used for open inquiry—describing actions in order to gain insight into teaching practices; and it can be used to examine specific areas of interest. McTighe and Brown (2005), for example, describe responsive teaching as practice that:

> demands diagnostic and ongoing assessments of student progress in relationship to required content and performance standards. Through this process, teachers decrease skills and knowledge gaps, as well as accommodate individual students' demonstrated strengths, interests, and personal learning goals (p. 237).

The ALACT model can be used to describe and reflect upon individual student's progress in terms of the content and performance standards planned for in a lesson. Teachers may choose to specifically "Look back" at how students were enabled (or not) to develop the big ideas of a lesson.

ALACT can also be used individually or for collaborative reflection and action. Especially useful in collaborative teaching, teachers can each describe aspects of a lesson or day, then work together to gain awareness of essential aspects (some which may not be apparent to only one person), create alternative methods for action, and trial teach together. The benefit of having multiple insights and sources for generating ideas is tremendous.

Research Supporting UDL and Differentiated Instruction

There is a growing research base to support the impact of UDL and differentiated instruction on student learning. In addition to sociocultural and constructivist frameworks, other contemporary theories of learning support differentiation as an approach to teaching, including brain-based learning and multiple intelligences. For example, proponents of "brain-based instruction" propose that a comfortable learning environment, an appropriate level of challenge, and activities that allow students to attach meaning to concepts through significant associations enable students' cognitive process (Tomlinson and Kalbfleisch, 1998). Howard Gardner's (1983; 1999) theory of multiple intelligences describes eight factors that comprise different types of intelligence: verbal–linguistic, logical–mathematic, visual–spatial, musical, bodily–kinesthetic, naturalistic, interpersonal, and intrapersonal. Although the theory has been subject to much critique regarding an empirically confirmed neurological basis (see Waterhouse, 2006), the idea of thinking about varied competencies and student preferences while planning to differentiate instruction is quite useful (and ubiquitous among educators). Surely, learners respond to variations in formats of instruction. Campbell, Campbell, and Dickinson (cited in Lynch and Warner, 2008) point out:

> When teachers create opportunities for all learners through multiple forms of instruction and assessment, they are better able to respond to the needs of learners who may demonstrate different types of intelligence other than the linguistic and logical-mathematical abilities that traditionally have been valued in academic settings (p. 11).

Lynch and Warner (2008) further offer the following review of research that demonstrates support for differentiated instruction:

> Patricia Hodge (as cited in Subban 2006) found that students who had received differentiated instruction had increased gains in mathematics scores. McAdamis (2001) reported that differentiated instruction resulted in significant improvement in test scores for low-achieving students across grade levels. In addition to improvements in test scores, another result of differentiated instruction, according to other studies, is increased student engagement. Johnsen (2003) found that differentiated techniques were engaging and stimulated student interest. In a study by Linda Affholder (as cited in Subban 2006), teachers who used differentiated techniques experienced a greater sense of effectiveness and were more willing to try new instructional approaches (p. 11).

In addition to support for differentiated instruction, the benefit for planning curriculum for conceptual understanding and engaging students in active dialog through is well established. The REACH project—a multi-year study examining the conceptual learning of students with disabilities—has yielded successful demonstrations of the role and impact of dialog. In a brief summary, Morocco (2001) describes:

> Some studies in special education have focused on the effect of constructive conversation on the learning of students with disabilities. For example, Woodward and Baxter (1996) identify questioning strategies in teachers' conversations with young adolescent students with disabilities as a way to build students' conceptual understanding in mathematics. Echevarria (1995) successfully embedded dialogue within strategy instruction within a curriculum focused on conceptual understanding of concepts for Hispanic students with disabilities. Palincsar et al. (1998) described the role that conversation can play in enabling students to synthesize evidence from science experiments (p. 9).

In a classroom-based study, Morocco and Hindin (2002) explain the learning accomplished through students' active engagement in discussions. In working with a teacher who modeled and scaffolded language practices that supported engagement with others' ideas, students were able to deepen their understanding. The researchers observed:

> The students demonstrate their developing ability to negotiate interpretations of literature through specific discourse practices that include stating claims, elaborating upon one another's claims, countering one another's claims with alternative views, and using arguments to support their claims. By requiring precise wording ... these four students reveal their understanding of the value of close attention to their language (p. 156).

Additionally, because students are able to incorporate knowledge of their own lives in the open format of discussion, they were able "to better interpret and hypothesize about the choices that [the character] makes in the text," which enabled them to "deepen their understanding" (p. 156).

The promising work done by teachers, students, and researchers in the REACH project offers support for guided inquiry and the concept of the learning community as an inclusive space. That is, one that provides many open opportunities to engage with instruction, deepen learning, gain support for developing cognitive and social strategies, and activities that capitalize on students' contributions and experiences.

A final area of study in support of learning communities and cooperative learning relates to improving the school experiences specifically for students with disabilities. Though work on strategies useful to realizing inclusion have been underway for some time, positive social interaction among labeled and non-labeled students has not been a natural outcome. In 1980, Guingagh noted that most "mainstreamed" children begin their regular classes with slight and unplanned social contact with their peers, and found that "[helping] children become better friends is not central to instruction" (p. 2). Johnson and Johnson (1980), in fact, had found that placing students with disabilities into the mainstream without the proper support and preparation can be extremely harmful:

> Placing handicapped students in the regular classroom is the beginning of an opportunity. But, liked all opportunities, it carries the risk of making things worse as well as the possibility of making things better. If things go badly, handicapped students will be stigmatized, stereotyped, and rejected. Even worse, they may be ignored or treated with the paternalistic care one reserves for pets. If things go well, however, true friendships and positive relationships may develop between the non-handicapped and handicapped students. ... What is needed is an understanding of how the process of acceptance works in a classroom setting and an understanding of the specified teaching strategies that help to build positive relationships between handicapped and nonhandicapped students as they attend the regular classroom together (p. 10).

Notably, further attention has been given to aspects of learning communities in terms of opportunities for collaboration and friendship.

Techniques such as cooperative learning—where children engage in small-group activities in which they are the primary talkers and doers—that emphasize group accomplishment and de-emphasize competition nurture self-esteem by building confidence and inviting students to achieve their potential. As Slavin (1990) stated:

> Because cooperative learning methods are social interventions, they should provide social effects. The criteria for positive intergroup relations are similar to the widely accepted antecedents of friendship formation or cohesion. ... These include contact; perceived similarity; engaging in pleasant activities; and, once again, cooperation where individuals who work toward the same goal come to see one another as providers of rewards. Cooperative learning increases contact between students, gives them a shared basis of similarity (group membership), engages them in pleasant activities together, and has them work toward common goals. As such, it can clearly be hypothesized that they would increase positive affect among students (p. 49).

Van der Klift and Kunc (1994) also remind us, however, that friendships develop from mutual respect and reciprocity. "Friendship is not the same thing as help" (p. 393).

Though children can and should learn to help each other through collaboration, it is important that all children have occasions to help and to accept help from others. In using practices that emphasize collaboration among children, we teach in consideration of academics ... and more. Noddings (1994) also focuses her work on the importance of human relationships in learning. Through providing instructional arrangements where students support and interact with each other in continual, meaningful ways, teachers promote relationships that lead to mutual caring. When teachers model positive language and attitudes toward difference, students also are affirmed in the development of their peer relationships. A classroom discourse that dialogically and pedagogically explores and embraces differences nurtures relationships within the classroom community and leads students toward a broader appreciation of difference.

Conclusion

Creating a curriculum that caters to individual students seems a daunting process when considering a classroom of 25, and often more, students. Practice born in UDL begins with a holistic conception of the potential for many possible learning experiences, in which the emphasis shifts from a focus on the benefits to an individual to the benefit of the whole community; from determined outcomes to those interpreted through open inquiry in assessment.

When many possibilities are presented, learners are poised to interact with the multitude of variations in contexts that inform whether a task is achievable on one day, but not another. Teachers are positioned to assess and plan based on learner strengths that show themselves in context, occasionally in surprising ways.

Research demonstrates that a sociocultural framework effectively guides and supports all students' learning. By using instructional arrangements that provide opportunities to form cooperative relationships in which students support each other and serve as learning models, students have multiple models and guides to practice and encourage the development of new and emerging abilities (Gindis, 1999). By providing multiple opportunities to participate in the learning community, student learning is both social and individualized and is reinforced through interaction with knowledge in several ways, a favored method in current learning theory (Gardner and Hatch, 1989). The use of this model allows and encourages multiple ways to participate and also reinforces the value of difference in the classroom and society. In this way, difference is reconstructed as normal in the classroom community. As Sapon-Shevin (2000/2001) explains, educators can "move beyond discussions of diversity as a problem in the classroom to a conceptualization of differences as natural, inevitable, and desirable, enriching teaching and learning experiences for teachers and students alike" (p. 35).

10
Designing Curriculum to Cultivate Least Restrictive Attitudes

To develop and maintain inclusive schools and communities, children and teachers need to see themselves as change agents, willing and able to confront and challenge stereotypes and oppressive, discriminatory behavior. Before one can change attitudes toward persons with disabilities, one must understand the development and structure of those attitudes (Jones and Guskin, 1984). In other words, to change attitudes, we must teach what they are. The study of attitudes can promote an understanding of the socialization process, and can contribute to understanding prejudices acquired by one's social group and assimilation of values held by one's parents and peers (Thomas, 1980).

Ableism

Ableism is discrimination toward persons with disabilities and is akin to racism, sexism, and heterosexism. All such "-isms" are forms of discrimination based on beliefs that some ways of being or appearing are superior to others. Prior to the contemporary term, ableism, "handicapism" was coined by Bogdan and Biklen in 1977, who referred to it as "the stereotyping, prejudice, and discrimination practiced by society against disabled people" (p. 14). Ableism is often based on stereotypical representations of disability, which more often lead to negative beliefs and attitudes toward people with disabilities (Shapiro and Spelkoman, 1979). The majority of Americans are unaware these negative attitudes exist within us. The United States Commission on Civil Rights reported, "Many perceive handicapped people's [sic] disadvantaged social and economic status as resulting from innate limitations caused by handicaps. Authorities from every branch of government have concluded, however, that prejudice and discrimination are major causes of the disadvantages confronting handicapped people (Bell and Burgdorf, 1983: 17). When asked to draw a picture of a person with blindness, many grade schoolers will most likely portray a sad individual with dark glasses, a cane, and a tin cup for begging. Ordinarily, children's life experiences provide few real interactions with persons with visual impairments. Stereotyped images persist without exposure and interaction to help offset them (Salend, 1994).

Considerable prejudice exists among school-aged youngsters and tends to increase and become more rigid, as they progress through the grades.

222

In unstructured situations such as in lunchrooms or playgrounds, students deemed different are particularly subject to mistreatment or isolation. "Simply put, students with disabilities are not often chosen as friends" (Rowley-Kelly and Reigel, 1993: 245). The majority of studies indicate that students who do not have disabilities demonstrate negative attitudes toward their peers that do (Salend, 1994: 162). Van Etten (1988), for example, described how she had to face constant cruel teasing as a student with dwarfism:

> The day is clear in my mind, when a group of kids saw me walking onto the school grounds. I was alone and there were about six or seven of them. One child noticed me and made sure the rest didn't miss seeing me. She pointed at me, and they all jumped up and down laughing and making fun of me in their excitement. Most times, I would have just ignored them, but this day it was impossible. Their message was loud and clear—I looked funny. I couldn't take it and tears spilled out as I walked passed them and heard their jeers behind me (p. 35).

Some youngsters do not limit their expressions of cruel behavior to their school-age peers. Ellis (1990), a disability rights advocate with cerebral palsy, reported this personal frightening experience while driving:

> I was stuck in traffic on Route 1. A bus carrying a high school athletic team was stalled next to me. One of the guys on the bus saw me through the window. He pointed me out to his buddies. They crowded to the window, mimicking my awkwardness. The muscles in my neck and face tightened, further distorting my body. I couldn't escape them. Finally, the traffic began to move (B 3).

Unfortunately, cruel terms such as "tard cart," "mental rental," and "banana wagon" are commonly heard from school-aged youngsters describing the small yellow vans (often referred to as "short busses") that have become associated with transport to special education programs. Such intolerance is more a reflection of adult prejudices and of adult-imposed segregation than innate cruelty. Safford observed, "The name-calling may not reveal imitation of adult behavior so much as identification with adult attitudes" (p. 292). This is why the integration of Disabilities Studies into the Curriculum is critical.

General Conditions for Changing Attitudes

Although the need to educate youngsters by teaching about disability is important and perhaps even self-evident, issues regarding prejudicial attitudes and behavior tend to receive low priority in school curriculum. This is especially the case when the pressure to perform on standardized assessments is intense. Nonetheless, focused efforts to promote positive, or anti-ableist attitudes toward disability can be successful (Gallagher, 1995). Designing curriculum to target attitude change, however, must be conceived as more than a one-time event, as some awareness activities or special sporting days might be. Attention to anti-ableist action must go on continually in the school to help students become aware of stereotypes, prejudice, and discrimination and gain exposure to a variety of ways of being and living. Learning about disability can occur alongside key competencies in language arts, social studies, media literacy, and critical thinking. All age groups can be taught about disability in meaningful and developmentally appropriate ways.

Curricular Infusion

The study of disability can enhance many subject areas commonly addressed in school curriculum. When infusing information about disabilities, it is best to offer instruction at appropriate content points rather than offering "special" lessons or units. Earlier chapters of this book provide a wealth of information and ways of thinking about disability and disabled persons that can inform efforts to deepen content-area curriculum, especially in social studies, literature, and media studies.

In social studies, for example, historical study may include knowledge about disabled persons in different eras and cultures. Incorporating the roles and experiences of people with disabilities into studies on daily life and governance in past civilizations contributes to a fuller body of knowledge and exemplifies that disability has always been a part of human experience. When studying contemporary history, especially other movements for civil and human rights, it is useful to include disabilities rights movements and laws such as the Education for All Handicapped Children's Act, Section 504 of the Rehabilitation Act, and the Americans with Disabilities Act. Disability Rights and ableism can be a topic of investigation in the same way that some schools explore the issues of sexism and racism. Background information may include the meanings of the terms "disability," "stereotype," "prejudice," "discrimination," and "stigma."

Analyzing Literature (Fiction)

Studying literature offers innumerable opportunities to consider plot development, characterization, symbolism, and imagery related to disability. According to Fiedler (1996), for example, Shakespeare's characterization of the king in *Richard III* provided "the prototype for the innumerable maimed villains who follow" (p. 41). "Richard's deformity is inextricably tied to his malevolent lust" (Thurer, 1980: 13). Useful to literary analysis, however, Dearing (1981) points out:

> …Richard III was an able soldier, a skillful politician and a capable monarch, who in the two short troubled years of his reign still managed to enact a number of excellent laws still on the books in modern England. Only a man of unusual physical strength and intellectual power could have achieved the career objective history concedes him. The myth, of course, is that Richard was evil incarnate, that he was a cruel, unfeeling

villain, a disastrous and destructive leader and a grotesque hunchback born with a full set of sharp teeth. He was vilified as a hunchback toad, a venomous spider, and a savage wild boar. ... The truth seems to be that he had one shoulder a little higher than the other, largely because of an overdeveloped sword arm; he personally wielded the heavy weapons of the period in his many military campaigns as the principal; field general of his brother King Edward IV. His contemporary portraits reveal a handsome, somewhat ascetic countenance (pp. 32–33).

Thus, it becomes apparent that Shakespeare used physical deformity as a literary device—the twisted mind in the twisted body—to symbolize mental and spiritual ugliness. Shakespeare exploited his audiences' negative perceptions of physical disability by distorting the appearance of the king, who in life was not disabled (Rogers, 1978), to accentuate the evil side of his personality.

Melville, too, used disability to symbolize a warped personality. In *Moby Dick*, Ahab loses his mind over the white whale's destruction of his leg and sacrifices himself and his crew in a mad, obsessive pursuit of revenge. As Kriegel (1982) observed:

Melville's Captain Ahab is not merely crippled—his leg torn from his body by the white whale—he is "crippled" in the deepest metaphysical sense. His injury became his self-hood (p. 18).

The reader's fear of Ahab is further heightened by the description of Ahab's scar, which begins under the hair of his head and extends to the length of his body (Margolis and Shapiro, 1987), and when Ishmael describes hearing Ahab's wooden leg tapping back and forth across the deck in the middle of the night (Biklen and Bogdan, 1977).

Similarly, Biklen and Bogdan (1977) describe the disability images found in Stevenson's classic, *Treasure Island*. In evoking the terror and suspense that mark this book's opening pages, the key elements are the disabled characters Black Dog and Blind Pew. The former is introduced as a "tallow-faced man, wanting two fingers." This minor disability sets a tone that is built up when the second man is described as that "hunched and eyeless creature," and it is the latter who hands Billy Bones the dread black spot. In addition, when Long John Silver is introduced as a good guy, there is only a casual mention of the fact that he has a wooden leg. Later, when his treachery is revealed, the references to his "timber" leg become ominous and foreboding (p. 7).

Disability, Mitchell and Snyder (2001) point out, is both a "stock feature of characterization and [employed as] an opportunistic metaphorical device" (p. 47). Thomson (1997) demonstrates how literary plots benefit from stereotyped representations of characters with disabilities, as she asks:

How could Ahab operate effectively if the reader were allowed to see him as an ordinary fellow instead of an icon of monomaniacal revenge—if his disability lost its transcendent meaning? What would happen to the pure pity generated for Tiny Tim if he were portrayed as sometimes naughty, such as a "normal" child? Thus, the rhetorical function of the highly charged trait fixes relations between disabled figures and their readers. If disabled characters act as real people with disabilities often do, to counter their stigmatized status, the rhetorical potency of the stigma would be mitigated or lost (pp. 11–12).

Literary analysts such as Rosemarie Garland Thomson, David Mitchell, and Sharon Snyder, among many others, have demonstrated the importance of examining the powerful role disability plays in canonical works of literature, often studied in school.

Literature and Attitude Development

In addition to engaging students in critical, contemporary forms of literary analysis by attending to disability, teachers can also consider the messages transmitted in the works students read. Classical literature, in particular, transmits values provides interpretation, teaches in the form of allegory, and provides models for identification and behavior (Baskin, 1975). A message in a classic receives respectability and even prestige, making it doubly difficult for those with disabilities to overcome deeply entrenched, complex prejudices (Margolis and Shapiro, 1987). As Margolis and Shapiro (1987) emphasize, however:

> The issue is never that of banning or censoring but of discussing and explaining symbolism so that damaging messages are negated. When literature is taught without an explanation of the moralistic meaning assigned to disabilities, those with impairments may find it difficult to overcome deeply entrenched prejudices (p. 21).

Thus, instead of censoring the material that contains prejudiced ideas, teachers can use them as object lessons to offset stereotypes. This can be accomplished by teaching students to discern stereotypes and stereotypical representations related to disability, including those noted earlier: The object of pity—the diseased or sick patient; the subhuman organism; sinister or evil: the menace or the monster; the unspeakable object of dread; the holy innocent or the eternal child; the object of comedy, ridicule, and curiosity; the burden; the victim of violence; and the "supercrip" or the extraordinary disabled person.

Interdisciplinary explorations of literature and related historical contexts can enhance understanding of history, literature, and their embeddedness in social and cultural frames of understanding. For example, John Steinbeck's 1937 classic, *Of Mice and Men*, offers the opportunity for research on disability and its history to understand the characters' actions in the context of time and place. The character, Lennie, exemplifies a view of intellectually disabled persons as social menaces contributing to genetic decline and social disorganization that proliferated during the era of eugenics. Kanner (1964) captured the essence of this image. He noted that:

> [In the early 1900s] mental defectives were viewed as a menace to civilization, incorrigible at home, burdens to the school, sexually promiscuous, breeders of feeble-minded offspring, victims and spreaders of poverty, degeneracy, crime and disease (p. 88).

Further, the President's Committee on Mental Retardation (1977) provided three interesting "articles of belief" from 1912 during the eugenics movement, which guided practice in the treatment of "feeble-minded" individuals during the early part of this century:

> First, there is always danger of uncontrollable and impulsive brutality and dangerous aggressiveness, even in the most mild appearing mental defectives, especially as they reach adult age. They are of essentially violent nature.

> Second, the feeble-minded are prone to crime and delinquency, contributing to a large proportion of the criminal population. Since they do not distinguish right from wrong, their behavior tends to be dominated by primitive anti-social drives.

> Third, feeble-minded persons, especially females, have abnormally strong sex drives which they are unable to control. They tend, therefore, to be degenerate and prolific (pp. 138–139).

The moral quandary over whether George was justified in killing Lennie, which is often posed as a topic for study in relation to *Of Mice and Men*, can be animated and enlivened by featuring the views of disability in Steinbeck's time. Additionally, the opportunities posed to discuss changes in views of disability over time, modern "mercy killings" of disabled persons, and/or disabled persons' position in the contemporary criminal justice system can enhance interdisciplinary study in schools.

Works of literature that feature disabled characters are abundant. Margolis and Shapiro (1987) offer some general recommendations to examine disability as part of literary study, which include:

1. Carefully examine excerpts that introduce and describe persons with disabilities
   a. "Explain how each adjective, phrase, or expression influences their responses"
   b. "Enumerate the number of positive and negative qualities the author attributes to the person with the disability" (Margolis and Shapiro, 1987: 20)

2. Read works fiction, drama, poetry, and non-fiction to include works that realistically portray the experiences of persons or intentionally challenge stereotypes and tropes with disabilities alongside typical reading assigned in school
3. Ask students to rewrite the book or a book excerpt with the disabled character no longer disabled, and have them discuss "How does it affect the story?" (Students may also rewrite the story from the disabled character's point of view.)
4. Ask students in upper grades to analyze and review books with disabled characters for children in the lower grades

The following basic questions can help guide discussion:

1. How would you describe the character's disability? Does the author specifically state it or is it implied?
2. What specific words does the author use to describe the character with the disability? How realistic is the description of the impairment?
3. When was this book written? How are the attitudes toward disability related to the time in which it was written? How do the attitudes and language used in the book compare with current society?
4. What stereotype(s) of disability are portrayed (e.g., is the character pitiable, evil, amusing, weak, burdensome)?
5. Are the characters with disabilities portrayed as people or as literary devices (e.g., "the twisted mind in the twisted body" or "the foreteller of ominous events")? And/or, does the overall theme of the book rely on disability?
6. Is the character with the disability portrayed as interacting in ways that are mutually beneficial? (Disabled individuals are often depicted in literature as pitiable "receivers" in their relationships with able-bodied characters.)
7. Are disabled characters depicted as functioning freely in least restrictive settings?
8. "Why do you think the author chose to make this character disabled? (A frequent answer is, "Because many people are afraid of those who are different, the author used the disability to create an atmosphere of fear.")
9. "How do you think such depictions and descriptive passages influence the way you feel about people with disabilities?
10. "How do you think such depictions and descriptive passages influence the way persons with disabilities feel about themselves?" (Margolis and Shapiro, 1987: 20)

Analyzing Non-Fiction

Reading autobiographies and memoirs and engaging students in writing about their own lives and experiences is a typical part of school curriculum for all levels of study. Students may create picture books, illustrated works of their lives and experiences, memoirs, narratives, and/or photo essays. Planning units on memoir or life writing offer excellent opportunities to include picture books and autobiographical narratives by persons with disabilities. Literature consistently proves itself a powerful means for providing information and influencing the attitudes and development of individuals, and according to Friedberg, Mullins, and Sukiennik (1985):

> Nonfiction carries the unique power of verifiable authenticity, giving special effect to biography, autobiography, concept, and information books about people who are disabled. Children are born without prejudice toward disabilities, but as they meet those who differ from themselves in significant ways, they are affected by societal attitudes as well as by their own individual reactions. Books that sensitively and honestly depict persons with disabilities expand limited experience and can mitigate the uneasiness that stems from material that helps them deal with anxieties and suggests ways that problems can be solved and the good life lived, even in the face of imperfection and adversity (p. ix).

Thus, an excellent method of sensitizing youngsters to the issues of disability is to have them read and evaluate a variety of non-fiction books written by people with disabilities. Ensuring students read a variety of works would help demonstrate that there are many experiences of disability, which, in turn, deflects stereotypes.

For children with disabilities, reading accounts of others can support their efforts to develop a positive self-concept. Kokaska and Brolin (1985) offer the concept of bibliotherapy:

> [O]ne means of helping individuals with disabilities to understand their difficulties is by exposing them to works of literature in which characters with limitations confront and, in most instances, succeed in life's challenges. The key element to the process, aside from the physical act of reading the book, occurs when the individual identifies with the character or circumstance, transfers insights from the literature, and applies them to his own situation. ... Bibliotherapy has received expanded interest among teachers, counselors, and therapists who are attempting to broaden the individual's perspective of his situation and potential problem-solving behaviors that increase the student's self-confidence. This interest has been aided by the fact that a greater number of literary works by individuals with a disability have found their way into print (p. 136).

Grindler, Stratton, and McKenna (1997) listed five research conclusions regarding the effects of bibliotherapy on children:

1. Bibliotherapy can produce positive attitude change related to the reduction of children's fear.
2. Listening and reading used in conjunction with discussion may change attitudes more than listening or reading alone.
3. Positive changes in self-concept can be attributed to bibliotherapy.
4. Bibliotherapy provides children with knowledge of strategies they might employ in particular situations.
5. Books can be useful in helping children solve problems and in helping children realize the usefulness of books for this purpose (p. 7).

When assigning a non-fiction book for its bibliotherapeutic value, teachers may want to consider the following 15 questions in selecting a book:

1. Who wrote the book and for what purpose was the book written? (e.g., memoir/autobiography; informational or instructive; support or inspiration for others with similar experience; for adults, young adults, or children)
2. What is the nature of the disability, and how did it occur?
3. How did the disability affect the author's education, home life, friends, and job?
4. What problems were encountered by the author as a result of the disability?
5. What were the author's accomplishments, contributions, goals, and hopes?
6. What is the message of the book—and to what extent does it reinforce or challenge stereotypes or tropes related to disability?
7. Is the language and terminology used respectful and current?
8. Does the book offer multifaceted ways of understanding experiences related to disability?
9. Did you find the book meaningful, relevant, and realistic? Why or why not?
10. Do you believe that an individual in a context such as the author's would find this book bibliotherapeutically relevant? Why or why not?
11. What did you learn about the disability experience you were unaware of before?

When choosing to assign readings for bibliotherapeutic value, students might read two to three books by different authors to compare and contrast experiences and themes. Six questions to compare and contrast the authors' approaches, feelings, points of view, and attitudes include:

1. On what issues do they agree?
2. On what issues do they differ?

3. What views and what important issues do they share?
4. What experiences do they have in common? What experiences are unique?
5. What are their individual feelings toward the medical model?
6. What do they have to say about labeling and language?

Media Studies

Studying news, political cartoons, media, film, and television programs are excellent ways to incorporate multimedia materials in teaching and support students to develop critical thinking skills. Being able understand and interpret varied sources of information is a necessity for navigating the "information society" that characterizes the contemporary United States. Individuals and organizations involved with disability rights have become increasingly critical about the biased way the media cover disability issues and stories. Prominent among these complaints are demeaning language, inaccuracy, bias, stereotypical representation, and ethical lapses. The media has a long legacy of using disability to deliver messages of tragedy, pity, charity, or brave and inspiring struggles. Less often have people with disabilities been spotlighted for their take on serious issues (Biklen, 1986; Haller, 2010; Johnson & Elkins, 1974; Margolis, Shapiro, and Anderson, 1990).

Teachers can challenge negative, inaccurate, and stereotypical images of persons with disabilities perpetuated by newspapers, magazines, television programs, films, political cartoons, and other mass media by:

1. Identifying and discussing current examples of distortion, inaccuracy, or misdirected attention and using instructional techniques that help students examine their own thoughts, thought processes, and attributions to help students discover, in a safe way, the personal biases and beliefs they were unaware of.
2. Inviting persons from disability rights and news organizations to discuss the issues of media coverage.
3. Organizing instructional units that analyze and evaluate newspaper and magazine coverage and compare findings with explicit criteria (e.g., does this story ignore major as well as his or her disabilities?), and reviewing magazines concerned with disabled persons can add a unique perspective to the unit.

Analyzing the News Media

A lively project that lends itself to cooperative learning is analyzing the news media. Teachers at the junior or senior high school levels consistently confront prejudices already embedded in their students' minds, and examining the beliefs students already hold is the first step in unmasking stereotypes. Next comes organizing instructional units that analyze and evaluate newspaper, magazine, and television coverage of disabled persons that requires students to compare their findings with explicit criteria. Combating stereotypes of the disabled in newspapers and magazines can be different at each schooling level, but in every case, combating stereotypes means examining assumptions, discussing issues, and critically responding to societal injustices. For example, a teacher can use the following nine questions as beginning criteria for analyzing news stories:

1. Does this story ignore major issues facing persons with disabilities?
2. Does the story accurately reflect persons' abilities as well as disabilities?
3. Does it use the proper terminology?
4. Does it use person-first language used? (Are people described as "voters with disabilities" rather than "disabled voters?")
5. Is disability being portrayed in a positive sense rather than as a fate worse than death? (Do words such as "tragedy," "sufferer," and "afflicted" appear?)
6. Does disability appear in the story unnecessarily? (Is the person's disability referred to even though it has no relevance to the story?)
7. Is the disabled individual described in sentimental or pop terms? (Are words such as "courageous," "heroic," "inspiring," "special," or "brave" used?)
8. Is disability portrayed as overcoming barriers and a challenge? (Are terms such as "in spite of his handicap": and "overcame her disability" used?)
9. Is the terminology accurate? (Are terms such as "Down syndrome," "handicapped parking," and "disabled seating" used rather than "Down syndrome," "parking for disabled persons," and "accessible seating?")

Analyzing Editorial (Political) Cartoons

Another important area in the mass media for teachers to address when striving for an anti-ableist curriculum is the very common use of negative disability images in political or editorial cartoons. These images are based on common stereotypical visuals such as:

Turning a deaf ear
Lame duck
Crippled by fear
Blind to the situation

Editorial cartoonists do in pictures what writers do in words. They work in the language of symbols involving visual metaphors. The value of the cartoon is based on its instantaneous exposition of an idea. It is actually a direct attack on someone or something and says one thing at a glance reducing complex issues to a single image. It has the ability to convey meaning in an extraordinarily concentrated manner.

Editorial cartoons are *political* (and often referred to as political cartoons), because they focus on the relationship of *power* between dominant and marginalized groups. They use satire and metaphor to hold up for contempt what they believe are vices, follies, and stupidity. A political cartoon's most important elements, exaggeration, humor, and ridicule often use disability as a metaphor of *powerlessness* and *incompetence.* Depicting the target in a wheelchair, or wearing dark glasses with a cane, or on crutches often portrays this. In order to interpret a political cartoon, the following five issues should be addressed:

1. What is the issue or point the cartoonist is trying to get across?
2. What is the viewpoint or motivation of the cartoonist?
3. Does the use of exaggeration and visual symbolism depict disability as a negative trait?
4. If so, what does the cartoonist intend the symbol to stand for?
5. What other techniques could the cartoonist use to make the point of the cartoon?

In order to fashion an anti-ableist environment, teachers and students need to become aware of the ubiquitous subtle images that stereotype persons with disabilities in editorial cartoons and be able to discuss them. It develops critical thinking and is necessary to expose biased images.

Organizing a Media Watch

Few cooperative learning instructional techniques engage students at any level quicker than a media watch campaign. These campaigns can help students cooperatively correct misconceptions inadvertently perpetuated by newspapers and magazines about persons with disabilities and thus increase understanding. The concomitant benefits of these campaigns include the development of critical reading and thinking skills and improved attitudes toward persons with disabilities. Because media images of persons with disabilities are often superficial or biased, they provide teachers with continual examples of negative language, prejudice, and stereotypes.

A media watch campaign is a planned method of monitoring the media and then providing reporters, newscasters, editors, and producers with responses, often in the form of personal letters that commend appropriate disability terminology and portrayals or suggest positive, constructive alternatives when problems appear. In addition, a media watch campaign teaches about prejudice by encouraging students to challenge biased coverage of disabilities, especially in news reports and human-interest stories. As a cooperative educational technique, such a campaign can help students learn how to analyze critically what they read and view about persons with disabilities. It also provides, of course, an excellent opportunity for implementing cooperative learning experiences.

A media watch campaign can easily include various cooperative learning groups, each assigned to a different newspaper, television, or radio station, with follow-up responsibilities for the whole class.

A media watch campaign allows students cooperatively to exert a direct impact on improving public attitudes toward persons with disabilities and exposing ableism in the media. Students personally and directly become involved in the media's ability to communicate, influence, and shape social values in our society. The class gains the experience of becoming involved through direct interaction with media professionals who have often been criticized for creating and perpetuating stereotypes through inaccurate or sensationalized portrayals of persons with disabilities. Such interaction challenges those image-makers who consider themselves responsible and responsive to their audience. Media watch campaigns also provide a way for students to encourage positive media portrayals by communicating constructively with the media when their story or article is well written.

Establishing a media watch campaign takes a lot of work and commitment on the part of both the teacher and the class. The class must understand the purposes and structure of the cooperative campaign assignment. The first step is to decide what particular goals the class hopes to accomplish so it can focus on exactly what it wants to do. Letters and phone calls to the media must reflect clear goals to be attained. The class may have several possible purposes or goals. It may want to focus, for example, on any or all of these five purposes:

1. Improving images in the media of persons with disability
2. Correcting the terminology used by the media
3. Increasing the frequency of news features about people with disabilities
4. Encouraging the media to include features or present information for the benefit of disabled persons in the community (e.g., encouraging restaurant critics to provide accessibility information in their restaurant reviews, or encouraging chambers of commerce to promote accessible community activities in their promotional brochures)
5. Promoting coverage of policy decisions that affect persons with disabilities (e.g., broad coverage of how a recent mass transit decision affects disabled persons)

The next step in establishing a media watch campaign is to set the scope of activities. Once the goals of the project are established, the class must then cooperatively decide on the scope of its activities. Possible activities include monitoring, taking action, and evaluating what it does. Many questions need to be answered. For example, monitoring procedures need to be clearly established. Some guiding questions for monitors can include reports on the following:

1. What is the origin of the feature? Is it local or from a wire service?
2. What type of disability does the article cover?
3. What words, both positive and negative, are used to describe the disability or the person with the disability?
4. How is the person with a disability or the disability issue portrayed?
5. How important and persistent is the issue? The principal criterion for determining its importance is the daily impact it has on the lives of persons with disabilities. The class must also decide if it will treat a "repeat offender" different from one with a past record for covering disability issues fairly?

The class will need to decide which media sources will be monitored, whether to monitor several newspapers or one, and whether to monitor local or national magazines, and television and radio stations. When setting goals, the class should consider monitoring comparatively few media sources regularly. It will need to discuss other important issues relating to its goals as well. For example, if the class decides to monitor newspapers, on what items will it focus? The possibilities include local, national, and international news stories; regional features; sports and entertainment; editorials; business items and advertisements; and even comics and political cartoons.

The class must also decide how long to conduct its campaign. Will it monitor news features for a day, a week, or a month? Elkins, Jones, and Ulicny (1987) found that daily monitoring is best. However, once the class sets the schedule, it must be followed. Only a regular monitoring schedule can measure the project's effects accurately; success depends on the consistency of the classes' monitoring and response letters. The class needs to agree on how long the campaign will last and at what intervals it will decide whether to continue—say a whole school year, a half-year, or less?

The next step in the process is deciding on appropriate action. Having decided what and when to monitor, the class must then decide what specific kinds of action it intends to take. If a student monitor brings in an article with an obvious ableist bias, how will the follow-up be? It is critical that the entire class discuss the ableist aspects of the article and then vote on an appropriate action. Elkins, Jones, and Ulicny (1987) mentioned the following four options for action:

1. *Educating the media professionals.* Such education may include sending a brochure to the media. In addition, the class could invite a media professional to speak to the class or it could appoint a representative to meet personally with media professionals, or with an editorial board of a targeted paper or station. The more personal contacts the class makes, the better its chance of establishing a positive relationship with the media. Personal meetings increase the class's credibility and its opportunity to bring about change.

2. *Rewarding positive articles.* The class may send a personal letter to a reporter or editor complimenting a story.
3. *Providing corrective responses to negative or undesirable articles.* The class may send letters to a reporter or editor mentioning problems with a particular story or feature, identifying negative aspects (e.g., unacceptable portrayals and language), and then suggesting suitable alternatives. In addition, the class may want to quantify the problems and let the editor or reporter know how often such problems have occurred in the past.
4. *Providing corrective activities for uncooperative media professionals.* The class must also decide how it will deal with media professionals who remain uncooperative and insensitive to disability issues. The class, for example, may opt to contact an agency, organization, or individual with the influence or power to make change—such as an editor, a publisher, a sponsor who buys lots of advertising, or even the Federal Communications Commission.

Expanding the watch to monitor other groups who are subject to media bias offers a way to expand or diversify a media watch. Students might work in small groups to consider representations of race, sexuality, gender, nationality, religion, economic status, or geographical region.

The last step in establishing a media watch campaign is assessment. To determine whether or not the campaign has reached its goals, the class can develop a method of evaluating outcomes. A flow chart that tracks group reports can be helpful; it can, perhaps measure whether negative portrayals, language, and terminology have decreased, increased, or remained unchanged. The class can judge whether the media are changing their portrayals and terminology over time. Thus, both the teacher and students must monitor the monitors for accuracy and consistency.

Disability Awareness Programs

Infusing the study of disability into school curriculum aims to incorporate a facet of study that has been omitted in the past. A focus on diversifying curriculum is akin to the long-term societal benefits of educating students with disabilities in public schools and in inclusive settings to reduce fear, bias, and discrimination. Although incorporating the study of disability into content-area instruction is most desirable, schools may also choose to address disability during particular days, weeks, or months designated for "disability awareness." Disability awareness is observed in states including Indiana and Missouri and in cities across the United States in March. The US Congress designates October as National Disability Employment Awareness Month, and Idaho, North Carolina, and New York also name October as a time to focus on disability history.

Disability awareness events tend to offer activities such as charity drives to benefit cure research and guest presenters who share experiences related to disability. Schools may also utilize a disability awareness curriculum to spread knowledge about disability in classes or workshops, or may engage students in activities to alert them to disability discrimination, reduce fear about disability and disabled persons, and/or develop empathy for people with disabilities. Because attitude change often comes in the aftermath of targeting an abundance of messages upon an individual or audience, it is possible to use disability awareness events to promote positive attitudes toward persons with disability.

From the literature on disability awareness, one can adduce the following 20 goals for a comprehensive disability awareness program:

1. One's value as a human being is not earned, it is a given.
2. People are more alike than different.
3. Differences can be seen as both positive and negative. Different does not imply one is better or worse than another person. Differences need not be stigmatized.
4. All persons benefit from a diverse population.
5. Although people are different, an overall transcending humanness unites us all.
6. All persons can learn.
7. Disabilities are normal.
8. People are unique individuals, not labels. Everyone has a right to be judged on individual merit, not prejudged by group membership.
9. It is hurtful to judge others.
10. Feelings are important. A caring person avoids hurting others.
11. Self-esteem helps an individual grow.
12. Language is a critical ingredient in framing our thoughts and attitudes.
13. Disabling environments, as opposed to impairments, per se, are situational and environmental and therefore can be eliminated.
14. Disabled persons have basic rights that must be safeguarded for everyone's benefit.
15. Positive attitudes and understanding help us all develop empathy.
16. Developing empathy, understanding, compassion, and concern for others enhances our own growth. Cruelty to others hinders personal growth. Persons with disabilities deserve empathy rather than sympathy or pity, and exercise of empathy is a valuable and compassionate skill.
17. We can most fully experience life by concentrating on our abilities and doing what we can do.
18. Each disability group is unique, special, and significant, as is each individual member of that group. We can learn valuable lessons from each disability group and each disabled individual.

19. Negative attitudes toward persons with disabilities are deeply ingrained in our culture, language, media, and history.
20. Integration is preferable to segregation.

A comprehensive disability awareness program should stress goals that facilitate integration by establishing a classroom climate in which students with disabilities can find acceptance and respect as their peers learn about the benefits, advantages, and opportunities of living in a diverse and pluralistic society. To support and promote integration and inclusion, one can usefully consider the following guiding principles.

Emphasize Sameness

When teaching about disability awareness, continually emphasize sameness. For example, when teaching about persons with mobility impairments emphasize the commonalities in people. We may do some things differently, but we do the same things. Although some people get around with the use of a wheelchair, we all need transportation. Some people communicate with sign language, but we all need to communicate. In fact, although we are all different, we are also all the same and more alike than unlike. When teaching about a particular disability, raise questions that invite this kind of thinking. For example, discussion questions on blindness may include: "What could you still do if you became blind? What couldn't you do? What could you still do but have to do differently or with help? Would you still be you?" When introducing examples of differing disabilities at the younger grade levels, reinforce the concept of sameness by proceeding from the least to the most severe. Also, make sure you present disabling conditions most familiar to the students, such as blindness, earliest (Bookbinder, 1978).

Appreciate Individual Differences

Another important basic theme in teaching disability awareness program is the appreciation for all individual differences, not just disabilities. Educators need to emphasize the idea that people are individuals who represent themselves, not a group, and each has a right to be different. Lessons and activities should reflect an appreciation for differences and diversity and avoid stereotypes and stigmatizing. Information included should stress how every individual contributes to the culture and classroom, and every student is equally worthy. Students, in turn, need to become equipped with a positive way to express their curiosity, concern, and acceptance of those who appear different. Whatever the disability, the classroom discussion should encompass and emphasize individual differences and an appreciation of uniqueness. Similarly, when a guest with a disability comes to class, remind the students that he or she speaks only for himself or herself, not for all disabled people.

Get Involved

Students should, of course, become aware of the enormous impact public attitudes have on the potential for acceptance and inclusion of persons with disabilities into community life and how negative impressions lead to prejudice, discrimination, and segregation that persons with disabilities encounter every day. When students begin to understand the issues that affect their classmates and others with disabilities, they will be more likely to support social policies and programs that promote inclusion and independence. Further, people typically have to do something in order to change attitudes. Attending lectures or reading ideas, without engagement with them, seldom changes attitudes. Work toward attitude change must include active participation, including thinking, communicating, and taking positive action. This is precisely why longer-term curriculum that includes activities such as conducting a media watch is likely to be most productive and enriching.

Strategies for Changing Negative Attitudes Toward Persons with Disabilities

Some effective ways to influence attitudes toward disability are experiential (active participation) techniques [Schroedel (1979), Donaldson (1980), and Watts (1984)]. These include social gaming (e.g., role-playing, behavior rehearsing, and simulation activities, always followed by discussion); value confrontation and learning about inference; interaction with persons with disabilities (including cooperative learning with disabled peers and exposure to guest presenters with disabilities); the provision of basic information on disabilities by exposure to books, articles, and a wide variety of audio-visual media, including resources available on the World Wide Web; and exposure to assistive technology.

Assessing Existing Attitudes

Teachers must assess class members' general knowledge of and attitudes toward persons with disabilities. Specifically, they need to assess their students' current attitudes, common assumptions, and misconceptions before they can respond effectively and attempt to induce change. Engaging students in self-examination is a good starting point. What myths do students believe to be truth? What paradigms regarding disability do they have? What attitudes the teachers themselves hold might be ableist? For example, does the student or teacher regard stuttering as amusing? Does he or she believe that persons with mental retardation are dangerous or that persons with disabilities can never be happy? Does he or she consider it foolish to take an individual with blindness to an art museum? What is his or her belief regarding integration and segregation? For example, should children with disabilities go to separate schools, and if so, why?

Does he or she regard persons with disabilities as a homogeneous group of persons who lead lives quite different from those of the rest of society? Does he or she associate physical disability with evilness or retribution? Such self-examination should be as intense as possible and should always include discussion. Those who actively participate are far likelier to change attitudes, while no change is likely to occur in those who remain passive.

Four effective basic techniques successfully used for assessing student attitudes toward disabilities are direct observation, student "opinionnaires," sentence completion techniques, and drawings. All four encourage youngsters to reflect on their attitudes and thoughts toward persons with disabilities and then convey them to the teacher. Any method used to assess attitudes and beliefs may also prompt discussions of issues related to disabilities.

Direct observation. Observing students as they interact with each other, respond to representations of disability in literature, photos, or media sources, or with adults with disabilities is a way to assess their perceptions and comfort.

Student opinionnaires. The Measurement of Attitudes toward People with Disabilities, by Antonak and Livneh (1988), includes opinionnaires on all levels for assessing pertinent information. Most of these opinionnaires use a Likert rating scale that includes the familiar range of answers: strongly agree, agree, undecided, disagree, and strongly disagree. They should be used only for "instructional" purposes, not "comparative" or "normative" ones. Teachers may want to develop opinionnaires that include items appropriate for the level of the students they teach and based on the curricular material they teach. In addition, they may want to adapt an existing opinionnaire for younger students who require explanations of language and terms. Teachers may want to rephrase, explain, or simplify questions, or even change them to a true and false format (Antonak and Livneh, 1988).

Student sentence completion techniques. Sentence completion provides another method for adducing feelings and attitudes of students. A student reads a series of open-ended statements to complete. Again, the teacher may want to develop additional or different prompts to match the level of the class and or a specific curriculum.

Student drawings. Yet another valuable attitude assessment strategy is to ask younger students to draw a picture of a scene depicting persons with disabilities. For example, if the student draws a picture of a character with blindness, is the individual wearing dark glasses, holding a cane or tin cup, or using a guide dog? What is the expression on the character's face? If the child draws a picture of a parent of a child with a disability, is the parent sad? If both a parent and a disabled child appear, where are they spaced in relation to each other? If possible, the teacher may want to sit with the child as he or she draws. As DiLeo (1983) stated, "Articulate children are likely to talk as they draw. These comments should be noted as they may clarify what may or may not be visibly evident"

(p. 4). In addition, to assess the youngster's feelings accurately, a teacher should ask him or her to write a story explaining the picture (Salend, 1994).

Experiential Methods

Demystifying Aids, Appliances, and Adaptive Technology

Many students with disabilities benefit from using supportive devices, aids, materials, and appliances. These materials include audio books, hearing aids, speech synthesizers, wheelchairs, Braille, and adaptive technology devices. Children with little or no exposure to people with disabilities are often fascinated by all the "gear." Because their fascination focuses on the equipment, they sometimes seem unaware of the person using it. In other words, people often concentrate more on the wheelchair than its user.

One aspect of the stigma of disability lies in the mystification of its accompanying equipment—such as wheelchairs, crutches, braces, and walkers—to the extent that people may be afraid to touch these objects, as if they might "catch" the disability. Unfortunately, charity drives reinforce these attitudes. In their quest to make their disability the most debilitating so the public will donate, they often use aids and appliances in a shocking way in their advertising. For example, to dissuade teenagers from drinking and driving, a Blue Cross and Blue Shield of Pennsylvania ad featured an empty wheelchair with the caption "Is this the set of wheels you've been saving for?" Another ad shows a wheelchair with the caption "Thousands of youngsters are sentenced to the chair each year." The message is plain: living your life in a wheelchair is the worst thing in the world. An ad for the Muscular Dystrophy Association shows a glass-box-like terrarium with a child's leg brace in it. The top has a slit similar to a bank to collect money. A sign on the box reads "Help Jerry's Kids bury the brace." If such campaigns must convey their points in a negative way, they should focus on what causes the handicap and disability, not what helps the individual overcome it. Such ads make it imperative that teachers, introducing a unit on physical disabilities or sensory impairments, show prostheses and wheelchairs as positive objects that help people deal with environmental barriers.

Recently, various juvenile books have been written that familiarize children with different kinds of equipment. In addition, various magazines, targeted for persons with disabilities, carry ads and information on adaptive equipment. Teachers may have their students read them to learn about adaptive equipment. Such equipment may be shown in a light-hearted context (e.g., electric wheelchairs go quite fast, much faster than a person on foot, and can be pictured in races or tag games) to counteract the link between this equipment and injury, death, disease, and vulnerability. Having "practiced" with the equipment, children are less likely to find it strange or frightening. When something is overwhelming, children sometimes react with fear or aggression—in order to make themselves feel more secure. Relieved of their resistance or fear, they can learn to take the paraphernalia for granted and recognize the persons using it. Teachers can introduce these devices in interesting ways that help youngsters develop an appreciation for their purpose, to liberate persons with disabilities.

Inventors, engineers, designers, therapists, and imaginative laypeople have devised a wide range of ingenious aids to help disabled people in all phases of their lives—for example, at home, traveling, at work, at recreation. From a simple homemade reacher that retrieves dropped articles, to a sophisticated breath-controlled switch that operates a typewriter, these devices help persons with disabilities live more independently. Aids can simplify eating, grooming, dressing—in fact, almost all the basic tasks of daily living. A few specialized gadgets can make household chores such as cleaning, cooking, and laundering easier. Among the more sophisticated adaptive apparatuses are electronic systems, telephones, reading and writing contrivances, and alternative and augmentative communication devices. Automobile adaptations, special controls, and transfer aids make driving possible. Wheelchairs, walkers, hoists, lifts, and ramps increase outdoor and indoor mobility.

The literally thousands of these devices and aids range from expensive equipment obtainable only from specialists to simple gadgets illustrated in a variety of mail order catalogs and magazines catering to the need of persons with physical disabilities. The large number and wide variety of these products make it impossible to mention every one. For example, just in the area of automobile transportation, automated controls help a physically disabled person drive his or her own car. These include parking brake extensions, left-foot accelerators, built-up brake and gas pedals, left-hand shift levers, and light-weight folding van ramps.

Similarly, a wide assortment of kitchen and cooking aids include a safety-cutting fork designed with the cutting edge along one side designed specifically for either the right or left hand. For those with limited arm range, an angle-handled utensil of stainless steel with a plastic handle is available. Also obtainable are slip-on or large-handled utensils. An inner-lip or suction cup dinner plate keeps food from sliding. Microwave ovens come with tactile touchpads, tactile dials, and Braille kits for the controls. A talking bread and dough maker comes with an optional voice feature that can be activated to guide users through all phases of the baking process.

In addition, a talking microwave oven with a tactile keypad. There are also non-slip special jar openers, capscrew openers, plastic sack openers, milk carton holders, tactile measuring spoons, tab grabbers, and utensils with handles enlarged. Special dinnerware includes sectioned plates with raised sides to push a fork or spoon against. An arthritis mug features two handles with thumb rests. A variety of aids for dressing and other daily living needs includes an elongated no-stoop shoehorn, elastic shoe laces that permit shoes to be slipped on or off without tying or untying, zipper pull rings or a long reach zipper pulls with 18-inch plastic cords and metal hooks and rings. A one-handed dental flosser that features floss storage and tension control in one handle.

Thus, disabled students may be introduced to aids, appliances and assistive technology, and may take time to examine and try out the devices that persons with disabilities might use. In their own classrooms, they can learn to write in Braille and to use finger spelling and some sign language. They can learn to operate and take care of hearing aids. They use wheelchairs, walkers, and crutches. They can examine braces, artificial legs, and other prostheses. Schools may borrow the aids and appliances from local agencies, or special schools in the area. Students may even design adaptive equipment as science projects.

Leaders of the disability rights movement believe that technology will be the equalizer in the twenty-first century. Technology already enhances our independence and productivity, whether or not we have disabilities. When a person with a disability uses a technology application, it is commonly referred to as "assistive technology." Assistive technology may be high or low tech; it may be an item available at a local department store, such as a large-key telephone, or a specially designed product, such as an electric wheelchair equipped with a sip-and-puff control. In the next decade, this technological "liberation" is likely to free more and more of our citizens with disabilities. Combined with civil rights, improved access, and education, assistive technology can help us transcend the myths and prejudices that have limited persons with disabilities for so many years and usher in a new age of inclusion for those so labeled.

Wherever possible, it would be best for students with the disabilities using adaptive equipment to introduce and explain the aids and devices they use themselves. They can show their classmates the devices and allow them to touch and experiment with the equipment. For example, a student with a hearing impairment could explain the parts and maintenance of the hearing aid, and then invite other students to use a hearing aid briefly. If the student with the disability feels uncomfortable explaining the aids he or she uses, a physical therapist, teacher, guidance counselor, or parent might do so. Adaptive devices may be obtained from a variety of sources and placed in a central location within the room. Students could then examine and experiment with the devices at different times during the school day.

Such alternative communication systems, such as Braille, sign language, and finger spelling can be introduced to students in a variety of ways that simultaneously promote academic skills. Teachers can teach students the manual alphabet, then have them practice their spelling words by spelling them manually. Teachers can include hand signs for numbers as part of a math assignment. For example, rather than writing the numbers of a division computation on the board, the teacher could present the problem with numerical hand signs. Teachers could introduce the students to basic signs and then use them to give directions and assignments. Students who have learned Braille might be assigned the task of reading Braille books, and writing their names or compositions in Braille.

Behavior Rehearsing and Role-Playing

Role-playing offers an effective technique for changing attitudes. For example, Watts (1984) concluded that active participation, such as role-playing provides an effective approach to changing attitudes toward persons with disabilities. The proven effectiveness of these methods reinforce his recommendation and, more important, conclude the resulting changes appear to be relatively permanent. Clore and Jeffrey (1972) conducted a relevant study that focused on the attitudinal effects of role-playing. They demonstrated the dramatic effects of emotional role-playing upon individuals' attitudes.

When initiating a role-playing situation, the teacher should emphasize that role-playing includes no "right or wrong" judgment. The students should know that everyone is acting. The goal is to act out a situation and to talk about the results. It is important for the teacher to state the goal of and the reason for using the technique. For example, "By role-playing and acting out this situation, you will have a chance to observe and express some of the behaviors we have been discussing in class."

To begin the role-playing activity, the teacher should describe the situation to be enacted clearly and in detail, and never force a student to assume a role. While the role-players are provided with written or verbal descriptions of their roles, the observers should be provided with such specific tasks as watching the verbal and non-verbal responses of particular characters. Once the role-playing begins, it should continue until enough has happened to stimulate discussion, the situation has been adequately illustrated, or the action has become dull or repetitive to the point of diminishing its impact. After the role-playing situation is stopped, the class should debrief both the actors and the observers. All actors should describe their experiences and responses to particular behaviors and feelings. Asking actors for their feelings before discussing the role-play with the group lessens their anxiety about criticism. In addition, observers should report on what happened and be encouraged to ask questions, discuss what happened in the role-play, why it turned out the way it did, and whether they are satisfied with the way it turned out (Salend, 1994). The role-play is a way to encourage dialog about disability, beliefs, and action. The most important part to promoting anti-ableist attitudes is the discussion.

Scenarios for Role-Play

1. You are sitting with a group of friends as a fast food restaurant. One of your friends has cerebral palsy and is a wheelchair user. The manager approaches and asks if your group can finish eating and leave as quickly as possible because some young children having a birthday party nearby are upset about seeing your friend in the wheelchair. How do you react?

2. You are at a mall with friends and encounter a group of persons with developmental disabilities. A friend says, "Look at those retards. Don't they make you want to barf?" How do you respond?

3. A classmate who needs help to do schoolwork and participate in class works with others in class, but is ignored on the playground and at lunch. How would you handle this?

4. You are a class officer. At a planning meeting for your 3-day out-of-town class trip, your principal gives your committee the option of excluding "the special ed kids." How do you respond?

5. A friend tells you that he or she has a brother with a developmental disability as she's inviting you to her home. How would you react?

6. You are at a party. You extend your hand while being introduced to another guest and realize she has low vision and is unaware you want to shake hands. What do you do?

7. Your mother does not like to have animals in the house, especially dogs. You are planning a party and want to include a friend who uses a guide dog. How would you handle the situation? What would you say to your mother?

8. You see a police officer yelling at a man you know who is hard-of-hearing. Do you get involved? If so, how do you handle it?

9. While standing next to a bank of pay telephones, you notice that a woman of short stature cannot reach high enough to dial what appears to be an important call. Would you offer help? Why or why not?

10. A wheelchair user parked nearby to you falls out of his chair while transferring from his van. Would you get involved? If so, how?

11. You are at a store and the customer ahead of you is speaking with a severe stutter to the salesperson who abruptly walks away in the middle of a sentence and asks you if you need help. How would you react?

12. Your sister is asked to go out on a date by someone you know and like, and who is in a special education class. Do you tell her or your parents? Why or why not?

13. A friend asks you to raise money for the Muscular Dystrophy Association. Knowing that many persons with physical disabilities have negative feelings toward such fund-raising activities would you participate or decline? What would you say?

14. You are at a restaurant with a friend with a disability. The waiter points to your friend and asks you, "What does he want?" How do you respond?

15. On the trip home, your school bus stops for a traffic light. A group of kids on the bus notice out the back window that the driver of the car behind the bus has cerebral palsy and displays spastic movements.

They laugh and begin to mock and imitate him through the window. How would you handle the situation?

16. Your good friend, a wheelchair user, is the best trumpet player in the school. He tells you that the bandmaster refused to allow him to join the band "because he will mess up the formations when they march in parades." How would you respond?

17. A person with whom you are having a conversation has a communication disability and you can't quite understand what he is saying. How do you respond?

18. A number of Deaf students and their parents are petitioning your school board to have American Sign Language taught at your school for foreign language credit. You are at the board meeting. Do you address the board in support of their request? Why or why not?

19. A classmate complains that it is unfair that a student with learning disabilities had only half the number of problems for homework. How would you respond?

20. A friend remarks that he would rather die than be in a wheelchair. How do you respond?

21. A classmate expresses a feeling of discrimination, because a fellow student with a learning disability is the only one in the class with permission to use a calculator during a math exam. How do you respond?

22. You and a group of friends are going to movie. Do you invite a friend with visual impairment along? What if you are going skiing?

23. You hear someone say "Institutions for the mentally retarded are important because the retarded prefer to be with their own kind." How would you respond?

24. You and a group of friends are planning to go to a rock concert. Do you ask a friend with hearing impairment to join you? Why or why not?

25. A friend expresses the view that mentally retarded people should not be allowed to marry or vote. What is your response?

26. A number of your neighbors are holding a meeting to express their anger at the state for wanting to open a group home for eight young adults with autism in your community. Among their fears are the safety of their children and lowered property values. You have an opportunity to address the meeting. What do you say?

27. You visit a friend for the first time since his accident in which he lost his legs. Role-play both a "sympathetic" and an "empathetic" reaction to his physical impairment.

28. A young boy who uses a wheelchair moves next door to you. You like him. As your families get to know each other, the boy's mother

confides in you that her son has a difficult time making friends with youngsters his own age. She asks if you would introduce him to the youngsters in the neighborhood and ease the transition for him. You and he see a group of youngsters from the neighborhood playing the next day. Role-play what you would do and say.

Simulations

Experiencing simulations is much like role-playing. Both are forms of social gaming. Learning through simulations takes place by creating circumstances and working out solutions to problems that might arise in a particular situation. The difference between role-playing and simulations is in the role that participants occupy. Role-plays assume that the participants respond as themselves; simulations ask participants to "try-on" the experience of another. Burgstahler and Doe (2004) explained, "A simulation creates a representation of elements of reality to develop a learning activity so participants develop skills, gain knowledge or change attitudes about that reality" (p. 8). They further stressed, "Simulations have been found to stimulate interest in a topic and the desire to learn more. They are reputed to change perspectives, increase empathy, increase self-awareness, and increase tolerance for ambiguity" (p. 9). Thus, a simulation allows the learner to experience essential aspects of a situation during active participation, which, ideally, generates insight into the real world.

Popular simulation activities include engaging students in blind-folding, ear-plugging, wheelchair-riding, and/or tying back limbs or fingers, then sending them to complete either planned tasks, such as an obstacle course, or to try to follow a usual routine as an impaired person. The widely used Frustration Anxiety and Tension workshop, known as F.A.T. City (Lavoie, 1989), is a video that invites participants to make meaning of nonsense words and complete impossible activities to simulate the experience of students with learning disabilities. Although the most favorable outcomes of simulations can result in empathy and appreciation for the challenges disabled persons face from environmental barriers, this learning comes at a steep price. Simulations can also result in heightened fear and negative perceptions of disability.

Burgstahaler and Doe (2004) warn:

In actuality, most disability-related simulations are designed to result in negative feelings. By disabling participants and simulating problematic experiences, given their new limitations participants learn how difficult it is to maneuver a wheelchair, how frustrating it is to be unable to hear or read, how frightening it is to be visually impaired, or how impossible it is to participate without the use of their hands. They focus on what people with disabilities cannot do with appropriate access, technology, or skills (p. 11).

Brew-Parrish (1997; 2004), a disabled activist, recalls her daughter's experience of a disability simulation from which students emerged "terrified of their newly created disabilities," and with ideas that "persons with disabilities had horrible lives. A few thought they might be better off dead."

On the problems with disability simulations, Wright (1987) quoted Laura Raucher, a disability rights advocate with a physical impairment:

> I don't encourage simulations because I think they're based on a false assumption that fifteen minutes, or two hours, or two weeks in a wheelchair or walking around blindfolded could give someone any idea what it's like to be disabled. ... What a simulation approximates is not the reality of being disabled, but the trauma of becoming disabled—the awkwardness, humiliation, and fear of confronting a world that isn't set up for you and frankly looks down on you, with tools you haven't yet mastered. ... The point we are missing, in the terrifying blackness behind the blindfold or the sweaty confusion of our first bout with double doors, is that people learn to manage, and manage well with disabilities (p. 4).

French (1996) similarly found:

> Simulation exercises have the aim of informing non-disabled people of the situation of disabled people, but they clearly provide false information. At best these exercises only simulate the onset of disability, but even that is not achieved because the people concerned know very well that at the end of the day, or any time they choose, they can stop being 'disabled' and return to their non-disabled status. It is quite obvious that if a person is suddenly deprived of his or her hearing, sight, or ability to walk or use his or her hands, difficulties will be experienced and fear and frustration may be felt, but this is not the situation disabled people are in because they have had to develop coping strategies or unusual dexterity or strength in other areas of their bodies, and are therefore likely to be far more clam and able than the non-disabled person's experience would suggest, which is not to minimize the difficulties they do experience (p. 117).

Alternatives to Simulations

The most common goals for a disability simulation include providing students with experiential activities through which to develop awareness of environmental barriers; and to increase knowledge about how persons with disabilities experience daily life—including joys and struggles. Both of these goals can be achieved through experiential activities that do not require simulation. Art Blaser offers "Some Alternatives to Simulation Exercises" in *Ragged Edge Magazine*, some which are included in the following list.

1. Talk about doing simulations—without doing them.
2. Survey your school or neighborhood to assess everyday barriers. Students may note places inaccessible except by stairs, cars parked

over driveways, unleashed dogs, color contrast on stairs, branches that can hit a blind person, note audible cues, such as horns honking.

3. Survey your school or neighborhood to assess accessibility features. Students can count the number of businesses that have ramps or elevators; explore how to gain access to an elevator in a subway or train station; hunt for accessibility measures found in the environment, including curb cuts, "bumpy tiles" that indicate street intersections or train platforms, Braille plates or signs, the options for auditory instructions. They may evaluate restaurants for table heights and clarity of menus, and so on.

4. Listen to a person with a disability—one in your neighborhood, your class, around school. Develop a list of questions to ask them about their life—not focused only on medical aspects of the disability.

5. Take a tour of a familiar place with a person with a disability to gain insight into how she or he negotiates various places.

6. Find out what confronts a family traveling and living in motels or hotels. Visit a local hotel. Find out where TDD/TTY phones are, and how you would find one if you were deaf.

7. Search for a personal assistant in the classified ads. Find out what the job entails.

8. Evaluate your home for accessibility according to one or many kinds of impairment. Get an estimate of what it would cost to install accessibility features in your home.

9. Create or visit an arts exhibit that can be experienced by many senses: touch, hearing, sight, and maybe even smell. For example, consider the texture of oil painting, sculpture, and relief; incorporate sound or narration into an exhibit; or use essential oils to offer ambient scents to an exhibit.

10. Attend or watch a sporting event that features professional disabled athletes. The Paralympics, for example, features well-known sports such as basketball, rugby, and tennis, as well as lesser-known competitive team sports such as goal ball.

Inviting Guests with Disabilities

Another way to increase students' awareness and understanding on disability is to invite guests with disabilities to interact with or give a presentation to the class. Introducing persons with disabilities into the daily classroom routine provides an ideal first-hand learning opportunity. In general, students benefit from working with community and family volunteers who may work with students on everyday work (e.g., reading buddies) or assist with a special project related to a visitor's professional expertise (e.g., planning a business to learn about economics; planting a garden to study botany). Teachers may specifically invite volunteers, family members, or professionals with disabilities to provide opportunities for direct contact and interaction that does not relate only to disability.

Presenters can also be invited specific to disability awareness events. Class guests with different disabilities can provide experiential knowledge and offer students a chance to have personal contact and to interact with an individual who at first may seem to be different, but in actuality is much like them. The experience gives the youngsters an opportunity to learn how persons with impairments accommodate their disabilities and accomplish what non-disabled persons do differently. They get the chance to see persons with disabilities as individuals, each with their particular personalities, lifestyles, interests, jobs, problems, and ideas. It is best to seek out a visitor who is accustomed to working with children and offering presentations related to disability, especially for the first visit, or if only one guest is planned. Classroom meetings with guests with disabilities should be well planned, and the following text presents preparatory considerations.

Selecting a guest presenter. For the meeting to be meaningful, teachers should be cautious in the identification, selection, and preparation of guest speakers. A teacher can rely on a number of ways to identify potential speakers. Guests with disabilities can be located through local branches of national agencies such as the Association for Retarded Citizens (ARC) and the United Cerebral Palsy Association (UCP). In addition, every state has a Developmental Disabilities Council, and most publish directories of agencies and services within that state. Local agencies are also listed in the Yellow Pages under Human Service Organizations or Social Service Organizations.

Selecting the number of guests. Teachers sometimes conclude that the experience will be more valuable if they invite several guests with similar disabilities at the same time. They feel one visitor may be more comfortable with others. Nevertheless, this decision should be considered carefully. Guests expounding conflicting perspectives or personalities may not appreciate being on the same panel without warning; and unplanned tension can result in confusion and discomfort for everyone involved. If a debate is desired or a presentation of divergent perspectives is intended, it is essential that guests are informed and comfortable and that students know the purpose of the presentation.

Screening potential guests. Having identified potential guest presenters, a teacher should interview them informally. Contact the person, introducing yourself, and explain the interest of your class. Briefly describe the purposes and related activities so that the presenter knows the context into which he or she is entering. It is important to explain what preparation the students will have before the visit. Also explain what you expect in a guest presenter, to help the potential guest speaker decide whether he or she would be comfortable participating in the program, and the kinds of things he or she would like to talk about. From this initial conversation, you might determine that the guest's perspective and experience is not well aligned with the curriculum or students' interests. If the guest does seem like a good candidate, you could gain some principles to include in the curriculum, as well as consider how your class might best interact with the visitor. An introductory conversation should help you get an idea of the person's personality and comfort with children, which can support the planning of a positive experience for all.

Important characteristics to look for in a presenter. If the guest comes from an organization, he or she will probably be accustomed to working with groups, though it is useful to consider the age groups with which the presenter has worked before. Potential presenters who are not accustomed to working with children or being "in the spotlight" need to know ahead of time the kind of questions that students may ask. The introductory conversation can be a time to alert presenters to the likely need to be able to respond candidly, respectfully, and age-appropriately to questions that may seem inappropriate, naive, or intrusive by adult norms. Declining to answer some kinds of questions is, of course, acceptable, but ground rules should be made explicit to students and are best established by the presenter.

Making arrangements. In addition to establishing a date and time, compensation, and other arrangements, it may be particularly important to discuss transportation and access requirements. Teachers should be aware of whether public transportation is accessible and convenient to the school, in terms of the guest's needs. It is also essential to evaluate the accessibility of the school itself: consider entrances and exits, the classroom space, and restrooms. Also important is to consider and ask about interaction with students. Will students need an interpreter or other assistive technology to interact with the guest, for example? If so, how will those arrangements be made? If a service animal (e.g., a guide dog) will attend class, it is important to consider allergies and/or students' fears.

Preparing the presenter. Teachers should keep foremost in their minds the importance of planning and preparation. When inviting a guest who will be compensated for his or her work and time, she or he should know ahead of time what the class expects. Teachers should explain the class's purpose for the invitation and what students should experience or learn, and guests need to know how long a presentation should be (an hour is usually about right for young students; more time may be useful for older); how much of the time to allow for questions; and what kinds of questions will be asked. For example, consider whether the class will have been learning about environmental accessibility, adapting to daily life, vocations, discrimination, personal experiences, being a child, and so on. When inviting a guest who is volunteering his or her time, providing information about length of time and structure is also necessary, but it is essential to ask and respond to the *guest's* preferences for the type of presentation that will be made and the kind discussion that will be invited.

A volunteer should not be asked to prepare something outside of his or her areas of comfort, unless she or he offers.

Preparing the students. Inviting guests with disabilities should be part of an inclusive, multidimensional classroom experience. Therefore, the students should have already engaged in some learning to prepare for the visit. If students know something about visitor's life and characteristics, their interest will be heightened, and they will tend to ask more meaningful questions. It is useful to describe the guest to students—age, where she or he lives or grew up, profession or job, interests, hobbies, and disability. Student may then generate topics of interest or questions they may like to ask. Generating ideas for questions provides an opportunity to help students evaluate appropriate or inappropriate kinds of questions, as based on the teacher's knowledge about the guest.

Addressing feelings. Be sure to allow opportunities for both the guest and children to express their feelings about being with each other. Such a visit may be the first experience youngsters have had to interact with a person with a disability. If the experience is positive, open, and natural, it will influence the way the youngsters may approach others with disabilities when they meet them. It is better to talk openly in front of most guests than talk about them after they have left. Persons with disabilities live with a need to express their feelings, and teachers should understand that individuals with disabilities are more comfortable with questions than non-disabled adults realize. In fact, the conclusion that persons with disabilities avoid talking about their impairments or are ashamed of them is itself a form of prejudiced thinking. Moreover, discussing people now out of sight encourages shyness in children.

Expressing appreciation. Among the best ideas to follow up a visit is to invite students to write thank-you letters, emails, or record messages to your presenter. This experience provides the class to express gratitude, comment on what they learned, and maybe ask more questions and build a relationship.

Questions for Classroom Discussion

All classroom activities—including role-playing and hosting guests with disabilities—should include thorough debriefings and discussions. When presenting any information on disability as diversity awareness, teachers may find any or all of the following questions helpful for promoting classroom discussions. These questions also lend themselves nicely to writing assignments.

1. Human variation is normal

   o Why are all children normal and all children special?
   o What is meant by the statement "People are different in degree rather than kind"?
   o What is your definition of "normal"?
   o How are all people more alike than different?

- How can differences be seen as both positive and negative?
- Why is it important to see people as individuals, not labels?

2. Attitudes and actions

- How do our feelings influence our attitudes and behavior?
- How does our language reflect our attitudes?
- How are negative attitudes toward persons with disabilities deeply ingrained in our culture, language, and history?
- How is your perception of yourself shaped by the way others perceive you?
- In what ways might experiences at school affect the self-image of persons with disabilities?
- Why is it wrong to judge someone by something he or she cannot change?
- What is the difference between "laughing at" people and "laughing with" them?
- How can a disability obstruct people's views of each other?
- What causes peer cruelty? Why do we tend to laugh at something or someone who is different?
- Why is important to treat all persons as individuals?
- What are the implications of calling someone a "vegetable"?
- What do the concepts of "monster" and "freak" imply?
- What are the implications for persons with disabilities beliefs such as "social Darwinism," "eugenics," and "racial hygiene"?

3. Stereotypes and self-image

- Why do you think many people with disabilities describe themselves as "ordinary" and wonder why others do not see them in the same way?
- How do labels become stereotypes? What other negative effects do labels have?
- How do labels affect self-image?
- What are the different effects of being born with a disability and acquiring one later in life?
- Why is it wrong to base judgments of others on appearances?
- What is a "stigma"? How does it affect what we think about someone?
- Describe the concept of "stigma spread." How does a disability become an "all-defining" characteristic?

4. Disability rights and awareness

- Why must the basic rights of persons with disabilities be safeguarded for everyone's benefit?

○ Why do many people with physical disabilities view telethons and similar fund-raising methods as demeaning?

○ Why do most persons with disabilities want us to "empathize" with them rather than "sympathize" with them?

○ What is meant by the statement "An impairment is a characteristic of a person; a disability is a characteristic of the environment"?

○ What is meant by the statement "disabilities are situational?"

○ What are the differences and similarities between the concepts of ableism and racism, sexism, or heterosexism?

○ What are the differences between "equity" and "equality"?

○ Describe what a socially inclusive society would be like.

Conclusion

The development of positive attitudes toward persons with disabilities is essential in working toward integrated schools and society. Providing opportunities for students with and without disabilities to live and learn together in inclusive classrooms is an important element in developing values for all ways of being. There are also many ways that the study of disability and the experiences of disabled people can become part of school curriculum, especially in literature, social studies, and media studies. The experiential (active participation) techniques presented here in this chapter included social gaming; value confrontation, and learning about inference; and ways to interact with adults with disabilities, such as guest presenters with disabilities. All of these activities and efforts have proven themselves effective for changing attitudes. The more varied the experiences provided, the likelier the attitude change.

Final Thoughts

This is a book for all teachers. Attitudes toward persons with disabilities affect everyone. As stated in Chapter 1, schools have a responsibility for encouraging diversity and tolerance, eliminating discrimination, increasing among youngsters an understanding of those perceived to be different, and respecting and protecting the rights of all diverse populations within our pluralistic society. Each individual child is the responsibility of the school and has a right to attend without having to feel inferior. Considering the "three R's"—recognition, respect, and responsibility—as tenets to guide educational practice that can inform productive dialog and the building of collaborative relationships with students, families, and other professionals.

The emergence of Disability Studies challenges and resists the medical model and segregation, as well as examines the perpetuation of these paradigms in the media, our culture, and schools. Directions toward inclusive education, such as universal design for learning and differentiated instruction, offer promising practices for meeting the needs of diverse learners. In turn, developing practices that are responsive to the anticipated diversity of learners mitigates the need to separate children from one another. Scholars in fields of Disability Studies and Disability Studies in Education firmly acknowledge that schools and teachers do not, alone, shoulder all of the responsibility in working toward societal and school integration. The historical legacy of marginalization; the paradigms of disability that inform societal institutions, bureaucratic structures, and policy; and slow, sometimes contradictory forces of school reform movements—including standardization—all complicate efforts toward the realization of inclusive schools. In addition, negative attitudes among educators (and the public) toward the inclusion of students with disabilities persist. In the face of seemingly insurmountable challenges, however, there is possibility. The emergence of disability rights and progress made toward inclusive education over the past decades is testament to the ability of schools and societies to become places in which everybody belongs.

References

Recommended Resources for Teachers

Memoirs and Essays by Persons with Disabilities

Bauby, J. D. (1997). *The Diving Bell and the Butterfly: A Memoir of Life in Death*. New York: Alfred A. Knopf.

Biklen, D., with Attfield, R., Bissonnette, L., Blackman, L., Burke, J., Frugone, A., Rajarshi Mukhopadhyay, T. & Rubin, S. (2005). *Autism and the Myth of the Person Alone*. New York: University Press.

Crawford, V. (2002). *Embracing the Monster: Overcoming the Challenges of Hidden Disabilities*. Baltimore, MD: Paul H. Brookes Publishing Co.

Finger, A. (1998). *Past Due: A Story of Disability, Pregnancy and Birth*. Berkeley, CA: Seal Press.

Fries, K. (1997). *Body Remember: A Memior*. New York: Dutton.

Fries, K. (ed.). (1997). *Staring Back: The Disability Experience from the Inside Out*. New York: Plume.

Glasgow, E. (1954). *The Woman Within*. New York: Harcourt Brace and Co.

Grandin, T. (2008). *The Way I See It: A Personal Look at Autism and Asperger's*. Arlington, TX: Future Horizons.

Grealy, L. (1994). *Autobiography of a Face*. New York: Harper Perennial.

Groce, E. (1985). *Everyone Here Speaks Sign Language*. Cambridge, MA: Harvard University Press.

Handler, L. (1999). *Twitch and Shout: A Tourettor's Tale*. New York: Penguin Group.

Hockenberry, J. (1995). *Moving Violations: War Zones, Wheelchairs and Declarations of Independence*. New York: Hyperion.

Jacobson, D. S. (1999). *The Question of David: A Disabled Mother's Journey through Adoption, Family, and Life*. Berkley, CA: Creative Arts Book Company.

Kayson, S. (1994). *Girl Interrupted*. New York: Vintage Books.

Kleege, G. (1999). *Sight Unseen*. New Haven, CT: Yale University Press.

Klein, B. S. (1998). *Slow Dance: A Story of Stroke, Love and Disability*. Berkley, CA: Page Mill Press.

Knipfel, J. (1999). *Slackjaw: A Memoir*. New York: Berkley Books.

Kuusisto, S. (1998). *Planet of the Blind: A Memoir*. New York: Dial Press.

Lee, C. & Jackson, R. (1992). *Faking It: A Look into the Mind of a Creative Learner*. Portsmouth, NH: Boynton/Cook Publishers, Inc.

Linton, S. (2006). *My Body Politic*. Ann Arbor, MI: University of Michigan Press.

Little, J. (1996). *If it Weren't for the Honor I'd Rather have Walked: Previously Untold Tales of the Journey to the ADA*. Cambridge, MA: Brookline Books Inc.

Mairs, N. (1996). *Waist-High in the World: A Life among the Nondisabled*. Boston, MA: Beacon Press.

Manning, M. (1995). *Undercurrents: A Therapist's Reckoning with Depression*. San Francisco, CA: Harper Collins.

Merker, H. (1992). *Listening*. New York: Harper Collins.

Mooney, J. (2008). *The Short Bus*. Canada: H.B. Fenn and Co.

Olson, C. T. (1986). *How Can We Understand the Life of Illness*. Edmunton: University of Alberta.

Osborn, C. (1998). *Over My Head: A Doctor's Own Story of Traumatic Brain Injury from the Inside Looking Out*. Kansas City, MO: Andrews McMeel Publishing.

Padden, C. & Humphries, T. (1988). *Deaf in America: Voices from a Culture.* Cambridge, MA: Harvard University Press.

Panzarino, C. (1994). *The Me in the Mirror.* Seattle, WA: Seal Press.

Rodis, Garrod & Boscardin. *Learning Disabilities and Life Stories.* Boston, MA: Allyn and Bacon.

Schmitt, A. (1994). *Brilliant Idiot: An Autobiography of a Dyslexic.* Intercourse, PA: Good Books.

Simpson, E. (1979). *Reversals.* Boston, MA: Houghton Mifflin Co.

Upham, D. A. & Trumbull, V. H. (1997). *Making the Grade: Reflections on Being Learning Disabled.* Portsmouth, NH: Heinemann.

Wright, M. (1999). *Sounds Like Home: Growing up Black & Deaf in the South.* Washington, DC: Gallaudet University Press.

Resources for Teaching About Disabilities Through Literature, Drama, and Film

Bunch, G. (1996). *Kids, Disabilities and Regular Classes, an Annotated Bibliography of Selected Children's Literature on Disability.* Toronto, Canada: Inclusion Press.

Connor, D. J. & Bejoian, L. M. (2006). Pigs, pirates, and pills: Using film to teach the social context of disability. *Teaching Exceptional Children, 39*(2), 52–60.

Darke, P. (1998). Understanding cinematic representations of disability. In T. Shakespeare (ed.), *The Disability Reader: Social Science Perspectives* (pp. 181–197). London: Casell.

Friedberg, J., Mullins, J., & Sukiennik, A. (1985). *Accept Me as I Am: Best Books of Juvenile Nonfiction on Impairments and Disabilities.* New York: R. R. Bowker.

Friedberg, J., Mullins, J., & Sukiennik, A. (1992). *Portraying Persons with Disabilities: an Annotated Bibliography of Nonfiction for Children and Teenagers.* New York: R. R. Bowker.

Margolis, H. & Shapiro, A. (1987). Countering negative images of disability in classical literature. *The English Journal, 76*(3), 18–22.

Mitchell, D. T. & Snyder, S. L. (2001). *Narrative Prosthesis: Disability and the Dependencies of Discourse.* Ann Arbor, MI: University of Michigan Press.

Quick, J. (1985). *Disability in Modern Children's Fiction.* Cambridge, MA: Brookline Books Inc.

Robertson, D. (1992). *Portraying Persons with Disabilities: An Annotated Bibliography of Fiction for Children and Teenagers.* New Providence, NJ: R. R. Bowker.

Sandahl, C. & Auslander, P. (2005). *Bodies in Commotion: Disability and Performance.* Ann Arbor, MI: University of Michigan Press.

Saxton, M. & Howe, F. (eds.) (1987). *With Wings: An Anthology of Literature by and about Women with Disabilities.* New York: The Feminist Press at the City University of New York.

Thomson, R. G. (1996). *Extraordinary Bodies: Figuring Physical Disability in American Culture and Literature.* New York: Columbia University Press.

Resources for Teaching Disability Rights and History

Fleischer, D. Z. & Zames, F. (2001). *The Disability Rights Movement: From Charity to Confrontation.* Philadelphia, PA: Temple University Press.

Longmore, P. K. & Umansky, L. (eds.) (2001). *The New Disability History: American Perspectives.* New York: New York University Press.

Museum of disABILITY History. [Website] http://www.museumofdisability.org. Williamsville, NY.

Shapiro, J. P. (1993). *No Pity: People with Disabilities Forging a New Civil Rights Movement.* New York: Times Books.

The EDGE (Education for Disability and Gender Equity). [Website] http://www.disabilityhistory.org/dwa/edge/curriculum/culture.htm

Sourcebooks for Inclusive Teaching Practice

Danforth, S. & Smith, T. J. (2005). *Engaging Troubling Students: A Constructivist Approach.* Thousand Oaks, CA: Corwin Press.

Friend, M. & Cook, L. (2007). *Interactions: Collaboration Skills for School Professionals.* Boston, MA: Pearson.

Gabel, S. (2005). *Disability Studies in Education: Readings in Theory and Method.* New York: Peter Lang.

Grant, C. A. & Sleeter, C. E. (2008). *Turning on Learning: Five Approaches for Multicultural Teaching Plans for Race, Class, Gender and Disability* (5 ed.). Hoboken, NJ: Wiley.

Jorgensen, C. M. (ed.). (1998). *Restructuring Highs Schools for All Students.* Baltimore, MD: Brookes Publishing Co.

Jorgensen, C. M., Schuh, M. C., & Nisbit, J. A. (2005). *The Inclusion Facilitator's Guide.* Baltimore, MD: Brookes Publishing Co.

Kalyanpur, M. & Harry, B. (1999). *Culture in Special Education: Building Reciprocal Family-Professional Relationships.* Baltimore, MD: Paul H. Brookes.

Kluth, P., Straut, D. M., & Biklen, D. P. (eds.) (2003). *Access to Academics for all Students: Critical Approaches to Inclusive Curriculum, Instruction, and Policy.* Mahwah, NJ: Lawrence Erlbaum Associates.

McTighe, J. & Wiggins, G. (2004). *The Understanding by Design Professional Development Workbook.* Alexandria, VA: ASCD.

Pugach, M. C. & Warger, C. L. (eds.) (1996). *Curriculum Trends, Special Education, and Reform: Refocusing the Conversation.* New York: Teachers College Press.

Salend, S. J. (2007). *Creating Inclusive Classrooms: Effective and Reflective Practices for All Students* (6th ed.). Upper Saddle River, NJ: Prentice Hall.

Sapon-Shevin, M. (2007). *Widening the Circle: The Power of Inclusive Classrooms.* Boston, MA: Beacon Press.

Stainback, S. & Stainback, W. (1996). *Inclusion: A Guide for Educators.* Baltimore, MD: Paul H. Brookes.

Thomas, G. & Loxley, A. (2007). *Deconstructing Special Education and Constructing Inclusion* (2 ed.). Philadelphia, PA: Open University Press.

Thousand, J. S., Villa, R. A., & Nevin, A. I. (eds.) (1994). *Creativity and Collaborative Learning: A Practical Guide to Empowering Students and Teachers.* Baltimore, MD: Paul H. Brookes.

Tomlinson, C. A. (2004). *How to Differentiate Instruction in Mixed-Ability Classrooms* (2 ed.). Alexandria, VA: ASCD.

Tomlinson, C. A. & McTighe, J. (2006). *Integrating Differentiated Instruction and Understanding by Design.* Alexandria, VA: ASCD.

Turnbull, A. P., Turnbull, H. R., & Wehmeyer, M. L. (2009). *Exceptional Lives: Special Education in Today's Schools* (6 ed.). Upper Saddle River, NJ: Prentice Hall.

Villa, R. A., Thousand, J. S., & Nevin, A. I. (2008). *A Guide to Co-Teaching: Practical Tips for Facilitating Student Learning.* Thousand Oaks, CA: Corwin Press.

Wiggins, G. & McTighe, J. (1998). *Understanding by Design.* Alexandria, VA: ASCD.

Works Cited

ADAPT v. Skinner, 881 F.2d 1184, 3rd Cir. (1989).

Adler, S., Richard, Y., & Horowitz, J. (2008). *Tropic Thunder* director/star Ben Stiller says disability advocates' planned boycott is unwarranted. *MTV.com.* Retrieved 11 August 2008, from http://www.mtv.com/movies/news/articles/1592544/story.jhtml

Advisory Committee on Human Radiation Experiments (ACHRE). (1994). *Interim Report.* Washington, DC: U.S. Government Printing Office.

Advisory Committee on Human Radiation Experiments (ACHRE). (1996). *Executive Summary and Guide to Final Report.* Washington, DC: U.S. Government Printing Office.

Albrecht, G., Seelman, K., & Bury, M. (2001). *Handbook of Disability Studies.* Thousand Oaks, CA: Sage Publications.

Albright, K., Brown, L., Vandeventer, P., & Jorgensen, J. (1989). Characteristics of educational programs for students with severe intellectual disabilities. In D. Biklen, D. Ferguson, & A. Ford (eds.), *Schooling and Disability* (pp. 59–76). Chicago, IL: University of Chicago Press.

Aldrich, R. (Producer & Director). (1962). *Whatever Happened to Baby Jane*? (Motion picture). United States: Warner Home video.

Alghazo, E. M., Dodeen, H., & Algaryouti, I. A. (2003). Attitudes of pre-service teachers towards persons with disabilities: Predictions for the success of inclusion. *College Student Journal, 37*(4), 515–522.

Allan, J. (1999). *Actively Seeking Inclusion: Pupils with Special Needs in Mainstream Schools.* London: Falmer Press.

American Psychiatric Association. (2000). *Diagnostic and Statistical Manual of Mental Disorders (4th ed). (DSM-IV TR).* Washington, DC: Author.

American Psychiatric Association. (1994). *Quick Reference to the Diagnostic Criteria from DSM IV.* Washington, DC: Author.

Americans with Disabilities Act Amendments Act of 2008. PL. 110–325. Stat. 3406. (2008).

Americans with Disabilities Act of 1990. PL. 101–336. 104 Stat. 327. (1990).

Americans with Disabilities Act Checklist for Readily Achievable Barrier Removal (1992). Washington, DC: Adaptive Environments Center & Barrier Free Environments.

Andrews, J. E., Carmine, D. W., Coutinho, M. J., Edgar, E. B., Forness, S. R., Fuchs, L. S., et al. (2000). Bridging the special education divide. *Remedial and Special Education, 21*(5), 258–260, 267.

Antonak, R. & Livneh, H. (1988). *The Measurement of Attitudes toward People with Disabilities: Methods, Psychometrics and Scales.* Springfield, IL: Charles C. Thomas, Publisher.

Arad, A., Foster, G., Milchan, A. (Producers) & Johnson, M. S. (Director). (2003). *Daredevil* (Motion picture). United States: 20th Century Fox.

Arieno, M. (1989). *Victorian Lunatics: A Social Epidemiology of Mental Illness in Mid-Nineteenth Century England.* Cranbury, NJ: Associated University Presses.

Aristotle. (1992). *The Politics* (T. Sinclair, trans.). London: Penguin Classics.

Armstrong, F. & Barton, L. (2007). *Policy, Experience and Change: Reflection on Inclusive Education.* London, England: Springer.

Arnold, M. & Lassmann, M. E. (2000). Overrepresentation of minority students in special education. *Education, 124*(2), 230–236.

Aronson, J. (2000). *Sound and Fury* (Motion picture). United States: Aronson Film Associates.

Artiles, A. J. & Trent, S. C. (1994). Overrepresentation of minority students in special education: A continuing debate. *The Journal of Special Education, 27*(4), 410–438.

Asch, A. (2000). Why I haven't changed my mind about prenatal diagnosis: Reflections and refinements. In E. Parens & A. Asch (eds.), *Prenatal Testing and Disability Rights* (pp. 234–258). Washington, DC: Georgetown University Press.

Aspies for Freedom [Website]. Accessed 1 May 2009, at http://www.aspiesforfreedom.com/

Astor, C. (1985). *Who Makes People Different: Jewish Perspectives on the Disabled.* New York: United Synagogue of America, Department of Youth Activities.

Autistic Self Advocacy Network [Website]. Accessed 1 May 2009, at http://www.autisticadvocacy.org/

Ayres, A. J. & Tickle, L. S. (1980). Hyper-responsivity to touch and vestibular stimuli as predictor of positive response to sensory integration procedures by autistic children. *American Journal of Occupational Therapy, 34*, 375–381.

Baglieri, S. & Knopf, J. H. (2004). Normalizing difference in inclusive teaching. *Journal of Learning Disabilities, 37*(6), 525–529.

Baglieri, S. & Leber, J. (2008). *Conversations about Graduate School and Learning Disability* [Website]. Accessed 3 June 2008, at http://www.graduateschoolandld.com

Baker, B. (2002). The hunt for disability: The new eugenics and the normalization of school children. *Teachers College Record, 104*(4), 663–703.

Ballard, K. (ed.). (1999). *Inclusive Education: International Voices on Disability and Justice.* London: Falmer Press.

Baranek, G. T. (2002). Efficacy of sensory and motor interventions for children with autism. *Journal of Autism and Developmental Disorders, 32*(5), 397–422.

Barnes, E., Berrigan, C., & Biklen, D. (1978). *What's the Difference? Teaching Positive Attitudes toward People with Disabilities.* Syracuse, NY: Human Policy Press.

Barnes, C., Mercer, G., & Shakespeare, T. (1999). *Exploring Disability: A Sociological Introduction.* Malden, MA: Blackwell Publishers, Inc.

Barrie, J. M. (1911). *Peter and Wendy* (AKA Peter Pan). London, England: Hodder & Stoughton.

Barton, L. (1986). The Politics of Special Educational Needs. *Disability, Handicap and Society, 1*(3), 273–290.

Barton, L. (ed.). (1996). *Disability and Society: Emerging Issues and Insights.* New York: Addison-Wesley Longman.

Barton, L. & Armstrong, F. (2001). Disability, education and inclusion: Cross-cultural issues Dilemmas. In G. Albrecht, K. Seelman, & M. Bury (eds.), *Handbook of Disability Studies* (pp. 693–710). Thousand Oaks, CA: Sage Publications.

Baskin, B. (1975). The handicapped in children's literature. In *Proceedings of the Special Study Institute, Fostering Positive Attitudes toward the Handicapped in School Settings* (pp. 132–164). Rensselaerville, NY: New York State Education Department.

Baum, D. & Wells, C. (1985). Promoting handicap awareness in preschool children. *Teaching Exceptional Children, 17*(4), 282–287.

Bauman, M. L. & Kemper, T. L. (eds.). (2004). *The Neurobiology of Autism* (2 ed.). Baltimore, MD: Johns Hopkins University Press.

Baumeister, A. & Butterfield, E. (eds.). (1970). *Residential Facilities for the Mentally Retarded.* Chicago, IL: Aldine Publishing Co.

Baynton, D. (2001). Disability and the justification of inequality in American History. In P. Longmore & L. Umansky. (eds.), *The New Disability History: American Perspectives* (pp. 33–57). New York: New York University Press.

Beirne-Smith, M., Patton, J., & Ittenbach, R. (1994). *Mental Retardation* (4th ed.). New York: Macmillan College Publishing Company, Inc.

Bejoian, L. M. & Reid, D. K. (2005). A Disability Studies perspective on the Bush education agenda: The No Child Left Behind act of 2001. *Equity & Excellence in Education, 38*(3), 220–231.

Bell, C. & Burgdorf, R. (1983). *Accommodating the Spectrum of Individual Abilities.* (Clearinghouse Publication 81) Washington, DC: United States Commission on Civil Rights.

Ben-Moshe, L. (2006). Infusing disability in the curriculum: The case of Saramago's "Blindness". *Disability Studies Quarterly, 26*(2), Retrieved 1 April 2006 from http://www.dsq-sds.org/2006_spring_toc.html.

Beratan, G. D. (2006). Institutionalizing inequity: Ableism, racism, and IDEA 2004. *Disability Studies Quarterly, 26*(2), http://www.dsq-sds.org/_articles_html/2006/spring/beratan.asp.

Berenbaum, M. (1993). *The World Must Know: The History of the Holocaust as Told in the United States Holocaust Memorial Museum.* Boston, MA: Little Brown & Co.

Berman, P. (Producer) & Dieterle, W. (Director). (1939). *The Hunchback of Notre Dame* (Motion picture). United States: RKO Radio Pictures.

Biklen, D. (1981). The Supreme Court v. retarded children. *Journal of the Association for Persons with Severe Handicaps, 6*(2), 3–5.

Biklen, D. (1986). Framed: Journalism's treatment of disability. *Social Policy*, Winter, 45–51.

Biklen, D. (1989). Redefining schools. In D. Biklen, D. Ferguson, & A. Ford (eds.), *Schooling and Disability* (pp. 1–24). Chicago, IL: National Society for the Study of Education.

Biklen, D. (ed.). (2005). *Autism and the Myth of the Person Alone.* New York: New York University Press.

Biklen, D. & Bailey, L. (eds). (1981). *Rudely Stamp'd: Imaginal Disability and Prejudice.* Washington, DC: University Press of America, Inc.

Biklen, D. & Bogdan, R. (1977). Media portrayals of disabled people: A study in stereotypes. *Interracial Books of Children Bulletin, 8*(6 & 7), 4–9.

Biklen, D. & Burke, J. (2006). Presuming Competence. *Equity & Excellence in Education, 39*(2), 166–175.

Biklen, D. & Cardinal, D. N. (eds.). (1997). *Contested Words, Contested Science: Unraveling the Facilitated Communication Controversy.* New York: Teachers College Press.

Biklen, D., Ferguson, D., & Ford, A. (eds.). (1989). *Schooling and Disability.* Chicago, IL: National Society for the Study of Education, University of Chicago Press.

Binding, K. & Hoche, A. (1975). *The Release of the Destruction of Life Devoid of Value.* R. Sassone (ed.). Santa Ana, CA: Life Quality Paperbacks. (original work published 1920).

Blanchett, W. J. (2006). Disproportionate representation of African-American students in special education: Acknowledging the role of White privilege and racism. *Educational Researcher, 35*(6), 24–28.

Blatt, B. (1970). *Exodus from Pandemonium: Human Abuse and a Reformation of Public Policy.* Boston, MA: Allyn and Bacon.

Blatt, B. (1981). *In and Out of Mental Retardation: Essays on Educability, Disability, and Human Policy.* Baltimore, MD: University Park Press.

Bleul, H. (1973). *Sex and Society in Nazi Germany.* Philadelphia, PA: J. B. Lippincott, Co.

Board of Education v. Rowley, 458 U.S. 176 (2nd Circuit Court 1982).

Bogdan, R. (1986). Exhibiting mentally retarded people for amusement and profit, 1850–1940. *American Journal of Mental Deficiency, 91*(2), 120–126.

Bogdan, R. (1988). *Freak Show: Presenting Human Oddities for Amusement and Profit.* Chicago, IL: University of Chicago Press.

Bogdan, R. & Biklen, D. (1977). Handicapism. *Social Policy, 7*, 14–19.

Bogdan, R., Biklen, D., Shapiro, A., & Spelkoman, D. (1982). The disabled: Media's Monster. *Social Policy, 13*, 32–35.

Bogdan, R. & Taylor, S. (1994). *The Social Meaning of Mental Retardation: Two Life Stories.* New York: Teachers College Press, Columbia University.

Bookbinder, S. (1978). *Mainstreaming—What Every Child Needs to Know about Disabilities.* Providence, RI: Rhode Island Easter Seal Society.

Boudah, D. J., Schumacher, J. B., & Deshler, D. D. (1997). Collaborative instruction: Is it an effective option for inclusion in secondary classrooms? *Learning Disability Quarterly, 20,* 293–316.

Bowe, F. (1978). *Handicapping America: Barriers to Disabled People.* New York: Harper & Row.

Brantlinger, E. A. (2003). *Dividing Classes: How the Middle Class Negotiates and Rationalizes School Advantage.* New York: Routledge.

Brew-Parrish, V. (1997). The wrong message (Electronic Version). *Ragged Edge Online, March/ April.* Retrieved 10 April 2008 from http://www.raggededgemagazine.com /archive/aware. htm.

Brew-Parrish, V. (2004). The wrong message—Still (Electronic Version). *Ragged Edge Online.* Retrieved 10 April 2008 from http://www.raggededgemagazine.com /focus/wrongmessage 04.html.

Broderick, A. A. & Kasa-Hendrickson, C. (2006). "I am thinking that speech is asinine": Narrating complexities and rethinking the notion of "independence" in communication. *Equity & Excellence in Education, 39*(2), 176–186.

Brodkin, M. & Coleman Advocates for Children & Youth (1993). *Every Kid Counts: 31 Ways to Save Our Children.* San Francisco, CA: Harper Collins.

Brolin, D. (1995). *Career Education: A Functional Life Skills Approach.* Englewood Cliffs, NJ: Merrill/Prentice Hall.

Brookfield, S. (1990). Using critical incidents to explore learners' assumptions. In J. Mezirow & Associates (eds.), *Fostering Critical Reflection in Adulthood: A Guide to Transformative and Emancipatory Learning* (pp. 177–193). San Francisco, CA: Jossey-Bass.

Brookfield, S. D. (2004). *The Power of Critical Theory: Liberating Adult Learning.* San Francisco, CA: Jossey-Bass.

Browder, D. M., Mims, P. J., Spooner, F., Ahlgrim-Delzell, L., & Lee, A. (2008). Teaching elementary students with multiple disabilities to participate in shared stories. *Research & Practice for Persons with Severe Disabilities, 33*(1–2), 3–12.

Brown v. Board of Education of Topeka. 347 U.S. 483 (1954).

Buck v. Bell, 143 Va. 313, 130 S.E. 516, 517 (1925).

Bullock, C. & Mahon, M. (1997). *Introduction to Recreation Services for People with Disabilities: A Person-Centered Approach.* Champaign, IL: Sagamore Publishing.

Burgdorf, R. (1980). *The Legal Rights of Handicapped Persons: Cases, Materials and Text.* Baltimore, MD: Brookes Publishing Co.

Burgdorf, M. & Burgdorf, R. (1975). A history of unequal treatment: The qualifications of handicapped persons as a *Suspect Class* under the Equal Protection Clause, *Santa Clara Lawyer, 215*(4), 855–910.

Burgdorf, R. & Burgdorf, M. (1977). The wicked witch is almost dead: "Buck v. Bell" and the sterilization of handicapped persons. Philadelphia, PA: reprinted from the *Temple Law Quarterly, 50*(4), 995–1034.

Burgstahler, S. & Doe, T. (2004) Disability-related simulations: If, and how to use them in professional development. *Review of Disability Studies: An International Journal, 2*(2), 8–18.

Burleigh, M. (1994). *Death and Deliverance: "Euthanasia" in Germany 1900–1945.* New York: Cambridge University Press.

Burns, M. (2005). Looking at how students reason. *Educational Leadership, 53*(3), 26–31.

Burns, R. (1995). 16,000 used in radiation experiments, *The Times* (Trenton, N.J). p. 3B.

Buxton, W. (1985). *Talcott Parsons and the Capitalist Nation-State: Political Sociology as a Strategic Vocation.* Toronto, Canada: University of Toronto Press.

Calkins, L. (1986). *The Art of Teaching Writing.* Portsmouth, NH: Heinemann.

Carlisle, J. (1985). *Tangled Tongue: Living with a Stutter.* Reading, MA: Addison-Wesley Publishing Company, Inc.

Carrier, J. G. (1986). *Learning Disability: Social Class and the Construction of Inequality in American Education.* New York: Greenwood Press.

Carroll, A., Forlin, C., & Jobling, A. (2003). The impact of teacher training in special education on the attitudes of Australian preservice general educators towards people with disabilities. *Teacher Education Quarterly, Summer, 30*(3), 65–79.

Charkins, H. (1996). *Children with Facial Difference.* Bethesda, MD: Woodbine House.

Clark, C. T. (2003). Examining the role of authoritative discourse in the labeling and unlabeling of a "learning disabled" college learner. *Journal of Adolescent and Adult Literacy, 47*(2), 128–135.

Clore, G. L. & Jeffrey, K. M. (1972). Emotional role playing, attitude change and attraction toward a disabled person. *Journal of Personality and Social Psychology, 23*, 105–111.

Cohen, S. (1977). *Special People.* Englewood Cliffs, NJ: Prentice Hall.

Collins, K. M. (2003). *Ability Profiling and School Failure: One Child's Struggle to be Seen as Competent.* Mahwah, NJ: Lawrence Erlbaum Associates.

Conot, R. (1983). *Justice at Nuremberg.* New York: Carroll & Graf Publishers.

Conrad, B. (1988). Cooperative learning and prejudice reduction. *Social Education (April/May),* 283–286.

Conrad, P. (1996). The medicalization of deviance in American Culture. In E. Rubington & M. Weinberg (eds.) *Deviance: The Interactionist Perspective* (6th ed.). Boston, MA: Allyn and Bacon.

Conrad, P. & Schneider, J. (1992). *Deviance and Medicalization: From Badness to Sickness.* Philadelphia, PA: Temple University Press.

Cook, B. G. (2002). Inclusive attitudes, strengths, and weaknesses of pre-service general educators enrolled in a curriculum infusion teacher preparation program. *Teacher Education and Special Education, 25*(3), 262–277.

Corbett, J. (1996) *Bad-Mouthing: The Language of Special Needs.* Bristol, PA: Falmer Press.

Cornfield, S. (Producer), McLeod, E. (Producer), & Stiller, B. (Producer/Director). (2008). *Tropic Thunder* (Motion picture). United States: DreamWorks/Paramount Pictures.

Crissey, M. & Rosen, M. (1986). *Institutions for the Mentally Retarded: A Changing Role in Changing Times.* Austin, TX: Pro-Ed.

Crossley, R. (1997). *Speechless: Facilitating Communication for People without Voices.* New York: Dutton/Penguin Books.

Crutchfield, S. & Epstein, M. (2000). *Points of Contact: Disability, Art, and Culture.* Ann Arbor, MI: University of Michigan Press.

Cummings, C., Dyson, A., & Millward, A. (2003). Participation and democracy: What's inclusion got to do with it? In J. Allan (ed.), *Inclusion, Participation and Democracy: What is the Purpose?* Dordrecht, The Netherlands: Kluwer Academic Publishers.

Danforth, S. & Rhodes, W. C. (1997). Deconstructing disability: A Philosophy for inclusion. *Remedial and Special Education, 18*(6), 357–366.

Danforth, S. & Smith, T. J. (2005). *Engaging Troubling Students: A Constructivist Approach.* Thousand Oaks, CA: Corwin Press.

Daniel R.R. v State Board of Education, 874 F.2d 1036 (5th Circuit Court 1989).

Darke, P. (1998). Understanding cinematic representations of disability. In T. Shakespeare (ed.), *The Disability Reader: Social Science Perspectives* (pp. 181–197). London: Casell.

Davis, L. (1995). *Enforcing Normalcy: Disability, Deafness and the Body.* London, UK: Verso.

Davis, L. (ed.). (1997). *The Disability Studies Reader.* New York, NY: Routledge.

Davis, L. J. (ed.). (2002). *Bending over Backwards: Disability, Dismodernism, and Other Difficult Positions.* New York: New York University Press.

Dawson, M., Soulières, I., Gernsbacher, M. A., & Mottron, L. (2007). The level and nature of autistic intelligence. *Psychological Science, 18*, 657–662.

Dearing, B. (1981). Literary images as stereotypes. In Biklen, D. & Bailey, L. (eds.), *Rudely Stamp'd: Imaginal Disability and Prejudice* (pp. 33–47). Washington, DC: University Press of America, Inc.

Dei, G. J. S., James, I. M., Karumanchery, L. L., James-Wilson, S., & Zine, J. (2000). *Removing the margins: The challenges and possibilities of inclusive schooling.*Toronto: Canadian Scholars' Press.

Despart, L. (1965). *The Emotionally Disturbed Child—Then and Now.* New York, NY: Vantage Press.

Dewer, D. (1982). *The Quality Circle Guide to Participation Management.* Englewood Cliffs, NJ: Princeton Hall.

Dewey, J. (1916). *Democracy and Education.* New York: MacMillan.

Dickens, C. (1843). *Christmas Carol.* London, England: Chapman & Hall.

DiLeo, J. (1983). *Interpreting Children's Drawings.* New York: Brunner/Mazel Publishers.

Disabled in Action of Pennsylvania v. Coleman (E.D., Pa. 1976).

Dolmage, J. & DeGenaro, W. (eds.). (2005). Responding to *Million Dollar Baby*: A forum. *Disability Studies Quarterly, 25*(3). Retrieved 21 June 2009, from http://www.dsq-sds.org/article/view/590/767

Donaldson, J. (1980). Changing attitudes toward handicapped persons: A review and analysis of research. *Exceptional Children, 46* (7), 504–514.

Dudley-Marling, C. & Dippo, D. (1995). What learning disability does: Sustaining the ideology of schooling. *Journal of Learning Disabilities, 28*, 406–414.

Durant, W. (1944). *Caesar and Christ.* New York: Simon & Schuster.

Eastwood, C. (Director). (2004). *Million Dollar Baby* (Motion picture). Los Angeles: Warner Brothers Pictures.

Edwards, M. (1996). Ability and disability in the Ancient Greek military community. In E. Makas & L. Schlesinger (eds.), *End Results and Starting Points: Expanding the Field of Disability Studies* (pp. 29–33). Portland ME: The Society for Disabilities Studies and The Muskie Institute of Public Affairs.

Eiseland, N. (1994). *The Disabled God: Toward a Liberatory Theology of Disability.* Nashville, TN: Abington Press.

Eisner, E. (2005). Back to whole. *Educational Leadership, 63*(1), 14–18.

Elkins, S., Jones, M., & Ulicny, R. (1987). *The Media Watch Campaign Manual.* Lawrence, KA: The Research & Training Center on Independent Living, The University of Kansas.

Ellis, E. (1990). *Why the Disabled are Always Angry.* Trenton, NJ: *The Times*, p. B–3.

Evans, D. (1983). *The Lives of Mentally Retarded Persons.* Boulder, CO: Westview Press.

Evans, J. H. (1976). Changing attitudes toward disabled persons: An experimental study. *Rehabilitation Counseling Bulletin, 19*, 527–579.

Ferguson, A. A. (2001). *Bad Boys: Public Schools in the Making of Black Masculinity.* Ann Arbor, MI: University of Michigan Press.

Ferguson, D. L. (1995). The real challenge of inclusion: Confessions of a 'rabid inclusionist'. *Phi Delta Kappan, 77*, 281–287.

Ferguson, P. (1994). *Abandoned to Their Fate: Social Policy and Practice Toward Severely Retarded People in America, 1820–1920.* Philadelphia, PA: Temple University Press.

Ferri, B. A. & Connor, D. J. (2005). Tools of exclusion: Race, disability, and (re)segregated education. *Teachers College Record, 107*(3), 453–474.

Ferri, B. A. & Connor, D. J. (2006). *Reading Resistance: Discourses of Exclusion in Desegregation and Inclusion Debates.* New York: Peter Lang.

Fiedler, L. (1978). *Freaks: Myths and Images of the Secret Self.* New York: Simon & Schuster.

Fiedler, L. (1996). *Tyranny of the Normal: Essays on Bioethics, Theology, and Myth.* New Brunswick, NJ: Rutgers University Press.

Fiedorowicz, I. C., Benezra, E., MacDonald, W., & McElgunn, B. (2001). Neurobiological basis of learning disabilities: An update. *Learning Disabilities: A Multidisciplinary Journal, 11*(2), 61–74.

Finger, A. (1992). The idiot, the cretin and the cripple. *Disability Rag, 13*(6), 23–25.

Fish, W. W. (2008). The IEP meeting. Perceptions of parents of students who receive special education services. *Preventing School Failure, 53*(1), 8–14.

Fisher, D., Frey, N., & Thousand, J. (2003). What do special educators need to know and be prepared to do for inclusive schooling to work? *Teacher Education and Special Education, 26*(1), 42–50.

Fleischer, D. Z. & Zames, F. (2001). *The Disability Rights Movement: From Charity to Confrontation.* Philadelphia, PA: Temple University Press.

Fosnot, C. T. (ed.). (2005). *Constructivism: Theory, Perspectives, and Practice* (2 ed.). New York: Teachers College Press.

Foucault, M. (1965). *Madness and Civilization: A History of Insanity in the Age of Reason* (R. Howard, Trans.). New York: Vintage Books.

Francis, K. (2005). Autism interventions: A critical update. *Developmental Medicine & Child Neurology, 47*(7), 493–499.

Franklin, B. M. (1987). The first crusade for learning disabilities: The movement for the education of backward children. In T. Popkewitz (ed.), *The Formation of School Subjects: The Struggle for Creating an American Institution* (pp. 190–209). London: Falmer Press.

Franklin, B. M. (1994). *From "Backwardness" to "At-Risk": Childhood Learning Difficulties and the Contradictions of School Reform.* Albany, NY: State University of New York Press.

Franks, B. (1996). Disability and fairy tales: An analysis. In E. Makas & L. Schlesinger (eds.), *End Results and Starting Points: Expanding the Field of Disability Studies* (pp. 17–22). Portland, ME: The Society for Disabilities Studies and The Muskie Institute of Public Affairs.

Freeman, J., Merson, M., Ryan., T. C. (Producers) & Miller, R. E. (Director). (1968). *Heart Is a Lonely Hunter* (Motion picture). United States: Warner Bros.

French, R. (1932). *From Homer to Helen Keller: A Social and Educational Study of the Blind*. New York: American Foundation of the Blind.

French, S. (1996). Simulation exercises in disability awareness training: A critique. In *Beyond Disability: Towards an Enabling Society* (pp. 114–123). Thousand Oaks, CA: Sage Publications.

Friedberg, J., Mullins, J., & Sukiennik, A. (1985) *Accept Me as I Am: Best Books of Juvenile Nonfiction on Impairments and Disabilities*. New Providence, NJ: R. R. Bowker.

Friedberg, J., Mullins, J., & Sukiennik, A. (1992). *Portraying Persons with Disabilities (Nonfiction): An Annotated Bibliography of Nonfiction for Children and Teenagers*. New Providence, NJ: R. R. Bowker.

Friedlander, H. (1995). *The Origins of Nazi Genocide: From Euthanasia to the Final Solution*. Chapel Hill, NC: The University of North Carolina Press.

Fries, K. (ed.). (1997). *Staring Back: The Disability Experience from the Inside Out*. New York: Penguin Books.

Fuchs, L. S., Fuchs, D., & Speece, D. L. (2002). Treatment validity as a unifying construct for identifying learning disabilities. *Learning Disability Quarterly, 25*, 33–46.

Funk, R. (1987). Disability rights: From caste to class in the context of civil rights. In Gartner & Joe (eds.), *Images of the Disabled-Disabling Images* (pp. 7–30). New York: Praeger Publishers.

Gabel, S. (2005). *Disability Studies in Education: Readings in Theory and Method*. New York: Peter Lang.

Galinsky, A. D., Hugenberg, K., Groom, C., & Bodenhausen, G. V. (2003). The reappropriation of stigmatizing labels: Implications for social identity. In J. Polzer (ed.), *Research on Managing Groups and Teams* (Vol. 5, pp. 221–256). Amsterdam, The Netherlands: Elsevier Science Ltd.

Gallagher, D. J. (2001). Neutrality as a moral standpoint, conceptual confusion and the full inclusion debate. *Disability and Society, 16*(5), 637–654.

Gallagher, D. J. (2006). On using blindness as metaphor and difficult questions: A response to Ben-Moshe. *Disability Studies Quarterly, 26*(2), Retrieved 1 April 2006 from http://www.dsq-sds.org/2006_spring_toc.html.

Gallagher, H. (1995). *By Trust Betrayed: Patients, Physicians, and the License to Kill in the Third Reich*. Arlington, VA: Vandamere Press.

Gallaudet Research Institute. (2003). Regional and National Summary Report of Data from the 2001–2002 Annual Survey of Deaf and Hard of Hearing Children & Youth (Electronic Version). Retrieved 15 August 2006 from http://gri.gallaudet.edu/Demographics/2002_National_Summary.pdf.

Garderen, D. v. & Whittaker, C. (2006). Planning differentiated, multicultural instruction for secondary inclusive classrooms. *Teaching Exceptional Children, 38*(3), 12–20.

Gardner, H. (1983). *Frames of Mind*. New York: Basic Books.

Gardner, H. (1999). *Intelligence Reframed*. New York: Basic Books.

Gardner, H. & Hatch, T. (1989). Multiple intelligences go to school: Educational implications of the theory of multiple intelligences. *Educational Researcher, 18*(8), 4–9.

Garland, R. (1995). *The Eye of the Beholder: Deformity and Disability in the Greco-Roman World*. Ithaca, NY: Cornell University Press.

Gearheart, B., Mullen, R., & Gearheart, C. (1993). *Exceptional Individuals: An Introduction*. Belmont, CA: Brooks/Cole Publishing Co.

Gearheart, B. & Weishahn, M. (1984). *The Exceptional Student in the Regular Classroom*. St. Louis, MO: Times Mirror/College Publishing.

George, P. S. (2005). A rationale for differentiating instruction in the regular classroom. *Theory Into Practice, 44*(3), 185–193.

Gilhool, T. K. (1997). The events, forces and issues that triggered enactment of the Education for All Handicapped Children Act of 1975. In D.K. Lipsky & A. Gartner, *Inclusion and School Reform: Transforming America's Classrooms* (pp. 263–273). Baltimore, MD: Paul H. Brookes.

Gill, C. J. & Voss, L. A. (2005). Views of disabled people regarding legalized assisted suicide before and after a balanced informational presentation. *Journal of Disability Policy Studies, 16*(1), 6–15.

Gindis, B. (1999). Vygotsky's vision: Reshaping the practice of special education for the 21st century. *Remedial and Special Education, 20*(6), 333–340.

Gliedman, J. (1979). The wheelchair rebellion. *Psychology Today*, pp. 59, 60, 63, 64, 99, 101.

Gliedman, J. & Roth, W. (1980). *The Unexpected Minority: Handicapped Children in America*. New York: Harcourt, Brace Jovanovich.

Globus, Y., Golam, M. (Producers), & Jaeckin, J. (Director). (1981). *Lady Chatterly's Lover* (Motion picture). United States, France, West Germany: Cannon Films, Columbia Pictures.

Goddard, H. H. (1912). *The Kallikak Family: A Study in the Heredity of Feeble-Mindedness*. New York: Macmillan.

Goffman, E. (1961). *Asylums: Essays on the Social Situation of Mental Patients and Other Inmates*. Garden City, NY: Anchor Books, Doubleday & Co.

Goffman, E. (1963). *Stigma: Notes on the Management of Spoiled Identities*. Englewood Cliffs, NJ: Prentice Hall.

Gordon, B. O. & Rosenblum, K. E. (2001). Bringing disability into the sociological frame: A comparison of disability with race, sex, and sexual orientation statuses. *Disability & Society, 16*(1), 5–19.

Gould, S. (1981). *The Mismeasure of Man*. New York: W. W. Norton & Company.

Gould, W. (1933). Euthanasia. *Journal of the Institute of Homeopathy, 27*, 82.

Grandin, T. (1995). *Thinking in Pictures: And Other Reports from My Life with Autism*. New York: Vintage.

Grandin, T. (ed.). (2007). *Livestock Handling and Transport* (3rd ed.). Wallingford, Oxon, UK: CAB International.

Grandin, T. & Johnson, C. (2005). *Animals in Translation*. New York: Scriber.

Grandin, T. & Scariano, M. M. (1986). *Emergence: Labeled Autistic*. New York: Warner Books.

Grimms' Fairy Tales. (1945/1995). New York: Grosset & Dunlap, Publishers.

Grindler, M., Stratton, B., & McKenna, M. (1997). *The Right Book, The Right Time: Helping Children Cope*. Boston, MA: Allyn and Bacon.

Grob, G. (1994). *The Mad among Us: A History of the Care of America's Mentally Ill*. New York: The Free Press.

Grossman, H. (ed.). (1983). *Classification in Mental Retardation*. Washington, DC: American Association on Mental Retardation.

Gutierrez, K. D., Baquedano-Lopez, P., Alvarez, H. H., & Chiu, M. M. (1999). Building a culture of collaboration through hybrid language practices. *Theory into Practice, 38*(2), 87–93.

Hahn, D. (Producer), Trousdale, G., & Wise, K. (Director). (1996). *The Hunchback of Notre Dame* (Motion picture). United States: Walt Disney Pictures, Buena Vista Distribution.

Hahn, H. (1987). Civil rights for disabled Americans: The foundation of a political agenda. In A. Gartner & T. Joe, (eds.), *Images of the Disabled, Disabling Images* (pp. 181–203). New York: Praeger Publishers.

Hahn, H. (1988). The politics of physical difference. In M. Nagler (ed.) (1990). *Perspectives on Disability*. Palo Alto, CA: Health Markets Research.

Haj, F. (1970). *Disability in Antiquity*. New York: Philosophical Library. In D. Moores (1996). *Educating the Deaf: Psychology, Principles, and Practices* (4th ed.). Boston, MA: Houghton Mifflin Co.

Haller, M. (1963). *Eugenics: Hereditarian Attitudes in American Thought*. New Brunswick, NJ: Rutgers University Press.

Haller, B. (2000). False positive. *Ragged Edge Online*, January/February. Retrieved 20 April 2002, from http://www.raggededgemagazine.com/0100/c0100media.htm

Haller, B. A. (2010). *Representing disability in an ableist world: Essays on mass media*. Louisville, KY: Advocado Press.

Hardman, M., Drew, C., & Egan, M. (1996). *Human Exceptionality: Society, School, and Family (5th ed.)*. Needham Heights, MA: Allyn and Bacon, Simon & Schuster.

Harry, B. (1994). *The Disproportionate Representation of Minority Students in Special Education: Theories and Recommendations*. Alexandria, VA: Project FORUM, National Association of State Directors of Special Education.

Harry, B. & Klingner, J. (2005). *Why are So Many Minority Students in Special Education? Understanding Race and Disability in Schools*. New York: Teachers College Press.

Harry, B., Klingner, J. K., & Hart, J. (2005). African American families under fire: Ethnographic view of family strengths. *Remedial and Special Education, 26*(2), 101–112.

Hehir, T. (2003). Beyond inclusion. *School Administrator, 60*(3), 36–39.

Henderson, H. & Bryan, W. (1997). *Psychosocial Aspects of Disability*. Springfield, IL: Charles C. Thomas.

Heshusius, L. (1989). The Newtonian mechanistic paradigm, special education, and the contours of alternatives: An overview. *Journal of Learning Disabilities, 22,* 402–415.

Hewett, F. & Forness, S. (1977). *Education of Exceptional Learners* (2nd ed.). Boston, MA: Allyn and Bacon, Inc.

Hirsch, K. & Hirsch, J. (1995). Self-defining narratives: Disability identity in the postmodern era. *Disabilities Studies Quarterly, 15*(4), 21–27.

Hitler, A. (1925/1971). *Mein Kampf* (R. Manheim, trans.). Boston, MA: Houghton Mifflin Co. (Original work published 1925).

Hockenberry, J. (1995). *Moving Violations: A Memoir of War Zones, Wheelchairs, and Declarations of Independence.* New York: Hyperion.

Hogan, G. (2003). *The Inclusive Corporation: A Disability Handbook for Business Professionals.* Athens, OH: Swallow Press/Ohio University Press.

Hollander, R. (1989). Euthanasia and mental retardation: Suggesting the unthinkable. *Mental Retardation, 27*(2), 53–61.

Hoversten, P. (1995a). Radiation test report: 16,000 were subjects, *USA Today,* p. 1A.

Hoversten, P. (1995b). Hunting radiation records—and truth, *USA Today,* p. 3A.

Horowitz, S. M., Bility, K. M., Plichta, S. B., Leaf, P. J., & Haynes, N. (1998). Teacher's assessments of behavioral disorders. *American Journal of Orthopsychiatry, 68*(1),117–25.

Hughes, R. (1993). *Culture of Complaint: The Fraying of America.* New York, NY: Oxford University Press.

Hugo, V. (1831). *The Hunchback of Notre Dame.* New York: Bantam Classics (1986 ed.).

Hull, J. (1990). *Touching the Rock: An Experience of Blindness.* New York: Vintage Press.

Hunt, N. & Marshall, K. (1994). *Exceptional Children and Youth: An Introduction to Special Education.* Boston, MA: Houghton Mifflin Co.

Hunter, M. (1982). *Mastery Teaching.* Thousand Oaks, CA: Corwin Press.

Individuals with Disabilities Education Act (IDEA). PL 101-47-642, U.S.C. (1990).

Individuals with Disabilities Education Improvement Act of 2004, Pub. L. No. 108-446, 118 Stat. 2658 (2004).

Ingstad, B. & Whyte, S. (eds.). (1995). *Disability and Culture.* Berkeley, CA: University of California Press.

Institute on Community Integration (n.d.). *Integrated School Communities for Students with Developmental Disabilities: 10 Reasons Why.* Minneapolis, MI: University of Minnesota.

James, H. (1975). *The Little Victims: How America Treats its Children.* New York: David McKay Company, Inc.

Jernigan, K. (1983). Blindness: Disability or nuisance. In R. Jones (ed.), *Reflections on Growing up Disabled* (pp. 58–67). Reston, VA: Council for Exceptional Children.

Johnson, D. W. & Johnson, R. T. (1999). Making cooperative learning work. *Theory into Practice, 38*(2), 67–73.

Johnson, E. (1987). Life unworthy of life. *Disability Rag, 8*(1), 24–26.

Johnson, H. M. (2003). Unspeakable conversations. *The New York Times.*

Johnson, M. (1994). Communicative action and its utility in disability research. In E. Makas & L. Schlesinger (eds.), *Insights and Outlooks: Current Trends in Disability Studies.* Portland, ME: The Society for Disability Studies.

Johnson, M. & Elkins, S. (eds.). (1974). *Reporting on Disability: Approaches and Issues. (A Sourcebook).* Louisville, KY: Advocado Press, Inc.

Johnson, R. & Johnson, D. (1980). The social integration of handicapped students into the mainstream. In M. Reynolds (ed.), *Social Environment of the Schools* (pp. 9–37). Reston, VA: The Council for Exceptional Children.

Johnson, W. (1956). An open letter to the mother of a stuttering child. In W. Johnson, S. Brown, J. Curtis, C. Edney, & S. Keaster (1959 ed.), *Speech Handicapped School Children.* New York: Harper & Bros. Reprinted by the National Society for Crippled Children and Adults.

Jones, R. & Guskin, S. (1984). Attitude and attitude change in special education. In R. L. Jones (ed.), *Attitude and Attitude Change in Special Education: Theory and Practice* (pp. 1–20). Reston, VA: Council for Exceptional Children.

Jorgensen, C. M. (1996). Designing inclusive curricula right from the start: Practical strategies and examples for the high school classroom. In S. Stainback & W. Stainback (eds.), *Inclusion: A Guide for Educators* (pp. 221–236). Baltimore, MD: Paul H. Brookes.

Jorgensen, C. M., McSheehan, M., & Sonnenmeier, R. M. (2007). Presumed competence reflected in the educational programs of students with IDD before and after the Beyond Access professional development intervention. *Journal of Intellectual & Developmental Disability,* 32(4), 248–262.

Jubala, K. A., Bishop, K. D., & Falvey, M. A. (1995). Creating a supportive classroom environment. In M. A. Falvey (ed.), *Inclusive and Heterogenous Schooling: Assessment, Curriculum, and Instruction.* Baltimore, MD: Paul H. Brookes.

Kalyanpur, M. & Harry, B. (1999). *Culture in Special Education: Building Reciprocal Family-Professional Relationships.* Baltimore, MD: Paul H. Brookes.

Kane, H. & Tangdhanakanond, K. (2008). A comparison of discrepancy procedures for learning disabilities: Evidence from the United States. *International Journal of Special Education,* 23(2), 70–77.

Kanner, L. (1964). *A History of the Care and Study of the Mentally Retarded.* Springfield, IL: Charles C. Thomas.

Karagiannis, A., Stainback, S., & Stainback, W. (1996). Historical overview of inclusion. In S. Stainback & W. Stainback (eds.), *Inclusion: A Guide for Educators* (pp. 17–28). Baltimore, MD: Paul H. Brookes.

Kasa-Hendrickson, C. (2005). 'There's no way this kid's retarded': teachers' optimistic constructions of students' ability. *International Journal of Inclusive Education,* 9(1), 55–69.

Kater, M. (1989). *Doctors under Hitler.* Chapel Hill, NC: The University of North Carolina Press.

Kavale, K. A. (2002). Mainstreaming to full inclusion: From orthogenesis to pathogenesis of an idea. *International Journal of Disability, Development and Education,* 49(2), 201–214.

Kelsay, D. M. R. & Tyler, R. S. (1996). Advantages and disadvantages expected and realized by pediatric cochlear implant recipients as reported by their parents. *American Journal of Otology,* 17(6), 866–873.

Kennedy, K., Marshall, F., Molen, G. R. (Producers), & Spielberg, S. (Director). (1991). *Hook* (Motion picture). United States: TriStar Pictures.

Kiger, G. (1989). Disability in film and social life: A dramaturgical perspective. In S. Hey, G. Kiger, & D. Evans (eds.), *The Changing World of Impaired and Disabled People in Society* (pp. 149–159). Salem, OR: The Society for Disability Studies and Willamette University.

Kirchner, C. (1996). Looking under the street lamp: Inappropriate uses of measures just because they are there. *Journal of Disability Policy Studies,* 7(1), 77–90.

Kirk, S. A. & Gallagher, J. E., Anastasiow, N. J., Coleman, M. R. (2009). *Educating Exceptional Children* (11th ed.). Boston, MA: Houghton Mifflin Co.

Kirschner, K. L., Brashler, R., & Savage, T. A. (2007). Ashley X. *American Journal of Physical Medicine & Rehabilitation,* 86(12), 1023–1029.

Kisor, H. (1990). *What's that Pig Outdoors? A Memoir of Deafness.* New York: Hill & Wang.

Kliebard, H. M. (1995). *The Struggle for the American Curriculum: 1893–1958* (2nd ed.). New York: Routledge.

Kliewer, C., Biklen, D., & Kasa-Hendrickson, C. (2006). Who may be literate? Disability and resistance to the cultural denial of competence. *American Educational Research Journal,* 43(2), 163–192.

Klobas, L. (1988). *Disability Drama in Television and Film.* Jefferson, NC: McFarland & Company, Inc.

Koegel, L. K., Koegel, R. L., Harrower, J. K., & Carter, C. M. (1999). Pivotal Response Intervention I: Overview of approach. *The Journal of the Association for Persons with Severe Handicaps,* 24(3), 174–185.

Koegel, L. K., Koegel, R. L., Shoshan, Y., & McNerney, E. (1999). Pivotal Response Intervention II: Preliminary long-term outcome data. *The Journal of the Association for Persons with Severe Handicaps,* 24(3), 186–198.

Kokaska, C. & Brolin, D. (1985). *Career Education for Handicapped Individuals* (2nd ed.) New York: Merrill, Macmillan Publishing Co.

Korthagen, F. A. J. (1999). Linking reflection and technical competence: The logbook as an instrument in teacher education. *European Journal of Teacher Education,* 22(2/3), 191–207.

Kozol, J. (1991). *Savage Inequalities.* New York: Crown.

Kozol, J. (2005). *The Shame of the Nation: The Restoration of Apartheid Schooling in America* New York: Crown.

Kriegel, L. (1982). The wolf in the pit in the zoo. *Social Policy,* 13, 16–23.

Kriegel, L. (1991). *Falling into Life.* San Francisco, CA: North Point Press.

Kroeger, S. D., Leibold, C. K., & Ryan, B. (1999). Creating a sense of ownership in the IEP process. *Teaching Exceptional Children, 32*(1), 4–9.

Kudlick, C. J. (2003). Disability history: Why we need another "other". Retrieved 22 August 2003, from http://www.historycoop.org/journals/ahr/108.3/kudlick.html

Kuhl, S. (1994). *The Nazi Connection: Eugenics, American Racism, and German National Socialism.* New York: Oxford University Press.

L'Abate, L. & Curtis, L. (1975). *Teaching the Exceptional Child.* Philadelphia, PA: W. B. Saunders Co.

Landsman, J. & Gorski, P. (2007). Countering standardization. *Educational Leadership, 64*(8), 40–44.

Lavoie, R. (Writer). (1989). How difficult can this be? The F.A.T. City workshop (DVD). United States: www.ricklavoie.com.

Lederer, J. M. (2000). Reciprocal teaching of social studies in inclusive elementary classrooms. *Journal of Learning Disabilities, 33*(1), 91–106.

Lessen, E. (1994). *Exceptional Persons in Society.* Needham Heights, MA: Simon & Schuster.

Levinson, B. (Director). (1988). *Rainman* (Motion picture). MGM.

Lewin, K. (1948). *Resolving Social Conflicts.* New York: Harper & Row.

Lickona, T. (1991). *Educating for Character.* New York: Bantam Books.

Lifton, R. (1986). *The Nazi Doctors: Medical Killing and the Psychology of Genocide.* New York: Basic Books.

Lifton, R. (1990). Sterilization and euthanasia. In M. Berenbaum (ed.), *A Mosaic of Victims: Non-Jews Persecuted and Murdered by the Nazis* (pp. 222–228). New York: New York University Press.

Linton, S. (2007). *My Body Politic: A Memoir.* Ann Arbor, MI: Univeristy of Michigan Press.

Linton, S. (1998). *Claiming Disability: Knowledge and Identity.* New York: New York University Press.

Linton, S. (2008). Simi Linton: Disability/Arts [Website]. Accessed 13 March 2008, at http://www.similinton.com/dac.htm

Linton, S., Mello, S., & O'Neill, J. (1995). Disability studies: Expanding the parameters of diversity. *Radical Teacher, 47,* 4–10.

Litvak, A., Wallis, H. B. (Producer), & Litvak, A. (Director). (1948). *Sorry Wrong Number* (Motion picture). United States: Paramount Pictures.

Long, E. (1985/1990). Riding the iron worm. In A. Brightman (ed.), *Ordinary Moments: The Disabled Experience* (pp. 79–98). Syracuse, NY: Human Policy Press.

Long, N. (1988). Introduction to Smith, Teaching the fourth R: Relationships. *The Pointer, 32*(3), 23–33.

Longmore, P. (1987). Screening stereotypes: Images of disabled people in television and motion pictures. In Gartner & Joe (eds.), *Images of the Disabled, Disabling Images* (pp. 65–78). New York: Praeger.

Longmore, P. (2005). The cultural framing of disability: Telethons as a case study. *Publications of the Modern Language Association of America, 120*(2), 502–517.

Longmore, P. K. & Umansky, L. (eds.). (2001). *The New Disability History: American Perspectives.* New York: New York University Press.

Losen, D. J. & Orfield, G. (eds.). (2002). *Racial Inequity in Special Education.* Boston, MA: Harvard Educational Publishing Group.

Lynch, S. A. & Warner, L. (2008). Creating lesson plans for all learners. *Kappa Delta Pi Record, 45*(1), 10–15.

MacFarlane, S. (Producer). (1999). *Family Guy* (Television series). Los Angeles: Fox Broadcasting Company.

Mackelprang, R. & Salsgiver, O. (1996). People with disabilities and social work: Historical and contemporary issues. *Social Work, 41*(1), 7–14. Corporation. (Original work Published 1753).

Mahn, H. (2000). Vygotsky's methodological contribution to sociocultural theory. *Remedial and Special Education, 20*(6), 341–350.

Makas, E. (1990) Positive attitudes toward disabled people: Disabled and nondisabled persons' perspectives. In M. Nagler (ed.), *Perspectives on Disability* (pp. 24–31). Palo Alto, CA: Health Markets Research.

Maloff, C. & Wood, S. (1988). *Business and Social Etiquette with Disabled People: A Guide to Getting along with Persons who have Impairments of Mobility, Vision, Hearing, or Speech.* Springfield, IL: Charles C. Thomas.

Margolis, H. & Shapiro, A. (1987). Countering negative images of disability in classical literature. *The English Journal, 76*(3), 5–10.

Margolis, H., Shapiro, A., & Anderson, P. (1990). Reading, writing, and thinking about prejudice: Stereotyped images of disability in the popular press. *Social Education*, 54(1), 28–30.

Mariage, T., V., Paxton-Buursma, D. J., & Bouck, E. C. (2004). Interanimation: Repositioning possibilities in educational contexts. *Journal of Learning Disabilities, 37*(6), 534–549.

Mason, C. Y., MaGahee-Kovac, M., & Johnson, L. (2004). How to help students lead their IEP meetings. *Teaching Exceptional Children, 36*(3), 18–25.

Matalon, D., Ohsson, B., Teper, M. (Producer), & Hallström, L. (Director). (1993) *What's Eating Gilbert Grape?* (Motion picture). United States: Paramount pictures, J&M Entertainment.

Matthew, N. & Clow, S. (2007). Putting disabled children in the picture: Promoting inclusive children's books and media. *International Journal of Early Childhood, 39*(2), 65–78.

McConnell, S. R. (2002). Interventions to facilitate social interaction for young children with autism: Review of available research and recommendations for educational intervention and future research. *Journal of Autism and Developmental Disorders, 32*(5), 351–372.

McCormic, P., Fisher, L., Wick, D. (Producer), & Hogan, P. J. (Director). (2003). *Peter Pan* (Motion picture). United States: Universal Studios, Columbia Pictures.

McDermott, R. & Varenne, H. (1995). Culture "as" disability. *Anthropology and Education Quarterly, 26*(3), 324–348.

McGuire, J. M., Scott, S. S., & Shaw, S. F. (2006). Universal design and its applications in educational enviroments. *Remedial and Special Education, 27*(3), 166–175.

McLaughlin, M. W. & Talbert, J. E. (1992). *Social Constructions of Students: Challenges to Policy Coherence.* Paper presented at the American Educational Research Association Annual Meeting, Washington, DC.

McLeskey, J. & Waldron, N. L. (2002). Inclusion and school change: Teacher perceptions regarding curricular and instructional adaptations. *Teacher Education and Special Education, 25*(1), 41–54.

McTighe, J. & Brown, J. L. (2005). Differentiated instruction and educational standards: Is detente possible? *Theory into Practice, 44*(3), 234–244.

McTighe, J. & Wiggins, G. (2004). *The Understanding by Design Professional Development Workbook.* Alexandria, VA: ASCD.

Meier, D. & Wood, G. (eds.). (2004). *Many Children Left Behind: How the No Child Left Behind Act is Damaging Our Children and Our Schools.* Boston, MA: Beacon Press.

Metcalf, U. (1818). The interior of Bethlehem Hospital. In D. Peterson (ed.) (1982), *A Mad People's History of Madness.* Pittsburgh, PA: University of Pittsburgh Press.

Metz, M. H. (1994). Desegregation as necessity and challenge. *Journal of Negro Education, 63*(1), 64–76.

Meyers, D. (1987). *Social Psychology.* New York: McGraw-Hill Book Company.

Mezirow, J. (1991). *Transformative Dimensions of Adult Learning.* San Francisco, CA: Jossey-Bass.

Mezirow, J. (1998). On critical reflection. *Adult Education Quarterly, 48*(3), 185–198.

Miles, M. (1995). Disability studies among the Asian religions and philosophies. *Disability Studies Quarterly, 15*(3), 27–32.

Miller, H. M. (2001). Including "the included". *The Reading Teacher, 54*(8), 820–822.

Mills v. Board of Education of District of Columbia, 348 F. Supp. 866 (D.D.C. 1972).

Mitchell, D. T. & Snyder, S. L. (Producers). (1995). *Vital Signs: Crip Culture Talks Back* (Motion picture). 4196 Washington St. Ste. 2, Boston, MA: Fanlight Productions.

Mitchell, D. T. & Snyder, S. L. (2001). *Narrative Prosthesis: Disability and the Dependencies of Discourse.* Ann Arbor, MI: University of Michigan Press.

Monestier, M. (1987). *Human Oddities: A Book of Nature's Anomalies.* Secaucus, NJ: Citadel Press.

Moores, D. (1996). *Educating the Deaf: Psychology, Principles, and Practices.* Boston, MA: Houghton Mifflin Co.

Morgan, S. (1987). *Abuse and Neglect of Handicapped Children.* Boston, MA: Little, Brown and Company.

Morocco, C. C. (2001). Teaching for understanding with students with disabilities: New directions for research on access to the general education curriculum. *Learning Disability Quarterly, 24*(1), 5–13.

Morocco, C. C. & Hindin, A. (2002). The role of conversation in a thematic understanding of literature. *Learning Disabilities Research and Practice, 17*(3), 144–159.

Morris, J. (1991). *Pride Against Prejudice: Transforming Attitudes to Disability.* Philadelphia, PA: New Society Publishers.

Mr. Snafoo. (1997). *The New York Times*, Section 6, p 21.

Mueller, T. G. (2009). IEP facilitation: A promising approach to resolving conflicts between families and schools. *Teaching Exceptional Children*, *41*(3), 60–67.

Mullen, C. A. (2001). Disabilities awareness and the pre-service teacher: A blueprint of a mentoring intervention. *Journal of Education for Teaching*, *27*(1), 39–61.

Müller, I. (1991). *Hitler's Justice: The Courts of the Third Reich*. Cambridge, MA: Harvard University Press.

Mullins, J. B. (1979). Making language work to eliminate handicapism. *Education Unlimited*, *1*(2), 20–24.

National Association of the Deaf. (2000). *Cochlear Implants: NAD Position Statement*. Retrieved 5 June 2009, from http://www.nad.org/ciposition.

Nario-Redmond, M. (2008). *Consensus for Disability Stereotypes: Maintaining Group Boundaries and Legitimizing the Status Quo*. Paper presented at the meeting of the Society for Disability Studies, New York, NY.

National Child Traumatic Stress Network. (2004). Facts on Trauma and Deaf Children (Electronic Version). Retrieved 1 August 2008, from www.NCTSNet.org.

Nelson, J. (Director). (2001). *I Am Sam* (Motion picture). United States: New Line Production.

Noddings, N. (1994). An ethic of caring and its implications for instructional arrangements. In *The Education Feminism Reader* (pp. 171–183). New York: Routledge.

Noguera, P. A. (2008). *The Trouble with Black Boys: And Other Reflections on Race, Equity and the Future of Public Education*. Hoboken, NJ: John Wiley & Sons.

Obermann, C. (1965). *A History of Vocational Rehabilitation in America*. Minneapolis, MN: T. S. Denison.

Oberti vs. Board of Education of the Borough of Clementon School District (3rd Circuit Court, 1993).

O'Brien, R. (ed.). (2004). *Voices from the Edge: Narratives about the Americans with Disabilities Act*. Oxford: Oxford University Press.

Ogle, D. (1986). K-W-L: A teaching model that develops active reading of expository text. *The Reading Teacher 39*, 564–570.

Oliver, M. (1990). *The Politics of Disablement: A Sociological Approach*. New York: St. Martin's Press.

Oliver, M. (1996). *Understanding Disability. From Theory to Practice*. Basingstoke, England: Macmillan.

Onosko, J. J. & Jorgensen, C. M. (1998). Unit and lesson planning in the inclusive classroom: Maximixing learning opportunities for all students. In C. M. Jorgensen (ed.), *Restructuring Highs Schools for All Students* (pp. 71–105). Baltimore, MD: Brookes Publishing Co.

Opp, G. (1994). Historical roots of the field of learning disabilities: Some nineteenth-century German contributions. *Journal of Learning Disabilities*, *27*(January), 10–19.

Oyler, C. (2001). Democratic classrooms and accessible instruction. *Democracy & Education*, *14*(28–31).

Padden, C. & Humphries, T. (1988). *Deaf in America: Voices from a Culture*. Cambridge, MA: Harvard University Press.

Palincsar, A. M. & Brown, A. L. (1984). Reciprocal teaching of comprehension and monitoring activities. *Cognition and Instruction*, *1*(2), 117–175.

Palincsar, A. S. (1998). Social constructivist perspectives on teaching and learning. *Annual Review of Psychology*, *49*, 345–375.

Palincsar, A. S., Magnusson, S. J., Collins, K. M., & Cutter, J. (2001). Promoting deep understanding of science in students with disabilities in inclusion classrooms. *Learning Disabilities Quarterly*, *41*(1), 15–32.

Paré, A. (1840/1982). *On Monsters and Marvels* (J. Pallister, trans.). Chicago, IL: University of Chicago Press. (Original work published 1840).

Parens, E. & Asch, A. (eds.). (2000). *Prenatal Testing and Disability Rights*. Washington, DC: Georgetown University Press.

Parsons, T. (1951). *The Social System*. Glencoe, IL: Free Press.

Patton, J., Blackbourn, J., & Fad, K. (1996). *Exceptional Individuals in Focus* (6th ed.). Englewood Cliffs, NJ: Prentice Hall.

Paul, P. V. & Ward, M. E. (1996). Inclusion paradigms in conflict. *Theory Into Practice*, *35*(1), 4–11.

Pearson, N. (Producer) & Sheridan, J. (Director). (1989). *My Left Foot* (Motion picture). Ireland, United Kingdom: Granada Films (UK), Miramax Films.

Pennsylvania Association for Retarded Children v. Commonwealth of Pennsylvania, 334 F. Supp. 1257 (E.D. Pa. 1971), 343; F. Supp. 279 (E.D. Pa. 1972).

People in Motion: Viewers Guide. (1995). New York: Thirteen: WNET.

Pernick, M. (1996). *The Black Stork: Eugenics and the Death of "Defective" Babies in American Medicine and Motion Pictures Since 1915*. New York: Oxford University Press.

Perry, R. (1992). A short history of the term "politically correct." In P. Aufderheide (ed.), *Beyond PC: Towards a Politics of Understanding* (pp. 71–79). St. Paul, MN: Graywolf Press.

Peters, S. (2000). Is there a disability culture? A syncretisation of three possible world views. *Disability & Society, 15*(4), 583–601.

Pisha, B. & Coyne, P. (2001). Smart from the start: The promise of universal design for learning. *Remedial and Special Education, 22*(4), 197–203.

Pope, A. & Tarlov, A. (eds.). (1991). *Disability in America.* Washington, DC: Committee on a National Agenda for the Prevention of Disabilities, Division of Health Promotion and Disease Prevention, Institute of Medicine, National Academy Press.

Preen, B. (1976). *Schooling for the Mentally Retarded: A Historical Perspective*. New York: St. Martin's Press.

President's Committee on Employment of the Handicapped (1977). *Disabled Americans: A History*. Washington, DC: Author.

President's Committee on Mental Retardation (1975). *Mental Retardation: The Known and the Unknown*. (DHEW Publication Nos. [OHD] 76-21008). Washington, DC: U. S. Government Printing Office.

President's Committee on Mental Retardation (1977). *Mental Retardation Past and Present*. Washington, DC: U.S. Government Printing Office.

Price, C., Goodson, B., & Stewart, G. (2007). *Infant Environmental Exposure to Thimerosal and Neuropsychological Outcomes at Ages 7 to 10 years.* (Technical report. Vol. I.). Bethesda, MD.

Proctor, R. (1988). *Racial Hygiene: Medicine under the Nazis*. Cambridge, MA: Harvard University Press.

Proctor, R. (1992). Nazi biomedical policies. In A. Caplan (ed.), *When Medicine Went Mad: Bioethics and the Holocaust*. Totowa, NJ: Humana Press.

Pross, C. (1992). Nazi doctors, German medicine, and historical truth. In G. Annas & M. Grodin (eds.), *The Nazi Doctors and the Nuremberg Code: Human Rights in Human Experimentation* (pp. 32–59). New York: Oxford University Press.

Pugach, M. C. & Warger, C. L. (2001). Curriculum matters: Raising expectations for students with disabilities. *Remedial and Special Education, 22*(4), 194–196.

Raven, J. C. (1958). *The Standard Progressive Matrices*. London: H. K. Lewis.

Reid, D. K. & Knight, M. G. (2006). Disability justifies exclusion of minority students: A critical history grounded in disability studies. *Educational Researcher, 35*(6), 18–23.

Reid, D. K. & Valle, J. W. (2004). The discursive practice of learning disability: Implications for instruction and parent-school relations. *Journal of Learning Disabilities, Special Issue, 37*(6), 466–481.

Reiman, J. W., Beck, L., Coppola, T., & Engiles, A. (2010). *Parents' Experiences with the IEP Process: Considerations for Improving Practice*. Eugene, OR: CADRE.

Reisberg, L. (1998). Facilitating inclusion with integrated curriculum: A multidisciplinary approach. *Intervention and School Clinic, 33*(5), 272–277.

Remak, J. (ed.). (1969). *The Nazi Years*. Englewood Cliffs, NJ: Prentice Hall.

Renzi, M., Green, S. (Producer), & Sayles, J. (Director). (1992). *Passion Fish* (Motion picture). United States: Miramax films.

Reschly, D. J. (1996). Identification and assessment of children with disabilities. *The Future of Children: Special Education for Children with Disabilities, 6*(1), 40–53.

Retarded school alumni told they consumed radiation with their oatmeal. (1994). *The Star Ledger*, p. 27.

Rice, N. (2006). 'Reining in' special education: Constructions of "Special Education" in *New York Times* editorials, 1975–2004 (Electronic Version). *Disability Studies Quarterly, 26*. Retrieved 30 June 2006 from http://www.dsq-sds-archives.org/test4dpubs/2006_spring_toc.html.

Rickover, H. G. (1957). *The Education of Our Talented Children*. Paper presented at the The Seventh Institute of The Thomas Alva Edison Foundation, Hotel Suburban, East Orange, NY.

Rioux, M. (1996). Services and supports in a human rights framework. *Disability Studies Quarterly, 16*(1), 4–10.

Rogasky, B. (1988). *Smoke and Ashes: The Story of the Holocaust*. New York: Holiday House.

Rogers, R. (2002). Between contexts: A critical discourse analysis of family literacy, discursive practices, and literate subjectivities. *Reading Research Quarterly, 37*(3), 248–277.

Rogers, B. (1978). Richard III: Shakespeare was quite wrong. *In Britain, 33,* 31–35.

Rosen, R. S. (2006). An unintended consequence of IDEA: American Sign Language, the Deaf community, and Deaf culture into mainstream education (Electronic Version). *Disability Studies Quarterly, 26.* Retrieved 5 June 2009 from http://www.dsq-sds.org/article/view/685/862.

Ross, R. (1978). Civilization's treatment of the handicapped. In G. McDevitt & L. McDevitt (eds.), *The Handicapped Experience: Some Human Perspectives* (pp. 7–13). Baltimore, MD: University of Baltimore.

Ross, R. & Freelander, R. (1977). *Handicapped People in Society: A Curriculum Guide.* Burlington, VT: University of Vermont.

Rothman, D. (ed.). (1990). *The Discovery of the Asylum: Social Order and Disorder in the New Republic.* Boston, MA: Little Brown & Company.

Rowley-Kelly, F. & Reigel, D. (1993). *Teaching the Student with Spina Bifida.* Baltimore, MD: Paul H. Brookes.

Rubenfeld, P. (1994). Special education: An institution whose time has come—and gone. In E. Makas & L. Schlesinger (eds.), *Insights and Outlooks: Current Trends in Disability Studies* (pp. 235–238). Portland, ME: The Society for Disability Studies.

Ruch, F. (1967). *Psychology and Life* (7th ed.). Glenview, IL: Scott Foresman.

Russell, M. (1998). *Beyond Ramps: Disability at the End of the Social Contract.* Monroe, ME: Common Courage Press.

Sacramento City Unified School District v. Holland, 14 F.3d 1398 (9th Cir.), cert denied, 512 U.S. 1207 (1994).

Sadker, M. & Sadker, D. (1992). *Teachers, Schools, and Society* (2nd ed.). New York: McGraw-Hill.

Safford, P. (1978). *Teaching Young Children with Special Needs.* St. Louis, MO: C.V. Mosby Co.

Safilios-Rothschild, C. (1970). *The Sociology and Social Psychology of Disability and Rehabilitation.* New York: Random House.

Saini, A. (2001). Advocating for full inclusion: Mothers' narratives. In *Semiotics & Disability: Interrogating Categories of Difference* (pp. 135–156). Albany, NY: State University of New York Press.

Salend, S. J. (1994). *Effective Mainstreaming: Creating Inclusive Classrooms* (2nd ed.). New York: Macmillan.

Sapon-Shevin, M. (1989). Mild disabilities: In and out of special education. In Biklen, Ferguson, & Ford (eds.), *Schooling and Disability* (pp. 77–107). Chicago, IL: Chicago University Press.

Sapon-Shevin, M. (2000/2001). Schools fit for all. *Educational Leadership, 58*(4), 34–39.

Sarason, S. & Doris, J. (1979). *Educational Handicap, Public Policy, and Social History: A Broadened Perspective on Mental Retardation.* New York: The Free Press.

Saville, V. (Producer) & Fleming, V. (Director). (1941). *Dr. Jekyll and Mr. Hyde* (Motion picture). United States: Metro-Goldwyn-Mayer.

Scheerenberger, R. (1983). *A History of Mental Retardation.* Baltimore, MD: Paul H. Brookes.

Scholl, G. (ed.). (1986). *Foundations of Education for Blind and Visually Handicapped Children and Youth: Theory and Practice.* New York: American Foundation for the Blind.

Schou, S. J. (2006, February 15). Disabled Los Angeles playwright and activist John Belluso dies. *AP Worldstream.* Retrieved from http://www.highbeam.com/doc/1P1-118511159.html

Schramm, D., Fitzpatrick, E., & Seguin, C. (2002). Cochlear implantation for adolescents and adults with prelinguistic deafness. *Otology & Neurotology, 23*(5), 698–703.

Schroedel, J. (ed.). (1979). *Attitudes toward Persons with Disabilities: A Compendium of Related Literature.* Albertson, NY: National Center on Employment of the Handicapped at the Human Resource Center.

Schultz, B. D. (2008). *Spectacular Things Happen along the Way: Lessons from an Urban Classroom.* New York: Teachers College Press.

Schumaker, J. B., Deshler, D. D., Bulgren, J. A., Davis, B., Lenz, B. K., & Grossen, B. (2002). Access of adolescents with disabilities to general education curriculum: Myth or reality? *Focus on Exceptional Children, 35*(3), 1–16.

Schwarz, P. (2006). *From Disability to Possibility: The Power of Inclusive Classrooms.* Portsmouth, NH: Heinemann; England, London: Penguin Books.

Shakespeare, T. (1994). Cultural representation of disabled people: Dustbins for disavowal. *Disability & Society, 9*(3), 283–299.

Shapiro, A. (1999). *Everybody Belongs: Changing Negative Attitudes toward Classmates with Disabilities* (Vol. 14). New York: Routledge.

Shapiro, A. & Barton, E. (1991). Changing lives by eliminating handicapism. *New Jersey Journal of Lifelong Learning, Winter*, 2–4.

Shapiro, A. & Margolis, H. (1988). Changing negative peer attitudes toward students with learning disabilities. *Reading & Writing Quarterly, 4*(2), 133–146.

Shapiro, A. & Spelkoman, D. (1979). Why must we exploit them? *The New York Times*, p. NJ26.

Shapiro, J. (1993). *No Pity: People with Disabilities Forging a New Civil Rights Movement*. New York: Random House.

Shea, T. & Bauer, A. (1997). *An Introduction to Special Education: A Social Systems Perspective*. Madison, WI: Brown & Benchmark Publishers.

Skrtic, T. M. (1991). *Behind Special Education: A Critical Analysis of Professional Culture and School Organization*. Denver, CO: Love Publishing Company.

Slater, W. H. & Horstman, F. R. (2002). Teaching reading and writing to struggling middle school and high school students: The case for reciprocal teaching. *Preventing School Failure, 46*(4), 163–166.

Slavin, R. (1990). *Cooperative Learning: Theory, Research and Practice*. Boston, MA: Allyn and Bacon.

Slavin, R. E. (1999). Comprehensive approaches to cooperative learning. *Theory into Practice, 38*(2), 74–79.

Slee, R. (ed.). (1993). *Is there a Desk with My Name on It? The Politics of Integration*. London: Falmer Press.

Sleeter, C. E. (1987). Why is there learning disabilities? A critical analysis of the birth of the field in its social context. In T. Popkewitz (ed.), *The Formation of School Subjects: The Struggle for Creating an American Institution* (pp. 210–237). London: Falmer Press.

Smart, J. (2001). *Disability, Society, and the Individual*. Austin, TX: Pro-E.

Smith, D. & Luckasson, R. (1995). *Introduction to Special Education: Teaching in an Age of Challenge* (2nd ed.). Needham Height, MA: Allyn and Bacon, Simon & Schuster.

Smith, J. (1985). *Minds Made Simple: The Myth and Legacy of the Kallikaks*, Austin, TX: Pro-Ed.

Smith, J. (1994). *Pieces of Purgatory: Mental Retardation in and out of Institutions*. Belmont, CA: Brooks/Cole Publishing, a Division of Wadsworth.

Snow, K. (2001). *Creating New Lives for Children and their Families: Revolutionary Common Sense for Raising Successful Children with Disabilities*. Woodland Park, CO: Brave Heart Press.

Snyder, S. L. & Mitchell, D. T. (2006). *Cultural locations of disability*. Chicago: University of Chicago Press.

Spooner, F., Baker, J. N., Harris, A. A., Ahlgrim-Delzell, L., & Browder, D. M. (2007). Effects of training in universal design for learning on lesson plan development. *Remedial and Special Education, 28*(2), 108–116.

Stainback, S. & Stainback, W. (1996). *Inclusion: A Guide for Educators*. Baltimore, MD: Paul H. Brookes.

Stanovich, P. J. & Jordan, A. (2002). Preparing general educators to teach in inclusive classrooms: Some food for thought. *The Teacher Educator, 37*(3), 173–185.

Steeves, P. (2006). Sliding Doors: Opening Our World. *Equity & Excellence in Education, 39*(2), 105–114.

Steinbeck, J. (1937). *Of Mice and Men*. New York: Triangle Books.

Stiker, H.-J. (1997). *A History of Disability*. Ann Arbor, MI: University of Michigan Press.

Stubblefield, A. (2007). "Beyond the pale": Tainted whiteness, cognitive disability, and eugenic sterilization. *Hypatia, 22*(2), 162–181.

Sutherland, A. (1984). *Disabled We Stand*. Bloomington, IN: Indiana University Press.

Sutton v. United Airlines, 527 U.S. 471 (1999).

Szasz, T. (1970). *The Manufacture of Madness*. New York: Harper & Row.

Taylor, S. J. (1988/2004). Caught in the continuum: A critical analysis of the principle of the least restrictive environment. *Reasearch and Practice for Persons with Severe Disabilities, 29*(4), 218–230.

Thomas, C. & Corker, M. (2002). A journey around the social model. In M. Corker & T. Shakespeare (eds.), *Disability/Postmodernity: Embodying Disability Theory* (pp. 18–31). London: Continuum.

Thomas, D. (1980). *The Social Psychology of Childhood Disability*, New York, NY: Schoken Books.

Thompson, C. (1968). *Giants, Dwarfs and Other Oddities*. New York: Citadel Press.

Thompson, C. (1994). *The Mystery and Lore of Monsters*. New York: Barnes & Nobel Books.

Thompson, D. (1985). Anger. In S. Browne, D. Connors, & N. Stern (eds.), *With the Power of Each Breath: A Disabled Women's Anthology* (pp. 78–85). Pittsburgh, PA: Cleis Press.

Thomson, R. G. (1997). *Extraordinary Bodies: Figuring Physical Disability in American Culture and Literature*. New York, NY: Columbia University Press.

Thurer, S. (1980). Disability and monstrosity: A look at literary distortions of handicapping conditions. *Rehabilitation Literature*, January/February, 49–52.

Titchkosky, T. (2001). Disability: A rose by any other name? "People-first" language in Canadian society. *Canadian Review of Sociology and Anthropology, 38*(2), 125–140.

Tomlinson, C. A. (1999). *The Differentiated Classroom: Responding to the Needs of All Learners*. Alexandria, VA: ASCD.

Tomlinson, C. A. (2004). The mobius effect: Addressing learner variance in schools. *Journal of Learning Disabilities, 37*(6), 516–524.

Tomlinson, C. A. & Kalbfleisch, M. L. (1998). Teach me, teach my brain. A call for differentiated classrooms. *Educational Leadership, 56*(3), 56–60.

Tomlinson, C. A. & McTighe, J. (2006). *Integrating Differentiated Instruction and Understanding by Design*. Alexandria, VA: ASCD.

Toyota Motor Manufacturing v. Williams, 534 U.S. 184 (2002).

Trattner, W. (1994). *From Poor Laws to Welfare State: A History of Social Welfare in America*. New York: The Free Press, A Division of Simon & Schuster.

Trent, J. (1994). *Inventing the Feeble Mind: A History of Mental Retardation in the United States*. Berkeley, CA: University of California Press.

UN Decade of Disabled Persons 1983–1992. (1983). *World Programme of Action Concerning Disabled Persons*. New York: United Nations.

UNESCO. (1995). *Overcoming Obstacles to the Integration of Disabled People*. (Report to The World Summit on Social Development). Copenhagen, Denmark: Author.

United Nations. (2007) *Convention on Rights of Person with Disabilities*. New York, NY.

United Nations General Assembly. (1948). *UN Declaration on Human Rights*.

United Nations Ministry of Educational, Scientific and Education and Science Cultural Organization (UNESCO). (1994). *The Salamanca Statement and Framework for Action on Special Needs Education*. Salamanca, Spain.

United States Congress (1973). *Public Law 93-112, Vocational Rehabilitation Act 1973, Section 504*.

United States Congress (1974). *Public Law 94-142, The Education for All Handicapped Children Act of 1975*.

Snyder, S. L. & Mitchell, D. T. (2006). Cultural locations of disability. Chicago: University of Chicago Press.

Valle, J. W. (2009). What mothers say about special education: From the 1960s to the present. New York: Palgrave Macmillan.

Van der Klift, E. & Kunc, N. (1994). Beyond Benevolence: Friendship and the Politics of Help. In J. S. Thousand, R. A. Villa, & A. I. Nevin (eds.), *Creativity and Collaborative Learning: A Practical Guide to Empowering Students and Teachers*. Baltimore, MD: Paul H. Brookes Publishing Co.

Van Etten, A. (1988). *Dwarfs Don't Live in Doll Houses*. Rochester, NY: Adaptive Living.

Van Riper, C. & Emerick, L. (1984). *Speech Correction: An Introduction to Speech Pathology and Audiology*. Englewood Cliffs, NJ: Prentice Hall.

Varenne, H. & McDermott, R. (1998). *Successful Failure: The School America Builds*. Boulder, CO: Westview.

Vash, C. (1981). *The Psychology of Disability*. New York: Springer Publishing Company. *Virginia Sterilization Act, va. Acts 569-71*. (1924, repealed 1968).

Vavrus, F. & Cole, K. (2002). "I didn't do nothin": The discursive construction of school suspension. *The Urban Review, 34*(2), 87–111.

Walther-Thomas, C. S. (1997). Co-teaching expereinces: The benefits and problems that teachers and principals report over time. *Journal of Learning Disabilities, 30*(4), 395–407.

Wang, M. C. & Reynolds, M. C. (1996). Progressive inclusion: Meeting new challenges in special education. *Theory into Practice, 35*(1), 20–25.

Ware, L. (2001). Writing, identity, and the other: Dare we do Disability Studies. *Journal of Teacher Education, 52*(2), 107–123.

Waterhouse, L. (2006). Inadequate Evidence for Multiple Intelligences, Mozart Effect, and Emotional Intelligence Theories. *Educational Psychologist, 41*(4), 247–255.

Watts, W. (1984). Attitude change: Theories and methods. In R. Jones (ed.), *Attitudes and Attitude Change in Special Education* (pp. 41–69). Reston, VA: Council for Exceptional Children.

Waxman, B. (1991). Hatred: The unacknowledged dimension in violence against disabled people. *Human Science Press*, May, 185–199.

Waxman, B. (1992). Hate. *The Disability Rag, 13*(3), 4–5, 7.

Webber, A. L. (Producer) & Schumacher, J. (Director). (2004). *The Phantom of the Opera* (Motion picture). United States, United Kingdom: Warner Bros.

Wechsler, D., Kaplan, E., Fein, D., Kramer, J., Morris, R., Delis, D. & Maerlender, A. (2004). *Wechsler Intelligence Scales for Children-Integrated* (4th ed). San Antonio, TX: Harcourt Assessment, Inc.

Wehmeyer, M. L. (2006). Beyond access: Ensuring progress in the general education curriculum for students with severe disabilities. *Research & Practice for Persons with Severe Disabilities, 31*(4), 322–326.

Weindling, P. (1989). *Health, Race and German Politics Between National Unification and Nazism, 1870–1945.* Cambridge, Great Britain: Cambridge University Press.

Welch, A. B. (2000). Responding to student concerns about fairness. *Exceptional Children, 33*(2), 36–40.

Wendell, S. (1997). Toward a feminist theory of disability. In L. Davis (ed.), *The Disability Studies Reader* (pp. 260–292). New York, NY: Routledge.

Wertham, F. (1980). *The German Euthanasia Program: Excerpts from "A Sign from Cain".* Cincinnati, OH: Hayes Publishing Company, Inc.

Westridge Young Writers Workshop (1994). *Kids Explore the Gifts of Children with Special Needs.* Santa Fe, NM: John Muir Publications.

White, G. (1993). *Justice Oliver Wendell Holmes.* New York: Oxford University Press.

Wiggins, G. & McTighe, J. (1998). *Understanding by Design.* Alexandria, VA: ASCD.

Will, M. (1986). *Educating Students with Learning Problems: A Shared Responsibility.* Washington, DC: U.S. Department of Education, Office of Special Education and Rehabilitation Services.

Winzer, M. A. (1993). *The History of Special Education: From Isolation to Integration.* Washington, DC: Gallaudet University Press.

Wolfensberger, W. (1980). Extermination: Disabled people in Nazi Germany. *Polestar, 1 (9).* Developmental Disabilities Training Systems and Technical Research Center, Region III, New York.

Wolfensberger, W. (1981). The extermination of handicapped people in World War II Germany. *Mental Retardation, 19* (February), 1–7.

Wolfensberger, W., Nirje, B., Olshansky, S., Perske, R., & Roos, P. (1972). *Normalization: The Principle of Normalization in Human Services.* Toronto, Canada: National Institute on Mental Retardation.

Woodcock, R., McGrew, K., & Mather, N. (2003). *Woodcock-Johnson Tests of Cognitive Abilities* (3rd ed.) Chicago, IL: Riverside Publishing Company.

Woodcock, R. W., McGrew, K. S., & Mather, N. (2001). *Woodcock-Johnson III Tests of Achievement.* Itasca, IL: Riverside Publishing.

Wotherspoon, T. & Schissel, B. (2001). The business of placing Canadian children and youth "at-risk". *Canadian Journal of Education, 26*(3), 321–339.

Wright, B. (1983). *Physical Disability—A Psychosocial Approach.* New York: Harper & Row.

Wright, M. H. (1999). *Sounds Like Home: Growing up Black and Deaf in the South.* Washington, DC: Galludet University Press.

Wright, P. (1987). Disabling attitudes. *Contact, XII*(3), 4–9.

Wurzburg, G. (Producer/Director) & Biklen, D. (Co-Producer). (2004). *Autism is a World* (DVD). United States: State of the Art/CNN Presents.

Yeargin-Allsopp, M., Rice, C., Karapurkar, T., et al. (2003). Prevalence of autism in a US metropolitan area. *JAMA, 289*(1). 49–55.

Yell, M. & Drasgow, E. (1999). A legal analysis of inclusion. *Preventing School Failure, 43*(3), 118–123.

Young, T. (Director). (1967). *Wait until dark* [Motion picture]. USA: Warner Bros. Pictures.

Young, R. (2005). Neurobiology of savant syndrome. In C. Stough (ed.), *Neurobiology of Exceptionality* (pp. 199–215). New York: Kluwer Academic/Plenum Publishers.

Yuker, H. & Block, J. (1979). *Challenging Barriers to Change: Attitudes Toward the Disabled.* Albertson, NY: National Center on the Employment of the Handicapped at Human Resources Center.

Zemeckis, R. (Director). (1994). *Forrest Gump* (Motion picture). United States: Paramount Pictures.

Zola, I. (ed.). (1982a). *Ordinary Lives: Voices of Disability and Disease.* Cambridge, MA: Applewood Books.

Zola, I. (1982b). *Missing Pieces: A Chronicle of Living with a Disability.* Philadelphia, PA: Temple University Press.

Index

ableism 222–3
activism 11, 17–18, 26, 89; *see also* civil
    rights; Disability Rights Movement
Africa 56
albinism 56
almshouses 67–8
American Breeders Association 72
American colonies 66–7
American Foundation for the Blind (AFB)
    85, 86
American Indians 56
American Sign Language (ASL) 50, 93,
    106, 155–6, 158
Americans with Disabilities Act (1990)
    89–92
Americans with Disabilities Act Amendments
    Act (2008) 40, 92
amputations 143
ancient Greece and Rome 56–7, 62, 63
animism 54
anxiety 38, 163
aphasia 152–3
apprenticeship 195
arthritis 141
arts and culture 99–101
Asperger's syndrome 49, 120; *see also* autism
assistive technology 122, 241–3
Assyrians 54–5
asylums 68, 69
attitude change 8–9, 37–9; ableism 222–3;
    assessing existing attitudes 239–41;
    curricular infusion 224; analyzing
    literary fiction 224–8; analyzing non-
    fiction 229–31; media studies *see* media
    studies; disability awareness programs
    236–8; appreciating individual
    differences 238; emphasizing sameness
    238; involvement of students 239;
    experiential methods; demystification
    241–3; role-play
    244–7; simulations 247–9; inviting
    guests with disabilities 249–52; necessary
    conditions 223–4; questions for class
    discussion 252–4; strategies 239

attitudes; affective component 5; behavioral
    component 5; cognitive component 5;
    history *see* historical attitudes; learned
    in early life 6–7, 9; negative attitudes and
    self-concept 7-8; positive attitudes 10–11
audiologists 136
Augustus Caesar 64
authentic tasks 206
autism 120–3; autistic behavior 158, 161–2;
    communication boards 159; echolalia
    159; Facilitated Communication
    159–60; preference for strict routines
    158, 171–2; Savant syndrome 159; self-
    stimulating and self-injurious behaviors
    158; Sensory Integration therapy
    162; speech and communication 158,
    159–60; splinter skills 158–9
autism spectrum disorders 121, 122
aversion 38
Aztec culture 56, 63

Babylonians 55
Barnum, P.T. 65
begging 64
behavioral disorders 118–20, 162–5
Bell, Alexander Graham 72
Belluso, John 100
Bennett, William J. 93
Bertholde 64
Bethlehem Hospital 64, 65–6
Bettelheim, Bruno 121
bibliotherapy 229–30
Biklen, Douglas 160
Bipolar Disorder 163
Blatt, B. 82–3
blindness *see* visual impairments
Braille 91, 243
brain-based instruction 217
brain injury 106–7
Brookfield, Steven 9
Buck, Carrie 73–4
Buddhism 61
Burke, Jamie 160
Bush, George W. 90

cartoons 232–3
Celsus, Aurelius Cornelius 109
Center for Applied Special Technology (CAST) 197
cerebral palsy 141–2
Charles V of France 63
Charles VI of Vienna 64
Cherry, James 87
children's attitudes 6–7, 9; negative attitudes and self-concept 7–8; see also attitude change
Christianity 59–60
civil rights 3, 11, 14, 17–18, 26, 85, 191; see also Disability Rights Movement
Civil Rights Act (1964) 90, 92
cleft palate/lip 144
cochlear implants 155
cognitive disability 109–13; see also intellectual disabilities
cognitive strategies 206–7
collaborative teaching 135
communication disorders 152–4; assistive technology 243; autism and autistic behavior 158, 159–60; see also deafness/Deafness; social interaction; speech or language impairments
Conduct Disorder 164
conductive hearing loss 154
conflict resolution 131–4
Confucianism 61
consciousness-raising 101
constructive conversation 207
constructivism 194–5, 205
Convention on the Rights of Persons with Disabilities 11, 41, 95
cooperative learning 172, 196, 205; attitudes toward students with disabilities 211–12; face-to-face promotive interaction 210; group processing 210–11; individual accountability 210; positive interdependence 210; social skills 210; see also guided inquiry
counselors 136
craniofacial disorders 144
cruelty 82–3, 223
cued speech 157
cultural deprivation 186–7
cultural mediation 196
culture 4–5; history see historical attitudes; medical model of disability see medical model
curiosity 34–5, 146

curriculum; attitude change see attitude change; constructivism 194–5, 205; cooperative learning 196, 205; attitudes toward students with disabilities 211-12; face-to-face promotive interaction 210; group processing 210–11; individual accountability 210; positive interdependence 210; social skills 210; democratic schooling 192–4; differentiated instruction 199, 209; research base 217–20, 221; variety in expressing learning 212–13; guided inquiry 196, 205; authentic tasks 206; cognitive strategies 206–7; constructive conversation 207; lesson planning 207–8; social mediation 207; history of special education 185; contemporary issues 189–92; early twentieth century 185–6; 'high-stakes' schooling 186–7; legislation 187; low expectations 190; mainstreaming 12, 187; Regular Education Initiative (REI) 187–9; segregation 186–7; norms 192; planning 199; assessment 203–5; big ideas 200–1; culminating projects 201; developing coherence 200–1; essential questions 200, 201; individuation 201–2; instructional methods and materials 202–3; reflective practice 215–17; Understanding by Design 201; units of study 200; social constructivism 195–6, 205; standardization and accountability 190–1; Universal Design for Learning (UDL) 196–9; materials 213–15; research base 217–20, 221; variety in expressing learning 212–13; whole child 191

Dart, Justin 90
Davenport, Charles 72
Deaf-Blindness 106
deafness/Deafness 49–50; American Sign Language (ASL) 50, 93, 106, 155–6, 158; cochlear implants 155; communication and social behavior 152, 153, 154–8; conductive hearing loss 154; deaf/Deaf distinction 50, 155; definitions 105–6; Free Appropriate Public Education (FAPE) 93; hearing aids 154–5; lip-reading 156–7, 167–8; sensorineural hearing loss 154; social interaction see social interaction

dehumanization 82–3
deinstitutionalization 82–4
democratic schooling 192–4
demystification 241–3
depression 163
Dewey, John 192, 194, 199
differentiated instruction 199, 209; research
    base 217–20, 221; variety in
    expressing learning 212–13
disability; civil rights 3, 11, 14, 17–18, 26,
    85, 191; see also Disability Rights
    Movement; definitions; Deaf-
    Blindness 106; emotional disturbance
    and behavioral disorder 118–20;
    hearing impairments 105–6; multiple
    disabilities 107; mental retardation,
    cognitive disability, intellectual
    disability 109–13; orthopedic
    impairments 106; other health
    impairment 107; soft disability 108–9,
    114, 120, 121–2, 123; specific learning
    disabilities 113–18; speech or language
    impairments 106; traumatic brain
    injury 106–7; visual impairments 105;
    discrimination 8, 9, 13, 36; emotional
    reactions to 38; history see historical
    attitudes; impairment and 27, 40, 41;
    medical model see medical model;
    paradigms 29–30; physical see physical
    disability; social models see social
    models of disability; societal norms
    5, 15; see also attitudes; stereotypes;
    stereotypes see stereotypes; terminology
    see terminology; visual
    see visual impairments
disability arts 99–101
disability awareness programs 236–8;
    appreciating individual differences
    238; emphasizing sameness 238;
    involvement of students 239
Disability Pride Parade 100
Disability Rights Movement 85–6;
    Americans with Disabilities Act
    (1990) 89–92; arts and culture 99–101;
    education 93–5; Education for All
    Handicapped Children Act (1975)
    88–9; post-legislation activism 89;
    section 504 of the Rehabilitation Act
    (1973) 86–8, 89, 90
disability studies 16–18, 28, 189, 254–5
disabled veterans 81
discomfort 38
discrimination 8, 9, 13, 36; racial 114, 115–16,
    119–20, 123, 186–7, 190

diversity 9–10
divination 55
Dix, Dorothea 68
Donaldson, J. 9
Down syndrome 94, 98, 142
DSM-IV classifications 23, 111, 114, 120, 122,
    123, 164
Duns Scotus, John 109
Durrell, Donald 199
dwarfs 6, 32, 63–4, 143–4

early civilizations 54–5, 61–2
echolalia 159
education see inclusive education; schools
Education for All Handicapped Children
    Act (1975) 88–9, 187
Egypt 55–6, 62
Emerman, Anne 84
emotional disturbance 118–20, 162–5
emotional reactions 38
employment 92
entertainment industry 96–7; see also
    fictional characters
eugenics 33, 70–1, 81, 82; controlling
    feeble-mindedness and the unfit
    71–3, 110, 227; modern variants
    96, 97–9; Nazism 33, 74–9; social
    menace 71; sterilization 33, 73–4,
    75, 77
euphemisms 44–7
euthanasia 75, 76, 78, 79
exceptionality 5
exclusion 16
extraordinary bodies 143–4

facilitated communication 122
fairytales 6, 32
Fay, Fred 87
fear 38
'feeble-mindedness' 67, 69, 71, 72, 73,
    109–10, 227
Fernald School 83
fictional characters 6, 31–6, 96–7, 159; literary
    analysis in the curriculum 224–8
Fiorito, Eunice 87
freak shows 34, 64–5
Free Appropriate Public Education (FAPE) 93,
    94, 95, 187
friendships 14, 223
frustration 153, 154, 172

Gall, Franz Joseph 115
Gallaudet, Thomas 69
Gallaudet College 69, 84

Galton, Francis 70
Gardner, Eileen Marie 93–4
gay pride 49
Goddard, Henry Herbert 71, 110
Godeau 64
Goffman, Erving 42
Goldwater Memorial Hospital 84
Grandin, Temple 123
group identity 44, 48–50
group processing 210–11
guide dogs 148, 151
guided inquiry 196, 205; authentic tasks 206;
    constructive conversation 207; lesson
    planning 207–8; social mediation
    207; see also cooperative learning
guilt 38

handicap 40, 41
health professionals 137–8
hearing aids 154–5
hearing impairments 105–6; see also
    deafness/Deafness
Heber, Rick 110
Henry VIII 66
Herodotus 56
Heumann, Judith E. 86, 87
Hinshelwood, John 115
historical attitudes 53, 79–80; early
    civilizations 54–5, 61–2; Greek and
    Roman practices 56–7, 62, 63; eugenics
    see eugenics; infanticide 54, 55-6, 57;
    objects of fascination 62; entertaining
    the aristocracy 62–4; medical
    curiosities and freak shows 64–5;
    primitive societies 54; religious attitudes
    see religious attitudes; segregation and
    institutionalization 65–6; American
    colonies 66–7; deinstitutionalization
    and reforms 82–4; large institutions
    69–70; residential facilities 68–9;
    residential placements 67–8; social
    context 53–4; twentieth century 81–2;
    deinstitutionalization and reforms
    82–4; Disability Rights Movement
    see Disability Rights Movement;
    independent living 84–5; twenty-first
    century 95–6, 101–2
Hitler, Adolf 74, 75, 76, 78
Holland, Rachel 94–5
Holocaust 79
Hotchkiss, Ralf D. 87
Howe, Samuel Gridley 68, 69, 109
Hunter, Madeline 207
identity 44, 48–50

'idiots' 69, 109, 110
'imbeciles' 109, 110
impairment 27, 40, 41
inclusion 3, 12–13, 18; see also integration
inclusive education 3–4, 12–13, 18, 28–9;
    acceptance of individual differences
    14; attitude change see attitude change;
    communication and social interaction
    see social interaction; critiques 4;
    curriculum see curriculum; disabilities
    affecting academic performance
    176–7; see also intellectual disabilities;
    learning disabilities; Disability
    Rights Movement 93–5; friendship
    development 14; goals 13–14; growth
    for peers 13–14; improved learning 13;
    Individualized Educational Programs
    see Individualized Educational
    Programs; normalizing human
    variation 139–40, 181–2; preparation
    for adult living 13; recognition 19;
    respect 19; responsibility 19; support of
    civil rights 14; teaching diversity 9–10;
    utilizing the help and support of
    others 140–1
independent living 84–5
India 55
Individualized Educational Programs (IEPs)
    125–6, 188; building relationships
    between schools and families 130;
    collaborative IEP meetings 127–8;
    collaborative problem solving 131–4;
    negative experiences of IEP meetings
    127, 129; professional collaboration
    134; collaborative teaching or
    co-teaching 135; consulting and
    supportive roles 135; paraprofessionals
    or school aides 136–8; specialists and
    related services 135–6; student-led IEP
    meetings 128–9; students and families
    as experts 126–7
Individuals with Disabilities in Education
    Improvement Act (2004) 21–2, 39,
    105, 141, 187, 188, 191; autism,
    autism spectrum disorder, Pervasive
    Developmental Disorder 120–3;
    Deaf-Blindness 106; emotional
    disturbance and behavioral disorder
    118–20; hearing impairments
    (including deafness) 105–6; IEPs see
    Individualized Educational Programs;
    mental retardation, cognitive disability,
    intellectual disability 109–13;
    multiple disabilities 107; orthopedic

impairments 106; other health
impairment 107; soft disability 108–9,
114 120, 121–2, 123; specific learning
disability 113–18; speech or language
impairments 106; traumatic brain
injury 106–7; visual impairments 105
infanticide 54, 55–6, 57, 98
institutionalization 65–6; American colonies
66–7; deinstitutionalization and
reforms 82–4; large institutions 69–70;
residential facilities 68–9; residential
placements 67–8
instructional methods and materials 202–3;
see also cooperative learning;
differentiated instruction; guided
inquiry; Universal Design for Learning
integration 10–12; see also inclusion
intellectual disabilities 109–13, 180–1
interpreters 136
IQ scores 110, 111, 112, 113, 116–17, 122
Islam 60
Ivy, Andrew 79

James IV of Scotland 63
Japan 60
Jennings, Harry 82
Judaism 58–9

Kallikak, Deborah 71
Kussmaul, Adolph 115

labels 42–3, 123
language practices see terminology
learning activities 9
learning disabilities 113–18, 177; aspects of
perception and academic performance
177–8; common-sense responses
to 178–80; discrepancy method of
diagnosis 116–17; race and social class
114, 115–16, 119–20, 123, 186–7, 190;
responsiveness to intervention 117
least restrictive attitudes see attitude change
Least Restrictive Environment (LRE) 12, 39,
94, 188
Lehrer, Riva 100
lesson planning 207–8
Lewin, K. 8
Linton, Simi 100
lip-reading 156–7, 167–8
lisps 152
literature; fictional characters 6, 31–6, 96–7,
159; literary analysis in the curriculum
224–8; non-fiction 229–31

Lovaas, O. Ivar 101
low vision see visual impairments

Mace, Ronald 197
mainstreaming 12, 187
Major Depressive Disorder 163
March of Dimes (1937) 82
mathematics 206
media studies 231; analyzing editorial and
political cartoons 232–3; analyzing
news media 231–2; organizing a media
watch 233–5; corrective action 236;
educating the media professionals 235
mediated learning 196
medical experiments 83
medical model 15–16, 20–1; diagnosis
and assessment 21–2; Individuals
with Disabilities in Education
Improvement Act (2004) 21–2, 39;
influence in school placement practice
22–3, 189; influence on social policy 36,
37, 39; medicalization as a social and
cultural trend 23–5, 96; shamanism 54
Melanesian culture 55
mental illness 64, 65–6, 68
mental retardation 109–13; see also intellectual
disabilities
Mesopotamians 55
Meyer, Anne 197
Mezirow, Jack 9
Mistler, Sharon 87
Mitchell, David 226
monstrous births 55
Montessori method 195
Morgan, W. Pringle 115
'morons' 71, 110
multiple disabilities 107
multiple intelligences 217
multiple sclerosis 142
muscular dystrophy 142

National Association for the Deaf (NAD)
85, 86, 155
Native Americans 56
Nazism 33, 49, 74–9
negative attitudes see attitudes; stereotypes
news media 231–2
Nixon, Richard 87
normalization 139–40
norms 5; history see historical attitudes;
medical model see medical model;
school curriculum 192; see also
attitudes; stereotypes

Oberti, Rafael 94
Obsessive-Compulsive Disorder (OCD) 163
occupational therapists 137
Oppositional Defiant Disorder (ODD) 164
orthopedic impairments 106
Orton-Gillingham reading program 186
overcompensation 36
Oyler, C. 193, 198

paradigms 29–30; influence on social
    structures and systems 36–7; shift 37–9;
    see also attitude change
paternalism 34
peer relationships 14, 223
people-first language 43–4, 45, 47, 48
Perkins Institute 69
Pervasive Developmental Disorder 120–1
Peterson, Roger 87
physical disability; barrier-free environments
    145–7; personal experiences 144–5;
    range of disabilities 141–4
physical environment 17, 145–7, 168–9, 197
physical therapists 137
Piaget, Jean 194
Pimentel, Al 87
pity 31
pluralistic society 10
political activism 11, 17–18, 26, 89; *see also*
    civil rights; Disability Rights
    Movement
political correctness 46
Post Traumatic Stress Disorder (PTSD) 163
poverty 92
prejudice 7, 8, 9, 13, 36; *see also* attitude
    change; attitudes; stereotypes
prenatal screening 97, 98
primitive societies 54
professionals 8, 134; consulting and
    supportive roles 135; medical model 24;
    paraprofessionals or school aides
    136–8; specialists and related services
    135–6
psychiatric hospitals 68
psychologists 136
public accommodations 91
public policy 37

racial discrimination 114, 115–16, 119–20,
    123, 186–7, 190
Reagan, Ronald 90
Reciprocal Teaching 206–7
reflective practice 215–17
Regular Education Initiative (REI) 187–9

Rehabilitation Act: section 504 (1973) 86–8,
    89, 90
religious attitudes 57–8, 81; Buddhism 61;
    Christianity 59–60; Confucianism 61;
    Islam 60; Judaism 58–9;
    Shinto 60
Ris, Jacof 64
Roberts, Edward 85, 99
role-play 244–7
Rolling Quads 85
Roosevelt, Eleanor 82
Roosevelt, Franklin D. 82
Rose, David 197
Rowley, Amy 93

Salamanca Statement and Framework for
    Action on Special Needs Education
    (UNESCO) 11, 95–6
Savant syndrome 159
Saviola, Marilyn 84
scaffolding 195
schizophrenia 163
schools; curriculum *see* curriculum; inclusive
    education *see* inclusive education
special education 3, 15–16, 22–3; Free
    Appropriate Public Education (FAPE)
    93, 94, 95
'Section 504': Rehabilitation Act (1973) 86–8,
    89, 90
segregation 65–6, 123; American colonies
    66–7; deinstitutionalization and
    reforms 82–4; education *see* special
    education; large institutions 69–70;
    residential facilities 68–9; residential
    placements 67–8
seizure disorder 142–3
self-concept 7–8
Seneca the Elder 57
sensorineural hearing loss 154
Sensory Integration therapy 162
shamanism 54
Shinto 60
sign language 50, 93, 106, 155–6, 158, 243
simulation exercises 247–9
Snyder, Sharon 226
social constructivism 195–6, 205
social inequality 115, 119–20, 123, 186–7
social interaction 152, 153, 154, 165; class
    activities and routines 170–2; class rules
    170, 172, 173; cooperative learning
    172; encouraging various ways of
    communicating 166; environmental
    barriers 168–9; interventions for

undesirable interactions 172–6;
pausing and taking turns 167; positive
reinforcement 170; promoting
acceptance, tolerance, and empathy
165–6; respectful communication
167–8; slowing down the pace of
talk 166–7
social mediation 207
social models of disability 25–6, 29, 37, 39,
108; disability studies 16–18, 28;
inclusion 28–9; *see also* inclusion;
inclusive education; postmodernist
view of marginalization 27–8;
sociopolitics 26–7; *see also* political
activism
social policy 37
social skills 210
social stigma *see* stigma
social workers 136
societal norms 5; history *see* historical
attitudes; medical model *see* medical
model; *see also* attitudes; stereotypes
sociocultural perspectives 196, 205
soft disability 108–9, 114, 120, 121–2, 123
solitary confinement 83
Sparta 56
special education 3, 15–16, 22–3; curriculum
see curriculum; Free Appopriate
Public Education (FAPE) 93, 94, 95;
segregation 186–7
specific learning disabilities *see* learning
disabilities
Speech-Language Pathologists 136
speech or language impairments 35, 106,
152–4; social interaction *see* social
interaction
spina bifida 143
Steinbeck, John 31–2, 226, 227
stereotypes 3, 4, 6, 9, 13, 30–1; burden to
society 35; changing attitudes *see*
attitude change; fictional characters 6,
31–6, 96–7, 159; literary analysis in the
curriculum 224–8; holy innocent or
eternal child 33–4; influence on social
structures and systems 36–7; labels 42;
object of comedy, ridicule and curiosity
34–5, 62; entertaining the aristocracy
62–4; medical curiosities and freak
shows 34, 64–5; object of dread 33;
object of pity 31; sinister or evil 32–3;

subhuman organism 31–2; Supercrip or
Extraordinary Disabled 35–6; victims
of violence 35; *see also* attitude change;
attitudes
sterilization 33, 73–4, 75, 77
stigma 42, 112, 121, 123, 153
stuttering 153–4, 168

teaching methods *see* cooperative learning;
differentiated instruction; guided
inquiry; Universal Design for Learning
telecommunications 92
teratoscopy 55
terminology 40, 41; euphemisms 44–7;
handicap 40, 41; impairment 40, 41;
labels 42–3, 123; language and identity
44, 48–50; people-first language 43–4,
45, 47, 48; reappropriation of negative
language 49; stigma 42
Thomson, Rosemarie Garland 226
Tiberius 64
token economies 170
Tourette syndrome 143
transformative learning 38
transportation services 91–2
traumatic brain injury 106–7

UN Convention on the Rights of Persons with
Disabilities 11, 41, 95
unemployment 92
Universal Design for Learning (UDL) 196–9;
materials 213–15; research base 217–20,
221; variety in expressing learning
212–13

verbal non-fluency 152, 154, 168
visual impairments 43–4, 55–6, 60–1, 147–8;
common-sense responses 149–51;
Deaf-Blindness 106; definitions 105;
mannerisms 151; myths 147, 148;
personal experiences 149
Vygotsky, Lev 189, 195

war veterans 81
wheelchair users 84, 85, 197
wheelchairs 82, 146–7, 241
Will, Madeline 187–8

Zola, Irving 100
Zone of Proximal Development 195

eBooks – at www.eBookstore.tandf.co.uk

A library at your fingertips!

eBooks are electronic versions of printed books. You can store them on your PC/laptop or browse them online.

They have advantages for anyone needing rapid access to a wide variety of published, copyright information.

eBooks can help your research by enabling you to bookmark chapters, annotate text and use instant searches to find specific words or phrases. Several eBook files would fit on even a small laptop or PDA.

NEW: Save money by eSubscribing: cheap, online access to any eBook for as long as you need it.

Annual subscription packages

We now offer special low-cost bulk subscriptions to packages of eBooks in certain subject areas. These are available to libraries or to individuals.

For more information please contact webmaster.ebooks@tandf.co.uk

We're continually developing the eBook concept, so keep up to date by visiting the website.

www.eBookstore.tandf.co.uk